HENRY ANSGAR KELLY

The Matrimonial Trials
of Henry VIII

❧✻❧

Stanford University Press

STANFORD, CALIFORNIA

1976

Stanford University Press
Stanford, California
© 1976 by the Board of Trustees of the
Leland Stanford Junior University
Printed in the United States of America
ISBN 0-8047-0895-9   LC 75-7483

Published with the assistance of
The Andrew W. Mellon Foundation

FOR SARAH

Acknowledgments

The major portion of this book was researched and written in the Vatican Library and Archives and the English College in Rome during the last half of 1969, when I was on sabbatical leave from the University of California at Los Angeles. The original manuscript was revised and much expanded after a summer of research at the British Museum, the Lambeth Palace Library, the Westminster Diocesan Archives, and the Public Record Office in 1971, during which time I was assisted by a grant from the John Simon Guggenheim Memorial Foundation. I should like to express my gratitude to all these institutions for the help and cooperation they have given me. I am especially grateful to the above-mentioned libraries and archives, and to the Cambridge University Library and the Vienna Haus-, Hof- und Staatsarchiv for permission to draw upon unpublished material for this study.

The manuscript was prepared with the aid of Raachel Nathan Jurovics, James Mininger, and Margaret Diener, research assistants generously provided me by the Center for Medieval and Renaissance Studies at U.C.L.A. Finally, I should like to thank all those friends who have read and criticized the manuscript and encouraged me in my conclusions, especially Robert M. Adams, Walter Anderson, David Mellinkoff, Mortimer Levine, John T. Noonan, Jr., Michael M. Sheehan, A. J. Slavin, Lynn White, Jr., and, importantly, my wife, Marea Tancred.

Henry Ansgar Kelly

Los Angeles
February 3, 1975
Feast of St. Ansgar

Contents

Abbreviations   xi

Introduction   1

Part One. First Efforts

1. Henry's Scruple   21
2. Dispensations for Anne   38
3. Pre-Trial Maneuvers   54
4. The Opening of the Legatine Court   75
5. The Charges Against the Marriage   89
6. The Attack on the Dispensations   101

Part Two. The Appeal to Rome

7. The Advocation   135
8. Nonconsummation: Pros and Cons   148
9. The Trial at the Papal Court   164

Part Three. The King's Way

10. The Search for Academic Approval   173
11. Further Efforts Toward Consummation   190
12. Annulment and Ratification   204
13. Cranmer and the King's Conscience   222

Part Four. Aftermath

14. The Second Annulment   241
15. The Third Annulment   261

    Epilogue   279

    Appendix A. The Queen's Libellus   289
    Appendix B. Statement of Archbishop Cranmer   296
    Works Cited   299
    Index   311

Abbreviations

Burnet   Gilbert Burnet, *The History of the Reformation of the Church of England*, ed. Nicholas Pocock, 7 vols. (Oxford, 1865).

Cavendish   George Cavendish, *The Life and Death of Cardinal Wolsey*, ed. Richard S. Sylvester, Early English Text Society, no. 243 (London, 1958).

Chichele Register   *The Register of Henry Chichele, Archbishop of Canterbury, 1414–1443*, ed. E. F. Jacob, Canterbury and York Society, nos. 42, 45–47, 4 vols. (Oxford, 1937–47).

CIC   *Corpus iuris canonici*: (1) Gratian, *Decretum*; (2) X: Decretals of Gregory IX; (3) Sextus: Decretals of Boniface VIII; (4) Clementinae: Decretals of Clement V; ed. Emil Friedberg, 2 vols. (Leipzig, 1879–81; repr. Graz, 1959). The glosses are cited from the unreliable post-Tridentine Roman edition (e.g. Lyons, 1606).

DNB   *Dictionary of National Biography*.

Ehses   Stephan Ehses, *Römische Dokumente zur Geschichte der Ehescheidung Heinrichs VIII von England* (Paderborn, 1893).

EHR   *English Historical Review*.

Gairdner, *EHR* 5   James Gairdner, "The Draft Dispensation for Henry VIII's Marriage with Anne Boleyn," *EHR* 5 (1890), 544–50.

Gairdner, *EHR* 11, 12   James Gairdner, "New Lights on the Divorce of Henry VIII," *EHR* 11 (1896), 673–702; 12 (1897), 1–16, 237–53.

Granville   British Museum, Granville Library.

Kelly, *Traditio*   Henry Ansgar Kelly, "Canonical Implications of Richard III's Plan to Marry His Niece," *Traditio*, 23 (1967), 269–311.

LP *Letters and Papers, Foreign and Domestic, of the Reign of Henry VIII*, ed. J. S. Brewer, James Gairdner, R. H. Brodie, vols. 2–21 (London, 1864–1910); vol. 1, 2d ed. (1920); *Addenda*, vol. 1 (1929–32); whole series reprinted with corrections, Vaduz, 1965. Citations are to volume and number of document.

Pocock Nicholas Pocock, *Records of the Reformation: The Divorce, 1527–1533*, 2 vols. (Oxford, 1870).

Rymer Thomas Rymer, *Foedera*, 2d ed., 20 vols. (London, 1726–35).

Scarisbrick J. J. Scarisbrick, *Henry VIII* (London, 1968).

SC *Calendar of Letters, Dispatches, and State Papers Relating to the Negotiations Between England and Spain*, ed. G. A. Bergenroth, P. de Gayangos, et al., 13 vols. and *Supplement* to vols. 1–2 (London, 1862–1954); *Further Supplement*, 1513–42, ed. Garrett Mattingly (London, 1940).

SP *State Papers: King Henry VIII*, 11 vols. (London, 1830–52).

Statutes *The Statutes of the Realm*, 11 vols. (London, 1810–28; repr. 1963).

Surtz Edward Surtz, "Henry VIII's Great Matter in Italy: An Introduction to Representative Italians in the King's Divorce, Mainly 1527–1535." Xerox University Microfilms Monograph Series, LD00025 (Ann Arbor, Mich., 1975).

Wilkins David Wilkins, *Concilia Magnae Britanniae et Hiberniae*, 4 vols. (London, 1737).

*The Matrimonial Trials
of Henry VIII*

Introduction

Henry VIII celebrated his marriage to Catherine of Aragon in 1509. In 1533 he had the marriage annulled on grounds that she had been the wife of his elder brother Arthur. Henry contended that, as Catherine's brother-in-law, he fell under the interdict of incest, which, even according to our present-day definition, could conceivably include in-laws; for incest, quite simply, is "cohabitation of a man and woman so closely related that marriage between them would be illegal." Henry was able to cite a law decreed by God himself that brought his case under an irremovable ban.

But the ban against the marriage had been removed at the time by no less an authority than Christ's vicar on earth, Pope Julius II. What were Henry's grounds for putting aside the papal dispensation? Were they no more than flimsy excuses to gratify his passion for Anne Boleyn? Or were there substantial reasons which could convince the Defender of the Faith that he had been living in sin for two decades with the wife whom he had married "in the face of the Church"?

Though there have been many attempts at an explanation, Henry's mind in the matter has remained a mystery. He has been seen as a complete hypocrite and a Machiavellian of the first water; he has also been characterized as a great upholder of the faith of Christ against the corrupt power of the papacy. The truth of the matter lies somewhere between these two extremes: Henry was partly hypocritical and partly conscientious. He was unquestionably convinced in his conscience that his marriage with Catherine was sinful in the eyes of God. He was the kind of man who could do nothing of set and official purpose that he did not feel to be completely justified before God; but he possessed massive powers of rationalization, and was prepared to resort to cant and skulduggery to attain ends that he believed were fundamentally righteous.[1]

The nature of Henry's self-defense has never been truly understood, first of all because the implications of his relationships with Catherine and Anne have been improperly evaluated, and secondly because key documents detailing his program of justification have been ignored or forgotten. Often, it is not the absence but the superabundance of materials that causes the greater difficulty in attempting to come to grips with the intricacies of Tudor history.

In this book I make use of hitherto unknown or unexploited documentary evidence which not only shows precisely the way in which Henry justified his actions in public and in the courtroom, but also indicates how he justified them to himself, in the privacy of his own conscience. The effect of this new (and old) information is to require substantial alterations in the traditional accounts, not only of his first marriage and annulment, but of the later ones as well; for the religious and legal principles involved remained matters of lasting concern to him.

The advances that I have been able to make in our understanding of these events have been due largely to my peculiar approach. I am not a Tudor historian, and I have not tried to write a Tudor history. Those readers who wish a fuller treatment of more general social and political issues of the time must consult more general (or more specialized) works. For biographical details, for instance, there are Garrett Mattingly's *Catherine of Aragon* (1941) and J. J. Scarisbrick's *Henry VIII* (1968), and for matters of governmental policy the works of G. R. Elton.[2] In Geoffrey de C. Parmiter's *The King's Great Matter* (1967), one can find, as the subtitle indicates, "A Study of Anglo-Papal Rela-

[1] For recent judicious discussions of Henry's conscience in general, see Lacey Baldwin Smith, *Henry VIII: The Mask of Royalty* (London, 1971), pp. 99–117, and Mortimer Levine, *Tudor Dynastic Problems, 1460–1571*, Historical Problems: Studies and Documents no. 21, ed. G. R. Elton (London, 1973), pp. 56–59.

[2] See e.g. Elton's collected essays in his *Studies in Tudor and Stuart Politics and Government*, 2 vols. (Cambridge, 1974), and the review by S. B. Chrimes, *Times Literary Supplement*, 6 December 1974, p. 1392.

tions, 1527–1534."[3] If, in a volume of this length, I had gone into such questions with any greater thoroughness than I do, it would have been at the sacrifice of a full discussion of other, newer material. I trust that I have given enough of the already known context to provide an easily followable story and to prevent the more obvious distortions that such a limited focus might give rise to.

I have come at the subject from the field of intellectual history, the limits of which are not time and space, but concepts and interests. I first approached Henry VIII while writing a history of legal incest. In the course of that study I realized that Henry's conspicuous role in the history would have to be reanalyzed. The major shortcoming of previous accounts of Henry's annulments is that the procedural and canonical aspects have been neglected. The principal reason for this neglect, it seems, is that Tudor historians have been for one reason or another generally disinclined to come to grips with the intricacies of canon law, and historians of canon law have seldom been interested in problems later than the thirteenth century, when the "classical period" of ecclesiastical lawmaking came to an end.

The neglect may be illustrated by a look at the records of the three trials convened in England to pass judgment on Henry's first marriage. The first trial was secretly initiated by Cardinal Wolsey in May 1527, acting on his permanent legatine authority. The official record of the process was brought to light by J. S. Brewer in the nineteenth century, in his *Letters and Papers of Henry VIII*. But Brewer transcribed only half of the badly damaged manuscript, and since then, to my knowledge, no one has attempted further decipherment.

The second trial, the one convened by Cardinals Wolsey and Campeggio by special commission of Pope Clement VII in May 1529, has been discussed at length by many historians, but they have relied chiefly on fragmentary reports instead of investigating the complete record that reposes in the Cambridge University Library. This record was selectively compiled and edited by the English clerks of the trial more than four years after the official process had come to an inconclusive end, presumably for trans-

---

[3] Although Parmiter does an excellent job of sorting out the printed sources for his period, he makes no significant use of archival material, and does not concentrate on the legal and judicial processes.

mittal to Rome as ordered by the papal court in mid-1533. Since its arrival at Cambridge two and a half centuries ago, it has remained almost unnoticed by scholars. Brewer and his successor, James Gairdner, for example, merely cite, at the appropriate dates of May 31, 1529, and October 1, 1533, in the *Letters and Papers*, the description of the manuscript given in the library catalogue.

So, too, has the record of the third English trial of the case, that convened by Archbishop Cranmer in May 1533, remained unused. Gairdner notes the existence of the document in the Cotton collection of the British Museum, but later scholars have only used, and been misled by, the various bits and scraps of documents that Gairdner and others have seen fit to publish.

So long neglected, these records can provide us with a great deal of new information on the events of the trials, and they can also help us to determine the precise form that the trials took. They did not follow an arbitrary format invented by Wolsey for the occasion, as has often been suspected or suggested, but rather were in strict accord with canonical procedure. Essentially, two kinds of juridical process were available to Henry. One was to make an instance case out of his scruple and bring a suit of annulment before one or other of his prelates. In that case, he would be the plaintiff and the queen the defendant. Or he could arrange to be summoned by the prelate and charged with having entered into an invalid and sinful union. This would make him the defendant along with the queen, compelling him either to plead guilty or to resist the charge by arguing in favor of the marriage.

It was the latter course that Henry chose for his first marriage, and similarly for his marriages to Anne Boleyn and to Anne of Cleves. In the case of Anne of Cleves, a formal accusation was leveled against the union by third parties, that is, by the six commissioners who negotiated the marriage in the first place. In the three English trials of Catherine's marriage, and in the single trial of Anne Boleyn, the accusers were identified only as "men worthy of credence," and the judges formulated the charges from the reports that these anonymous but "trustworthy" men gave them.

Such a process was termed an *ex officio* inquisition. It was instituted by Pope Innocent III at the turn of the thirteenth century, and by the fourteenth it had become the most common sort of trial in the English ecclesiastical courts. Chaucer's account of the archdeacon and summoner in the *Friar's Tale* can give us an idea of the sort of abuses that were prosecuted. The archdeacon, we are told, boldly did execution

> In punysshynge of fornicacioun,
> Of wicchecraft, and eek of bawderye,
> Of diffamacioun, and avowtrye,
> Of chirche reves, and of testamentz,
> Of contractes and of lakke of sacramentz,
> Of usure, and of symonye also.

Apart from the sexual offenses here named—fornication, pimping, adultery, and clandestine marriage ("contracts")—people were often summoned on charges of having entered, or of wishing to enter, an impeded marriage.[4] The most common impediment to marriage was a former marriage. When, for example, Henry Percy, Earl of Northumberland, was made to appear before Archbishops Warham and Lee in the summer of 1532 upon the accusation of having entered into a clandestine marriage with Anne Boleyn, the validity not only of Percy's marriage to Mary Talbot but also of Anne's intended marriage to Henry VIII was in question. Summonses were also issued on the basis of suspected incest, that is, carnal connection or marriage between persons related within the forbidden degrees of consanguinity and affinity.

In order to have a clearer understanding of the nature of the chief dispute that arose over Henry's marriage with Catherine, we should take a brief look at the history of the regulations concerning incest, which shows that Henry had a great deal of traditional support for his position.

By the time that canon law was codified by the Bolognese jurist Gratian in the middle of the twelfth century, Christian society had become completely exogamous, at least in theory. By reason of the impediment of consanguinity, no man could marry a woman more closely akin to him than seventh cousin. The law of affinity was

---

[4] For an example of the variety of such "office trials," see my article "Clandestine Marriage and Chaucer's *Troilus*," *Viator*, 4 (1973), 435–57, esp. 439–40, incorporated into my *Love and Marriage in the Age of Chaucer* (Ithaca, N.Y., 1975), pp. 169–70; see also Michael M. Sheehan, "The Formation and Stability of Marriage in Fourteenth-Century England: Evidence of an Ely Register," *Mediaeval Studies*, 33 (1971), 228–63.

equally severe: a widower was prohibited from marrying any of his deceased wife's relatives up to and including the seventh degree (that is, sixth cousins). For all practical purposes, this placed every known kinsman off bounds, since few men are acquainted with their seventh cousins.

The rules were based not so much on an absolute taboo against intermarriage as on a misguided zeal for the letter of the law. From the sixth century onward the standard was taken from Leviticus 18: "No man shall approach to her that is near of kin to him, to uncover her turpitude." Instead of placing the limit at the fifteen or so relationships listed specifically or clearly implied in the book of Leviticus,[5] however, the Church called upon the Roman laws of inheritance to set bounds to the marriage restriction. These laws spoke of descendents to the sixth or seventh degree; and since brother and sister were in the second degree, uncle and niece in the third, and so on, the restriction extended only to second cousins, or to third at the most. But the Germanic system of computation was replacing the Roman, under the influence of the Lombards; for them, the seventh degree meant the seventh generation. Brother and sister were then related in the first degree, uncle and niece in the first mixed with the second, first cousins in the second, and so on to sixth cousins.

In the ninth century, a Frankish forger of papal decrees, now known as Pseudo-Isidore, was so convinced that the prohibition should extend to the seventh generation that he fabricated a letter from Pope Gregory the Great, declaring that the concession which he had granted to Augustine of Canterbury permitting marriages between second and third cousins was merely a temporary provision, to be used in facilitating the conversions of the Angles and Saxons. This false decree was accepted as authentic, and by the eleventh century the rigorous rule setting the boundary at sixth cousins was stabilized; but it proved to be unworkable. Dispensations or other relaxations had to be made. The practice of Gregory the Great, even as modified by Pseudo-Isidore, showed that large

---

[5] The Act of Succession of 1534 prohibited a man from marrying his mother, stepmother, sister, son's daughter, daughter's daughter, half sister, paternal aunt, maternal aunt, uncle's wife, son's wife, brother's wife, stepdaughter, stepson's daughter, stepdaughter's daughter, or wife's sister. Among the more obvious omissions were daughter and mother-in-law; the latter is mentioned in Leviticus, the former is not. See below, Chap. 12 after n. 36.

dispensations were permissible at the discretion of the pope; and at the Fourth Lateran Council of 1215, called by Innocent III, the greatest of the lawyer-popes, it was decided to grant a general reduction in the degrees. Now marriages were to be forbidden only through the fourth degree of consanguinity and affinity; beyond the third-cousin level, there was no longer any impediment.

It was recognized at the same time, however, that still further inroads could be made in the regulations: Pope Gregory I had allowed unions between second cousins among the newly converted Englishmen, and in certain cases even first-cousin unions were considered admissible. Canonists and theologians therefore decided that the specific relationships named in Leviticus were to be taken as the limits of a divinely imposed barrier which no human power had authority to cross. This opinion was universal in the thirteenth century.

At the turn of the fourteenth century the liberal theologian John Duns Scotus stated that only direct-line (parent-child, grandparent-grandchild) marriages were prohibited by the law of nature as formulated in the book of Genesis; collateral degrees of consanguinity and all degrees of affinity were prohibited only by the Church, since Christ did not explicitly renew the Mosaic law of Leviticus. In later times, up to the present day, it was assumed that Scotus believed the pope able to grant dispensations in all degrees except the direct of consanguinity. But he did not draw this conclusion himself, and he clearly held that even before the time of Moses, given the Fall and the multiplication of mankind, several other degrees were in force in the law of nature, on moral grounds.[6]

More importantly, it was not Scotus or his line of reasoning that first led to papal dispensations in the Levitical law. The decisive argument was provided by a contemporary of Scotus, John Andreae (1270–1348), who was not a theologian but a lawyer (and not a celibate cleric but a married layman): he was *doctor utriusque iuris*, professor of canon law at the University of Bo-

---

[6] For the pertinent texts, see my article "Canonical Implications of Richard III's Plan to Marry His Niece," *Traditio*, 23 (1967), 269–311, esp. 274–75. The history of dispensation that follows in the text above is for the most part a condensation of this article, and I refer any reader to it who wishes to follow up the precedents in greater detail.

logna, and one of the most erudite and authoritative jurists of the Middle Ages. Andreae, though he followed the traditional view that the Levitical degrees were still binding upon all men by divine law, developed a theory that the pope could grant a dispensation from such laws in specific instances for a suitable cause. His suggestion, however, was not acted upon in the papal court for another century.

The first pope seriously to consider the possibility of such a dispensation seems to have been Clement VII—not the contemporary of Henry VIII, but the first of the schismatic Avignonese popes, who reigned from 1378 to 1394. In 1392, Bernard, Count of Armagnac, requested a dispensation to marry his older brother's widow. Clement was well disposed toward granting the dispensation, but upon consulting with some of his advisers (including Giles Bellemère, Bishop of Avignon, who reported the incident), he denied it.[7] The matter was discussed before William Noellet, Cardinal of Sant' Angelo, and centered on two questions: did the pope have the power to grant such a dispensation, and was it expedient to do so? The first question was presented by Martin de Zalva (or Salba), Cardinal of Pamplona, who found the arguments for the affirmative more convincing than those against. The question of expediency was presented by Bernard Alemanni, Bishop of Condom, who concluded against it. The matter was then thrown open to the others present, consisting of three theologians and five canonists (or six if Bellemère was present). All but one of the theologians decided that the pope did not have such power of dispensation. The lone holdout (along with Zalva, presumably) was John Acton (or Hatton), O.P., the English penitentiary at the court of Avignon, who like Zalva maintained that the degree of affinity involved was not a moral but rather a judicial law. (Scotus was cited against this opinion, not for it.) Another of Zalva's arguments was that even if the prohibition were still binding by divine law, the pope could dispense from it, as he does with other divine laws. It was acknowledged on both sides that John Andreae and others admitted the power of dispensation for certain kinds of divine law, but not for the Levitical degrees.[8]

[7] Aegidius Bellemère, *Super Decretales Gregorii IX lecturae*, 4.1.8 (*Sponsam*), Vatican MS Ross. 832, f. 39rb–va.

[8] Bellemère gives a long, rambling account of this discussion in his *Consilia*, no. 89, Vatican MS Lat. 2345, ff. 234va–239rv. It is summarized in part by Henri

Andreae's reasoning was not understood and approved of until the reign of John XXIII, who was elected pope by the Council of Pisa in preference to two other claimants to the tiara. In the year 1410 John XXIII received a request from two of the sons of King Henry IV of England, Henry, Prince of Wales, and Thomas, Duke of Clarence, who begged the pontiff to allow Thomas to marry a certain Margaret Holland, in spite of their being related to each other in the second and third degrees of consanguinity and the second degree of affinity. The consanguinity caused no difficulty, but upon further inquiry the pope discovered that the affinity was in the second degree touching the first: Margaret was the widow of John Beaufort, Earl of Somerset, who, being Henry IV's brother,

---

Gilles, "Gilles Bellemère et le tribunal de la Rote à la fin du xive siècle," *Mélanges d'archéologie et d'histoire*, 67 (1955), 281–319, esp. 300–303. Bellemère does not say that he was present at the discussion, though no doubt he was. He says at the beginning that he is drawing on the "factum" given him in which is recorded Count Bernard's petition ("Ex facto mihi tradito in quo dominus Bernardus comes Almaniaci petit," etc.), from which factum two doubts arise: whether the pope can dispense and whether he should. The arguments against the papal power given on ff. 234vb–235ra and the six arguments in favor of the power on ff. 235rb–236vb presumably were contained in Cardinal Zalva's presentation. Zalva ends by citing John Andreae's opinion that questions of power are to be left ultimately to the one whose power is being discussed (f. 236vb). The Bishop of Condom's presentation follows (ff. 236vb–237va), and he cites Andreae on the necessity of reasonable cause (f. 237ra) and against unwise dispensations (f. 237rb). The opinion of the majority is then given (ff. 237va–238va), followed by Acton's (f. 238vab). Then comes a refutation of Acton, which seems to consist mainly of Bellemère's own reasoning (ff. 238vb–239ra). Finally, Bellemère gives his cautious conclusion to the *consilium*: If the pope asks for counsel before acting, "it can probably be answered that he should believe and hold that this dispensation is not permitted to him." If he has already acted, he should not be opposed, for it is up to him to declare the truth in doubtful matters. If he has acted and then has doubts and seeks advice, Bellemère does not know what stand to take (f. 239rab; see Gilles, pp. 302–3). Scotus is cited by both Zalva and the majority as supporting the opinion that the affinity in question is a moral or natural law (ff. 234vb, 237vb). The majority cite Andreae's statement that the pope cannot dispense consanguinity in the first degree direct (parent-child, grandparent-grandchild, etc.) in support of their opinion that he cannot dispense in-laws (f. 237vb). Zalva appeals to Andreae and others as allowing papal dispensations from such divine laws as those governing oaths and even the solemn vow (of celibacy) that comes with holy orders, according to the opinion of all, and also from the vow made in religious profession, according to the more common opinion, and from nonconsummated marriage (f. 236ra). The majority also cite Andreae as justifying dispensations from oaths and vows, which, they say, the Church admits; but they assert that the Church does not admit dispensations in the present case (f. 238rb). For more information on John Acton, see A. B. Emden, *A Biographical Register of the University of Oxford to* A.D. *1500* (Oxford, 1957–59), p. 12.

was Thomas's uncle. The marriage was forbidden by the law of God.

The pope called in to advise him Peter of Ancarano, who like John Andreae before him was professor of canon law at the University of Bologna and a highly respected authority. Peter's *consilium* or formal response to the pontiff, which drew upon Andreae's opinion as well as weighty reasons of his own, concluded that the pope did indeed have the power to grant such a dispensation as was being requested, given a proper reason.

John XXIII's decree, following Peter's opinion, was considered binding even in light of subsequent events. That is, in spite of John's deposition by the ecumenical Council of Constance, which he himself had called, the decisions that he took with due respect for the law—for instance, his excommunication of John Hus in 1411—were considered valid. Even with his alleged public and private defects (including incest), he was still pope, for in the sixteenth century the Pisan popes were held to have been the legitimate rulers of the Church. Proof of this can be seen in Rodrigo Borgia's assumption of the name of Alexander VI, by which he recognized the papal status of John XXIII's Pisan predecessor Alexander V.[9]

When, therefore, on November 11, 1411, Pope John XXIII authorized his nuncio to England to dispense the impediments that stood in the way of the Duke of Clarence's marriage to his uncle's widow, it was an historic event, a breakthrough in the legal tradition of the Church, and it was recognized and respected as such.

In the spring or early summer of 1412, Thomas, Duke of Clarence, acted upon his dispensation and married his aunt-in-law, the widow Beaufort. It is one of the ironies of history that she, the first woman in Christendom to marry legitimately within the Levitical degrees, was the great-great-grandmother of Henry VIII. Her son by her previous marriage, John Beaufort, Duke of Somerset, was the father of Margaret, Countess of Richmond, mother of Henry VII, who, of course, was Henry VIII's father.

A half dozen years after Henry's forebear was dispensed from the law that Henry was to maintain was indispensable, Martin V,

---

[9] We must not be misled by the fact that a pope in the twentieth century considered John to be an antipope and did him the final indignity of removing him from the canonical list of St. Peter's successors, taking his name as the true John XXIII.

the pope who had been elected at Constance after John XXIII's deposition, declared that the theologians, canonists, and prelates whom he had consulted at the council were in agreement that he could permit a man to marry two sisters in succession. (The man in question was Count John I of Foix, who had requested permission to marry Blanche of Navarre, his deceased wife's sister.) No doubt the memory of the English dispensation had an important bearing upon this opinion. But less than two decades later, when a similar request involving two of Margaret Beaufort's granddaughters was brought to Pope Eugenius IV, it was emphatically rejected as being contrary to the law of God and outside the pope's power.

The petitioner in this latter case was the Dauphin of France, the future King Louis XI. His first wife, Margaret, had died in 1445, and he sought permission to marry one of her sisters (both were daughters of King James I of Scotland and his queen Joan Beaufort, daughter of Margaret Beaufort née Holland).[10] The dauphin's royal in-laws could have had little enthusiasm for the marriage of yet another daughter to this sinister prince, whose neglect and ill treatment had contributed, it was thought, to young Margaret's early death. They need not have worried, for the pope entrusted the case to Cardinal John de Torquemada, a man at least as stern and literal in the pursuit of truth and justice as his nephew Thomas, the Grand Inquisitor of Spain. The cardinal's judgment was decisive and admitted of no contradiction: the Levitical degrees were set by the law of God himself, and no pope could tamper with them.[11]

[10] James was captured by the English in 1406, at the age of twelve, and held prisoner for the next eighteen years. It has been thought that his love for the Lady Joan is allegorized in *The Kingis Quair*, a long poem written in rhyme royal, a verse form made popular by Chaucer but so named because of James's supposed use of it.

[11] We should not think that Torquemada maintained any sternness toward the marriage state as such. His tomb in the church of Santa Maria sopra Minerva in Rome reveals that he was a rather gentle soul in this regard. The portrait above the chapel altar shows the cardinal as patron of a pious society founded to raise dowries for girls whose parents were too impoverished to provide for them; he is portrayed in the act of presenting three young maidens to the care of the Holy Virgin. In the same church, behind the high altar, are Sangallo's triumphal tombs of the Medici popes Leo X and Clement VII. The latter, of course, was the pope who was driven to an early grave by Henry VIII—a martyr, in effect, to the principle that the Levitical degrees did in fact admit of papal dispensation.

Henry VIII and his advocates in later times were much encouraged when they discovered Torquemada's account of this case, in which the offspring of the sovereigns of two nations were summarily refused permission to marry on the very same grounds upon which Henry was resting his case. John Fisher, the learned Bishop of Rochester, who not long before had helped to make the king Defender of the Faith, opposed this argument—just as he opposed all the arguments that were brought up in support of Henry's position. If Torquemada had only studied the sacred text more closely, Fisher said, he would have seen that Leviticus forbade marriage with the wife's sister only while the wife was still alive.[12] The Jews, in fact, practiced polygamy and allowed divorce, and the Levitical restriction upon affinity dealt with something quite different from what Christian lawmakers had traditionally believed. Literally taken, it meant that Henry had been forbidden to marry Catherine only while his brother Arthur was alive.

Cardinal Torquemada apparently was not cognizant of the grants made by Popes John XXIII and Martin V against the letter (as he saw it) of the Levitical law. But he was aware of oversimplified arguments that canonists had been using in claiming that the pope had this power, and he dismissed them with contempt. In response to the allegation that the power had already been exercised recently in allowing an uncle to marry his niece, the cardinal replied brusquely that he did not know of any such case.

This too was seized upon by Henry's men, and Fisher remarked that if the cardinal had only lived till his day (he was writing in 1531), he would have seen many examples of such dispensations for uncle-niece marriages.[13] If Fisher and his opponents had read a little further in Torquemada, they would have seen that the cardinal himself was later called upon by another pope, Pius II, to consider a request of this sort. This time he did go back to his Bible, there to discover that although unions between nephew and aunt were interdicted, those between uncle and niece were not. Torquemada, like most other theologians and canonists, had misinterpreted the word *neptis* in the lists of prohibited persons

---

[12] John Fisher, *Responsum ad libellum impressum Londini 1530*, London, British Museum MS Arundel 151, f. 262v.

[13] *Ibid.*, f. 263.

given in the glosses on canon law, reading it as niece rather than granddaughter. Following this discovery, at Torquemada's recommendation, Pope Pius permitted a count of Piacenza to marry his sister's daughter.

This action seems not to have become widely known, however, and twenty years later, in 1485, when Richard III of England thought of marrying Elizabeth, the daughter of his brother Edward IV, he was told by his theological advisers that the pope would be unable to permit it. His niece was therefore reserved for greater things, and thus it was that her son Henry VIII received the benefit—or curse as he came to see it—of the pope's newly found and still disputed powers of relaxing the boundaries that God had set against incest.

If the memory of the precedent established within the English royal family had been lost to it (Margaret Holland was the sister-in-law of Richard III's grandmother), it was not lost to Rome. In 1481 there appeared a commentary upon canon law by Felino Sandeo, in which he stated: "The pope for a reason can interpret and delimit divine law by constitution or rescript, although he cannot entirely abrogate it . . . because divine law is immutable." After acknowledging the authority of John Andreae, he went on to say: "You will find a good deal of support for this position in the *consilium* of Peter of Ancarano . . . in which he took great pains on behalf of the son of the King of England to advise that the pope could for a reason dispense a nephew, that is, the son of a brother, to marry the wife of his dead uncle." The edition of Peter's *Consilia* published in Pavia in 1496 also revealed that "this was a question which concerned the son of the King of England."[14]

Felino Sandeo was an auditor of the Roman Rota (the papal

---

[14] Kelly, *Traditio*, 23: 284–85. Luis Vives, one of Catherine of Aragon's humanist advocates, cited Peter's *consilium* and the agreement of Sandeo and the Speculator (William Durantis) on the pope's general power of dispensation and then quoted a marginal gloss (from what source he did not say) affirming that a dispensation to marry one's uncle's widow could be granted, as was done for a nephew of the king of England. Vives, *Non esse neque divino neque naturae iure prohibitum quin summus pontifex dispensare possit ut frater demortui sine liberis fratris uxorem legitimo matrimonio sibi possit adiungere, adversus aliquot academiarum censuras tumultuaria ac perbrevis apologia sive confutatio* (Lüneburg, September 1532), sig. r ii. This treatise, along with many other early printed works on the dispute, is in the Granville Library of the British Museum (no. 1234). On the Lüneburg imprint, which is suspect, see below, Chap. 11, n. 14.

court of appeals that pronounced upon questions of canon law) until the end of 1502, shortly before his death. During his tenure the pope's power in the realm of forbidden marriages had been reactivated: in 1496, Ferrante, the twenty-six-year-old King of Naples, was allowed by the Spanish pope Alexander VI to marry his nineteen-year-old aunt, Joanna, who was the niece of Ferdinand the Catholic; and in 1500, Ferdinand's daughter Maria married King Emmanuel I of Portugal, who had previously been married to another of Ferdinand's daughters, Isabella. In 1504, still another daughter of Ferdinand's, Catherine, was finally dispensed after some hesitation by a new pope, Julius II, to marry her former husband's brother, Henry, Prince of Wales.

Such, then, is the history of theological and legal thought and practice concerning marriage and incest up to the time of Henry VIII, as we now know it.[15] Henry knew much less than we know, especially at the time when he first became convinced of the illegality of his marriage. He was under the impression that the law against marriage within the Levitical degrees had first been relaxed only a few years before his own dispensation was granted, at the request of his future wife's family, by the notoriously corrupt Borgia pope Alexander VI, as a favor from one Spaniard to another. Against these few exemptions—or rather violations—of the law, Henry had the witness not only of God himself but of fifteen centuries of Christian teaching.

But Henry's case was not to be resolved so simply as he thought. Peter of Ancarano, in demonstrating to Pope John XXIII the legality of allowing Henry's ancestor, the widowed Countess of Somerset, to marry her husband's nephew, had argued that Pope Inno-

[15] It is sometimes thought that Louis XII of France was allowed in 1499 to marry his brother's widow, Anne of Brittany; in fact, however, Anne was the widow of his cousin Charles VIII. See my article in *Traditio*, p. 308, n. 1. Louis's first wife, Jeanne of Valois, enters our story for a different reason: her marriage to the king was annulled on grounds that the match had been forced upon him and not consummated. Henry VIII used similar grounds in dissolving his union to Anne of Cleves, and he also urged Catherine of Aragon to enter a convent, following Jeanne's supposed example—hoping that her religious vows would effect the divorce. Finally, it is worth noting that no impediment was caused by the circumstance that Louis's second wife was sister-in-law of his first wife. J. J. Scarisbrick (*Henry VIII*, p. 358) is mistaken in finding a double affinity between Henry and the Duchess of Milan, Catherine's grandniece. The affinity came only from Catherine's union to Henry, and not from her marriage to Arthur, even assuming that that marriage was consummated.

cent III had permitted converts to the faith to remain married to their brothers' widows. The pope had made this concession only if the conditions of the law of levirate had been present—the law, that is, of Deuteronomy which commanded the younger brother to marry the wife of the elder brother when the latter had died without begetting any children. It was the only exception to the Levitical prohibitions that was recognized in the Middle Ages, and this recognition was denied by few; Torquemada, for example, strongly affirmed it.

Unfortunately for Henry's wishes, his situation conformed to the requirements of levirate. He tried to prove in various ways that the law did not apply to him—that it was, for instance, a dispensation that only God could give and that in fact God had revoked, since the Jews no longer practiced it. It was true that the Jews no longer practiced polygamy, having adopted the Christian view in the matter; but it was not true that they had abandoned the law of levirate, and Henry's argument was dashed when two such marriages were reported in Italy.

He attempted to buttress his position with Hebraic scholarship, and summoned learned rabbis for the purpose (he had to import them, since his predecessor Edward I had anticipated Catherine's parents by two centuries in expelling all the Jews from his kingdom). One such rabbi, after studying the problem, emerged with the solution that even though Henry had legitimately married Catherine, he had done so to fulfill the law of levirate, and was simply acting in Arthur's place; Catherine was still Arthur's wife, and Henry was free to have another wife for himself. When the exegete was informed that his answer was not satisfactory, he tried again, and pronounced this time that the king's marriage was indeed invalid, for the reason that he had not had the intention of raising up children to his brother's name. The disappointed monarch realized that he would get nothing from him against the validity of levirate itself, which was what he so dearly desired.

Again, Henry alleged that the leviratical dispensation applied only to Jews—he was, he declared time and again, the only Christian man who had been allowed to marry his brother's wife. But then two other cases were turned up in Venice by the agents of Catherine's nephew, the Emperor Charles V.

Still another way out of the levirate impasse was suggested: this was to assert that the command of Deuteronomy applied only to the brother's wife whose marriage had not been completed by sexual union. This solution received no encouragement from the king. For the truth of the matter, though he was now admitting it to no one, was that Catherine's marriage to Arthur had never been consummated and therefore no affinity had been contracted, since in the opinion of the authorities on canon law affinity arose from intercourse, not marriage. In other words, Henry knew that the only impediment between him and Catherine was the impediment that arose from the marriage contract, namely, "public honesty," which everyone affirmed to be a man-imposed obstacle easily removed by the pope.

As a further complication, years before Henry had become infatuated with Anne Boleyn, he had taken her sister Mary as his mistress. Therefore, since affinity was caused even by extramarital intercourse, there existed an adamantine Levitical barrier between Henry and Anne, the same kind that he had supposed to be between him and Catherine.

There was another problem still: Anne Boleyn was already married. She had, Henry was informed quite early in the piece, secretly entered into but not consummated a matrimonial contract. (Such unions were valid even without priest or witnesses.) She was married in the same way therefore that Catherine had been married to Arthur; but Anne's husband, whoever he was, was still alive. Therefore, at the same time that Henry sought an annulment for his own marriage, he also had to take steps to get a divorce for Anne's marriage.[16] But the pope's power to dissolve a nonconsummated marriage contract was even more strongly disputed than his power to dispense from the Levitical degrees; some canonists said that it could be done, but many others, along with almost all theologians, said no. The rigorists therefore who agreed with Henry's first idea that no mere man, not even the Vicar of Christ, could allow him to have his brother's wife, would free him from Catherine only to deny him Anne, for they would

[16] It will be seen that "divorce" in Henry's day had not only the modern meaning of dissolution of an admittedly valid marriage but also the meaning of annulment, that is, the judicial declaration that a marriage had been null and void from the beginning. In the pages that follow, for the sake of clarity, I shall favor the term "annulment" over "divorce" when nullity and not dissolution is under discussion.

not admit that he could have another man's wife—or, for that matter, the sister of his concubine.[17] If, on the other hand, Henry himself were to adopt a broader notion of the Holy Father's powers, and if something were to be found defective in the bull that allowed him to marry Catherine, then he could be released from her and the barriers between him and Anne could be lowered.

These then are some of the difficulties that Henry encountered when he began his attempt to free himself of his first wife and to take another more to his liking. Let us begin to follow him in detail as he attempted to steer a course toward the remedy he sought, and hope that the complicated maze of his conscience will, at least in part, be laid open to us.[18]

[17] I cannot forbear at this point from taking issue with James A. Brundage, "Concubinage and Marriage in Medieval Canon Law," *Journal of Medieval History*, 1 (1975), 1–17, who holds that lay concubinage, in the sense of sexual cohabitation without marriage, was not finally and fully prohibited until the Council of Trent in 1563 (see esp. p. 10). It was only clandestine marriage that was held to be valid, though illicit, before Trent. No approbation or validity of any kind was attached to nonmarital sexual intercourse, apart from the matter of affinity; it is true, of course, that even priests could enter into *financial* contracts with their concubines that might be considered binding (see my *Love and Marriage in the Age of Chaucer*, pp. 200–201). It was a principle of canon law that priests could bestow their private property upon whomever they chose (CIC X 3.27.1).

[18] Chronological surveys of events can be found in the Index under appropriate entries, especially Catherine of Aragon, Clement VII (Medici), consummation, Cranmer, Henry VIII, Julius II, legatine court, Parliament, public honesty, trials, and Wolsey.

FIRST EFFORTS

But, conscience, conscience!
Oh, 'tis a tender place; and I must leave her.

It seems the marriage with his brother's wife
Has crept too near his conscience.
No, his conscience
Has crept too near another lady.

Thus hulling in
The wild sea of my conscience, I did steer
Toward this remedy.

—Shakespeare & Fletcher, HENRY VIII

CHAPTER ONE

Henry's Scruple

EARLY IN the year 1527, Henry VIII, after eighteen years of marriage to Catherine of Aragon, made a disturbing revelation to a handful of his counselors: he had come to the conclusion that his marriage had been entered into against the law of God, and he therefore wished to have it annulled. Catherine and many others, when they discovered the king's intention, immediately concluded that the idea had been planted in his mind by the Cardinal Archbishop of York, Thomas Wolsey, who, as Henry's Lord Chancellor, was his chief adviser. The cardinal's desire to be revenged for the diplomatic betrayals practiced upon England by the Emperor Charles V, Catherine's nephew, was thought sufficient motivation for such a scheme. But the truth of the matter seems to be that Henry's plan came as a surprise to the cardinal, and that he was basically opposed to it.

Henry was fully capable of coming to his conclusion alone and unaided. For he needed only a strong reason for pursuing a given course of conduct and he would immediately begin to find justification for it. Wolsey knew this, and knew too that once his sovereign had set his mind on an object it was advisable to fall into line and make the best of it. The cardinal accordingly began to investigate the matter, and in May 1527 he summoned the king to appear before him at a secret ecclesiastical trial held in Wolsey's own house at Westminster.

The trial was, as I have mentioned in the Introduction, an *ex officio* inquisition, a form that had been established by Pope Innocent III and confirmed at the Fourth Lateran Council in 1215. It enabled a prelate to take action against a crime or an abuse without the formality of having an accusation or denunciation brought against the implicated party by a specific individual. Public infamy, as reported to the prelate by trustworthy persons, was sufficient. The accused, or rather the defamed, would then be summoned to appear before him as judge to hear the charges and to be informed of the names and testimony of whatever witnesses were to appear in the matter. The procedure differed from the sort of inquest that survives in our own day, in that the judge was empowered to pronounce sentence and impose a fitting penalty if guilt were established. It was, in other words, a real trial, and essentially the same sort of process as that used by inquisitors both in England and on the Continent against suspected heretics, except that in heresy cases the rights of the accused could be, but need not be, greatly restricted.[1]

Wolsey convened his tribunal as papal legate *a latere*, which gave him jurisdiction over all England. He had at his command a kind of legatine chancery: when his faculties as legate were extended by Pope Leo X in 1521, he was given the power to grant certain dispensations, including the right to marry within the ecclesiastically prohibited degrees of consanguinity and affinity, and he set up a faculty office with a legal staff to administer these powers.[2] Since all kinds of serious and nonserious abuses,

[1] Pope Innocent's decree was incorporated into the *Decretals of Gregory IX*, CIC X 5.1.24: "Qualiter et quando debeat praelatus procedere ad inquirendum et puniendum subditorum excessus." The gloss on this chapter gives a clear explanation of the procedure to be followed. See also "Inquisition," *Dictionnaire de droit canonique*, VII, 1419–20. For evidence that the concessions allowed to the *inquisitor haereticae pravitatis* were available to the English bishops, see my forthcoming "English Kings and the Fear of Sorcery," *Mediaeval Studies*, 39 (1977). This article also describes standard *ex officio* procedures in fifteenth-century England, which remained the same in the sixteenth century. See also Brian L. Woodcock, *Medieval Ecclesiastical Courts in the Diocese of Canterbury* (Oxford, 1952); Colin Morris, "A Consistory Court in the Middle Ages," *Journal of Ecclesiastical History*, 14 (1963), 150–59; Margaret Bowker, *An Episcopal Court Book for the Diocese of Lincoln, 1514–1520*, Lincoln Record Society, no. 61 (Lincoln, 1967). Morris's supposition (p. 153), followed by Bowker, p. xix, that the bishop's consistory court in Lincoln lost the power to hear *ex officio* cases after the middle of the fourteenth century, is surely wrong. One of his reasons, that the sole surviving consistory roll (1430–31) contains only instance cases, can doubtless be disposed of by what Woodcock, p. 31, has to say about Canterbury: that *ex officio* records were kept separately from instance acts, and were much less careful and complete.

[2] D. S. Chambers, *Faculty Office Registers, 1534–1549* (Oxford, 1966), pp. xvii–xviii.

including "consanguinity between spouses and other matrimonial impediments," could be investigated by a formal inquisition,[3] and were so investigated in England as a matter of course, the cardinal would clearly have had much experience in conducting this kind of trial. He proceeded in the "modern" fashion for important cases, once the preliminary charge was contested, by appointing a "promoter of his office" to assist him in the conduct of the trial. This official, eventually called the "promoter of justice," finds no mention in the judicial directories of the thirteenth century; he appeared later, but long before Wolsey's time, to fulfill a function analogous to that of the prosecuting attorney in present-day practice, and also comparable to the "promoter of the faith" or "devil's advocate" in canonization trials.[4] But there is a very great difference: unlike modern criminal proceedings, where the prosecutor presents the state's or crown's accusations and evidence against the defendant independently of the judge, in the *inquisitio ex officio* it is the judge himself, or, after the initial charges, the promoter *acting as the judge's aide*, who levels all accusations and gathers the evidence to support them.

In one way Wolsey neglected to fulfill the requirements for an *inquisitio ex officio*: all persons implicated in the abuse or crime were supposed to be summoned, and the trial could not proceed in their absence, unless they absented themselves through contumacy (contempt of court). Not only was Catherine not summoned, but every effort was made to keep the knowledge of the affair secret from her. For all their precautions, she did find out about the trial not long after it came to an end. Perhaps it was the nature of the proceedings, in which Wolsey impugned the marriage and Henry appeared as the defender of the bond, that convinced Catherine that the cardinal was the instigator of the annulment.

The record of the trial is extant. It was committed in its final form to parchment by the court clerks, Stephen Gardiner, Wolsey's secretary, and William Clayburgh. Though it has been badly

[3] William Durantis (1237–96), *Speculum iuris*, III, part 1: *De inquisitione* 2.3 (Venice, 1585), p. 31. See also my Introduction, n. 4.

[4] See *Dictionnaire de droit canonique*, VI, 1421; VII, 356–60. The promoter of the faith was even more recently evolved than the promoter of justice: his role was first defined by Leo X, the pope who granted Wolsey his legatine powers for life.

damaged by damp and vermin, it is possible to make out the main lines of the proceedings.[5]

The trial convened on May 17. The clerks were first sworn in, in the presence of the king and William Warham, Archbishop of Canterbury, with three other doctors of law as witnesses. Wolsey then addressed the king and explained the purpose of the trial, the necessity of which was dictated by the responsibility he felt for his legatine office. He recounted that he had come to be troubled in his mind and conscience over a matter that concerned the salvation of Henry's soul. Accordingly, in the company of the Archbishop of Canterbury, he had approached the king at Greenwich and requested him to present himself at Westminster on this day, to begin cognizance of the case according to the order and custom of trials and the manner of procedure established by the Church, for the settling of their consciences and especially for the safety of the king's soul. The cardinal then requested that Warham be permitted to serve as his assessor (that is, assistant and counselor), and the king agreed.[6] Thereafter, Wolsey would announce before all his decisions that he was acting upon the counsel of his fellow archbishop.

The cardinal then presented to Henry in a single article the facts of his marriage and the objection that had been raised against it. It was notorious, he charged, by the evidence of the fact itself, that Catherine, who for eighteen years had had Henry for husband and had raised offspring to him, had previously contracted marriage with Henry's deceased brother, with whom she had lived and by whom she had been carnally known. Unless therefore a sufficient dispensation had been obtained from the Apostolic See completely removing the impediment raised by Catherine's first marriage, the second would not be valid. But because, in the opinion of some, such a marriage was forbidden by divine law as well as by ecclesiastical statute, a scruple ought to arise in the king's conscience and he should fear the divine vengeance, which, though sometimes slow in coming, customarily made up for the delay by its severity. The cardinal therefore for-

---

[5] *Acta iudicialia*, London, Public Record Office SP 1, Folio C.1, partially transcribed by J. S. Brewer, LP IV, 3140. At the beginning of his summary, for "registrar" read "registrars," to include Gardiner along with Clayburgh. In their oath, p. 3, the clerks refer to the trial as a "iudiciaria cognitio."

[6] *Acta iudicialia* 4–6.

mally requested the king to reply to the charge and offer whatever justification he could for his marriage.

The king had a preliminary reply ready in writing. He seems to have admitted the truth and notoriety of fact as set forth by the cardinal, but said that he would offer justification for the marriage in due time through his proctor, Dr. John Bell.[7]

Wolsey then appointed Dr. Richard Wolman to be the promoter of his office in order to assist in the examination of the cause.[8] Wolman immediately requested the aforesaid article to be judged notorious, since it was so conceded *ex adversis*, that is, by the party against whom it was directed. Apparently Wolsey agreed, and then adjourned the trial until May 20. When the trial resumed, Bell appeared with Henry's justification. This repeated Wolsey's statement of fact and apparently admitted its truth and notoriety, but except for mention of a dispensation, the substance of the justification is almost completely unintelligible. The promoter then requested that the evidence for the justification be examined, and Wolsey set the following Thursday, May 23, for the purpose.[9]

On that day Wolsey allowed the justificatory material to be produced by Bell, and apparently set a term for any more such material to be submitted, namely, the octave of the feast of Saint Michael, if it should happen to be a juridical day; otherwise it was to be the first juridical day following. That is to say, they had until October 6 or later to justify the marriage. But Bell immediately brought forth Pope Julius II's bull of dispensation for exhibition. Thereupon Wolman requested a term to be set for hearing the objections that could be raised against the bull. Wolsey complied by naming the day after Ascension Thursday, namely May 31.[10]

---

[7] *Ibid.* 6–7. Cf. Brewer's transcription, pp. 1427–28.

[8] *Ibid.* 8. Brewer is mistaken in calling Wolman "promoter of the suit"; this kind of trial did not have a suit presented by a plaintiff or accuser. Wolsey's announcement of Wolman's appointment reads: "Ut causa, cuius examinationem nobis suscepimus ex debito iuris ordine atque officio nostri, debite in omnibus et per omnia diligenter examinetur, Vos, Richardum Wulmanne decretorum doctorem quem nostre Jurisdictionis cum effectu exequende solicitum et diligentem fore speramus, ac multum antehoc argumentis f * * * * * * * * * et circumspectum cognoscimus, promotorem necessarium officii nostri in hac causa assignamus ac deputamus."

[9] *Ibid.* 8–11.

[10] *Ibid.* 11–15.

On the assigned day Wolman appeared and exhibited material against the bull, on the basis of which he petitioned Wolsey to do whatever justice demanded in the matter. The promoter had arranged his objections in the form of a number of articles which contained matter both of fact and of law. He intended to prove them before Wolsey, so far as it was necessary and he was bound by law, by means of witnesses, legal instruments, and other species of proof. He proposed all that was contained in the articles to have the full effect of the law, but did not bind himself to prove everything that he alleged. Rather he insisted that everything which did admit of proof should hold good.[11]

In the first article he repeated what had been shown to be notorious by the evidence of the fact and the judicially submitted confession of the implicated party. In the second article (most of which is undecipherable) he stated what was clearly provided by the law in the matter. The third article cited authorities who held that such a marriage could not be allowed even by the pope, because it was forbidden by divine law. He cited Innocent III's decretal *Litteras*, where the pope stated that a dispensation could not be given in degrees forbidden by divine law;[12] and he adduced Cardinal Torquemada's strong assertion to the same effect.[13]

The first part of the fourth article is also undecipherable, but in the second half Wolman said that the bull of dispensation had been obtained for Henry when he had not yet completed his twelfth year, and that in his twelfth year or later (*citra*), in obedience (to his father, presumably) he contracted spousals with Catherine. Upon attaining his fourteenth year, by the counsel of his

---

[11] *Ibid.* 16: "Articulos infrascriptos et contenta in eijsdem tam facti quam Juris materiam continentes producit et exhibet. Et quatenus necesse erit aut de Jure tenetur, testibus, instrumentis, et alijs probationis speciebus coram Vobis probare intendit. Que omnia in infrascriptis articulis comprehensa proponit ad omnem Juris effectum coniunctim et divisim. Non ar[c]tans se ad omnia inferius deducta probanda. Sed eatenus obtineat quatenus probaverit, etc." See the similar formulas of the promoters in the heresy trials of Friar William Russell before Archbishop Chichele in London in 1425 and before the papal delegate Cardinal Branda in Rome in 1426, in the *Chichele Register*, III, 104–55, esp. 126–28 and 140–44. These trials, as well as others in the same volume, provide valuable illustrations of the various forms of procedure to be met with in Henry's marriage trials.

[12] CIC X 2.13.13 (in the title *De restitutione spoliatorum*). See Kelly, *Traditio*, 23: 274.

[13] *Acta iudicialia* 16–17.

greater maturity, he had protested against the spousals in the presence of witnesses.[14] The promoter did not draw any legal objections at this point from these facts, or from the fact stated in the fifth article, that Isabella and Henry VII had died (before the marriage actually took place). He rather saved the charges for succeeding articles. In the mutilated passage that follows, the sense seems to be that he placed all the above ("premisit omnia") along with the previously adduced factual matter ("in facti materia"). Or perhaps it is a better rendering to say that these items were to be added to the content of the factum. A *factum*, as we shall see later, is a statement of the accepted facts of a case, to be recited before a legal discussion of the said facts takes place. Wolman went on to say that this material would be necessary in proving the papal bull surreptitious (that is, obtained under false pretenses through the suppression of vital information).

In the next paragraph, beginning "Principio" (in the first place), which I count as the sixth article, he dealt with the "surreption" that stemmed from telling the pope something that would cause him to grant the dispensation more easily. He seems to have given an example from the above facts, but it cannot be made out what it was. He clearly did so in the next, alleging that Henry's young age, an especially important consideration in matrimonial dispensations, was passed over in silence. In the eighth article he charged that the certainty of consummation in Catherine's first marriage, from which affinity arose, was concealed, and instead it was expressed to the pope as doubtful by use of the word *forsan* ("perhaps").[15]

In the ninth article, he spoke of the need to have all the impediments removed, and objected that the bull made no mention of public honesty (the impediment that arose from the marriage contract, as contrasted with affinity, which arose from the consummation of the marriage). Therefore this obstacle continued to stand in the way of the marriage.[16] The tenth article objected that insuf-

---

[14] *Ibid.* 18. On the meaning of *citra*, see below, Chap. 4, n. 13.

[15] *Acta iudicialia* 18–19.

[16] *Ibid.* 20. I assume that this was the form of the objection from the fact that carnal copula with resulting affinity is taken as established. In the second line of the article occur the words "removendi omnia impedimenta." The impediment of "publice honestatis iustitia" (the righteousness of public decency) is named three times—e.g. "publice honestatis Ulla sit facta [mentio]." Cf. the

ficient diligence and caution had been used in the granting of such a highly unusual and rarely conceded dispensation; and the fact that the usual form and style had not been followed made the grant suspect. The next article is similar: in dispensations of this sort the popes were accustomed to add clauses derogating from any contrary provisions in the acts of general councils or in previous papal pronouncements; Julius's bull was considerably defective on this score; and since the impediment was based on divine law, he should have added the phrase "notwithstanding that it is prohibited by divine law."[17]

In the twelfth article he spoke of the great distance between England and Spain and the impossibility of a sudden attack by one against the other. There were no disputed titles in either country, and commerce was carried on between them. The promoter's objection seems to have been that there was no urgent need for a marriage of this sort to conserve the peace, as it was alleged in the bull.[18] Finally, in the last two articles, Wolman charged that even if the dispensation had been valid at the time it was granted, it was nullified by subsequent events. First of all, and this is the substance of the thirteenth article, it was established in the foregoing factum ("iam ex facti serie, ut predictum est, constat") that by the protestation which Henry made upon reaching puberty, he freed himself from the spousals he had contracted with Catherine. The dispensation thereupon was invalidated, and it could not regain its efficacy by anything that followed (that is, by Henry's decision to go ahead with the marriage after all). The fourteenth and last article centered upon the fact that Queen Isabella and King Henry VII had died before the papal concession had been put into effect. But the pope in granting the bull for the conservation of peace intended this effect for the specific rulers named in the bull. Therefore, once these persons had died, the grant became null and void, for it was now lacking its final cause.[19]

In summation, Dr. Wolman requested the cardinal to balance the arguments he had set forth and to decide which were light and which were weighty, to receive evidence establishing their proof,

---

form of the objection raised, presumably by the promoter, in the legatine trial of 1529 (see Appendix A, the eighth doubt).

[17] *Acta iudicialia* 20.

[18] *Ibid.* 20–21.

[19] *Ibid.* 21–22.

and finally to decree the execution of whatever the law prescribed in the matter.

Dr. Bell then asked for a copy of the promoter's articles. Wolsey gave order for it, and then abruptly adjourned the proceedings *sine die*. He stated that, upon consultation with his assessor, since the cognizance of the case was very difficult and depended upon the interpretation of the sacred canons, he hereby decreed that learned theologians and lawyers should be summoned to elucidate the matter. Among those whom he named were Bishops Fisher of Rochester, Longland of Lincoln, and Tunstall of London.[20]

Wolsey himself had already consulted with Fisher, and Fisher had written to him twice on the subject. He first told the cardinal of the great dissidence that he had found in the published authorities: many held that such a marriage was prohibited by divine law, while others vigorously asserted that it was in no way contrary to it. In the second letter, which Wolsey forwarded to the king on June 2, two days after the trial was adjourned, Fisher summed up his previous report and gave his own opinion in the matter: it could not be proved by any reason that there was a divine law still in force prohibiting a man from marrying his brother's childless widow. Therefore, no one could deny the pope the power to grant it for a pressing reason. Even if the arguments for and against this view were conceded to be of equal force, the fact that the pope had often exercised the power would satisfy him that he did so legitimately.[21]

Wolsey clearly saw that Henry's case would not easily stand up in court—especially in a papal court[22]—unless the actual document of dispensation could be disqualified in some way. On this point the cardinal was worried by one problem in particular,

20 *Ibid*. 22–23.

21 Pocock, I, 9–10; SP I, 189 (LP IV, 3147). Wolsey had not yet told Fisher that Henry's marriage was in any way impugned, but the bishop guessed that an annulment was being sought. Wolsey assured him a month later that it was only the French ambassador, the Bishop of Tarbes, who had questioned the marriage. Wolsey to Henry VIII, 5 July 1527, LP IV, 3231 (also Brewer's Intro., IV, cclxvi–cclxvii).

22 A few days before the last session of the Westminster inquisition, word had reached England that Rome had been sacked by the forces of the Emperor Charles V, Catherine of Aragon's nephew, and that Clement VII and his cardinals had taken refuge in the Castel Sant' Angelo. See the letter of Bishop John Clerk to Wolsey, 28 May 1527, LP IV, 3136.

which concerned the precise nature of the queen's first marriage. Although at the trial the king through his proctor had specifically admitted the accuracy of all the facts contained in the indictment, including Arthur's carnal knowledge of his wife, common opinion, supported by the assertions of both Catherine and Henry himself, was that the marriage had not been consummated. Apparently when Henry first hit upon the idea of a divorce he had not realized the crucial importance of this point, but Wolsey no doubt did, as can be gathered from the questions put by Wolman, well over a month before the beginning of the trial, to Richard Fox, the aged and now blind Bishop of Winchester. Fox had opposed the match between Henry and Catherine when it was first suggested, shortly after Arthur's death, but when the dispensation was finally obtained, he consented to it. One of the matters upon which the bishop was now interrogated was whether the marriage between Arthur and Catherine was consummated. He replied that the couple had lived together, and that he believed that consummation had followed from this cohabitation. Further on, he was asked whether a dispensation had been obtained from the pope for the impediment of affinity or of public honesty. Fox replied that he thought that a bull had been obtained for the impediment of affinity.[23]

I have shown the use to which Wolman put this information at the trial: since Catherine had acquired both impediments, the bull was invalid because it dispensed only for affinity and not for public honesty. Other of his charges were based upon the claim that the affinity was an obstacle established by the law of God. But if consummation had not occurred, then this argument was apparently worthless, for only the impediment of public honesty would be present; and it was admitted by all modern authorities that this was a barrier erected not by divine decree but rather by man-made —or church-made—law that could be suspended at will by the supreme pontiff.

The difficulty had not occurred to Henry. Would it, Wolsey won-

23 Record Office SP 1/54, ff. 362–63; cited in Scarisbrick, p. 194; cf. LP IV, 5791, and see below, Chap. 6 at n. 48. Wolman phrased the question, "an ob removendum impedimentum affinitatis sive publice honestatis aliqua a summo pontifice dispensatio fuit impetrata." The use of *sive* rather than the adversative *aut* indicates that it was not an "either/or" question but "one or both."

dered, occur to Catherine when it came time to break the news to her of the doubt that had been cast upon her marriage? It would indeed, he soon found out. Within a month after the trial was adjourned, he discovered what her reaction was: Richard Sampson, Henry's chaplain, reported that "the queen was very stiff and obstinate" in her determination to defend her marriage; she affirmed that Arthur had never known her carnally, and, furthermore, she desired to have professional advice, not only such counsel as could be provided in England, but expert assistance from abroad as well.

Wolsey realized immediately that Catherine had already been counseled: someone with a clear knowledge of the canon law of the case had instructed her how to defend herself. She could not otherwise, he felt, have put her finger so unerringly upon the weakest link in the chain of argument that had been forged against the marriage. The king's offensive would have to be altered radically if the queen's assertion were substantiated. Wolsey knew all along the defense that would have to be made: he would have to adjust the argument that Wolman had offered at the inquisition in his ninth article. The cardinal explained his reasoning to Sampson: the bull of Pope Julius dispensed Henry and Catherine only from affinity and made no mention of public honesty; but if there had been no affinity but only public honesty, then the latter impediment was never dispensed from, and still stood in the way of the marriage.[24]

In his recent biography of Henry, J. J. Scarisbrick expresses great confidence in this argument. He elaborates upon it with the enthusiasm and cautious optimism of one of the king's more competent legal advisers, and propounds it as a line of defense which he is reasonably certain would have won the day for his royal subject, if only it had been pursued. "Why," he asks, "did not the scores of nimble doctors, the international team of theologians and canonists whom Henry called up to cut his Gordian knot, leap upon this point?"[25]

The answer is that they did—and found it wanting. A closer look at the records reveals that the argument of public honesty was a key element in the defense of the case in the trials held both in

24 Wolsey to Henry VIII, SP I, 194.
25 Scarisbrick, p. 193.

England and in Rome, and the point became one of utmost concern to Henry's conscience.

Henry first heard of the new difficulty from Sampson, who had reported, as directed by Wolsey, the conversation that the cardinal had had with him. Henry's response was a forecast of things to come: he became angered with Wolsey for questioning his secret matter, and sent Wolman to deliver him a sharp rebuke. Wolsey wrote back, protested his entire devotion to the cause, and repeated precisely what he had said to Sampson: if Arthur never knew the queen carnally, the nature of the impediment was altered.[26]

This time, no doubt, the justice of the cardinal's insight struck home. What effect would it have had upon his views on the divine institution of marriage? Let us see if we can arrive at some understanding of what his meditations on God's ways with man and woman must have been.

In the earliest phase of his efforts to get out of his marriage, Henry was unquestionably much impressed by the texts of Leviticus that forbade a union with one's brother's wife, but it is by no means evident that he was convinced that it was an absolute prohibition that admitted of no exception. It seems clear that he was still willing to admit that the pope had the power to allow such a marriage; but if so, he was sure that it had been wrongly or improperly done in his case, and for this reason God had punished him in leaving him virtually childless, the penalty promised by Leviticus; for, apart from her many miscarriages, five of the six children born to him by Catherine had died, and only one daughter, Mary, survived.

No woman had ever formally ruled England (*pace* the champions of the Empress Matilda or Margaret of Anjou). The precedent for successful female sovereigns would in fact be set by Mary, but that was something that Henry could not know or even hope for with much confidence. His virtual childlessness, then, and especially his failure to produce a male heir, must have had frightening implications for him, who was only the second king in a new royal line. This dynastic crisis, which really lasted throughout his reign, must never be lost sight of as a powerful reason for his discontent

26 The letter cited in n. 24 above, which was written on 1 July 1527.

with unfruitful unions and his desires to enter into more promising marriages.

Catherine had long passed the age of childbearing, and the thought that God had been punishing him for maintaining an unholy alliance gained a strong hold over Henry's mind. He felt a burning need to bring an end to the punishment by ridding himself of his present wife and taking another—and one was waiting for him in the wings.

He knew that it was possible for him to produce a healthy son. He had already done so by one of his mistresses: young Henry Fitzroy (that is, *fils du roi*) was striking evidence of his potency in this respect.[27] It did not occur to him, apparently, to question the whimsicalness of God's punishment in letting a son survive from a patently sinful amour and wreaking his vengeance instead upon a marriage which, though it might be objectively wrong, had been entered into in good faith on his part. He saw only the effects of the threatened biblical punishment in his marriage.

When Wolsey brought up the question of the nature of Catherine's marriage to Arthur, Henry must have rushed back to look at his Bible once again. The language of Leviticus is clear enough: "Thou shalt not uncover the turpitude of thy brother's wife," and, "A man who marries his brother's wife does an illicit thing; they shall be without children." John the Baptist confirmed this teaching in the New Testament by forbidding Herod his brother's wife. In all these texts the operative word is "wife." It does not exclude a wife who is still a virgin. How did it come about, then, that the canonists and theologians made a distinction between different kinds of wives?

An historical note may be of interest here. The Roman Church had originally adopted a straightforward method of determining affinity, one corresponding to the language of Leviticus. A man acquired in-laws by marriage, not by sexual union. Germanic

---

27 An indication of what was thought of the pope's power over marriage can be seen from the circumstance that as late as October 1528 there was still talk (on Wolsey's part, to be sure) of settling Henry's dynastic worries by obtaining a dispensation from the pope to allow Mary to marry her brother Henry. The pope, indeed, declared himself willing to consider it if the king would put aside his demands for the annulment of his marriage. See my article "Kinship, Incest, and the Dictates of Law," *American Journal of Jurisprudence*, 14 (1969), 73.

Christians adopted a different notion, starting no doubt from the text "They shall be two in one flesh." According to this view (at least logically), the most casual extramarital encounter brought with it a host of new relatives who were immediately placed beyond the pale of matrimonial eligibility, whereas a man who had not yet had sexual intercourse with his wife was still considered free of legal ties to her kinswomen.

Sometime during the eleventh century, when the northern concept began to prevail in Italy, a series of papal letters was forged in an attempt to give more standing to the old system. They were successful to the extent that the two methods were eventually combined: unmarriageable in-laws were to be had not only from consummated marriages (here the two systems overlapped), but also from premarital and extramarital copula, from nonconsummated marriage, and—to make matters worse—even from betrothal. For the counterfeiter of the decretals, which were incorporated into Gratian's *Decretum*, was of the view that an agreement to marry in the future (*de futuro*) was fully as binding as a contract to enter into a match at once (*de praesenti*).[28]

The impedimental relationship arising from carnal copula was called affinity; that stemming from betrothal was termed *iustitia publicae honestatis*, the righteousness of public honesty. There was some lack of agreement on the name to be given to the impediment caused by a nonconsummated marriage, that is, a contract *de praesenti*; a few, like St. Thomas Aquinas, retained the old view that affinity began with marriage, but by far the majority considered the impediment at this stage to be simply public honesty.

If we grant that Henry knew Catherine to be a virgin when she became his wife, he would naturally be moved to accept the common-sense reading of the text, namely, that the prohibition is caused by the fact of marriage, not by the fact of carnal knowledge. This conclusion, moreover, would also clear his conscience for his projected marriage with Anne Boleyn: for Anne was related to Henry in the same degree of canonical affinity as Catherine would have been had her marriage with Arthur been consummated. In having seduced Anne's sister Mary, he was barred from marrying Anne by the impediment of affinity in the first degree collateral,

[28] CIC Gratian 2.27.2.11, 12, 14, 15. See George Hayward Joyce, *Christian Marriage*, 2d ed. (London, 1948), pp. 93–94, 534–44.

and if Leviticus were to be interpreted canonically, there would be a divine ban against the marriage. Leviticus says clearly: "Thou shalt not take the sister of thy wife as a concubine, nor uncover her turpitude whilst thy wife still liveth." Henry, being a superb literalist when the spirit moved him, could assure himself that he was doing no such thing; on the contrary, he was intending to take the sister of his concubine as a wife. Therefore he could in all honesty apply to the pope for a dispensation from the ecclesiastical impediment of affinity *ex coitu illicito*, from unlawful intercourse, at the same time that he was impeaching the bull of Julius II. If the attack against the bull failed, he could still fall back on the argument that the law did not admit of dispensation, secure in the knowledge that his alliance with Anne was not really against the letter of the law.

So much for Henry's internal forum. As for the external forum, would the world of experts in law and theology accept his reasoning that brothers' virginal wives fell within the divine law and mistresses' sisters did not? If he were to use Wolsey's argument of public honesty against the bull and admit Catherine's virginity, and if the argument subsequently failed to hold good in court, could he expect to gain the support of those scholars, to whom Wolsey referred at the trial, who believed that the pope did not have the power to dispense for such a marriage?

Henry found out quite early that the answer to these questions was likely to be in the negative. We can see this clearly from the case of Robert Wakefield, who was the most learned man in the kingdom in Hebrew and other Oriental languages. Wakefield's education had been supported by Queen Catherine and Bishop Fisher, and when the question of the interpretation of the Levitical law first arose, he took the queen's side. But then he collaborated with Richard Pace, another humanist who had been patronized by Catherine, in writing a treatise showing that there was no justification in the Hebrew text for the Greek title of Deuteronomy ("Second Law") for the fifth book of Moses. It therefore could not be claimed that the law of levirate in Deuteronomy superseded the laws of Leviticus.

Pace sent the work to Henry, along with a covering letter in which he acknowledged Wakefield's share in its composition and said that Wakefield was prepared to defend its conclusions against any opponent. Wakefield was hesitant to pursue the question further, Pace said, unless he had Henry's assurance that he would not be offended if the truth of the matter were found to be against him rather than for him. Pace therefore asked the king to set Wakefield's mind at rest and to take advantage of his unparalleled learning.[29]

Wakefield, some seven years later in a justificatory letter addressed to Bishop Fisher and published at that time, explained that the book that he assisted Pace in composing was written before he was informed "not only by the king himself but also by many other trustworthy witnesses" that the queen had been carnally known by Henry's brother.[30] When the information was revealed to him in 1527, he quickly sent a letter to the king declaring his support: "I as your true and faithful subject will and can defend your cause or question in all the universities in Christendom against all men by good and sufficient authority." Previously, he said, he had defended the queen's cause, "not knowing that she was carnally known of Prince Arthur, your brother." He was already at work on what promised to be an enormous volume in answer to the Bishop of Rochester's book, and he was confident that he would so thoroughly refute him "that I trust he shall be ashamed to wade or meddle any further in the matter." But he begged Henry to keep it all a secret for the time being, for he was

[29] Wakefield printed Pace's letter twice, once in English and again in Latin, in two works that he published "about seven years" after the event, therefore, circa 1534. One he terms a "fragment of a codex": *Kotser codicis R. Wakfeldi quo, praeter ecclesiae sacrosanctae decretum, probatur coniugium cum fratria carnaliter cognita illicitum, omnino inhibitum, interdictumque esse, tum naturae iure, tum iure divino, legeque evangelica atque consuetudine catholica ecclesiae orthodoxae* (Granville no. 1252). The other was called *Syntagma de hebraeorum codicum incorruptione* (Granville no. 1226), which was a continuation of another treatise that he had published earlier (see *DNB*). Both the *Kotser* and the *Syntagma* were printed in London, the former by Thomas Berthelet and the latter by Wynkyn de Worde. The English version of Pace's letter is in *Kotser*, sig. P iii–iv, and has the date 1527. The Latin version forms part of the prefatory material of the *Syntagma*, sig. [D iv]–E i, and has the incorrect date 1526 (cf. LP IV, 3233). Wakefield dedicated the *Kotser* to Thomas Boleyn, in a letter in which he referred to his daughter Anne as queen (sig. [O iv^v]–P i), but in the following letter addressed to Bishop Fisher (sig. P iv–iii), he committed the indiscretion of calling Catherine queen as well.

[30] *Kotser* P ii^v: "antequam mihi non a rege ipso tantum sed et aliis quam plurimis fide dignis testibus narraretur eam a fratre suo defuncto carnaliter fuisse cognitam."

afraid of the outcry that would be raised against him by the people, who knew that he had originally defended the queen: "Surely I should be stoned of them to death, or else have such a slander and obloquy raised upon me that I had rather to die a thousand times ere suffer it."[31]

It was the fact of carnal cognition, then, that won for Henry Wakefield's support; and, as the full title of his *Kotser codicis* shows, it was a painfully prominent element in his refutation of Fisher. Therefore, even though Henry knew or suspected that Catherine had not consummated her first marriage, it would be dangerous to admit it. In due time, conscience or prudence would prevent him from asserting, from his own certain knowledge, that she had lost her virginity to Arthur. But he knew the importance of continuing the pretense of certainty. Unless the opposite were proved, Wolsey's public-honesty argument would have to be kept in the background, to be used only in a state of emergency.

[31] *Kotser* [P iv^{rv}]; cf. LP IV, 3234. The *Kotser* presumably is the reply that Wakefield referred to in his letter to Henry. In the letter addressed to Fisher seven years later, he begged the bishop to reply to his book. He also asked him to send him the other book that he had reportedly composed on the question (*Kotser* P iv). (Actually, by that time Fisher had composed six more books on the subject, by his own testimony.) In the same letter, Wakefield recalled that at the time in question (i.e. 1527), he was approached by Edward Fox, now Henry's almoner, accompanied by "Belus" (John Bell?), and asked to establish three conclusions: (1) that the Levitical prohibitions should be taken as referring not so much to incestuous coitus as to illicit matrimony, (2) that these commands were moral laws, as demonstrated in the Hebrew, Greek, and Chaldean texts, and (3) that they were more concerned with deceased than with living relatives. Wakefield complied, but Fox—true to his name, having always been envious of him—told the king that it was the work of John Stokesley. Stokesley was honest enough to admit that it was not his, but Wakefield's (*Kotser* P ii). In the preface to the *Syntagma*, Wakefield published a short treatise that dealt with the topics outlined by Fox, but he specified that it was written in answer to a question proposed by Fisher, viz: "An matrimonium in quo dispensavit pontifex ut frater fratris uxorem duceret firmum sit et indissolubile?" The vehemence of Wakefield's negative response makes it clear that he was writing after he had sent his letter to Henry (*Syntagma* [A iv–D iv]). Fisher was early apprised of some of Wakefield's reasonings, which he refuted in a letter to a friend (LP IV, 3232).

CHAPTER TWO

Dispensations for Anne

W OLSEY's explanation to Henry of the impediment of public honesty must have set the king to thinking about the public honesty and other impediments existing between himself and an intended bride of whom Wolsey as yet had no knowledge. It could hardly have occurred to Wolsey that the king was bent on passing up the chance of a powerful new alliance so that he could marry his latest courtesan, a woman whom Wolsey knew only too well, and whose cause he would soon be championing.

Unknown to Wolsey, Henry determined to seek a dispensation from the pope, and for that purpose he dispatched his secretary, William Knight, to Rome. Wolsey had been sent to Compiègne to see what could be done about rescuing the pope from the emperor and to begin negotiations for a French princess for Henry's hand. His first inkling of Anne's role in the annulment probably came when Knight arrived at Compiègne on September 10, 1527, ostensibly to receive instructions before continuing on to the pope; since Wolsey himself had already sent agents to Rome to urge a commission to decide the king's matter, he must have realized that it was all being taken out of his hands. The discovery that the king's intentions were more domestic put him in much the same position as the Earl of Warwick in *Henry VI* when he learns that Edward IV has chosen Elizabeth Woodville over a French bride.[1] But Wol-

---

[1] Shakespeare, *III Henry VI* 3.3. Shakespeare, like his sources, Hall and Holinshed, telescoped the order of events in this scene: Warwick no doubt did not like the Woodville marriage of 1464, but it was another marriage, that of Edward's sister Margaret to Charles the Bold, Duke of Burgundy, in 1468, that frustrated Warwick's pro-French policy and helped motivate his rebellion in 1469. I should say here at the beginning of this chapter that I am grateful to

sey, far from indulging in any indignation in Warwick's lavish manner, hurried home to assist his king in attaining his goal.

Knight, Wolsey found out, had been instructed to persuade Pope Clement to dispense Henry not only from the ordinary kinds of impediment (affinity, public honesty, and so on) that might stand in the way of a new marriage, but also from the ban set up by his present marriage. Wolsey convinced the king that such a request would never be granted, but instead of collaborating with Wolsey in drawing up a more reasonable document of dispensation, Henry secretly prepared such a document on his own and sent it to Knight, expressing confidence that since he knew who informed Wolsey about Knight's original mission, the cardinal would not find out about this one.

There were, then, three bulls of dispensation drawn up by Henry, and he spoke of them in these terms to Knight:

Surely, to be plain with you, we are of the opinion that the cardinal is of touching the first bull, for surely we think it is too much to be required and unreasonable to be granted, and therefore he and I jointly shall devise another, which hereafter we shall send to you (and that ere it be long), willing you to make all diligence to you possible for impetrating of this first which presently I send you [i.e. Henry's second draft, revised according to Wolsey's advice but without Wolsey's knowledge, and enclosed in the present letter], for that is it which I above all things do desire, and if you cannot attain it, then solicit the other which my Lord Cardinal and I shall send you, which, peradventure, shall not be much discrepant from this, but that shall be made *pro forma tantum*—and so to cloak other matters if you possibly may attain this, desiring you heartily to use all ways to you possible to get access to the pope's person, and then to solicit both the protestation and this bull with all diligence.[2]

Of these three drafts we possess only the third, that prepared jointly by Henry and Wolsey. Of the first we know only that it was to be granted *constante matrimonio*, as Knight phrased it, that is, with Henry's present marriage still standing. The secretary was writing to Henry shortly after his encounter with Wolsey, and he told the king that it would be much easier to obtain the dispensation *soluto matrimonio*, that is, after he had been freed of his first marriage.[3] Perhaps Wolsey even by then had guessed precisely what Knight's

Professor Mortimer Levine, who is writing a biography of Anne Boleyn, for offering many valuable criticisms of my treatment of Henry's second queen.

[2] Gairdner, *EHR* 11: 685.

[3] Letter of 13 September 1527, SP VII, 3; LP IV, 3422.

mission was, or had wormed it out of him, and had spoken to him
of the difficulty of accomplishing such a purpose.

It is not accurate to say that Henry was asking for a license for
a bigamous marriage, though he was to inquire about the possibility a year later. To the king's mind, no bigamy would be involved,
since he was not validly married to Catherine, and the nullity of
the marriage would eventually be recognized. He no longer treated
Catherine as his true wife, and he desired only permission to take
a legitimate spouse before the formalities of the annulment were
begun or accomplished. Anyone familiar with the delays of Roman
annulment procedures in modern times can readily understand
Henry's request. Indeed, Clement VII himself was to suggest not
long afterward—according to Sir Gregory Casale, although his
account should probably be viewed with some skepticism—that
immediate and unlicensed remarriage would be the best course for
Henry to follow. If the king were certain in his conscience that he
was free to marry, the pope allegedly said, he should go ahead and
marry, and thereby force the trial in England. The queen would
doubtless appeal the case, on the grounds that the place of trial and
the judges were suspect, thus requiring that the case be transferred
to Clement himself, who would hand down a fair sentence.[4] This
was hardly the sort of papal approval that Henry was looking for.
He would be acting on his own responsibility, not the pope's, and
the pope could easily declare his action invalid when the matter
was finally adjudicated.

The new dispensation drawn up by the king himself without
Wolsey's knowledge was enclosed in the same packet as the letter
just cited, and both were carried to Knight by John Barlow. Henry
made it clear in his letter that the draft of the revised dispensation
did not mention his present marriage, and if the pope should hesitate because the marriage was not yet dissolved, he could consult
with Bishop John Staphileus, the so-called Dean of the Rota, who,
Henry was confident, would assure the pope that "this bull is not
desired except I be *legitime absolutus ab hoc matrimonio Kath-
erinae*," that is, legally freed from this marriage with Catherine.

---

[4] Casale to Wolsey, 13 January 1528, Burnet, IV, 41. Cf. CIC X 4.1.18 (the
decretal *Cum in apostolica* of Urban III): A second marriage contracted during
annulment proceedings is valid if the first marriage is declared null. For Henry's
inquiry into bigamy, see LP IV, 4977.

It is puzzling that Henry desired this version of the bull to be kept from Wolsey, since, as he admitted himself, the bull that he and Wolsey would draw up together might not be very much different from it. When Henry said that he would join Wolsey in composing another bull in order to "cloak other matters," what other matters was he referring to? Not the secret bull, if it was to be the same sort of thing as the joint bull. Perhaps he was referring to the "protestation" that Knight was to attempt to get from the pope along with the secret bull. But the nature of the protestation, too, is unexplained. We have to infer that it formed part of Knight's original mission, and that it was never obtained.

The second dispensation that Henry drafted has been lost, but there are extant several copies of the bull that was issued as a result of the king's request. The transcript in the Corsini Library in Rome was made from a copy docketed by the papal secretary, Motta. The bull itself is dated December 17, 1527, but, according to Motta, it was taken from a draft in the hand of Laurence Pucci, Cardinal of the Church of the Four Crowned Saints, dated December 23 (when it was actually expedited). Motta went on to say that the draft had been corrected in the margin by Pope Clement himself "in his own hand with the utmost secrecy."[5] Another copy, this one in the Public Record Office in London, is accompanied by copious marginal notes, in the same Italian hand as the copy, which complain of the form and content of the document.[6] If the handwriting is not Wolsey's, the voice of the complainer most certainly is.

It has been assumed that the document as issued by the pope corresponded fairly closely to the draft that Henry secretly sent to Knight by way of Barlow. But Clement's bull held forth at length about Henry's marriage to Catherine, and made the dispensation contingent upon the annulment of that marriage. I inferred that

[5] Corsini MS 244 (36 D 2), ff. 148v–152v. For the text of the docket, see Ehses, p. 16. Neither Pucci's nor Motta's handwriting appears here, of course; the whole copy is in the same hand as the rest of this seventeenth-century MS.

[6] Record Office SP 1/45, ff. 237–242v; Pocock, I, 22. Gairdner, *EHR* 11: 691, assumes that the author is Wolsey. Scarisbrick, pp. 203–4, was misled into thinking that the writer of this copy was Pucci. It should also be pointed out that the preamble of the bull did not "state as a fact that the present marriage was invalid," as Scarisbrick thinks, but simply recounted that Henry was convinced that this was so.

Henry's document carefully avoided the express mention of this condition, as did the draft composed jointly by Henry and Wolsey.[7] The commentator of the Record Office copy objected strongly to the annulment condition and said that the dispensation should be unconditional and not joined to the question of the nullity of the present marriage.[8]

It seems, then, that Pucci made numerous changes in the document, making explicit what Henry wanted to remain implicit (so he said) on the question of his union with Catherine. If so, it is also possible that he changed the text dealing with the relaxation of other impediments that might stand in the way of Henry's marrying another woman.

The chief difference in this respect between the bull issued by Clement in December 1527 and the one drawn up with Wolsey's aid (which reached Knight only after he had already secured the other) is that the papal version dispensed Henry from a wide range of impediments, including first-cousin consanguinity, giving the impression that the king had not yet selected another bride, whereas Wolsey's draft obviously had one woman in mind, namely, Anne Boleyn.

Doubtless it would have been more politic for Henry to have asked for the dispensation in a general form, in order not to give the game away by pointing out the object of his desires; but in view of his eagerness to make sure that the papal relaxation struck home, it seems likely that his draft was fairly specific, and that Pucci made it more general in order to put a better face on the proceedings.

The dispensation revised by Cardinal Pucci and approved by Clement at the end of 1527 stated that Henry requested, "in the event of a declaration of nullity of such a marriage [that is, with Catherine, his brother's widow], to be dispensed to marry any other woman whatever, even though she has already contracted marriage with another, as long as she has not consummated it by carnal copula, or even though she be related to you in the second or more remote degrees of consanguinity, or in the first degree of affinity,

---

[7] This draft, as well as the papal version based on it (issued April 13, 1528), referred to Henry's present union to Catherine only to condemn anyone who might impugn the dispensation on the grounds that Henry was "not free or released from marriage at the time of this concession."

[8] Pocock, I, 23.

arising from whatever licit or illicit intercourse, as long as she is not the widow of your aforesaid brother, and even if she be related to you by spiritual or legal kinship, and the impediment of the righteousness of public honesty be present."[9]

It is noteworthy that the impediment of affinity from extramarital intercourse was for all practical purposes given the same status as affinity arising from a consummated marriage; this was, as we have seen, consonant with the current view of canon law, but it was not consonant with the idea that Henry no doubt had in the back of his mind, namely, that the pope did not have the power to dispense him to marry Catherine, but that he did have the power to allow him to marry Anne. It is amusing to see that the one person excluded from this dispensation was his brother's widow, to whom he was at least in name already married. One would like to see the hand of Henry himself here, taking pains to make sure that his present marriage would not be inadvertently legitimated by this decree.

Let us now examine the draft prepared jointly by Henry and Wolsey in order to see precisely what impediments were thought to stand in the way of a union with Anne Boleyn. We shall first study the original form of the document, and then the corrections that were inserted into the text.[10]

The first relaxation sought was from the impediment of consanguinity in the fourth degree—meaning that Henry knew or feared that Anne was his third cousin. Given the knowledge that the king's great-grandparents Richard Woodville and Jacquetta, the widowed Duchess of Bedford, had had fourteen or fifteen children between them, who was to know with certainty if one of Henry's sixteen great-great-grandparents was not shared by Anne? At any rate, there was no sense in taking a chance. They seem, in fact, to have been related no closer than in the eighth and ninth degrees—that is, they were seventh cousins once removed, by virtue of Anne's descent, which she shared with all five of Henry's other wives, from Edward I.[11]

9 Ehses, p. 15.

10 This document is quoted in large part by Brewer (LP IV, 3643.1) and is collated by Gairdner with the version granted by the pope on April 13, 1528 (*EHR* 5: 546). Gairdner, however, does not adequately reproduce the text as it existed before the interlineations were added.

11 See F. P. Barnard, "The Kinship of Henry VIII and His Wives," *Miscellanea genealogia et heraldica*, series 5, 3 (1918–19), 194–96.

The second impediment mentioned was that of "the righteousness of public honesty arising from espousals clandestinely contracted before the age of seven or otherwise, which would impede and invalidate matrimony or render it illicit." Later on the document summarized the impediment as "the righteousness of public honesty arising from a secret contract." That is to say, it was thought that there had been a private arrangement made for Anne, while she was still at a very young age, to be affianced to a third cousin or an even closer relative of Henry's; for the impediment of public honesty, like those of consanguinity and affinity, prohibited marriage through the fourth degree of kinship.

The phrase *in septennio* has been taken to refer to a betrothal made in 1520 between Anne and Sir James Butler, son of the Earl of Ormond. If so, the drafters badly misunderstood the phrase; *in septennio* does not mean "within the last seven years," but rather "within the first seven years of age." According to canon law the impediment of public honesty did not arise when the engagement took place *in septennio* unless the party consented to it after reaching the age of seven.[12]

Any marriage agreement made without ecclesiastical form was technically clandestine; but apart from the fact that Anne was long past the age of seven when we first hear of negotiations for her marriage to young Butler,[13] the intended groom does not seem to have been related by blood to Henry. At most, the king's first cousin Elizabeth St. John (granddaughter of Elizabeth Woodville) was the stepmother of the boy's mother, Margaret Fitzgerald (Table 1). This relationship would have raised no canonical barrier; but Henry may again have been simply playing it safe.

The other known candidate for Anne's hand at this time was Henry Percy, son of the fifth Earl of Northumberland, who, if he treated of marriage with Anne, certainly did it secretly; but he came into the picture even later than the Butler youth. Percy was

---

12 CIC X 4.2.4–6 (decretals of Alexander III in the title *De desponsatione impuberum*). Public honesty did arise, however, if a man took his under-seven-year-old fiancée home to live with him (X 4.1.3).

13 Shortly after Henry VIII married Anne's sister Mary to Mr. Carew (before Feb. 4, 1520), he wished to know if Sir Piers Butler, Earl of Ormond, would consent to a match between his son and Anne (who was then still in France). Brewer, LP III, Intro., pp. ccccxxxii f. The match was given up at the end of 1522; see Paul Friedmann, *Anne Boleyn* (London, 1884), I, 43. On the technicalities of clandestinity, see my *Love and Marriage in the Age of Chaucer*, pp. 163–76.

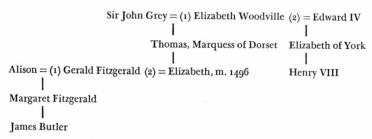

Table 1. Lack of consanguinity between Henry VIII and James Butler through Elizabeth Woodville.

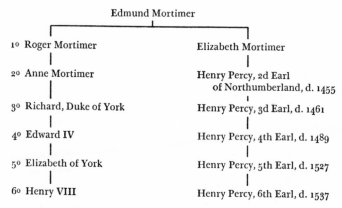

Table 2. Consanguinity between Henry VIII and Henry Percy through the Mortimers in the sixth and sixth degrees: fifth cousins.

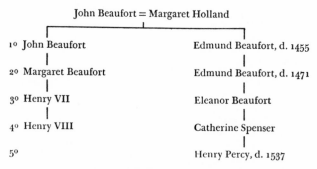

Table 3. Consanguinity between Henry VIII and Henry Percy through the Beauforts in the fourth and fifth degrees: third cousins once removed.

Henry's fifth cousin by virtue of their common descent from Phi-
lippa, Edward III's granddaughter (Table 2), but this tie was outside the then current range of marriage impediments; he was also,
however, Henry's third cousin, by reason of his descent from Henry's great-great-grandparents John Beaufort, Earl of Somerset, and
Margaret Holland, the same lady who later received the first dispensation ever given from the Levitical degrees.[14] Percy's mother,
Catherine Spenser, was the daughter of Eleanor Beaufort, who in
turn was the daughter of Edmund Beaufort, son of Edmund Beaufort, Duke of Somerset, whose parents were the above-named John
and Margaret (Table 3). But the extra generation in Percy's line
made John and Margaret his great-great-great-grandparents, meaning that he was Henry's third cousin *once removed*, and so once
more the king would be outside the forbidden degrees, since the
law was that the prohibition of marriage should not exceed the
fourth degree of consanguinity and affinity.[15] Perhaps the law was
not clear to Henry and his advisers.[16] Or perhaps they were confused by the two Edmund Beauforts and did not realize that there
was a surplus degree.

At all events, if Henry was afraid that Anne was third or even
second cousin to him (see below) when in fact she was only his
seventh once removed, one can readily infer that he would want
to take a similar precaution in Percy's case. The question of Percy's involvement with Anne would be brought up with some insistence in later years, as we shall see.[17]

The final impediment to be dispensed from was "affinity arising
from illicit intercourse." Wolsey and the king added it here as if

14 See above, Introduction, after n. 8.

15 CIC X 4.14.8 (Innocent III's decree at the Fourth Lateran Council, in the
title *De consanguinitate et affinitate*).

16 See H. A. Kelly, "Kinship, Incest, and the Dictates of Law," p. 70. About
forty years later Pius V would formally decree that when the degrees were mixed
only the more remote need be mentioned for a dispensation to be valid (e.g.,
Henry and Percy could then be said to be related in the fifth degree, meaning
fourth and fifth). But apparently this had long been curial policy. In the *Chichele Register* (IV, 288–89) there is a letter from Martin V dated 1428 reassuring
a couple who had failed to specify their fourth-degree affinity as being in the
third and fourth degrees: in accord with the policy of Clement VI (1342–52),
such failure to mention the third degree did not invalidate the dispensation.
In 1540, the papal law of prohibited degrees was stated accurately by Parliament
as extending only to the "fourth and fourth degree." See below, Chap. 15 at n. 3.

17 Below, Chap. 14.

it were of less importance than the first two, and they failed to specify the degrees that might possibly be involved.

The original draft was then modified—perhaps one of the collaborators (Henry or Wolsey) had drawn up the document alone, and the other required the changes to be made; or perhaps further discussions with Mistress Anne had brought new complications to light.

The dispensation from the impediment of consanguinity was extended to cover the third degree, that is, second cousins. The third impediment was now specified to be "affinity arising from illicit intercourse in whatever degree, even the first." Thus Henry would clearly be protected from the consequences of his relationship with Mary, Anne's sister—by which, as we know, Anne was related to him in the first degree collateral of affinity. And, since they do not state what kind of degree is meant, the same would also hold true of his relationship with Anne's mother, Elizabeth Howard, if there were any truth to the story that she too had been his mistress. Anne would then be related to him in the first degree direct of affinity.

Nicholas Sanders, who in his *Origin and Progress of the English Schism* was the most energetic reporter of the story that Anne's mother had been Henry's concubine, doubted that the pope had the power to dispense upon the resulting impediment.[18] (He topped his story with evidence taken from Judge William Rastell's biography of Thomas More that the fruit of this amour was none other than Anne Boleyn herself! He had no doubts whatsoever about the pope's lack of power in these circumstances.) The Roman editor of Sanders's manuscript protested against his position on affinity, upon the very good grounds that it was "contrary to the daily practice of the Penitentiary and Datary, where this dispensation is very often obtained," most especially when the intercourse was kept secret, thereby allowing a man to marry a woman

---

[18] "Et in hac quidem causa non facile dixerim claues Pontificis habere dispensandi potestatem, propterea quod hoc affinitatis genus ipsam nuptiarum essentiam proprius attingere uideatur quam ut in eo dispensari quodammodo deceat." He goes on at length justifying this position. I quote from the MS (f. 49v) at the Venerable English College, Rome, which contains Sanders's text before it underwent revision by Edward Rishton for the first edition (Cologne, 1585). It also contains corrections and additions in another hand, and the MS thus adapted was used along with the Cologne edition in arriving at a text for the second edition (Rome, 1586).

whose mother or daughter he had carnally known beforehand. The concession was also given to many penitents already married who had lost the right to the marriage debt (that is to say, by having had intercourse with their mother-in-law or stepdaughter).[19]

Perhaps then such dispensations had become, if not the matter of course that they were in 1585, at least common enough by Henry's time for his request to be granted, much to his surprise, without a fuss, even though the affinity involved might have been thought to be in the direct line.

An affair between Henry and Elizabeth Howard has no very good historical source to recommend it as a fact. Sir George Throgmorton on one occasion warned Henry that his conscience would eventually be even more troubled than it now was if he married Anne, "for that it is thought that ye have meddled with both the mother and the sister." Henry's reply—"Never with the mother!"—quite clearly an admission of his interlude with the sister,[20] could perhaps be interpreted as an attempt to cover up an even more shameful truth. His failure to restrict his appeal to the collateral line when seeking a dispensation from affinity could be taken as support for this view. It seems more likely, however, that Henry had in fact never meddled with Anne's mother, and that in 1527 the rumor of such an alliance had not yet got under way. The affinity therefore would not be specifically denominated as collateral any more than would the consanguinity, since there would have been just as little thought that Anne was Henry's stepdaughter by affinity as that she was his great-granddaughter by consanguinity.

<hr>

[19] Sanders MS, f. 50 (a leaf inserted into the original MS, in the hand of the corrector): "Quod dicat se non facile dicere claues Pontificis habere potestatem dispensandi in hoc ut filia nubat ei viro qui eiusdem matrem semel carnaliter cognouerat—contra est quotidianus usus et penitentiariae et Datariae, vbi sepissime ea dispensatio obtinetur, potissimum quando alterutrum concubitus est occultus ante initas nuptias huius aut vnius mulieris, nempe tam vt matrem ducat qui eius filiam ante cognouit, quam vt filiam ducat in vxorem qui matrem eiusdem cognouisset. Nam quod dispensent in personas iam maritatis [sic] vt propterea petant debitum cuius ius perdiderant, hoc multis conceditur penitentiarijs, et vidimus praticarij in sancto Petro. Anno [unintelligible symbols follow; the date must be 1585 or 1586]." In the upper right-hand corner there are the initials "C: A:"—perhaps identifying the corrector. Jasper Ridley, *Thomas Cranmer* (Oxford, 1962), p. 108, mistakenly says that no theologian held that affinity caused by extramarital intercourse came under the divine prohibition. On the contrary, this was the normal view. See Kelly, *Traditio*, 23: 293.

[20] LP IV, Intro., p. cccxxix n.

The second impediment mentioned in the original draft, that of public honesty, was retained, but the words "before the age of seven or otherwise" were dropped; perhaps the king and cardinal realized their mistake in interpreting the meaning of the phrase. In addition, still another impediment was brought up for exemption, namely, "a marriage precontract secretly entered into but not consummated, which would impede and invalidate a second marriage."[21] In a summary statement later in the draft the precontract was further specified as one "made clandestinely or secretly with reference to the present time," that is, an actual private marriage. The added words, *per verba de praesenti*, also characterized the precontract in a second summary.[22]

It should be noted that in the summaries a marriage *per verba de praesenti* is termed a precontract, and *sponsalia* (spousals, or espousals), which, unless otherwise qualified, would ordinarily be thought of as entered into *per verba de futuro*, a contract. But "precontract" simply meant "previous contract," and spousals could also be made *per verba de praesenti*, in which case they were the same thing as a contract *de praesenti*. The question arises, therefore, whether only one contract was being discussed from two points of view. The answer would appear to be no, if we can judge from the wording of the text, which consistently distinguishes two contracts as different events. This is particularly true of the second summary, which speaks of "the aforesaid precontract contracted

---

[21] The revised section referring to public honesty, precontract, and affinity reads as follows: "Canones ... qui de impedimento publicae honestatis iustitiae ex sponsalibus clandestine contractis natae, matrimonium impedientes et dirimentes contractum; aut de praecontractu matrimoniali clandestine inito non consummato, secundum matrimonium impedituro et dirempturo; ac etiam illos qui de affinitate ex coitu illegitimo in quocumque gradu, etiamsi primo, proveniente, matrimoniorum irritatorio impedimento extant, ad matrimonia per te contrahenda non pertinere."

[22] The corrected first summary reads: "Propter praecontractum per verba de praesenti clandestine aut secrete factum, impedimentumve publicae honestatis iustitiae ex clandestino contractu provenientis, aut affinitatis in quocumque gradu, etiamsi primo, ex illicito coitu contingentis, gradumve consanguinitatis modo secundum aut tertium excesserit." Gairdner fails to note that the words "secundum aut" were added to the original draft. The second summary says the affinity is "ex persona tua causata," that is, caused by Henry. In both summaries the interlineations concerning the precontract are inserted *before* the mention of public honesty, but this change of position is probably of no significance, since consanguinity is put out of order even in the original version of the summaries and named last, whereas it comes first in the body of the draft.

per verba de praesenti or that contract from which public honesty would arise."[23] This conclusion, however, is by no means certain.

Another question that occurs is whether Anne's clandestine fiancé was the same person as her clandestine husband, or a different man entirely. If there were two men involved, we can reconstruct Anne's career as follows, granted that the impediments were such as Henry and Wolsey stated them. She was first secretly engaged, presumably *per verba de futuro*, to marry a relatively close cousin of Henry's, and thereafter she would not be free to marry any of her fiancé's relatives, including Henry, because of the impediment of public honesty. Then she secretly married another man, one who was not closely related to Henry, and this marriage persisted, in the estimation of Henry and Wolsey, at least up to the present time (the latter part of 1527), allegedly without ever having been consummated. The previous engagement *de futuro* would have been dissolved automatically by the *de praesenti* marriage, if it had not already been legally dissolved by mutual consent (or, if one of the parties were unwilling, by ecclesiastical decree).

Alternatively, Anne could have contracted such a marriage beforehand, and then abandoned her secret husband to become engaged to a cousin of Henry's before she was sought by Henry himself. An engagement of this kind would be null and void, of course, because of the earlier *de praesenti* contract; but the impediment of public honesty would still arise between Anne and Henry, since canon law declared that even invalid spousals created public honesty,[24] just as illicit intercourse gave rise to affinity.

If, on the other hand, only one man was involved, that man being Henry Percy, the situation might be reconstructed differently. Percy was the king's third cousin, or was thought to be such, and he first became secretly engaged to Anne (*sponsalia de futuro*) and then contracted marriage with her *per verba de praesenti*, that is, entered into a *de praesenti* contract (*sponsalia de praesenti*). Or, if only one contract was in question, he simply came straight to the point and married her without bothering about an engagement. But since there was said to have been no sexual union be-

23 "De scientia praedicti praecontractus per verba de praesenti contracti aut contractus illius unde publica honestas oriretur."

24 CIC Sextus 4.1.1 (decretal of Boniface VIII, in the title *De sponsalibus et matrimoniis*).

tween the couple after the vows had been exchanged, the marriage could, according to most canon lawyers, against the strong objections of the generality of theologians,[25] be dissolved by the pope for a reasonable cause; the obstacle of precontract would be removed thereby, and an exemption could also be given for the impediment of public honesty which supposedly arose from Percy's kinship to the king.

Henry took the course of not having an explicit divorce arranged for Anne, since this would have put the pope in the position of having to dissolve all existing nonconsummated marriages in the world. The king was unwilling to say that he was thinking of a specific precontract (and therefore a specific woman), and it was no doubt thought that to have Anne herself apply for a nullification would be even more of a giveaway. He therefore settled for asking the pope to let him marry another woman in spite of the fact that she was already married (quite apart from Henry's being already married himself). In granting this request, the pope was decreeing that the first marriage of Henry's intended bride would be dissolved at the moment when she married the king.

The precision with which Henry and Wolsey described the nature of Anne's former unions, especially in their pains to specify her marriage as a contract *de praesenti*, is an indication that they were not simply taking unnecessary precautions, as in the case of a nonexistent impediment of consanguinity, but were working from detailed information supplied by Anne herself. The dispensation granted by Pope Clement on December 23 allowed Henry to marry a woman who had contracted marriage (*matrimonium contraxerit*), and it later refers to an *impedimentum praecontractus matrimonii non consummati*. The commentator in the Record Office copy, whom we have assumed to be writing at Wolsey's dictation, insists that to the phrase *matrimonium contraxerit* "the words *de praesenti* should be added, lest it be taken to refer to a marriage contracted *per verba de futuro*."[26] As for the spousals, it was not necessary to specify them as *de futuro* or *de praesenti* in the context of public honesty; for no increase in the strength of this impediment resulted when the promise of future marriage was

25 See below, Chap. 10 at n. 19, and Cranmer's discussion in Chap. 13 at n. 12.
26 Pocock, I, 23.

fulfilled by words of present consent. Though Henry himself may have believed that public honesty changed to affinity at this point, it was still regarded as public honesty by the ecclesiastical laws.

In February of 1528 Wolsey set up a new embassy to the pope at Orvieto, where the court had taken refuge after being driven out of Rome by imperial forces; the delegation consisted of two of the cardinal's secretaries, Stephen Gardiner and Edward Fox. One of their charges was to obtain another dispensation for the king's remarriage, to take the place of the unsatisfactory one already granted.

The new dispensation was accorded without difficulty, and was issued on April 13. It is possible that Gardiner and Fox were entrusted by the cardinal with a draft identical to the one that he and Henry had prepared earlier, which we have just examined, and that the changes in content in the papal bull were made by Clement's advisers; but it seems more likely that Wolsey himself was responsible for the revisions. The wording bears study. Anne was still not mentioned in the document, but Wolsey knew that Clement had been aware of the object of the king's efforts for some time, and the cardinal went to great lengths in defending the virtue of the lady, in Gardiner and Fox's original instructions.[27]

The pope declared Henry exempt from all the canons, statutes, and other laws dealing "with the noncontracting of marriage between persons related by blood in the third or fourth degree; with the impediment of the righteousness of public honesty arising from spousals clandestinely contracted, viz., that which would impede and invalidate the contracting of marriage; and also those covering a matrimonial precontract entered into and contracted *per verba de praesenti*, but not consummated or solemnized, which would impede and invalidate a second marriage; and then those that deal with affinity arising from illicit coitus in whatever degree, even the first, an impediment similarly invalidating marriage; finally, those speaking of spiritual kinship, likewise impeding marriage."[28]

The addition of the impediment of spiritual kinship is odd. Was it thought that Henry was Anne's godfather? (Or that Catherine

[27] LP IV, 3913.
[28] Ehses, p. 34.

was her godmother?) Or had Anne participated in the baptism of one of Henry's ill-fated children? It would seem, at any rate, that the mention of spiritual kinship in the papal dispensation of December 23 awakened a fear that some obstacle of the sort might be found out, and it was decided to provide against it.

We notice that the previously contracted marriage was no longer said to have been clandestine, though the spousals were—a further indication, perhaps, that two different persons were involved. The marriage was also said not to have been solemnized; that is, no wedding ceremony had taken place in church.

By this document Henry and Anne were finally relieved of all the impediments that stood in the way of their marriage. But it was all conditioned upon the removal of the most serious obstacle of all, Henry's present marriage. His efforts to dissolve this *de praesenti* contract were to meet with a great many impediments in the years to come.

CHAPTER THREE

Pre-Trial Maneuvers

T HE MOST important task that faced Stephen Gardiner and Edward Fox when they arrived at Orvieto in March 1528 was not the securing of the king's dispensation, but the obtaining of a decretal commission. This was a bull by which the pope would appoint legates to hold an inquisition in England on the question of the marriage between Henry and Catherine to determine whether the allegations made against it were true. If even one of the charges were found to be true, the legates were to declare the union null and void, with no need or possibility for appeal. That is to say, the point of law would already have been decided in the commission; the legates would merely try to ascertain the facts. It was a form of procedure that had been employed in the early days of pontifical law but had long since fallen into disuse.

To justify the issuance of such a decretal, the English envoys presented five objections to the dispensation granted to Henry and Catherine by Julius II:

1. The reason given, that of making peace, is false, because there was no discord at the time between the sovereigns.

2. It is also false that Henry requested the dispensation; he was only eleven years old, and so incapable of marrying; it was not his request but his father's.

3. Because he was underage, the dispensation was not valid, and it could not become valid when he came of age.

4. Henry protested against the dispensation and said that he did not consent to it.

5. At the time of the contracting of the marriage, the reason of

making peace between Henry VII and Ferdinand and Isabella had
ceased to exist, because Isabella had died in the meantime.[1]

In a *consilium* given to Clement concerning these allegations,
the author, apparently Cardinal Pucci, changed their order, revers-
ing the first and second and fourth and fifth objections, thus putting Henry's protest against the dispensation when he came of age
in last place. He considers it the most weighty of the five objections, and gives over a good deal of space to discussing it.[2] The first
objection on Pucci's list—that Henry himself did not seek the marriage and was not even aware that such a dispensation had been
obtained—is left unanswered, though this was the very objection
that Wolsey thought to be the most important, and upon which
he placed his hopes for assuaging his own conscience.

Wolsey had by no means abandoned his public-honesty argument, although he was beginning to doubt the wisdom of pursuing
it. Fox had returned to England to report to Wolsey the progress
that had been made. On April 13, as we have seen, the pope issued
a fresh dispensation for Henry. He also granted a legatine commission on the same day. It was not, however, the hoped-for decretal bull but rather a general commission which authorized the
usual sort of papal inquisition, subject to various risks that Henry
was unwilling to take. A dispatch from Fox to Gardiner, dated May
11, 1528, set forth Wolsey's instructions, dictated on May 9, to
press on for the decretal letter. Also, Gardiner was to consult with
Staphileus and others on these questions:

first, in case the Queen's Grace, omitting all such benefit and privilege
which she might pretend to have by the dispensation of Julius and refusing to enter the disputation of the validity of the same, like as His Grace
[Wolsey] is perfectly informed by some of her counsel that she will do,
and recurring only to this allegation, *Quod non fuit cognita ab Arthuro*,
whether then, and in case the said allegation should be proved true, the
said bull be not *prorsus* invalidate by reason there is no mention made
in the same *de publica honestate*. For, sith the bull dispenseth only *cum
affinitate cuiusmodi*, if her allegation should be true, *nulla intercessit
inter contrahentes*, and [it] being necessary [for] the same to be dispensed
with, argueth the matrimony to be illegitimate, in His Grace's opinion.
Wherein His Grace would gladly be resolved by your and other learned

1 Ehses, p. 156.
2 *Ibid.*, pp. 21–22.

men's judgments there, to be by you inquired, and certificate thereof to be made to His Grace as before.[3]

The obvious inference from this is that Wolsey was not altogether convinced of either the need for, or the validity of, the argument concerning public honesty. He still had his hopes pinned on impugning the reasons that were given in Julius's bull, as Fox made clear:

And specially, above all things, forasmuch as His Grace intendeth in this cause of so high consequence, wherein dependeth the wealth or ruin of this realm, the conservation of his honor or else immortal ignominy and slander, the damnation of his soul or else everlasting merit, to proceed according to due order of justice and to ground and firm his conscience upon so perfect and infallible rule of equity that before God he may account himself discharged ne to have anything *reclamante conscientia*; and having, among other, in His Grace's own opinion one specially just and steadfast base and foundation to ground right wisely his conscience thereupon, viz. *quod rex ipse nescierit prorsus de impetratione bullae*, whereof he is ascertained not only by the king's relation, but also by My Lord of Winchester [Bishop Fox], His Grace willeth and desireth you ye will under most secret manner *et tacitis nominibus ne videatur viz. dubitare de iustitia causae quam toties depraedicavit*, inquire of Anconitane [Peter Accolti, Cardinal of Ancona] or else some other of like learning whether the said ground be so justifiable and of such sort as His Grace might well build his conscience upon without grudge or scruple hereafter.

One is not sure how to judge Wolsey's crisis of conscience. It seems likely that he was really troubled—whatever one may think of his histrionic protestation the next day (Sunday, May 10), which Fox also recounted, when the cardinal solemnly told the king that he would rather be torn to pieces than do anything in the matter against his conscience. No doubt Wolsey intended this scene to be recounted at the papal curia, for he clearly did not want to give the impression that he doubted in any way the cogency of the arguments against Julius's bull. But doubts he did have, and it is not difficult to believe that he had moral misgivings as well. Presumably he appeased his misgivings for the moment, as Fox's letter indicates, by expressing his confidence in the fact of the young Henry's ignorance of the dispensation—to the extent, at least, of being able to bring genuine fervor into his public assertion of dedication to justice and truth at court the following day. But he

[3] Fox to Gardiner, 11 May 1528, Pocock, I, 150.

had come to realize that not only his high post, but even his very life depended upon his success in fulfilling the king's desires in this matter; and even if the thought encouraged him to resort to every kind of chicanery that might prove helpful, it may also have prompted him to regard his last end, when he would have to answer to another Master.

Wolsey gave his reasons for believing that young Henry had not known about the dispensation his father was securing for him, but he did not say what the king's mind was regarding Catherine's virginity at the time of her second marriage. This was a matter on which the cardinal had no proof one way or the other. Henry, who almost certainly knew that she was still a virgin, did not dare to deny the fact to Wolsey or anyone else, though he was permitting and even encouraging the belief that she was not. But Wolsey, we notice, spoke of the possibility first that the queen's claim of virginity would "be proved true," and then that it might even "be true," as if it were seeming more and more likely.

Earlier in the same letter, Fox passed on to Gardiner the urgent reasons that Wolsey listed for the granting of the decretal commission, though surprisingly he did not recommend a change in the wording of the decretal, to bring it into conformity with his recent meditations, by restating the objection of Henry's ignorance. The text as it reads in the extant drafts[4] notes that Henry's advisers

[4] Four versions of the proposed decretal bull survive:

1. Cotton Vitellius B xii, ff. 172–184 (new foliation), ed. Burnet, IV, 48–52; addressed to Wolsey, with a space left for the name of his fellow legate, to be filled in by the pope.

2. Another copy earlier in the same MS, ff. 124–136, excerpted by Herbert Thurston, "The Canon Law of the Divorce," *EHR* 19 (1904), 641; made out to Wolsey and Campeggio together.

3. A copy in the Record Office, ed. Pocock, I, 28–32; the addressee is not named, so that the pope could simply write in the name of Wolsey or some other cardinal of his own choosing without further ado. The fellow legate is to be the Archbishop of Canterbury.

4. The second half of a copy in the Vatican Archives, in the volume *Addita ad dispensationem Henrici VIII Angliae regis* (AA Arm. I–XVIII, 3265), ff. 5–6; once again the addressee is not named, and his fellow legate is designated as the Archbishop of Canterbury or some other prelate of England ("aut alius quicunque illius Regni Prelatus"). This copy has not previously been noticed, I think. Cf. Wolsey's original instructions to Gardiner and Fox, where he gives as possibilities: (1) a legate is to be joined to Wolsey, or (2) a legate is to be sent alone, or (3) the commission is to be directed to Wolsey, and the Archbishop of Canterbury, or some other bishop, is to be joined with him. LP IV, 3913.

found the dispensation inadequate on the following counts: (1) the alleged threat to peace was nonexistent; (2) Henry did not seek to marry Catherine in order to preserve peace, since (*a*) he was at that time, as he asserts, unaware of the procurement of the dispensation, and (*b*) because of his youth he could not have acted from such a motive; (3) the dispensation would seem to have been nullified when Henry renounced it in his protestation; (4) the rulers among whom peace was to have been maintained died before the bull was put into effect.

The pope then goes on (in the words given to him by Wolsey) to commission his legates to declare the dispensation and the marriage void if the above objections or some of them are found to be true, namely, whether (1) the peace could have continued without the marriage, or (2) Henry, as it is alleged, did not desire to contract the marriage in order to conserve peace, or (3) the rulers or one of them had died before the bull was put into effect. It was no doubt thought that this last ground would be particularly easy to establish. We shall see, however, that Henry and Catherine were actually married *per verba de praesenti* in the autumn of 1504, before Isabella had died. It is true that the marriage occurred a month or two before the pope formally issued the dispensation, but it would have had retroactive effect, since he dated it 1503.

The objection that Henry knew nothing about the dispensation is omitted entirely in the all-important papal summary of the bull's defects, and it is used only to support the allegation that he did not desire the marriage to keep the peace (that is to say, the possibility was left open that he desired to marry the princess for other reasons).

This is the form that the objection had taken a year before when Wolsey urged it on John Fisher as the main defect in the bull. A few days after he had written to the king about the queen's virginity and public honesty, the cardinal had set off for France, but had stopped off on the way to have a not very satisfactory chat with the Bishop of Rochester. He wrote to Henry about it later: after Fisher had rejected the argument that the marriage was against the divine law, the cardinal brought up all the reasons against the bull that he later placed at the beginning of the draft of the decretal commission, except, surprisingly, the objection that there was no threat to peace at the time.[5] Perhaps he realized that Fisher knew better.

The harassed pope held out as long as he could against Gardiner's bullying. Finally, some time in June, he gave in, and issued the decretal bull. He made the stipulation, however, that it was not to be used in the trial, but was meant only to be shown to the king and then destroyed. He seems to have granted it at last only in order to save Wolsey from ruin. Even so, it was a mistake, which Clement soon came to regret. He was fortunate that neither Wolsey nor the king was able to put the document to improper use.

The operative bull, therefore, was the general commission of April 13, which appointed Wolsey and Cardinal Laurence Campeggio as joint inquisitors to try the matter of the marriage and deliver a just sentence. Campeggio, though in bad health, set out for England, and after a long and painful journey arrived there the following October and began to record his impressions of the situation and dispatch them to Rome.

After some preliminary meetings, first with Wolsey, then with Henry, and finally with Henry and Wolsey together, Campeggio and his fellow legate paid a formal call on the queen in hopes of persuading her to help solve the complexities of the case by entering a convent. Catherine was hardly more receptive to this alternative than Henry had been to Campeggio's offer to secure a new dispensation for him and Catherine making up for any defects in Julius's bull. Henry's response to this suggestion was a discourse upon the question whether the pope had the power to dispense; even granted that he did have such power, the king was interested only in finding out whether the dispensation was valid. One way or another, he was convinced that the marriage was null, and, as Campeggio wrote in a coded paragraph, "I believe that if an angel descended from heaven he would be unable to persuade him otherwise."[6]

After the legates' unsuccessful meeting with the queen, Henry himself went to see her the following day (October 25). In this interview he told her that she was not his wife, that all the jurists in the country had signed a statement to that effect; and (according

[5] Wolsey to Henry VIII, 5 July 1527, SP I, 196; LP IV, 3231.
[6] Ehses, pp. 54–56.

to Iñigo de Mendoza, the Spanish ambassador) he made many other equally groundless assertions.[7] He may have convinced himself that his rhetoric had carried the day where that of the cardinals had failed. At any rate, he gave her permission to go to confession to Campeggio, and the next day he appointed a distinguished group of churchmen and lawyers as her counsel. It was inevitable that she should be represented, of course, but perhaps it was Henry's momentary overconfidence that permitted him to include in her defense team the formidable John Fisher. Or it may be that he could not easily have excluded Fisher.

If Henry thought that the queen was going to confess at long last her abominable sin of incest, he was badly deceived. Her confession to Campeggio was nothing more than an assertion that she had remained untouched in her first marriage and had come to Henry a virgin. She made this declaration in the most solemn way, not only as a formal statement in the sacrament of confession but also as an oath taken between the cardinal's hands,[8] whereby she placed herself under the sanctions of sacrilege and perjury.

Less than a fortnight before this event, Mendoza had written to the emperor of his fear that Catherine intended to insist on the nonconsummation of her first marriage, if the case should ever come to a trial. The ambassador was afraid that the lawyers whom she was consulting were deliberately deceiving her, for he considered the queen's line of defense very bad strategy. In the first place, virginity was very difficult to prove. Second, an insistence from the outset of the trial that the first marriage had not been consummated might indicate that there was some doubt about the validity of the dispensation. The argument should be used only as a last resort, in case the dispensation were proved to be defective. By the time that he sent his next dispatch, Mendoza was convinced that his advice would be followed in court, even though Catherine insisted upon her virginity in private to Campeggio.[9]

But Catherine, as Wolsey himself knew full well, had no intention of holding the argument of her virginity in abeyance for what-

[7] Mendoza to Charles V, 18 November 1528, SC III, part 2, 842.

[8] Campeggio to Salviati, 26 October 1528, Ehses, pp. 58–59. Cf. SC III, part 2, 842–43; LP VI, 160 (p. 74). Catherine's oath to Campeggio may have been taken later; see his letter of 16 June 1529, cited below, Chap. 4 at n. 27.

[9] Mendoza to Charles, 13–16 October and 18 November 1528, SC III, part 2, 819, 843.

ever motive. While Campeggio was still on his way to England, Robert Shorton, Catherine's almoner and at one time the dean of Wolsey's chapel, had revealed to the cardinal the queen's mind in the matter of the coming legatine trial. He had often heard her say "that if in this cause she might attain and enjoy her natural defense and justice, she distrusted nothing but it should take such effect as should be acceptable both to God and man, and that for these causes: First, for that it was in the eyes of God most plain and evident that she was never known of Prince Arthur. Secondly, for that neither of the judges were competent, being both the king's subjects, beneficed within his realm [Campeggio held the bishopric of Salisbury], and delegate from the pope at the contemplation of the king, she being never heard ne admitted to her defense. Thirdly, for that she ne had, ne might not have, within this realm any indifferent counsel. Finally, for that she had in Spain two bulls, the one being latter date than the other, but both of such efficacy and strength as should soon remove all objections and cavillations to be made to the infringing of this matrimony."

Wolsey responded to Shorton at some length against the first three of these arguments. For instance, concerning her claim of nonconsummation, there were extremely strong presumptions of law against it, which "of congruence ought to weigh more in every equal judge's breast than her simple allegation." That is, as one of the judges, Wolsey had already made up his mind on the question. He alleged the fact that both Catherine and Arthur were of sufficient age to perform the act, and that it was notorious that they slept together for the third part of a year. The parents of both desired nothing more than such a consummation, and in fact Ferdinand's counselors in England sent the bedsheets stained with Catherine's blood to Spain as proof that it had occurred. Moreover, in the treaty of marriage that was made later between Catherine and Henry, the representatives of both Spain and England solemnly swore that the first marriage had been consummated. "Furthermore, the common voice through England is that the said Prince Arthur should ofttimes boast one morning how oft he had been the night before in the midst of Spain: insomuch that commonly his so premature death was imputed to *nimio coitu*" (that is, excessive intercourse). Finally, Henry VII for some time after Arthur's death would not permit young Henry to be named prince, for Catherine's closest attendants thought she might be pregnant.[10]

To Catherine's fourth argument Wolsey attempted no refutation; he assumed, no doubt, that any differences that existed in her two dispensations were simply the usual insignificant scribal variants. He soon found out differently. Around the seventh of November,[11] Catherine gave to Campeggio a hitherto unknown form of Julius II's dispensation. It was in the form of a brief rather than a bull; like the bull, it was predated December 26, 1503,[12] but it was couched in disturbingly different terms. It had the effect of exploding in an instant all the plans that Wolsey and the king had painstakingly laid, and Catherine felt the repercussions immediately. On the same day that she revealed the brief, some of her counsel, including Archbishop Warham of Canterbury and Bishop Tunstall of London, came to interrogate her, on orders from the king, concerning some points raised by the opposing counsel.

The visitors were actually delegated to deliver a somewhat silly rebuke to the queen. There had been a plot reported against the king's life, she was told, and they felt that they must point out to her that if anything came of it, it would be imputed to her. In fact, they went on, the king had begun to have his doubts about her, since she was proceeding about her business with her usual cheerfulness, while Henry had become very pensive and troubled about the matter of their marriage. She did not show him the love that she owed him as her husband (in his instructions Henry apparently forgot that he had recently told her that he was not her husband), but rather she exhorted her ladies to dance, and showed herself to the people, taking delight in their cries of approval and disapproval. One instance of her neglect was the fact that she had kept

10 Document from the Cambridge University Archives, published by Richard Fiddes, *The Life of Cardinal Wolsey* (London, 1724), II, 212–15. Cf. LP IV, 4685: Brewer calendars the report among the documents of August 1528, but it should no doubt be placed somewhat later.

11 Mendoza, writing on November 18, says he spoke to Campeggio "some time ago"; and "five or six days after this conversation," the events described here took place. SC III, part 2, 843–44.

12 Technically, the brief should have been dated 1504, since "brief-years" ordinarily began on December 25 or 26. Therefore "December 26, 1503" on a brief meant "December 26, 1502." Perhaps this is what Catherine meant when she stated that one of her dispensations was of a later date than the other. It was to cause some awkwardness, since Julius II was not yet pope in 1502.

the brief to herself, whereas she should have shown it to the king long ago, "for the exhibition thereof might have done much ease before this time." Henry, in sum, had come to the conclusion that the queen hated him, and he was determined to deny her access to him, because he feared for his life. Her daughter would also be kept away from her, and she herself was to remain in seclusion and not stir up the populace. She really should enter a religious order; she need not be afraid that Henry would marry someone else if she did so.

At the end of the memorandum containing the above message for the queen, there are some notes concerning further points that were to be brought up to her. They are written in the hand of John Clerk, Bishop of Bath and Wells, one of her counsel who on other occasions was to show no little courage on her behalf. For the moment, however, he was obliged to follow Henry's instructions, and tell the queen that it was stupid to contend with the king, and that it was thought that the brief was a forgery. She was to be asked how long she had had it, whom she had sent for it, what letters she had mailed by this messenger's means and to whom, who had given her the brief, and whether she possessed any more letters.[13] If Henry was to suffer any further shocks like this one, he wanted to get them over with immediately.

Catherine understood that she was being asked to answer two questions: first, whether it was true that she had planned to assassinate the king, in order to allow herself and her daughter to marry at will; second, why she had not shown the brief before, and how she had come by it. She answered the first by saying she was sure that such an abominable accusation could not have come from the king, her lord, because he knew well that she valued his life more than her own, and therefore there was no need to answer such a question. As to the second, she had not exhibited the brief before because she had no idea that it would be required; and as to who had given it to her, it was Don Iñigo, some six months ago.

The queen warned Mendoza that he would be questioned about the brief, and, as he wrote to Charles, he planned his answer, "that it may not disagree with the queen's declaration, nor make it appear as if she had stated an untruth."

---

[13] Pocock, I, 212 (cf. LP IV, 4981); Gairdner, *EHR* 12: 238, correctly assigns the paper to this occasion and identifies the writer of the notes as Clerk.

Did Catherine state an untruth? Her moral integrity would probably not have permitted her more than a diplomatic evasion. If there was such an evasion, perhaps it had to do with the nature of the copy of the brief. Mendoza was first sent a simple transcript, and later both he and the queen insisted upon the necessity of a notarized copy that would stand up in court. Charles wrote on the first of September that he was sending attested copies of both dispensations, but Mendoza reported on September 18 and again on October 16 that the attested brief had not yet arrived. It may be that this was the main reason why the brief was not produced earlier, because the copy that Catherine showed to Campeggio had not really been given to her six months before but had only just come into her hands.

There was something about the brief that disturbed Catherine; whereas the bull said that Henry and she had informed the pope that her first marriage with Arthur was "perhaps consummated," the brief omitted the qualification and had the princely petitioners state as a definite fact that consummation had taken place. To set the record straight, the queen took advantage of her new lawyers' visit to Bridewell. She had them summon a notary, and made sure too that Bishop Fisher was present. Then she solemnly took an oath upon the Gospels, "being neither asked nor required to do so, but of her own volition," and declared in a loud voice that the words which were inserted into the brief narrating as a fact that carnal intercourse had taken place were put there without her knowledge by the agents who had obtained the brief. Moreover, she protested that she did not intend by the exhibition of this brief before any persons whatever to consent or confess because of these words that she was ever carnally known by Prince Arthur. For the truth of the matter was that she was not so known, but that the petitioners who had acted in her name were "following the presumption of the law rather than the truth of what actually happened."[14]

The question of legal presumption versus truth in regard to

[14] Pocock, II, 431. The protestation is dated November 7, 1528. A year later, when speaking of this public act of the queen's and sending a copy of her statement to Charles, Eustace Chapuys, the new ambassador, mistook the meaning of the last part of it, thinking that Catherine repudiated all use of the brief because it denied her virginity: "La Royne mesme leur a proteste par instrument publicque, dont [j']en envoye la copie a vostre majesté, qu'elle ne vouloit

Catherine's virginity would be important later on. Though Catherine's fears would eventually be realized and the brief taken as an admission of consummation in her first marriage, what now concerned the king's cause most was that in the brief the pope gave the dispensation not only for the reasons named in the bull, which the decretal commission discounted as false or inaccurate, but also for other unnamed causes. It was this that set the minds of the king's men to work at top speed, in an attempt to shore up their crumbling defenses.

The day after the queen's protestation Henry decided to do some protesting himself. He had been very much disturbed by the warm reception that the people were giving to the queen, and by the discontent they manifested at the arrival of the papal legate. He felt that the rebuke delivered to the queen was not enough and that public opinion must be won over. He therefore summoned the mayor and aldermen of London to Bridewell and entered into a pious defense of his actions, in the presence of his privy council and a greater part of the lords of the land and various of his officials.

He spoke of his good relations with both Spain and France, and said that the learned bishop who had formerly been the French ambassador in England had terribly increased the scruple that he had long had on the subject of his marriage. For the said bishop had raised the matter with great insistence in his council (that is, when negotiating the marriage of the Princess Mary). Henry was very anxious to secure the succession of his realm, and therefore he wished to learn from his good subjects and friends how matters stood in the law and in reason; for he was determined to follow entirely what reason dictated. Meanwhile should any person speak of the matter in terms other than he ought to use of his prince, he would let him know that he was the master. Du Bellay, the Bishop of Bayonne, who reported this speech,[15] could hardly credit his own senses, but he thought that Henry phrased it thus: that there was no head so pretty (*si belle*) that he would not make it fly.

---

avoyer ledit bref ne s'en ayder pour autant que en icelluy est exprimé que le prince Arthur l'avoit cogneue, qu'elle dit estoit contre verité." Letter of 8 October 1529, Vienna, Haus-, Hof- und Staatsarchiv, England, Korrespondenz Karton 4; cf. SC IV, part 1, 275.

[15] LP IV, 4942 (p. 2145), du Bellay to Montmorency, 17 November 1528.

Another witness to Henry's speech on that day, the chronicler Edward Hall, claims to have set down the king's words as well as his wit could bear them away. Hall's wit never put his head in any danger from Henry's side, and perhaps for this reason he omitted the king's final threat. We must remember too that since Hall claimed for himself the classical historian's license of imagining what might well have been said upon a given occasion, he is not lightly to be trusted without corroborating evidence. His account differs from du Bellay's in having Henry say that the doubt was first raised in his mind by one of the French king's counselors, who said that his marriage to Catherine was against the law of God. It was only then that he began to be troubled in conscience and to fear for the loss of his inheritance: "For this only cause, I protest before God and in the word of a prince, I have asked counsel of the greatest clerks in Christendom, and for this cause I have sent for this legate as a man indifferent only to know the truth and so to settle my conscience, and for none other cause, as God can judge."[16]

It is likely that Hall was correct in having Henry bring up the possibility that his marriage was contrary to divine law, for he had suggested the same thing to Campeggio not long before, as we have seen. It was a sign that this argument was again coming to the fore. It had been, apparently, the first objection to the marriage that had occurred to the king, and it was given scope at the Westminster inquisition; but fairly soon afterward, it was seemingly dropped. It was thought best to assail the dispensation on purely formal terms—especially after Fisher's opinion on the subject had been made known, and after Charles V in a letter to Henry formally denied the validity of such an argument and asserted the inadvisability of questioning the marriage under any pretext.[17]

The argument of indispensability was kept always in readiness, however, and trotted out occasionally as a threat. Thus, in the

[16] *Hall's Chronicle*, ed. Henry Ellis (London, 1809), pp. 754–55. On Hall, see my *Divine Providence in the England of Shakespeare's Histories* (Cambridge, Mass., 1970), pp. 109–12.

[17] LP IV, 3312, letter of 29 July 1527. Mendoza reported this shift in Henry's tactics in his dispatch of 6 September 1527 (SC III, part 2, 377); see the correction made to this entry by Garrett Mattingly, *Catherine of Aragon* (Boston, 1941; repr. London, 1950), p. 192 and note.

drafts of the decretal bull itself the pope was assured that Henry did not question his power, but that those of his consultants who did, when united with others who considered the bull defective, made the vote against the marriage unanimous. Perhaps the revelation of the brief made the king decide to use both forms of attack at the legatine trial. At any rate, the less momentous question of the technical adequacy of Julius's bull was to remain the chief target while the case was in the hands of the legates.

Henry attempted to surmount the obstacle of the brief by having it declared a forgery, endeavoring all the while to get his hands upon the original. The tale of his efforts in these directions, with the shameful expedients that he employed and the heroic resistance he met with from Catherine's supporters (which would often be repeated), is a familiar one and has been well told before. The chief result of the queen's exhibition of the brief was that whereas heretofore Henry had been burning to get the trial under way, now he willingly accepted a delay.

Meanwhile, some progress had been made in the matter of public honesty. Cardinal Wolsey's argument against the bull of dispensation would, of course, apply equally well to the brief. It was not the cardinal's strategy that received fresh support, however, but rather Henry's theological position. I postulated earlier that the king must inevitably have come to the conclusion that public honesty in the Levitical degrees was a divinely imposed impediment against marriage. In good time, well before Catherine's revelation of the brief, one of Henry's men had found a pope who had held the same thing; moreover, his decree on the matter had been incorporated into canon law.

This discovery was set forth in a position paper, of which only a summary, in English, has as yet been found. Something of the nature of the Latin original can, however, be deduced from the reply made to it by Nicholas West, Bishop of Ely, as well as from the subsequent attack by the author on West's reply, and from West's answer to that attack.[18]

---

18 The summary of the position paper, *A Compendious Annotation*, is edited in Pocock, II, 94–99, from a MS in the Public Record Office. A copy also exists in the British Museum, Additional MS 4622, ff. 104ff. For some reason (not evident from either copy) Pocock dates the summary 1531. Be that as it may, the original version must have been composed some time before November 1528, when the king's party found out about the brief, since neither the author nor

The summary of the position paper is entitled *A Compendious Annotation of Such Points and Articles as Seemeth Most Vehemently to Impugn the Matrimony Between the King's Highness and the Queen's Grace*. The discussion is preceded by a "fact," that is, a factum: a narrative of the basic facts of the case.[19] Included is the assertion that the marriage between Arthur and Catherine was contracted, solemnized, and consummated with carnal knowledge. As a result, there were two impediments between Henry and Catherine: public honesty, arising from the contract; and affinity, "by reason of carnal conjunction."

Then comes an explanation of the laws involved:

For the examination of which question it is first to be considered that there is in the Church of God a prohibition of matrimony evident and manifest, which some doctors affirm to proceed of God's law directly, and all agree to be an old constitution of the holy canons, the authority whereof cannot be violate without deadly sin, that the brother may not marry his brother's wife. Which prohibition extendeth not only to that wife whom the brother hath carnally known, but also to that woman with whom the brother hath only contracted spousals, although he never carnally knew her, ne openly married her, like as the Pope manifestly declareth in the chapter *Ad audientiam*, in the title *De sponsalibus et matrimoniis*, where he writeth these words following: "Scriptum est quod sponsam fratris frater habere non potest,"[20] understanding that not only when the brother still liveth, but also after his death. So as between the

---

Bishop West made any reference to it in the controversy that followed. West's two treatises, which were eventually submitted on the queen's behalf at the legatine tribunal in 1529 (Public Record Office SP 1/54, f. 262; cf. LP IV, 5768.1.2), have recently turned up in a collection purchased by the Lambeth Palace Library. The first one, *In Dei nomine, amen. Cum ex facto*, etc., which I shall call 1 Ely, is in Lambeth MS 2341, ff. 1–44v. The second, *In Dei nomine, Amen. Ad ea que*, etc. (2 Ely), is in the same MS, ff. 46–179v, but separately foliated 1–136v. The response to 1 Ely, *Responsurus hijs que Reverendus pater Eliensis*, etc., is contained, as I was informed by the late Father Edward Surtz, S.J., in the archives of the Roman Catholic diocese of Westminster, Archbishop's House: Manuscripta archivi westmonasteriensis 1, A.D. 1509 ad A.D. 1569, pp. 37–140, separately foliated 1–52v. I should perhaps add that the Lambeth collection has a recent Italian provenance, which has given rise to the otherwise unsubstantiated conjecture that Cardinal Campeggio took the documents with him when he departed from England after the legatine trial.

19 The Oxford English Dictionary records the use of this term in England only from the eighteenth century on; see "factum" (2) and "fact" (7).

20 "It is written that the brother cannot have his brother's spouse." Cf. Lev. 18.16 and Mark 6.18, where the standard text has *uxor* (wife) rather than *sponsa*

brother and the brother's wife, where espousals or matrimony hath been contract, and carnal knowledge hath ensued upon the same, be two impediments in the law of like strength and effect; that is to say, of the contract, *publica honestas*, and of the carnal knowledge, affinity.[21]

As is clear from this summary, the author of the position paper had enough honesty of his own to admit that only some doctors believed the law against marrying one's brother's wife proceeded "of God's law directly," but he was less honest when he implied that all the doctors who took this stand considered it to extend to cases where no affinity but only public honesty had been contracted. Noticeable also is his disregard for the universal view that purely ecclesiastical canons, no matter how old or "holy," were subject to dispensation.

He was correct, however, in his assertion that Pope Alexander III believed the public honesty in this case to be a divinely imposed impediment which he could not remove, and that he understood it to apply when the brother was dead as well as while he lived. What he failed to explain was that when Alexander first contemplated the question, he did not believe that there was any impediment unless the first marriage had been consummated, and accordingly he issued a decretal allowing a man after the death of his *sponsa* (virgin bride) to marry her sister. Then later, under the influence of those same texts of Scripture which were to weigh so heavily with Henry VIII, the pope changed his mind and issued the contradictory decretal *Ad audientiam*, which Gregory IX included in his official collection. But the situation that Alexander was now dealing with was more complicated than in the previous case. A resident of Pavia named Hugo had vowed that if he could not marry his daughter to one of the sons of a fellow Pavian named Landacon, he would marry her to the other son. After the spousals were made with the first son, an objection of consanguinity was brought forth, and Hugo attempted to give her to another son, a half brother of the first. The pope forbade the marriage, on the grounds that Scripture did not allow a brother to marry his broth-

---

(spouse). Alexander was probably influenced by Gratian's comment after *Decretum* 2.27.2.10, where he purports to cite Leviticus as identifying *sponsa* and *uxor*: "Si quis sponsam alterius in agro oppresserit, morte moriatur, quia uxorem alterius violavit." Alexander's decretal is in CIC X 4.1.4.

[21] *Compendious Annotation*, Pocock, II, 94–95.

er's spouse, and he directed the Bishop-elect of Pavia to punish Hugo for making an illicit vow.

The canonists and popes of succeeding generations drew several lessons from this decretal but did not accept the view that such a marriage was forbidden by divine law. This was by no means the only time that Alexander III would be overruled by his successors. The *Glossa ordinaria* pointed out that even invalid espousals impeded marriage with blood relatives of one of the parties, but it was to be noted that they did so only by public honesty. That is, the glossator implied that a dispensation could be granted. Even the theologians, who in general took a stricter view than the canonists, agreed that public honesty rested only on the positive law of the Church.[22]

Following the appearance of the position paper the Bishop of Ely was commanded (by whom he did not say) to give his opinion on the questions that had arisen concerning the king's marriage. After taking an oath that he would favor neither side but seek only the truth, he began to refute the arguments of the *Compendious Annotation* one by one. First, however, he composed a factum of his own, as sincerely as he could. On the point of the nature of Catherine's first marriage, he said that it was consummated, "as it is presumed," and that therefore both public honesty and affinity stood in the way of her union to Henry. He also added a dramatic element to the account. He said, for instance, that Henry VII called his son to him and said, "Son Henry, I have agreed with the King of Aragon that you should marry Catherine, your brother's widow, in order that the peace between us might be continued. Do you wish to marry her in order to have the peace continued?" The prince responded by leaving all in his father's hands.[23] Ely of course was begging the question on this point as much as the author of the position paper did in taking consummation as a certain fact.

The discussion of Pope Alexander's decretal was something of a comedy of errors. In the original Latin version of the *Compendious Annotation* the author spoke first of the commentary of Praepositus (John Anthony of San Gregorio, d. 1509) on the chap-

22 On this whole matter, see Jean Dauvillier, *Le mariage dans le droit classique de l'église* (Paris, 1933), pp. 146–52.

23 1 Ely, ff. 1–2, 4.

ter *Ad audientiam* from the title *De rescriptis*, where he said that Praepositus "thinks" that the prohibition was one of divine law. Bishop West in reply said that he had studied the passage with a great deal of care and could find nothing of the sort. But even if it were so, it was only putative and not definite. In the exchange that followed, his adversary apologized for the scribe's error in referring to the title *De rescriptis* rather than *De sponsalibus*, but chided Ely for not understanding the meaning of *puto* ("I think"), whereupon the bishop in his second treatise replied with a good deal of indignation and a long dissertation on the significance of the word.[24]

Bishop West did go on in his first treatise, however, to take up Alexander III's canon *Ad audientiam* in the title *De sponsalibus*. Since the pope was using John the Baptist's denunciation of Herod, the bishop referred back to his earlier discussion of that passage: it was part of the Gospel narrative and not a Gospel command. But even if it were a definitive statement of divine law, it would have no bearing on Henry's case, because the Baptist spoke of the wife of a living brother.[25]

Rather abruptly, West dropped the subject at this point and went on to the next question. His adversary accused him of passing over the words of the pope in silence. The bishop replied that this was not true: he did give one answer (the one we have just seen). He had intended, however, to give a further response, as could be gathered from his words "Respondetur primo," but it was omitted through carelessness, whether his own or his scribe's. He had meant to add that Pope Alexander clearly understood John the Baptist to be speaking of a living brother, since this was the case in Pavia, so that clearly the decretal supported the bishop's position.[26]

Bishop West did not understand the full import of his adversary's intention in alleging the canon to extend divine law to non-consummated marriages. He left this supposition unchallenged, and the king's men would make use of it again.

The greater part of the *Compendious Annotation* dealt with reasons for the formal invalidity of the bull of dispensation, especially (1) the false suggestion that Henry desired to marry Cather-

---

[24] 1 Ely, ff. 4v, 9v; *Responsurus*, ff. 11v–12; 2 Ely, ff. 39v–44.
[25] 1 Ely, ff. 10–11.
[26] *Responsurus*, f. 11v; 2 Ely, ff. 35v–36v.

ine and desired peace, (2) Henry's protestation, and (3) the death of Henry VII. The author listed without elaboration other arguments that could be urged, namely, the petitioners' silence on Henry's youth, the fact that Henry had not authorized the request, the false statement that consummation was uncertain, and the mention of only one of the two impediments (there having been no word of public honesty).[27]

We have seen that Ely attempted to combat these arguments first of all by giving his own version of the factum. But he marshaled lengthy reasons against them all, including those left undefended by his opponent. Of these, the last two are of most interest to us. West pointed out to his opponent that the word "perhaps" (*forsitan* or *forsan*) in the clause "perhaps you consummated the marriage by carnal copula" could have two meanings. It could be expressive of doubt; if so, it would have no effect upon the pope's intention in giving the dispensation, for he expressed his willingness to grant it even if consummation had occurred. But the word sometimes had a purely affirmative meaning, examples of which could be seen in both canon and civil law.[28]

The author on the king's side replied that it did not matter what the pope's response was; the fact that a doubt had been introduced to make the pontiff more amenable automatically vitiated the grant. Furthermore, Ely's example from canon law (the chapter *Iuvenis*) confirmed *forsan* as an expression of doubt.[29] In answer, the bishop reiterated his stand: the pope showed himself willing to grant the dispensation whether consummation had occurred or not; this was proof that an unambiguous expression of consummation would not have rendered the grant more difficult. He admitted that some interpreters of canon law considered the *forsan* of *Iuvenis* to be a word of doubt, but others held it to be expressive of fact, and Ely for his part held it more likely that the latter was the pope's meaning. At the end of his argument he added a note in his own hand referring to another canon, *Super litteris*, which Catherine's counsel would use to oppose the same objection at the legatine court.[30] It is noteworthy that the bishop

27 *Compendious Annotation*, pp. 95, 99.

28 1 Ely, ff. 43v–44.

29 *Responsurus*, ff. 51–52. The chapter *Iuvenis* is in the title *De sponsalibus*, X 4.1.3. See above, Chap. 2, n. 12.

30 2 Ely, ff. 135v–136. See Appendix A, at n. 73.

did not try to prove that Catherine's first marriage had not been consummated, or that there was indeed a doubt about whether it had been consummated. Perhaps he agreed with Mendoza that it was not opportune to press the point at this stage.

The last objection that was mentioned in passing in the *Compendious Annotation* was that only affinity and not public honesty was mentioned by the pope. This, it should be remembered, was not the argument that Wolsey had suggested using in case the first marriage had not been consummated. Rather it was the argument that Wolman had used in the Westminster trial. It was assumed that consummation had occurred, and had thereby added the impediment of affinity to the already present obstacle of public honesty. Ely agreed that it was necessary to get a dispensation for both, but he denied that it was necessary to mention public honesty explicitly. He referred his adversary to the commentary of the "Abbot," that is, Nicholas Tudeschi, the fifteenth-century Abbot of Palermo (Panormitanus). The impediment could be clearly gathered from the narrated facts in the dispensation, and therefore it was tacitly removed.[31]

The bishop's opponent chose to omit giving a defense for this final argument. Perhaps he admitted the justice of Ely's answer. But, as we shall see, the point was to be brought up again at the legatine court.

The king's advocate ended his treatise by apologizing for any excesses against decorum that he might have committed in the heat of the debate, and prayed that Henry would attain to the truth; he added that it would be an unforgivable crime to harm His Majesty in this matter, and therefore he dedicated himself to embrace whatever the truth presented to him, and he prayed to Christ for assistance.[32]

Bishop West on his part addressed the king directly at the beginning of his response, but did not return to him at the end with any good wishes. He ended instead with a simple prayer to Christ for the elimination of error by the light of truth.[33]

Bishop West was one of the counselors appointed for the queen in October 1528. He was present at the appeal that Catherine made to the pope just before she was to appear in the legatine

31 1 Ely, f. 44rv.   32 *Responsurus*, f. 52.
33 2 Ely, ff. 1, 136v.

court. It is not clear whether he attended the early sessions of the trial, but, as was mentioned before, his two treatises were submitted at some time on the queen's behalf. His name appears among the signers of a document dated July 1, which recounted the origin of the king's scruple. He did appear on July 5, to be sworn in as a witness, and his deposition was taken outside of court on the same day. The testimony that he gave at this time has been misrepresented. The truth is that he remained consistent with his previous position: he declared that he believed and had always believed that Henry's marriage with Catherine was not against divine law.[34] On the question of consummation in Catherine's first marriage, he replied that he did not know. When pressed to say what he believed, he replied that he doubted it, because the queen had often told him on the testimony of her conscience that she had never been carnally known by Arthur. His answer to the final article was still more straightforward: he did not believe that the legates were competent judges, because the queen had appealed the case to the pope.

Bishop West was taken ill after this, and eight days later, on July 13, ten days before the end of the trial, we find him at Downham, near Ely, writing to Wolsey to thank him for his good wishes on hearing of his convalescence. Wolsey had sent Stephen Gardiner to West to impart these sentiments, and also to request him to come to London immediately to do some service for the king. Bishop West replied that he would come as speedily as his disease and the intemperate heat permitted,[35] and he was listed as present at the trial three days later, at the Friday session of July 16.

West had been one of the witnesses of the protestation that Henry had made against his marriage contract on the eve of his fourteenth birthday in 1505, and Wolsey wanted him to testify to that effect, and he did so on July 21. He was also present for the end of the trial on Friday, July 23.

We have here, then, a preview of the main concerns of the legatine trial. Let us now try to reconstruct the proceedings of the court day by day.

---

[34] Brewer, LP IV, 5774.6 (p. 2579), using British Museum Cotton MS Vit. xii, f. 130rv (new f. 123rv) failed to see the negative in the statement: "Examinatus super sexto dicit Articulum non continere in se veritatem quo ad Jus divinum, ut ipse constanter credit." It is this copy of West's testimony that is dated July 5.

[35] LP IV, 5776.

CHAPTER FOUR

The Opening of the Legatine Court

THE TRIBUNAL authorized by Pope Clement VII to investigate the marriage of Henry VIII and Catherine of Aragon finally met for the first time on May 31, 1529; it lasted for almost two months. Our knowledge of what happened at the court is fragmentary. We have the contemporary accounts of George Cavendish (who wrote almost thirty years after the event), of the French and Venetian ambassadors, of Campeggio himself, and of his secretary Floriano Montini, who was one of the official recorders of the process. Edward Hall gives a few snippets; and, although only one or two small fragments survive of William Rastell's life of Thomas More, the early biography of John Fisher and, more importantly, Nicholas Sanders's *Anglican Schism* draw upon it.[1]

In addition there are scattered unpublished documents concerning the case in various archives and libraries, not all of which have been carefully examined. The most important of these is the notarial copy of the acts compiled and arranged in one volume by Richard Watkins, notary public, and William Clayburgh, prothonotary public, the two English clerks of the trial, more than four years after the court was adjourned for the last time. Watkins's certification of the record on the last page says that the actual copying was done by George Lording, one of Watkins's servants, since Watkins himself was otherwise occupied on necessary business. But both he and Clayburgh collated the copy with the original documents, and noted their respective emendations folio by folio. In addition, Watkins signed each of the sixty-nine folios.

---

[1] F. van Ortroy, "Vie du bienheureux martyr Jean Fisher," *Analecta bollandiana*, 10 (1891), 312 n.; 12 (1893), 248–49.

The two notaries asserted that the legates performed all the acts contained in the record, "among other things," in the twelve sessions of the trial specified. The notaries could not be accused of lying through their teeth, for it was a true statement—as far as it went. But they could be accused of violating the honor of their profession by a sin of omission. The fact is, as we shall see, that there was a thirteenth session, that of June 21, about which they made no mention, or almost no mention. And the "other things" done in the court were often far more important and vital to the case than the events that they mentioned.

Between the statements of Clayburgh and Watkins is a testimonial letter from Nicholas Wootton, certifying the profession, competence, and good character of the two notaries. It is dated October 1, 1533. I shall speculate later on the possible reasons for compiling a doctored version of the legatine proceedings at that late date.

The Watkins-Clayburgh volume was first heard of when it was excerpted by Edward Herbert, first Baron Herbert of Cherbury, in his *Life and Reign of King Henry VIII*, published in 1649. After that, it eventually came into the hands of John Moore, who was Bishop of Ely from 1707 until his death in 1714. Bishop Moore allowed his fellow bishop Gilbert Burnet to consult the manuscript for the supplement to his *History of the Reformation*, which appeared in 1715. Meanwhile, shortly after his accession, King George I purchased Bishop Moore's library for six thousand guineas and bestowed it upon Cambridge University as a reward for supporting the House of Hanover "on Church of England principles." The legatine record was included in the bequest and it has remained in the university library since that time.[2]

2 See Cecil Moore, *Memoir of the Father of Black Letter Collectors (John Moore, Bishop of Ely)* (London, 1885), pp. 25–29. The record is Cambridge University Library MS Dd 13.26, cited hereafter as Court Record. It is calendared in LP IV, 5791.2 (p. 2589) and VI, 1198. Of the two foliations, I use the lower numbers, which are those followed by Watkins and Clayburgh themselves. Clayburgh's certification appears on f. 69rv, Wootton's letter on ff. 70v–71, and Watkins's statement on f. 72. Events and documents of the second and third days of the trial (that is, June 18 and 21), especially as they pertain to the queen, are to be found in "a register of certain acts subscribed by the discreet men, Messrs. John Talcarne and John Clerk, public notaries, and authenticated by a letter of legality by the honorable man, Peter Ligham, Official of the Court of Canterbury"; the authentication took place on October 21, 1531, and the acts were submitted at the papal trial in Rome on December 11, 1531, on Catherine's be-

The record begins with an account of the events of May 31. Cardinals Wolsey and Campeggio appeared in the Parliament Chamber of the priory of Blackfriars, which was situated east of the royal residence of Bridewell across the Fleet River. The two establishments had been connected by a bridge in 1522 to accommodate the Emperor Charles V when he was lodged at Blackfriars as a guest of the king.[3] Henry did not make an appearance at the May 31 meeting of the court. Instead, Bishop Longland of Lincoln, who happened to be the king's confessor, delivered the papal commission to the legates, who gave it to Floriano Montini to read. In the commission, which was the one issued in April and again in June of the previous year (1528), the pope declared that it had frequently been related to him by trustworthy persons that there was question about the validity of the marriage between King Henry and Queen Catherine. The case had not yet been brought to a public ecclesiastical trial, and because of the importance of the matter a rapid judgment was required. Since therefore the pope himself was not able to inquire into the truth of the facts (*factum*), and considering that the factum from which the law depended could be better found out in England, he delegated Cardinals Wolsey and Campeggio to investigate all the circumstances, and, having called the parties in question, to proceed summarily and plainly, without judicial fanfare and form ("summarie et de plano sine strepitu et figura iudicii"). They were to determine whether the marriage was valid or invalid, and if one or other of the parties should request it, they were either to con-

---

half. These legatine acts appear in a manuscript in the British Museum (Add. 37154) entitled *Extractum registri cause Anglie matrimonialis coram R. P. D. Paulo Capisuccho*, which describes the proceedings at Rome from July 5, 1529, to August 28, 1533. It was brought to light by Edward Surtz in his elaborate prosopography "Henry VIII's Great Matter in Italy: An Introduction to Representative Italians in the King's Divorce, Mainly 1527–1535," which he completed shortly before his death in January 1973. His work was made available in xerograph form by Xerox University Microfilms, Ann Arbor, in 1975, and I received a copy just as the present study was being given to the printer. Surtz analyzes the *Extractum registri* on pp. 976–1011, and describes the legatine materials mentioned above, which occur on ff. 105v–135 of the manuscript, on pp. 996–99. For the importance of these legatine acts in the Roman trial, see below, Chap. 9 at n. 8.

[3] E. K. Chambers, *The Elizabethan Stage* (Oxford, 1923), II, 476, and Irwin Smith, *Shakespeare's Blackfriars Playhouse: Its History and Its Design* (New York, 1964), p. 13.

firm the marriage or declare it null, according to their findings. In the latter case, they were to give a sentence of divorce. One of the legates could proceed to judgment even if the other were impeded, and all possibility of refusal and appeal was removed.[4]

The terms in which the pope phrased this commission, in alleging that there was not a single accuser of the marriage but rather numerous reports, show that the trial was to be an *ex officio* inquisition of the sort that Wolsey had held two years before. The model that Innocent III had had in mind for establishing this kind of trial-inquest was the practice of God himself: "And the Lord said, 'The cry of Sodom and Gomorrah is multiplied, and their sin is become exceedingly grievous, I will go down and see whether they have done according to the cry that is come to me, or whether it be not so, that I may know.' "[5] The formula enjoining summary process was applied to all the more common ecclesiastical cases, including those concerning marriage, by order of Pope Clement V (1305–14),[6] and the same pope defined the phrase to mean simply that the judge was permitted to eliminate all unnecessary delays.[7] This authorization included the power to hold court even during time of vacation ("tempore etiam feriarum"), a point that Wolsey was apparently to overlook and Campeggio deliberately to ignore.

Though Campeggio was to speak later of the speed with which the trial was proceeding, it seems that all the normal rules for this kind of office-inquisition were observed. The two legates commissioned Bishops Longland and Clerk to cite Henry and Catherine to appear before them there in the Parliament Chamber on June 18, and the bishops later reported that they executed their commissions and presented summonses to the royal couple, who were both lodged at Bridewell, on June 1.[8]

Two days before the date on which the court was to reconvene, the legates were still in the dark as to what the queen would do.[9] But on that very day, June 16, Catherine made her move, following instructions from her friends in Flanders. At Baynard's Castle

---

4 Ehses, pp. 28–30.

5 Genesis 18.20–21. See CIC X 5.1.24; 5.3.31.

6 CIC Clementinae 2.1.2; cf. my "English Kings and the Fear of Sorcery," *Mediaeval Studies*, 39 (1977).

7 CIC Clementinae 5.11.2.

8 Court Record, ff. 1–3v; cf. LP 5613.1–6, 5694.

9 Campeggio to Salviati, 16 June 1529, Ehses, p. 102, LP IV, 5681.

(located on the Thames to the east of Blackfriars), in the presence of Archbishop Warham and Bishops Tunstall, West, Clerk, Fisher, Standish, and Athequa, along with her almoner Robert Shorton, with Bishop Clerk and John Talcarne serving as notaries, the queen solemnly appealed the case from the legates to the pope.[10]

On the morning of June 18, after Longland and Clerk had notified the court that the king and queen had been cited, the legates asked if anyone wished to appear for the king. Richard Sampson stepped forward with Henry's powers of attorney for himself and for John Bell. There was no need for the legates to ask if anyone was appearing for the queen, since Catherine was there in person. She read a protest, the essence of which was that her appearance there and anything that she should say were not to be taken as an indication of approval of the legates as competent judges in the case, nor to derogate from any allegations, protestations, provocations, appeals, complaints, supplications, recusations, and reclamations made to the pope; she would adhere to them, and whatever was to be done in this court by her or in her name was to be included under this same protest. She requested that the protest be inserted into the acts of the court; it was so done, but nothing else that was said by her or on her behalf in the trial was to be recorded in this way again. Or rather, if it was, it was not included in the acts compiled by Watkins and Clayburgh four years later.

The acts do mention that the queen did other things besides make a protest, but they do not say what they were. There are preserved elsewhere, however, two drafts of the proceedings of this day in court, in which it is recorded that after the queen read her protestation, she asked that another protestation that she had previously prepared be inserted into the records. One of the drafts gives part of the text: in substance it is very similar to the one discussed above. The queen proceeded next to exhibit a "provocation" or appeal and asked that it be notarized then and there. She then produced another provocation and appeal. Finally, she requested that these documents be registered and returned to her; the judges agreed, and it was so done.[11] A list of the various ap-

10 Pocock, II, 609.

11 London, British Museum, Cotton MS Vit. B xii, ff. 35–39v, 62v–63; ed. Pocock, I, 216–18. One of the queen's appeals is given later in the same codex (Pocock, I, 219–22). Brewer (LP IV, 5695.3) mistakenly interprets the queen as saying that the legates had already rejected her appeal. What she said was that

peals and protestations submitted by the queen to the court is to be found in the Public Record Office; also listed is the power of attorney enabling a proctor to appear for her, together with the protestation which her proctor, one John Faytor, submitted to the court on his own behalf.[12] When Catherine read her own protestation before the cardinals on June 18, she specified at the beginning that she was speaking "citra revocationem procuratoris mei alias in hac parte constituti," that is, after (or before) recalling the proctor that she had previously empowered to appear for her in this court.[13] Since no version of the acts gives an account of her proctor's role, it is evident that they cannot be relied upon to supply all of the essential events of the trial.

After the queen had submitted her documents, the cardinals appointed Montini, Clayburgh, and Watkins as scribes of the process, and named John Hughes "as the promoter or coadjutor of their most reverend office, whole and entire, up to the end of the aforesaid cause, inclusively." According to the draft signed by Montini as well as by the two English scribes, which gives the actions of the queen more fully, the cardinals then assigned Catherine the following Monday, June 21, to hear their decision upon her matter and petition, and they admonished her to be present. She, however, objected to this assignment and entered the same protestation as before.[14]

Not only does the notarial record of Clayburgh and Watkins fail to record the assignment, but also it omits all the proceedings of the next session on June 21. We must go to different sources for an account of the momentous events of that day, which

she had already made an appeal to the pope. The *Extractum registri* preserves the texts of the queen's exhibits of June 18: the protestation (ff. 110–111), the appeal declining the jurisdiction of the cardinals (ff. 111–118), the appeal of June 16 (ff. 118–121v), and a *provocatio et appellatio* embodying the petition made to the pope in the previous year by the imperial ambassador Muscetula, notarized July 20, 1528 (ff. 122–125v; Surtz, pp. 997–98).

12 LP IV, 5768.2.3. For Faytor (Fayter), see A. B. Emden, *A Biographical Register of the University of Oxford, A.D. 1501–1540* (Oxford, 1974).

13 Court Record, f. 4v. The word *citra* can have either the classical and medieval meaning of "before" (that is, "this side of," when looking ahead in time) or the purely postclassical meaning of "after" (looking back in time); the latter use can be seen in Warham's testimony (Court Record, f. 26v). See R. E. Latham, *Revised Medieval Latin Word List* (London, 1965).

14 Cotton Vit. B xii, f. 63v; cf. LP IV, 5694; see also Henry's account of 23 June, LP IV, 5707.

came perilously close to *strepitus iudicii*. According to Campeggio, the court met in the morning, as usual, and both the king and the queen appeared in person, along with a great crowd of officials and spectators. Henry proceeded to make an oration, justifying himself with great gravity and vehemence. Cardinal Wolsey answered, and thanked him; then he swore and protested that he would take no consideration in this case for anything except justice.[15]

This sort of protestation was becoming almost a spring ritual with Wolsey. In May of 1527 he had begun his secret inquisition with a similar asseveration: his conscience was disturbed by the matter and he was concerned for the safety of the king's soul, which he cared for as his own.[16] A year later, we recall, he enacted a similar scene, presumably for the benefit of any critics that he might have at the papal court. The repeat performance of the current year was likewise reported to Rome, by his fellow legate Campeggio.

According to Cavendish, Wolsey asked Henry to exculpate him of the charge that he had originated his scruple: "Sir, I most humbly beseech Your Highness to declare me before all this audience whether I have been the chief inventor or first mover of this matter unto Your Majesty, for I am greatly suspected of all men herein." Henry replied by repeating much of what he had said at Bridewell the year before about the origin of his doubt, to judge from the words attributed to him by Cavendish and Hall. He reiterated his willingness to take Catherine back to him if this court found that the marriage was valid, and said once again that it was the French ambassador who had first raised the scruple in his mind. He had confided it to Bishop Longland, his confessor, who had advised him to seek the counsel of other bishops. He had asked the Archbishop of Canterbury, who was his metropolitan, for license "to put this matter in question," which he granted in writing, as did all the bishops present.

At this point, Cavendish says, Bishop Fisher indignantly denied

---

[15] Campeggio, in Ehses, p. 106. See LP IV, 5695.13 for a draft of Wolsey's projected reply to a speech that Sampson was expected to make on the king's behalf (Pocock, I, 228, for some reason thinks that Wolsey was answering the queen's proctor).

[16] LP IV, 3140: "cum animo conscientiaeque meae id haberem iniectum, quod animae vestrae salutem respiceret, quam ut meam ipsius curare et velim et debeam."

that he had done any such thing and rebuked Warham for saying that he allowed him to sign his name for him. Henry tried to bluster his way past the bishop, who would not budge, and in his embarrassment the king attempted to pass the incident off as unimportant: "Well, well, it shall make no matter; we will not stand with you in argument herein, for you are but one man."[17]

What was the document alluded to in this exchange? The only thing of the sort that has thus far turned up is a statement dated July 1, 1529, ten days after Henry made his speech, and there is no indication in the surviving accounts that the king ever appeared again in court in his own person. The document in question is a statement to the effect that when Henry conceived his scruple concerning his marriage the undersigned prelates were consulted about it. They agreed that he had good reason to be disturbed, and said that it seemed necessary to submit it to the judgment of the pope. The instrument is signed by Archbishop Warham and Bishop Tunstall (who on this same day, July 1, departed for France, along with Thomas More), as well as by Bishops West, Standish, Fisher, Clerk, Voysey, Kite, and Longland. All but the last two were members of the original group of counselors appointed for the queen the previous October.[18]

It clearly is the kind of document that Fisher would have objected to, because, as far as we can tell, his advice to the king was quite against his beginning any annulment proceedings. Wolsey reported to Henry in his letter of July 5, 1527, that when he brought up the arguments against the marriage, Fisher rejected outright the notion that it was against the divine law; and, though he admitted that "he had ever heard that a dispensation is nought *si preces veritate non nitantur,*" that is, if the reasons alleged were not verified, his conclusion was not to call the validity of the marriage into question, or to say that the pope should investigate it, but simply to lament "the negligence of them that so handled that thing in the beginning, being of so high importance and great weight, whereupon might insurge doubt or question upon the succession of Your Highness."[19]

17 Cavendish, pp. 82–85.
18 Rymer, XIV, 301. Garrett Mattingly, *Catherine of Aragon,* p. 201, fills in Campeggio's list of counselors with West, Standish, and Voysey.
19 SP I, 201.

In spite of Wolsey's warnings not to speak to the queen about the matter, Fisher had written his encouragement to her: there was no doubt of the pope's power to dispense; she should stand firm on the bull of Julius II, and secretly apply to Pope Clement for another bull repairing any accidental defects in the first.[20] It is true that Fisher had written in a private letter to one of the queen's supporters that if the king "has formed a scruple of conscience because of those Levitical prohibitions, who will deny that he does the right thing if, as a true Christian and orthodox prince should, he submits himself to the pope's interpretation? I do not see that anyone should object to such a proceeding [*institutum*], especially since the king seems to have woven together [*pretexere*] some basis for his scruple from Scripture." The bishop did not mean to say, however, that Henry's scruple had any real justification, nor would he encourage the king to put it to the test. "For," as he went on to say, "kings usually think that they are permitted to do whatever pleases them, because of the magnitude of their power. Therefore it is good for these kings, in my opinion, to submit themselves to the decrees of the Church, and this is beyond a doubt to be praised in them, lest otherwise they kick over the traces and do what they please, as long as they can weave together some appearance and color of right." He concluded by telling his correspondent that it was far from true that all the bishops who had resisted the pleasure (*voluptas*) of the king in this matter had now recanted and believed either that the marriage was invalid or that the Levitical prohibitions forbade it; but the matter was of such great moment and vitally concerned so many persons that no one could affirm it without openly endangering himself.[21]

The document of July 1, 1529, therefore, is surely the one that figures in Cavendish's story; it is in fact listed among the documents exhibited by the legates.[22] Fisher's signature must have been

[20] Mattingly, *Catherine of Aragon*, p. 192.

[21] Record Office SP 1/42, f. 166v. Brewer calendars the letter in early July 1527 (LP IV, 3232). I cited the same letter above (Chap. 1, n. 31) for Fisher's refutation of Wakefield.

[22] Record Office SP 1/54, f. 263: "Littere testimoniales sigillis episcoporum sigillate testantes conscienciam Regie maiestatis in causa coram Judicibus agitata, quarum Jnitium est *Vniuersis*, etc." Cf. LP IV, 5768.2.1. The letter in Rymer begins, *Universis et singulis ad quorum notitiam praesentes litterae pervenerint.*

forged to it, when he would not go along with the scheme of making it appear that even the episcopal counselors of the queen had advised Henry to ask the pope for a judgment on the question. This is what the king did, of course, and the pope graciously responded by commissioning two legates *a latere* to hear and decide the case in his name. What the exact circumstances of Fisher's repudiation of the document were we do not know. It certainly must have taken place during July, however, as I shall attempt to show.

Cavendish seems to be mistaken, too, in the order of the speeches of June 21. He says that the queen spoke first, then Wolsey, and finally the king; according to the report of Louis Falier, the Venetian ambassador, the order was exactly the reverse. Henry spoke first, and, according to Falier, his main point was that he wished to remain no longer in mortal sin as he had done for the past twenty years. He asserted that he would never rest easy until the matter was decided in court, which he urged the judges to do with dispatch. Wolsey then answered: he admitted that he had received great favors from the king and was held to be suspect in this matter (he was referring to the queen's reasons for refusing the judges), yet he and Cardinal Campeggio had been appointed to decide this question by the pope, and he would do whatever he thought was demanded by justice. Then the queen rose and threw herself on her knees before the king, and said that she did not deserve to be repudiated after twenty years of marriage.[23]

According to Bishop du Bellay, before the queen knelt before him, the king answered her complaint and appeal by saying that his great love for her had prevented him from revealing his scruple about the marriage before this time. But he desired nothing so much as to have the marriage declared valid. He objected to the judges that it was unreasonable to have the case tried in Rome, because of the emperor's power there. It was at this point, the bishop said, that Catherine knelt before the king and begged him to consider her honor, and that of her daughter and his own as well. He should not be displeased with her for defending the marriage; because of his own willingness to see the bond confirmed,

---

23 Louis Falier, letter of 22 June 1529, in *I diarii di Marino Sanuto*, ed. F. Stefani et al., LI (Venice, 1898), 178. Cf. Rawdon Brown, *Calendar of State Papers and Manuscripts Relating to English Affairs Existing in the Archives and Collections of Venice*, IV (London, 1871), 219.

she had appealed the case to Rome. It was more suitable to decide it there, since England was subject to suspicion. Moreover, the case was already in the hands of the pope.[24] Campeggio's account is different still. He is not altogether reliable since, by his own admission, he had difficulty in understanding what was said, all of it being in English; but his English may not have been substantially worse than the Venetian's or the Frenchman's. The legate described the events of June 21 in two letters he wrote that same day. In one, as we saw above, he described the speeches of Henry and Wolsey. In the other, he said that after the queen had refused the judges and appealed the case on June 18, they summoned her to the court on June 21 to hear their decision upon her allegations. On that day, it was pronounced that they were competent judges, and all the forms that she had submitted were rejected. We know that it was Campeggio himself who denied her motions, saying that he had Wolsey's concurrence. He was moved to this action by the nature of the papal commission and by "certain other causes" (the same saving phrase that was used in Julius II's brief). The queen responded by presenting another appeal which covered all contingencies, together with a supplication to the pope, and then departed. But first she went to Henry and knelt before him. When he raised her up she knelt once more, and once again he was forced to lift her up; he then granted her request for permission to write to the pope in defense of her honor and her conscience.[25]

Cavendish reports that the queen made a long and eloquent speech as she was kneeling before the king. She spoke in broken English, and Cavendish pretends to give no more than the effect of it. She told the king, among other things:

When ye had me at the first, I take God to be my judge, I was a true maid without touch of man, and whether it be true or no I put it to your conscience. If there be any just cause by the law that ye can allege against me, either of dishonesty or any other impediment, to banish and put me from you, I am well content to depart, to my great shame and dishonor. And if

---

24 Du Bellay to Francis I, 22 June 1529, LP IV, 5702.

25 Campeggio, in Ehses, pp. 108–9; draft of the court record, Pocock, I, 223–24 (LP IV, 5695.2). According to the *Extractum registri*, Catherine appeared and asked to have the acts of the previous Friday read and copies made; Campeggio then rejected her appeal, and Catherine entered her protest, petition, and appeal (ff. 126v–130; Surtz, p. 998).

there be none, then here I most lowly beseech you let me remain in my former estate and to receive justice at your princely hands.[26]

Presumably, in speaking of "dishonesty," Catherine was alluding to the impediment of public honesty, which had allegedly not been cleared by the dispensation. According to Hall she had justified her marriage by citing the papal bull, which provided "that I, being the one brother's wife, and peradventure carnally known, might without scruple of conscience marry with the other brother lawfully." That is to say, she was dispensed, whether from public honesty or from affinity, depending on whether the first marriage had been consummated or not.

It is very credible that Catherine declared her virginity openly in court and defied Henry to deny it. Just two days before her first appearance at the trial, on the day on which she made her appeal at Baynard's Castle, she saw Campeggio and made a similar statement to him. The cardinal reported to the papal secretary, "She regards this fact as the great solace of her mind and as the firm foundation of her righteousness, that from the embraces of her first husband she entered this marriage as a virgin and an immaculate woman. This she very solemnly swears. She formerly made the same declaration, and still declares and affirms it even

[26] Cavendish, p. 81. Other parts of her speech bear some resemblance to the words that, according to Hall (*Chronicle*, p. 755), she spoke to the two legates when they visited her at Bridewell shortly after the king's speech of November 8, 1528. Hall says that the Bridewell exchange was spoken in French and recorded by Campeggio's secretary. Perhaps Hall was drawing on a record of the legatine court for June 21 and applied it to the Bridewell encounter. In his own account of the legatine trial, Hall says that Catherine made no speech on the day that she and Henry appeared in court together. According to his report of her words at Bridewell, she strongly condemned Cardinal Wolsey's role in the matter, and Wolsey's alleged response combines the elements of his speech of June 21, 1529, as reported by Cavendish and Falier. Cavendish too reports an encounter at Bridewell, but says it occurred after the trial had progressed for some time, and that he himself accompanied the two cardinals on their visit to the queen. If Montini went with them into her inner chamber, it may have been at this time that he wrote down the record seen by Hall. But according to Cavendish, English and not French was spoken: when Wolsey started to speak in Latin, Catherine said, "Nay, my good lord, speak to me in English, I beseech you, although I understand Latin" (p. 88). If Cavendish has remembered the time of this conversation correctly, he may be mistaken about the place; for after her departure from the court, Catherine retired to Greenwich, and it was there that she received the citations, from June 22 to July 2 (but see n. 31 below).

to the king himself, and it appears that this thing raises some scruple in the king's mind."[27]

When Catherine had had her say, she left the court, and refused to return, though repeatedly called; for this she was pronounced contumacious. Her new appeal had already been rejected, and order was given for her citation to the next session, Friday, June 25. The subpoena was prepared that very day (Monday, June 21) and presented, "with all due reverence," to the queen the next day by Bishop Clerk, who was received by her in the dining chamber of the royal residence at Greenwich.[28]

The Venetian ambassador, Falier, in the letter cited above, which was written on Tuesday, June 22, said that after the queen had made her final departure from the court at the Monday session, Henry gathered his counsel together and discussed matters with them for half an hour. Then the judges adjourned the court until the next day, June 22. On that day the Bishops of Rochester and Bath appeared as advocates and proctors of the queen. They declared that in order to prevent the king from falling into mortal sin, they wished to defend the rights of the queen and show that she was his legitimate and true wife. The bishops then presented her written appeal, which objected to the judges as suspect; and nothing further was done that day.[29]

If there was a meeting of the court on June 22, it was not one at which the king and queen or their proctors were expected to appear, for, as we have seen, the queen did not receive her citation until this day, and it was for June 25. Moreover, it was the Bishop of Bath, John Clerk, who delivered the subpoena, and who would continue to deliver similar citations after further meetings of the court. Furthermore, the queen would be held in contempt of court at each of these meetings for failure to appear or to send a proctor to appear for her. Still, the report may be essentially correct, since it sounds like a dress rehearsal of Fisher's defense of the queen at the session of June 28. The Bishop of St. Asaph, Henry Standish, also spoke on the queen's behalf on that

---

27 Campeggio to Salviati, 16 June 1529, Ehses, p. 102, LP IV, 5681.

28 Cavendish, p. 82; Henry VIII to his envoys in Rome, 23 June 1529, LP IV, 5707; draft of court record, Pocock, I, 223–24; LP IV, 5695.7–8; Court Record, f. 5v (narration of the citatory letter).

29 Falier, pp. 178–79.

day. Perhaps, then, it was Standish and Fisher who appeared before the legates on June 22, not as proctors, but simply as advocates for the queen. The fact that upon a later occasion the king claimed that a proctor for the queen acted officially for her[30] does not weigh seriously against this conclusion. An indication that Clerk could act on Catherine's behalf as well as for the court is to be had from the fact that he notarized her instrument of appeal on June 16, and did so again on June 21 (or 24) when Catherine produced an identical document at Baynard's Castle.[31]

June 22 was also the day of Stephen Gardiner's arrival in London, having returned from his post in Rome. Cavendish mistakenly designates him as the principal scribe for the court. Perhaps he is confused by the fact that Gardiner and Clayburgh were the court clerks for the 1527 inquisition. It is possible, of course, that Gardiner sat in court by virtue of his official position as Wolsey's secretary. At all events, he was definitely to play a role in the matters that were brought up during the course of the trial.

[30] See below, Chap. 13 at n. 26 (and Appendix B); earlier, Henry had referred to the same action as performed simply by Catherine's counsel (see below, Chap. 8 at n. 14).

[31] *Extractum registri*, ff. 131–135. Surtz, pp. 998–99, is rather confused in his summary; he speaks of the queen's withdrawal on June 21, which he mistakenly calls June 24 in his notes, p. 1028, n. 98; he goes on to speak of her appeal at Baynard's Castle on June 24; then he says that twenty persons were present, most of whom had been present in court on June 18—almost as if he were saying that Catherine produced her appeal in court on June 24 (which Surtz has confused with June 21). Finally, he says that the notaries were the same, namely, Talcarne and Clerk, and the letter of authentication was by Peter Ligham; but it seems that this latter notarization and authentication must refer to the whole legatine document, which Ligham executed in 1531 (see above, n. 2).

CHAPTER FIVE

The Charges Against the Marriage

❧❧

Cʜᴀᴏᴛɪᴄ ᴀs the first days of the trial might seem, it had gone according to the usual pattern of an inquisition. The delegated judges had convened their tribunal and summoned the implicated parties to appear before them. King Henry had accepted their jurisdiction and Queen Catherine had challenged it, according to the prescribed forms. The judges had rejected her protests, refusals, and appeals, and summoned her anew. On Friday, June 25, at the fourth official session of the court, Bishop Clerk assured the cardinals that the citation had been served upon the queen; when she did not appear, she was declared contumacious. The business of the court could then proceed even in her absence.

The legates, we saw, had appointed as their promoter John Hughes, who was an employee of Wolsey's faculty office.[1] He has left a memorandum on the method of carrying on the trial. According to the papal commission the whole case was to proceed, up to the demand for a divorce, in the manner of an inquisition from the side of the judges themselves, and not at the petition of one of the parties. When the parties appeared, articles were to be administered to them by the judges or the promoter, and these articles were to be such as one of the parties would allege against the dispensation and the marriage, if he had impugned the marriage.[2] In other words, if the papal commission had stated that the investigation had been requested by Henry or by some third party, this accuser, or plaintiff, would have been required by the legates to submit to them a *libellus* detailing his charges against

---

1 D. S. Chambers, *Faculty Office Registers, 1534–1549*, pp. xviii, xxvii.
2 LP IV, 5613.7.

the marriage, and the suit would then be contested by the defendant or defendants. As it was, however, the inquisition was to proceed *ex officio* on the part of the judges, as in Wolsey's tribunal of two years before.[3]

In accordance with this procedure, after the queen was declared contumacious on June 25, the legates, in the presence of Dr. Sampson, the lawyer-priest who was serving as the king's proctor, and by virtue of their office alone ("ex officio nostro mero"), introduced twelve articles against the marriage. The purpose of the articles was to detail point by point the facts that were the object of the defamation. But they were also meant to serve as questions put to the king and queen about their marriage, and they were to be used in interrogating witnesses. They were stated in categorical fashion, but rather clumsily, some being addressed only to Henry or Catherine, some to both, and others to no one at all—or rather to everyone in general.

Thus, the first article was addressed to Henry, stating that he and Arthur were brothers, born of the same parents. The second article was addressed to the queen, and stated the same thing. The third objection was likewise directed to Catherine, and deserves to be cited in full: "Likewise, most serene lady, Queen Catherine, we object, explain, articulate, and administer to you, with the aforesaid effect, that you and the above-mentioned Arthur of illustrious memory, who at that time was of legitimate age, legitimately contracted a true, pure, and legitimate marriage through words *de praesenti* which were fit for the purpose and which accordingly expressed true mutual consent, and that you had it solemnized in the face of the Church, and that you consummated it with carnal copula and openly lived together for some time and were commonly regarded and believed to be man and wife and legitimate spouses from that time until the time of the death or decease of the said Arthur, and that these things were and are true, public, and notorious, and that the public voice and fame have labored and still labor under and upon the same." (This statement of notoriety concluded each of the articles.) The fourth article was addressed to Henry, and had the same content as the third, with a very significant difference: it was objected that

3 See William Durantis, *Speculum iuris*, III, part 1: *De inquisitione* 3.6; 4.1: *De libellorum conceptione* 9.1–2 (Venice, 1585), pp. 33, 61.

Catherine and Arthur had contracted marriage, "and that they had it solemnized in the face of the Church ∽ ∽ ∽ ∽ ∽ ∽ between themselves ∽ and that they openly lived together for some time," and so on.[4] Why did the court clerks or the copy scribe, George Lording, put space-fillers in that part of the article that should specify the consummation of the marriage? The most logical answer is that someone deleted the words from the original text, and the copyist simply wanted to indicate that something was missing. We know that there had been some indecision about whether to have the king commit himself on the question of consummation, for in a rough draft of these articles we see that the original text of the fourth article simply stated that Catherine and Arthur contracted marriage "and had it solemnized in the face of the Church and openly lived together for some time," and so forth. But then between these two clauses another was careted in: "and consummated it with carnal copula."[5] The clause was apparently retained when the articles were first announced in court on June 25. I shall hypothesize later upon what happened to it after that.

The fifth article was addressed to both Henry and Catherine and stated simply that in 1509 they contracted and solemnized marriage and later consummated it and had offspring. The sixth told them that the aforesaid marriage "is prohibited and banned by both divine and ecclesiastical law, and that this was and is true and public," and so forth. The seventh stated that this marriage, "unless it can otherwise be validated and justified, was and is by reason of the foregoing altogether null and invalid and deserves to be held and adjudged as such."

The eighth article objected to the royal couple that at the time in which they were negotiating the marriage, "a grave, immense, and widespread scandal arose amongst the clergy and the people of the kingdom of England and in other places concerning such a marriage, and that obloquy and insistent murmuring against it

---

4 "Ac illud in facie Eccesie solennizari fecerunt ∽ ∽ ∽ ∽ ∽ ∽ inter se ∽ et per nonnulla tempora insimul cohabitaverunt," etc. Court Record, f. 6.

5 British Museum Cotton MS Vit. B xii, f. 72: "Ac [illud] in facie ecclesie inter se solennisari fecerunt *ac carnali copula consummarunt* [?] et per nonnulla tempora [insimul] cohabitarunt." I have indicated the careted clause by italics. The right edge of f. 72 is missing, which I indicate by brackets; I have filled in the obvious missing words. Cf. the edition by Pocock, I, 225.

arose amongst the nations." In the ninth place, they were told that in spite of this they married and stayed married until the present time.

The tenth article was a general statement: all the above came to the ears of the pope. In the eleventh, Henry and Catherine were informed that the pope ordered them to appear before the legates to explain themselves. The final article was an assertion that the legates were competent judges in the case. This being so, Henry and Catherine were cited to appear before them on Monday next, June 28. Campeggio was apparently displeased by the form that these articles took. He wrote to Salviati the same day, June 25, complaining that his associates were conducting the trial in such a manner that it was impossible to act according to the evidence, except after their own fashion.

On June 28 the queen again did not appear, but while the business of declaring her contumacious was being repeated, Bishop Fisher, along with other counselors for the queen, came forth—not however, as her proctor (Bishop du Bellay insisted on this point), but simply to give his response to the invitation that the king had made in his speech of June 21. Henry had asked not only the judges but everyone else to throw what light they could on the matter in order to relieve the burden on his conscience. Fisher felt obliged, in his own conscience, in the face of such an appeal, to come forward and reveal what conclusions he had come to after studying the problem with great diligence for the last two years. He declared therefore, with compelling reasons, that the marriage was good and that no power whatsoever could dissolve it, and that, just as John the Baptist had died in the cause of marriage, he too would be willing to become a martyr for it. He finally handed in a book that he had written demonstrating all his assertions. The cardinals were apparently somewhat cowed by this eloquence. They made him a "rather modest" answer, saying that it was not up to him to speak so definitively upon the question, since he had not been appointed to judge it. Fisher was followed by Henry Standish, Bishop of St. Asaph, and then the Dean of the Arches (Peter Ligham) spoke on behalf of the queen, but neither of them used the same force or eloquence that Fisher had commanded.[6]

[6] Reports of Montini (Ehses, pp. 116–17) and du Bellay (LP IV, 5741).

Cavendish says that it was Dr. Ridley who spoke after the two bishops in the queen's defense. He means Robert Ridley, the uncle of the future Protestant martyr, Nicholas. Robert was a kinsman of Bishop Tunstall of London, by whom he had been appointed his assessor in trials against heretics. Tunstall had also assigned him to assist Polydore Vergil in editing the *De calamitate Britanniae* of Gildas, which together they published in 1525. He remained a close associate of Vergil and other humanists in later years.[7] Cavendish describes him as "a very small person in stature, but surely a great and an excellent clerk in divinity."

According to Cavendish, Fisher interrupted a wrangle that had developed over the queen's consummation of her first marriage. If that is true, it must have occurred later in the session than Montini reported, unless no one was listening to the contumacy proceedings. Let us hear what Cavendish says: The matter of the queen's virginity was "very sore touched and maintained by the king's counsel, and the contrary defended by such as took upon them to be on that other part with the good queen. And to prove the same carnal copulation they alleged many colored reasons and similitudes of truth. It was answered again negatively on the other side, by which it seemed that all their former allegations to be very doubtful to be tried, so that it was said that no man could know the truth." That is, a case was being made for legal presumption. It was at this point that Bishop Fisher interrupted by declaring, "I know the truth," and citing the text asserting that what God had joined together no man could put asunder. Wolsey answered him by saying that his reasoning was not sufficient in this case: "For the king's counsel doth allege divers presumptions to prove the marriage not good at the beginning; ergo, say they, it was not joined by God at the beginning, and therefore it is not lawful; for God ordaineth nor joineth nothing without a just order. Therefore it is not to be doubted but that their presumptions must be true, as it plainly appears; and nothing can be more true in case their allegations cannot be avoided. Therefore to say that the matrimony was joined of God, ye must prove it further than by that

[7] See Jasper Ridley, *Nicholas Ridley* (London, 1957); Denys Hay, *Polydore Vergil* (Oxford, 1952); John E. Paul, *Catherine of Aragon and Her Friends* (London, 1966). J. Ridley asserts that Robert was Catherine's proctor at the trial (p. 44), but we have seen that this was not so.

text which ye have alleged for your matter; for ye must first avoid their presumptions."

Cavendish is doubtless not completely accurate in reporting Wolsey's statement when he characterizes the king's counsel as attempting to impugn the marriage. We shall soon see that the pattern of the 1527 inquisition was being maintained here; that is, though the king would admit that certain of the articles were true, he would still take the stance ostensibly of defending the marriage. In any dispute that arose over the queen's first marriage, then, Henry's counsel would simply be insisting upon the fact of consummation, and not upon the invalidity of her second marriage. In fact, after the trial, Henry made a point of declaring that he had not attacked the marriage during the trial.[8]

It was after Wolsey's explanation of the legal state of the question that Ridley broke in. He was not impressed with the cardinal's "therefore's," and said that it was a great dishonor "that any such presumptions should be alleged in this open court, which be to all good and honest men most detestable to be rehearsed." The Cardinal of York took him up and told him to speak more reverently. "No, no, My Lord," he answered, "there belongeth no reverence to be given to these abominable presumptions, for an unreverent tale would be unreverently answered."[9]

Montini reported that Fisher's speech was completely unexpected and left everyone sitting in amazement. The English clerks, reporting in 1533, merely stated that "there were present there at this time the very reverend fathers and lords in Christ, Lord John and Lord Henry, Bishops by the divine permission of the Churches of Rochester and St. Asaph, and the noble men Edward Earl of Derby and John Hussey, Knight, and many others gathered together in a numerous multitude."[10] According to their record for this meeting of June 28, after Catherine had been declared contumacious, "and after other things had been expedited by them," the judges swore in witnesses to testify on the articles. They were

[8] Chapuys to Charles V, 8 October 1529, SC IV, part 1, 274–75.

[9] Cavendish, pp. 80, 85–86. For his reference to Henry's "suit" before the judges, see below, Chap. 6 at n. 56.

[10] Court Record, f. 8. The phrase about the numerous multitude was standard, and was used even when the courtroom was not crowded, as, for example, in Cranmer's inquisition at Dunstable in 1533.

Thomas Grey, Marquess of Dorset; John de Vere, Earl of Oxford; George Talbot, Earl of Shrewsbury; Robert Radcliffe, Viscount Fitzwalter; Thomas Lord Darcy; William Blount Lord Mountjoy; Sir Henry Guildford; Sir Anthony Poyntz; and Sir William Thomas. John Taylor was assigned to take their testimony outside of court, and the court clerks were to record it. Then the legates made an announcement concerning the king's response to the articles. This is the first and only mention in the record of any such response, but if the legates followed their prearranged schedule (which is still extant), they had arranged for the king to be sworn in and officially examined upon the articles, and Sampson was required to hand in the written record of Henry's answers to the cardinals on the fifth day (that is, this session of June 28) after the queen had been declared contumacious and before witnesses were received.[11] The record, however, gives no hint that the judges delivered the deposition to the clerks for inclusion in the acts, though it is listed elsewhere as one of the documents exhibited by the legates; further, there is clear evidence that the king's deposition was originally included among the officially collected but yet unbound acts and exhibits of the court,[12] and that all reference to its exhibition was deliberately omitted when the record from which I am quoting was made. This record merely indicates that the legates asserted that Henry's answer to the seventh article alleged a papal dispensation to justify his marriage to Catherine and that they ordered Sampson to produce it and any other dispensations pertaining to the validity of the said marriage.[13]

What, one wonders, did the king have to say about the fourth article? Is it possible that he answered it fully and truthfully, to the extent of committing himself on the question of the consummation of Catherine's first marriage? Floriano Montini, the third clerk of the court and personal secretary to Cardinal Campeggio, reported it so all over Italy a year later: Richard Croke wrote to Henry that, according to Montini, Campeggio had the king's own handwriting "constantly affirming that the queen was a maid when she was married unto Your Highness."[14] Why, then, if the cardinal

[11] LP IV, 5695.9–10; cf. Court Record, ff. 7v–8.

[12] The king's response to the articles is named in the list of exhibits, Record Office SP 1/54, f. 264; cf. LP 5768.2.2. See below, Chap. 12 at n. 12.

[13] Court Record, ff. 7–8.   [14] Pocock, II, 29.

had such information, did he not make something of it, at least
after the case had been removed to Rome? A possible reason is
that he could not because Henry had taken the precaution of receiving from him a signed statement that he had not already and
would not write to the pope about his opinion on the case or di-
vulge any of the king's secrets, and that if the trial should be withdrawn to Rome he would use all his efforts to prevent the queen
from prosecuting it or carrying it on before the pope, and that he
would do all that he could to advance the king's interests, as be-
fitted one of his sworn councillors.[15]

Perhaps, then, Wolsey too found out only at the June 28 meeting the answer to his question about the queen's virginity. But it
seems much more probable that if Henry did answer the question
put to him, he said that he did not know for certain whether Catherine consummated the marriage or not, since he could not be sure
of the queen's virginity when she married him. This, at least, was
what the king was to say later, according to John Casale (see Chapter 7 below).

Let us return to the puzzle of the deleted clause concerning consummation in the fourth article. If Henry answered the article as
originally posed, then the deletion must have occurred at a later
time, no doubt at the same time that the king's responses were
removed from the acts. There is, however, another possible explanation for what happened. It may be that Wolsey or Henry himself
deleted the passage touching upon consummation before he answered it, so that he would not have to commit himself on the
point. Perhaps, then, other documentary evidence had come in
before the legates from the queen's counsel, some early letters of
Henry's, it may be, which admitted her virginity. We shall see later
that her counsel did formally assert at the trial that the king had
confessed it several times, and no doubt they backed up the assertion with proof.

We must not forget that it was at the June 28 meeting that Fisher
and the others made their speeches, and that according to Cavendish the main subject before the court was the consummation of
the queen's first marriage. What was it that triggered this discussion at this particular time? It is possible that it was Henry's answer

15 LP IV, 5820.

to the fourth article, if he answered the question on consummation and if his answer was read in court. Or alternatively, it might have been his failure to answer the question, or the cardinal's refusal to announce the answer (or the failure to answer).

Fisher, of course, had long been prepared to attack the case against the marriage. As expected, the fundamental charge that the cardinals had made on June 25 was that the marriage was against both divine and ecclesiastical law, and the book that Fisher submitted on June 28 addressed itself to both laws. Like the notarial record, this treatise is preserved in the Cambridge University Library.[16] We need not go into Fisher's arguments, except to note the way in which he explained the discrepancy in language between the bull and the brief in regard to the consummation of the queen's first marriage. King Ferdinand had been persuaded, he said, that Prince Arthur and Catherine had consummated their marriage; this was not unlikely, since they had long lived together on familiar terms. But Henry VII, who took careful note of all the circumstances, did not dare to affirm it, and therefore he had a word of doubt, *forsan*, added to the bull. All this proved, Fisher concluded, that there was nothing surreptitious or obreptitious in the papal dispensations, since the parents of neither party had any wish to deceive the pope.[17]

The truth of the matter seems to be that when the dying Isabella received the brief, she insisted upon a modification in the dispensation because in her view the statement of consummation was not true. That is, it was at her demand that the *forsan* was inserted into the bull.

On the whole, the session of June 28 had been a very trying one for Cardinal Wolsey, and rather than have the court meet as usual on Friday, he and Campeggio adjourned the trial for a whole week. He needed time to think and prepare his strategy. Fisher would have to be answered, and something would have to be done about the question of the queen's first marriage. He would carry on with the plan of gathering the presumptive evidence for consummation

---

16 John Fisher, *Licitum fuisse matrimonium Henrici octavi cum Catharina relicta fratris sui Arthuri*, Cambridge University Library MS Ff 5.25, ff. 152–197v (= pp. 1–88). Analyzed in Edward Surtz, *The Works and Days of John Fisher* (Cambridge, Mass., 1967), p. 351.

17 *Licitum*, pp. 68–69.

which Ridley objected to, and which Wolsey had detailed to the queen's almoner in the previous year. But in the event this evidence was found wanting he needed an alternative, another method of attack against the marriage.

Fisher's speech and book enraged the king. The part about the bishop's likening himself to John the Baptist stung him especially, for that was clearly intended to suggest a resemblance between Henry and Herod. Henry gave the book to Stephen Gardiner and ordered him to write a rebuttal in the king's name.

Gardiner took up his pen with zeal and delivered a bitter and, if not always cogent, often ingenious reply against the man who had been his chancellor at Cambridge. One copy of the reply was given to Fisher and annotated by him with short marginal comments that pointed out some of the misstatements in the work. The same or possibly another copy was submitted to the legatine court, where it was recorded anonymously as "a book in which Rochester's conclusions are blotted out." Gardiner also submitted a continuation of his reply in his own name, and it is so listed among the exhibits. The continuation was entered before the first part of the treatise, curiously enough, and the work itself is preserved in this reverse order earlier in the same codex.[18]

Henry (through his ghost-writer Gardiner) protested to the legates that he had explained the whole matter of his marriage to the Bishop of Rochester many times, some months ago (Fisher comments: "About a year has passed," *Preterijt annus ferme*). The bishop, Henry said, admitted that the reasons which had convinced

---

[18] Record Office SP 1/54, f. 262 (LP IV, 5768.1.1):

> Libellus D. Stephani Gardineri incipiens *Quod ad illud axima* [sic], etc.
> Libellus quo delentur deducta per Roffensem incipiens *Postquam in hac materia*, etc.

The first part of the reply, titled *Liber contra Roffensis orationem . . . compositus vt videtur per Regem ipsum*, beginning *Postquam in hac matrimonii causa*, is on ff. 166–214 of the same codex in which the list of court exhibits is given (i.e. SP 1/54). This copy, which is not in Gardiner's hand, contains Fisher's marginalia. It is followed, however, on ff. 218–229v, by a fragmentary copy in Gardiner's hand, corresponding to ff. 203–214 of the first copy. The concluding part of the treatise, *Quod ad illud axioma*, found on ff. 129–164, is also in Gardiner's hand, and likewise contains Fisher's marginalia. The work is analyzed by Pierre Janelle, *Obedience in Church and State: Three Political Tracts by Stephen Gardiner* (Cambridge, 1930), pp. xviii–xx, 2–9, and *L'Angleterre catholique à la veille du schisme* (Paris, 1935), pp. 115–30; cf. LP IV, 5729.

him that his marriage was illegitimate and incestuous were so grave and forceful that the question should be submitted to the judgment of the pope in order to restore him to his original tranquillity of mind. (Fisher remarks, "I did not say this; certainly the cardinal wanted me to say it.")[19]

It is likely that Henry appeared in court in person during one of the July sessions to read this answer, and that it was then that there occurred the argument over whether Fisher had signed the statement saying that the marriage should be pronounced upon by the pope. In any case, the document of July 1 to this effect was, to judge by Fisher's comment, a device got up by Wolsey to give support to the king's statement in Gardiner's treatise.

Gardiner asserted at one point in his book, when he was showing that the law of Deuteronomy did not contradict the law of Leviticus: "The Levitical law forbids the uncovering of the brother's turpitude, thereby prohibiting marriage with the brother's wife who was corrupted and polluted by the former brother. Are we not compelled to say, then, that the law of Deuteronomy requires no brother or relative to take the brother's widow unless he had left her intact and whole?"[20] This was a dangerous argument, and doubtless one that neither Henry nor Wolsey wished to urge with any force. Gardiner saved himself by saying a bit later that nowadays the law punished anyone who entered into such a marriage. He was citing civil law, and Fisher comments: "The prince [that is, the author of the law] did not wish it to be done, but he could have dispensed from the law."[21]

Where Gardiner took up the reason given in the bull for the dispensation, that is, the keeping of peace, Fisher noted in the margin that the brief spoke of other reasons that moved the pope.[22] This argument, which had long been foreseen, would have to be countered later in the trial. Gardiner tacitly made use of the brief, however, for when rehearsing the statement of the dispensation that the marriage between Arthur and Catherine had been consummated, he omitted the *forsan* of the bull.[23]

Only in passing, and very briefly, did Gardiner mention that the

---

19 *Liber contra Roffensis orationem*, f. 166v.
20 *Ibid.*, f. 185. 21 *Ibid.*, f. 185v.
22 *Ibid.*, f. 134v. 23 *Ibid.*, f. 144v.

impediment of public honesty as well as the impediment of affinity stood in the way of the king's marriage.[24] Wolsey had commissioned him to investigate the problem in Rome, but perhaps he had been instructed not to reveal the attack that was planned on this front until it was presented in court.

24 *Ibid.*, f. 146v.

CHAPTER SIX

The Attack on the Dispensations

❦

A T T H E E N D of the eventful session of June 28 the judges decreed, at the "promotion" or petition of John Hughes, that Catherine was to be cited to appear on Monday, July 5, to witness the exhibition of the dispensation or dispensations that Henry referred to and to present any dispensations that she thought would be advantageous to her. She was to be warned that if she did not appear, they would proceed to sentence in her absence. When the court reconvened on July 5, for the sixth session of the trial, Bishop Clerk reported that he had presented the citation to Catherine, who was still at Greenwich, on Friday, July 2. Thereupon the judges, again at Hughes's request, declared her contumacious for the last time.[1] She was to be cited to this court no more. Richard Sampson then exhibited the bull of Julius II, as well as a transcript of the brief. At Hughes's motion, the cardinals ordered Sampson to appear on the following Friday to see the further proceedings in the case. Finally, eight additional witnesses were sworn in to testify on the articles administered on June 25. They were Archbishop Warham, Bishop West, Archbishop-Bishop John Kite of Carlisle, Thomas Howard, Duke of Norfolk (Anne Boleyn's uncle), Thomas Boleyn, Viscount Rochford (her father), Charles Brandon, Duke of Suffolk (Henry's brother-in-law), Sir David Owen, and Sir Richard Sacheverell. They were admonished not to reveal their testimonies before their publication. Fisher and Standish were listed as having been present at this meeting of the court.[2]

At the Friday session of July 9, according to the record, the car-

1 Court Record, ff. 8–9v.
2 *Ibid.*, ff. 10–12.

dinals immediately presented articles objecting to the bull and the brief. But it is likely that the administration of these articles was preceded by other events, which involved the queen's defense. Perhaps we can receive some guidance from the trial of 1527. We recall that as soon as the king's proctor produced the bull of dispensation, the promoter petitioned that a term be set for hearing the objections that could be raised against it. On the appointed day, the promoter presented a summary of the facts of the case, detailed the charges against the dispensation, and asked Wolsey to weigh them and select the most important for substantiation. It is likely that Hughes did the same thing at the legatine trial. In his memorandum, cited above, he stated that he as well as the legates could present charges against the marriage.

My hypothesis is that Hughes presented to the legates a factum together with a series of objections against the bull and another factum with objections against the brief. Such documents have not yet been found, to my knowledge, but a rebuttal made by the queen's counsel to objections against the bull is extant, and it contains a factum, which I take to be the same as Hughes's (at least in essence), as well as a copy of the bull; then comes a list of objections that arise from the factum, each of which is followed by a refutation. According to William Durantis in his *Speculum iuris*, the advocate of the accused is to summarize each point proposed by the opposition and destroy it as best he can. He must deal with everything pertaining to the facts adduced for the opposition ("et sic de aliis quae in facto consistunt pro parte actoris inductis"). He should also try to reword the factum in the best possible light: "Studeat quoque advocatus factum suum aliter quam actor proposuerit asseverare, quibuscumque modis poterit."[3]

<hr/>

[3] Durantis, *Speculum iuris*, II, part 2: *De litis contestatione*, § *De disputationibus et allegationibus advocatorum*, section 4: *Post hoc autem rei advocatus*, §§ 1, 23 (Venice, 1585), pp. 748, 752. Durantis is dealing specifically with instance cases, but at this stage in the trial the procedure is the same as in *ex officio* inquisitions. The section *De renuntiatione et conclusione*, § 2 (p. 758), is perhaps also pertinent: if the question is intricate, the judge should require in writing a brief and true account of the contents of the factum, and the allegations and replies of the parties ("Brevem et veram facti continentiam, allegationes quoque et replicationes partium in scriptis faciat sibi dari"). See the similar presentation in Tancred of Bologna, writing in 1214–16, *Ordo iudiciarius*, 3.15: *De allegationibus*, ed. Friedrich Bergmann, *Pilii, Tancredi, Gratiae libri de iudiciorum ordine* (Göttingen, 1842), pp. 261–68, and *Der Ordo*

By Henry's own admission two or three years later, a *libellus* was "presented afore the legates sitting in judgment by the late [queen's counsel, in] which be contained divers answers [to the] objections then made against the pope's bulls of dispensation." He also spoke of the queen, though how accurately can only be conjectured, as "consenting [and] assenting that they should be exhib[ited afore the] said legates, as her own counsel doth k[nowledge]."[4] We shall see that Henry and his councillors were particularly insistent on the point because they were under the mistaken impression that the *libellus* compromised the queen's defense, and therefore they might have been exaggerating Catherine's role in approving its contents.

A copy of the queen's *libellus* was sent to Charles V by Eustace Chapuys, the new imperial ambassador to England, not long after the legatine trial concluded. Henry sent another copy to his agents in Rome in 1532, and still another (or perhaps the same one) to Charles V in 1533. It is this last-named copy that survives, in the Vienna Archives, and it seems to be the original version that was submitted to the court.[5] I reproduce it in Appendix A below.

The factum stated very clearly all the facts of the case, without assuming any of the points that were being contested. It was the fairest summary of the matter yet to come out of the debate. It declared simply that Catherine first married Arthur when he was already of age (no mention was made of consummation), and after his death without children a treaty of marriage was made between Catherine and Henry upon condition that a dispensation be obtained for the impediments of affinity and public honesty that existed between them. A papal bull of dispensation was received, and upon this basis Henry and Catherine contracted *sponsalia per verba de praesenti* while Henry had still not reached the age of puberty. Then, after two years, at the beginning of his puberty, unknown to Catherine, he objected against such spousals, protesting that he did not and never did wish to marry her. After Henry

---

iudiciarius des Aegidius de Fuscarariis (ca. 1262–66), ed. Ludwig Wahrmund, Quellen zur Gesch. des römisch-kanonischen Prozesses im Mittelalter no. 3 (Innsbruck, 1916; repr. Aalen, 1962), pp. 116–25.

4 See below, Chap. 8 at n. 14.

5 Vienna, Haus-, Hof- und Staatsarchiv, Memorandum of Henry VIII to Charles V, England, Varia Karton 2. Cf. SP IV, part 1, 215 (no. 154), where there is given the signature "Henricus VII [*sic*] Anglie Rex."

VII died, Henry VIII succeeded him, and his mature age prompted him to the marriage, which he solemnly contracted according to the Church ritual. It was consummated, and Princess Mary was born of it.

The events of those early days and their proper chronology were confusing two decades later and they remain confusing to this day. A quick review is therefore warranted.

Arthur, aged fifteen, married Catherine, also aged fifteen, on November 14, 1501. Arthur died, still aged fifteen, in April 1502, leaving Catherine a widow at the age of sixteen.

The treaty of marriage between Henry, aged eleven, and Catherine was concluded on June 23, 1503. Their *sponsalia de futuro* were celebrated shortly afterward, before Henry's twelfth birthday, which occurred on June 28, 1503.[6]

The treaty specified that Henry and Catherine were to marry *per verba de praesenti* when a suitable dispensation was obtained. The marriage was to be *solemnized* (that is, by the nuptial ceremonies in church) when Henry *completed his fifteenth year*, that is, when he became fifteen years of age, on June 28, 1506.[7]

On July 6, 1504, Julius II wrote to Henry VII that the dispensation would be granted.[8] Henry seems to have taken this as the equivalent of a dispensation. In August we hear of marriage preparations,[9] and in October they were said to be now married *per verba de praesenti*, at a time when Henry was aged thirteen.[10]

Julius II sent a brief of dispensation to the dying Isabella, which was predated December 26, 1503. Ferdinand wrote to Henry VII of its reception on November 24, 1504, and of Isabella's death two days later.[11]

---

6 SC I, 316.

7 Treaty in Rymer, XIII, 82, 83. The last-named clause reads: "Solempnizatio erit cum praefatus dominus Henricus quintumdecimum aetatis annum compleverit." Many historians have been misled by SC I, 307, which mistakenly puts the "fourteenth" year.

8 SC I, 328.

9 Estrada to Isabella, 10 August 1504, SC I, 328.

10 De Puebla to Ferdinand and Isabella, 23 October 1504, SC I, 333 (Henry VII told the French ambassador that a marriage had already been concluded between Henry and Catherine, and that they were already wedded). Ferdinand and Isabella, 16 November 1504, SC I, 337 (they speak of Catherine and Henry as already married *per verba de praesenti*).

11 SC I, 338, 339.

In March 1505 Julius II ordered Bishop Silvester Gigli to take the bull of dispensation to Henry VII.[12] Like the brief, it was predated December 26, 1503. On June 27, 1505, the day before his fourteenth birthday, Prince Henry made his protestation. He declared that he had contracted marriage during his minority to Catherine; but, now that he was near the age of puberty, he declared that he would not ratify the said marriage contract but rather denounced it as null and void.[13] This was a year and a day before the solemnization was due to take place. Catherine was never told of the protestation, and it seems that it was simply held in reserve as a possible weapon in the dispute over Catherine's dowry. Prince Henry continued to refer to Catherine as his wife (*femme*) after this time.[14]

It was true, then, as the factum stated, that Henry contracted *sponsalia de praesenti* while still in his minority. But according to a decretal of Innocent III, when anyone contracted *per verba de praesenti* with someone below the age of puberty, it was to be interpreted not as marriage but as espousals (that is, *de futuro*). The marriage would have been confirmed as *de praesenti* after Henry reached puberty, if it were evident that he and Catherine persisted in their intention to marry; hence the precaution of having Henry make his protestation. According to a decretal of Alexander III, such a protestation would not be valid if made before the age of puberty.[15]

To return to the queen's *libellus*: after the factum, the text of the bull was given, with no mention made of the brief. Finally, there were presented fourteen doubts that arose from the factum, along with suggested answers to them, all of which I translate or summarize as follows:

1. "Is it prohibited by divine law to marry the widow of one's childless brother? The opposite side says yes, citing Leviticus 18

---

[12] Gigli to Henry VII, 17 March 1505, SC I, 349.

[13] SC I, 338–39. See the further discussion below, at n. 51.

[14] Letter of 9 April 1506, ed. James Gairdner, *Letters and Papers Illustrative of the Reigns of Richard III and Henry VII*, Rolls Series no. 24 (London, 1861–63), I, 285.

[15] Innocent III, CIC X 4.2.14 (chapter *Tuae* in the title *De desponsatione impuberum*); Alexander III, X 4.2.7 (*De illis*). On the validation after reaching puberty, see Boniface VIII, chapter *Si infantes* ¶ *Idem*, title *De despons. imp.*, CIC Sextus 4.2.1.

and 20. We say the contrary, since the precept is not a moral one that obliges at all times." As St. Thomas says, such a law does not bind except by ecclesiastical statute. Also, Deuteronomy commands the contrary. It may be, however, that the law of levirate was instituted as a "type" (*in figura*), and also that God may have conceded it by way of dispensation and because of necessity. [It was generous of Catherine's counsel to admit these doubts at the end of their defense.]

2. Presupposing that there is a prohibition of divine law in the case, could the pope dispense from it by his absolute or ordinary power? And would such a dispensation, even if it were given without cause, hold good at least in a court of law? There are many opinions both for and against, as can be seen in commentaries on Lombard's *Sentences* and in *summae* and various decretals.

3. Would the dispensation be invalid supposing that there was no fear of war at the time? Or would not the keeping of the peace be a sufficient cause, especially in the case of kings? Kings furthermore are not to be denied dispensations that have been granted to others on the same grounds. Moreover, memory of the war that existed before Arthur and Catherine were married caused concern, and the second marriage was also desired in order to eliminate the dispute that could arise over the imminent restitution of Catherine's dowry and jewelry. The pope also said that he was "moved by other causes." [They are quoting the brief.]

4. Would the dispensation be invalid because it was allegedly asked for on Henry's behalf, whereas it cannot be established that he authorized the request? It would seem that the contrary could be affirmed, because a father can legitimately act for his son, and because the bull simply says "on behalf of Henry." The *onus probandi* therefore falls on the opposite side. Also, if a son knows what his father has done, he is considered to consent to it; and once Henry reached puberty he seems to have approved it, especially by going through with the marriage. Finally, the grant was for the son's liberation. [That is, it benefited rather than restrained him.]

5. Should the dispensation be considered surreptitious because Henry is said to have desired to marry and to conserve peace, even though he was underage and incapable of such desires? Or rather could not the contrary be affirmed, since he was close to the age of

puberty? [As such, he was considered responsible in the eyes of the law.]

6. Should the dispensation and espousals be considered null in virtue of the protestation that Henry made upon reaching puberty? Or rather did not his subsequent marriage and consummation of marriage show that he had changed his mind? Furthermore, the queen did not know of the protestation. [Betrothal, we remember, if valid, must be dissolved by mutual consent or ecclesiastical decree, or by another marriage.]

7. If Henry should be found to have renounced the dispensation, would his subsequent marriage be null? Or rather did his protest have no effect, because it was to the prejudice of the queen, and because it did not remove his *ability* to contract marriage, which was sufficient for validity?

8. Could the dispensation be said to be invalid because there existed two impediments, affinity and public honesty, and no dispensation was made for public honesty, as John Andreae says must be done? Or rather could not the contrary be held, since there seems to be both a tacit and an express mention of both impediments in the dispensation, and since public honesty constitutes a necessary consequence, as is pointed out by the commentators upon the law of Innocent III reducing the restrictions on consanguinity and affinity? [That is, the law was held to apply to public honesty as well.]

9. Should the marriage between Catherine and Arthur be presumed consummated from their having lived and slept together? Or should it not rather be believed that it was not consummated and that as a result there is no affinity and no divine prohibition between Catherine and Henry? [Hall, we shall see, says that the theologians at the trial were of the opinion that the marriage was against the law of God if Catherine had been carnally known by Arthur.] The reasons are that there is no proof for the consummation, and the queen stated upon oath that she had never been known by Arthur; furthermore, Henry himself confessed the same thing several times.[16]

---

[16] The laws that are cited after this last statement seem to have little bearing on the matter, especially the first, viz. the "Authentic" summary *Sed rem necesse* (a mistake for *Sed iam necesse*—see Appendix A, n. 62), since it deals

10. It is objected that the *espousals* [*de futuro*] were not valid because the dispensation was for *marriage*. A law is quoted to refute this argument ("What concerns marriage pertains to espousals as well"); furthermore, Henry and Catherine did in fact get married. [Sanders reports that Catherine's lawyers urged, among other arguments, the obvious truth that even if the espousals had not been valid, the marriage would be valid, since espousals were not necessary for marriage.][17]

11. Was the dispensation invalid because Henry was too young to contract marriage, or was it not sufficient that he was capable of having the impediment removed?

12. Did the intervening death of Henry VII and Isabella invalidate the marriage, or was it not enough that the impediment had already been removed?

13. If it should be established that Catherine was carnally known by Arthur, would not the dispensation be invalid because the fact was stated not categorically but rather as doubtful, by the use of the word *forsan*? Suitable laws are cited for the opposing view.

14. Should a dispensation granted for a false cause be upheld or not? There are canons saying that it should.

This was the substantial point-by-point defense of the bull of dispensation presented by the queen's counsel. They no doubt also answered whatever charges the promoter made against the brief, but that part of their response has not been preserved.

If, therefore, Hughes did submit objections to the dispensations on July 9, or even on July 5, the cardinals would have decreed a copy to be given to Sampson. And doubtless Fisher and the other advocates of the queen would have secured another for themselves, unless they had managed to write down the pertinent details as the document was being read in court. The answers given in the queen's *libellus* were composed hastily, and the laws were no doubt cited from memory, since mistakes were made and sometimes spaces were left blank or filled in by another hand. But if the main author (probably a lawyer, like Clerk or Ligham) began his reply during the July 9 session, he could hardly have had it

---

with dowries. The second, however, viz. the chapter *Is qui* of the title *De sponsalibus et matrimonio* (CIC X 4.1.30), does deal with the question of legal presumption in marriage.

17 I shall justify my use of Sanders below, at n. 26.

ready on that day, especially if it was true that it was first shown to Catherine (who may still have been at Greenwich). It seems reasonable to assume, therefore, that it was presented at the next meeting of the court, Monday, July 12, although it is very likely that the promoter's allegations were debated orally at the Friday session. I suggested earlier that the argument over the consummation of Catherine's first marriage, as reported by Cavendish, might have been inspired by Henry's reply or lack of reply on this point, and the promoter's urging of presumption in lieu of direct proof could have provided an impetus for another such discussion.

At the 1527 trial, the promoter was able to claim consummation as a fact because Henry admitted it. Hughes, it seems, was not able to do so at the legatine trial. Of the two accused parties, one, namely Catherine, strongly denied it, and Henry's position was ambiguous. Nevertheless Hughes, to judge from the *libellus* of the queen's counsel, repeated the public-honesty objection in the same form that Wolman had given it, which presumed the presence of affinity as well as public honesty. But when the cardinals at the July 9 session came to formulate their objections from the material provided by their promoter, they did not follow his example. Instead, they put it in the form that Wolsey had suggested to Henry when the problem of the queen's virginity was first raised. It was stated as follows: "We object, expound, and articulate that as the aforesaid dispensations should not suffice to remove the impediment of affinity for the above-mentioned causes, so too in case fuller proofs could show (contrary to what is now established and certain) that no carnal copula was had between you, most serene Lady Catherine, and Arthur, and that no impediment of affinity sprang therefrom: in this case the said exhibited dispensations would not suffice nor extend to the removal of the impediment of public honesty, for the reason that there was no express mention made of public honesty; nor could it be included or removed tacitly by the way, or as a consequence, since the principal matter does not exist and is not present."[18]

There is some evidence that Catherine's counsel presented a

18 Court Record, f. 13v: "Item obiicimus, exponimus et articulamur quod quemadmodum dispensationes prefate ad removendum impedimentum affinitatis ex causis predictis sufficere non debeant, ita casu quo plenioribus probationibus diversum eius quod nunc constat et certum [est] posset ostendi inter

refutation to the legates not only of the promoter's version of the objection but also of the legates' form, at least in substance. But first, let us look at all the charges that the cardinals *ex officio suo mero* leveled against the dispensations on July 9. They repeated what they had said in the previous articles, that the marriage was contracted in the face of an impediment or impediments "which were introduced and sanctioned not only by human and ecclesiastical but also by divine law." They went on to urge that the dispensations produced before them ought not to be sufficient for the justification of the said marriage, since they were invalid because of the reasons explained in the following articles. This prefatory remark corresponded to the promoter's first doubt, that the marriage was against divine law.

It is noteworthy that the second doubt of the *libellus*, that a divine law of this sort could not be dispensed upon by the pope, found no place in the cardinals' articles. Instead, the first article took up the third doubt of the *libellus*, and charged that there was no urgent need for the preservation of peace, and therefore there was no adequate reason for removing impediments imposed by divine law. Second, they charged that Henry had not yet reached his twelfth year (this was changed in a later session to read "thirteenth") and so was unable to contract marriage. The failure to state his age made the dispensations surreptitious. Third, the dispensations were also obreptitious, that is, obtained not only through the suppression of facts, but also through false information. It was claimed that Henry desired the marriage for the continuance of peace, whereas he was too young to entertain such a sentiment. These two articles corresponded to the *libellus's* fifth doubt (and also to the fourteenth, which alleged invalidity because the grant was for a false cause). Surprisingly, no use was made of the fourth doubt, which was the objection on which Wolsey had grounded his conscience in the spring of 1528: namely, that Henry was unaware that the dispensation was being requested for him.

---

vos, viz. serenissimam dominam Catherinam et Arthurum, nullam carnalem copulam intervenisse nec inde natum affinitatis impedimentum, eo casu dicte dispensationes exhibite ad removendum publice honestatis impedimentum non sufficere[n]t nec ad illud extendere[n]tur, eo viz. et ex eo quod de publica honestate nulla mentio expressa facta sit et sub eo includi aut virtute illius tacite removeri non possit incidenter aut consecutum, quod ipsum principale non est nec subsistit."

The fourth article corresponded to the twelfth doubt, and objected that the rulers of England and Spain, between whom peace was to be conserved, had died, or at least one of them had died, before the bull was put into effect: that is, before the marriage was celebrated in virtue of the dispensation. (The word "celebrate" was perhaps designed to get around the terms of the treaty reflected in the factum: namely, that the marriage was to be contracted *de praesenti* as soon as the dispensation was granted; but it was not to be solemnized by a Church ceremony until later.) The fifth article is the one dealing with public honesty, quoted above in full. It contained the substance not only of the eighth but also of the ninth doubt, since it asserted that consummation of the first marriage was certain. But the cardinals did not pursue the thirteenth doubt, which found the bull faulty for not stating categorically that consummation had occurred.

The legates also ignored the tenth and eleventh doubts, the former dealing with Henry's allegedly invalid espousals, and the latter with Henry's inability to contract marriage because of his youth. (In their second article, their only complaint was that the pope should have been told that the prince was under the marriageable age.) The judges also failed to use the sixth and seventh doubts, dealing with Henry's protestation; for, as subsequent events will show, they were not yet able to locate the document recording this act. Bishop West, one of the signers, had returned to Ely where he was detained through illness. The cardinals therefore must have decided to postpone formulating an article on the matter.

Instead they turned their attention to the objections that could be made against the brief. They selected four. The document was declared to be false (1) because it differed from the bull, (2) because it was not registered at Rome, (3) because it was not contained in the English archives, and (4) because the date did not follow the practice for dating briefs. A tenth article stated that all the above was well known.[19]

As with the first twelve articles, there is no indication in the notarial record that Henry was expected to testify on these articles.

[19] Court Record, ff. 12v–14. Listed as present at the July 9 session were the Duke of Norfolk, Bishops Longland and Kite, and the Earl of Shrewsbury.

It was simply stated that Sampson was to be present at the next session to see witnesses received to testify on the matter presented. Accordingly, on Monday, July 12, the judges administered oaths to the witnesses, most of whom had already been received on the first set of articles, namely: Norfolk, Suffolk, Shrewsbury, Rochford, Dorset, Fitzwalter, Kite, and Owen. New to the proceedings were Sir John Hussey and Sir Richard Weston. John Taylor was to take the testimony once again, and the court scribes were to record it. Then the judges ordered Sampson to be present at the next session, which was to be Wednesday rather than Friday, to see proposed and exhibited "omnia quae in facto consistunt," that is, everything pertaining to the facts of the case.[20]

On Tuesday, July 13, Cardinal Campeggio reported that the queen's interests were undefended. By this, however, he meant that her defense was not adequate, for he went on to admit that Fisher and Standish spoke on her behalf, and that they and some other doctors had submitted books in her cause, but that they had done so in fear.[21] The Public Record Office contains a list of *libelli* submitted to the court, but no contribution by Standish is mentioned, nor is the *libellus* answering the fourteen doubts about the bull; Bishop West's two treatises are named, however, as is one by Bishop Tunstall of London.[22] There is another attributed to several authors, of whom only Gwent is named (that is, Richard Gwent, who would succeed Ligham as Dean of the Arches). Finally, there are two by Fisher, the first being the one submitted on June 28, beginning with the words *Constat inclitissimum* (the Record Office list reads *inuictissimum*), and the second beginning,

[20] *Ibid.*, f. 14rv. Present were Longland and Thomas Arundell. The *propositio omnium in facto consistentium* seems to refer to a certain stage in a trial, after charges have been leveled and witnesses received, when any other allegations, proofs, or rebuttals can be presented. The term is frequently used in the more extensive instance trials held in the consistory court of the Diocese of Rochester in 1347–48, where the proposals of *consistentia in facto* can be made by both plaintiff and defendant. See *Registrum Hamonis Hethe diocesis Roffensis A.D. 1319–1352*, ed. Charles Johnson, Canterbury and York Society (Oxford, 1948), pp. 911–1043, esp. 915, 931, 942, 948, 953, 1010, 1014, 1018, 1024. I am grateful to Father Michael M. Sheehan for this reference.

[21] Ehses, pp. 119–20.

[22] The author of the life of John Fisher says that Tunstall had given Campeggio his book to be read in court, and that Campeggio commended his writing as that of another Ulpian, and wished to hear him speak. *Analecta bollandiana*, 10: 326.

like Tunstall's, with an acknowledgment of the legates: *Reverendissimis in Christo patribus*. It was obviously composed during the trial, and, since it dealt with the law of levirate in the Book of Deuteronomy, it is no doubt an indication that the question was debated in court. Fisher said that he was writing it to prevent the cardinals from being misled by certain persons who on the pretext of expertise in foreign languages might suggest to them that it was not commanded that a brother was to marry his brother's childless widow. Fisher's treatise, like the two by Bishop West, was recently acquired by the Lambeth Palace Library from an undisclosed Italian source. On the cover of Fisher's work it is designated as the fourth defense exhibited to the legates.[23] (In the Record Office list it is the sixth and last of the "consultations . . . judicially exhibited to the legates . . . on the part of the queen.")

The Record Office report also lists eight *libelli* submitted on the king's side (though the king was not supposed to be attacking the marriage). There is one each by Henry himself, Staphileus, Bell, and Clayburgh; also, Gardiner's two-part response to Fisher, discussed above; a treatise beginning *Veritatem rerum*, mentioned later in the Clayburgh-Watkins record; and a treatise "containing a declaration of the divine and human law in the king's business," beginning *Sed occurrit*.[24] The king's book is probably the one that he wrote more than a year before, which Pope Clement himself had read.[25] Clayburgh's treatise presumably addressed itself to a factum, since it begins *In facti*, but it need not have been the one

---

[23] London, Lambeth Palace Library MS 2342, ff. 1–21v. There is a copy of the same treatise on ff. 23–32v. Following this, on ff. 34–50, is a treatise dealing with a question like the fourteenth doubt in the queen's *libellus*: *Utrum in casu nostro in quo versamur supposito et non concesso quod dispensatio esset nulla, an possit ferri sententia divortii.* It is a question that the Bishop of Ely dealt with at great length in much the same way, and in fact it is in the same hand as his treatises in MS 2341. There follows in MS 2342 the last part of a work on the Levitical law, favoring Henry's side (ff. 53–75) followed by a few pages of notes on the same work (ff. 79–82v), and then, on ff. 84–108, another treatise favoring Henry, dealing with the Levitical law. It begins with the word *Queritur*. The rest of the codex is taken up by two copies of Julius II's bull of dispensation (ff. 109–113), and copies in a later hand of Clement VII's Pollicitation to Henry (Ehses, pp. 30–31), and the legatine commission (Ehses, pp. 28–30). The latter was taken from the version in the Vatican Archives, Lettere di principi 14, f. 128 (see Ehses, p. 30).

[24] Record Office SP 1/54, f. 262; cf. LP 5768.1.1–2.

[25] Casale, Gardiner, and Fox to Wolsey, 31 March 1528, Pocock, I, 100–101.

presumably composed by Hughes. It could even have been the one that Wolman compiled at the inquisition of 1527, since Clayburgh was the clerk of that process as well as of the legatine trial, just as Bell was Henry's proctor in both tribunals.

But apart from this war of rather dated *libelli*, and apart from the clash reported on June 28, Cardinal Campeggio's report of July 13 indicates that there was further debate. Nicholas Sanders's account provides perhaps the best indication that even the non-articled objections deriving from the factum were brought up and discussed in court. Sanders is often not a reliable guide, but he did use Rastell, who, though unreliable himself, might have witnessed the trial (he was about twenty-one at the time) or had access to witnesses or relevant documents. Be that as it may, the fact remains that Sanders lists six arguments that were submitted against the bull of Julius II, and two of them (the failure of the pope to dispense for espousals, and the charge that Catherine and the young Henry had not authorized the request for the dispensation) do not appear in the Court Record, although they appear among the doubts of the factum; furthermore, the objections are cited correctly and in a much fuller way than could be derived from these doubts, at least as they are repeated in the *libellus* of the queen's counsel.[26]

According to Sanders, then, even though the queen wanted nothing to do with the proceedings, her defense attorneys responded as soon as possible to the arguments put forth by the opposition, "so that it would not be thought that they lacked the support of law and equity." The objection concerning public honesty, as Sanders gives it, was not in the Wolseian form that appeared as one of the articles, which was to be used only in case the queen's consummation was disproved, but rather in the form attached to the factum in the queen's *libellus*. In the latter form, consummation was assumed and the argument was based upon the directive of John Andreae in his commentary on the "Tree of Affinity," which was always included in the *Corpus iuris canonici*: "If your wife dies and you want to marry one of her relatives with a dispen-

<hr>

[26] Sanders, English College MS, ff. 28v–29. The six objections are: (1) no mention of betrothal, (2) no mention of Henry's age, (3) Henry's protest, (4) the allegations that Henry did not wish peace, and that Henry VII and Isabella had died, (5) the allegation that the parents were not acting legally for the couple, (6) no mention of public honesty.

sation of the Church, and the Church allows you to marry her notwithstanding your relationship in such and such a degree of affinity, you still cannot marry, because in spite of the removal of the impediment of affinity, the impediment of public honesty has still not been removed. You should therefore have it said that you can marry with such a one notwithstanding the impediment of public honesty (because you were married to her blood relative in the fourth degree) and also notwithstanding the fact that you are related by affinity in the fourth degree (because you had carnal knowledge of the aforesaid wife)."[27]

Clearly the English and Spanish commissioners who put into effect the Anglo-Spanish treaty of 1503 had this passage in mind. For they provided that Henry VII and Ferdinand and Isabella should obtain a dispensation from the Holy See "after the manner of the Roman curia" and in terms the most conducive to validity, enabling young Henry and Catherine to marry "notwithstanding the impediment of the righteousness of public honesty, because the aforesaid most serene Lady Catherine had contracted marriage *per verba de praesenti* with the aforesaid Lord Arthur, the first-born son of the above-mentioned King of England and the brother and sibling of the same most valiant Henry; and notwithstanding also the fact that they are related by affinity in the first degree, because the same marriage between the above-named Lord Arthur and the most serene Lady Catherine was solemnized in the face of the Church and was afterwards consummated."[28]

As I noted above, the factum of the queen's *libellus* seems to have been based upon this passage, and appeal was made to John Andreae in the formulation of the doubt. A possible weakness of this form of the objection was that it had become a regular curial practice during the course of the fifteenth century to consider public honesty as included under affinity in cases involving consummated marriages.[29] On the other hand it does not seem that knowledge of this procedure was at all widespread. Bishop West did not know of it when he answered the same objection that appears in the *Compendious Annotation*, and the same lack of awareness can be seen in the treatise of the Spanish inquisitor, Ferdinand de Loazes, which he published in the queen's cause in

[27] John Andreae, CIC Appendix to Gratian, in Friedberg, I, 1433 ¶ 3.
[28] Rymer, XIII, 81.
[29] See Scarisbrick, p. 186.

1531. Although Loazes defended the marriage against Henry's charges with an extraordinary range of legal learning, when he came to this objection he fell back on the same arguments that had been employed by the Bishop of Ely and the queen's *libellus.* That is, he said, first of all, that since the dispensation spoke of Catherine and Arthur as having contracted marriage and having perhaps consummated it, it showed that Pope Julius was fully informed of all the circumstances and that he removed all the impediments that could arise from these circumstances. In support of this contention he cited laws and opinions showing that when a ruler allowed a forbidden action about which he had been thoroughly briefed, the action was legitimate even though the grant permitting it made no mention of the impediment standing in the way; such an impediment was considered to be tacitly removed. Second, Loazes called upon canonists like Panormitanus who held that public honesty was included under affinity.[30] Much earlier in the treatise he made the point that seemingly there was no affinity between Henry and Catherine, only public honesty,[31] but when he came to treat of public honesty he did not face the implications of this circumstance.

To return to Sanders: in describing the events of the legatine court, perhaps following Cavendish, he has it that the objections were first introduced by the proctors of the king. This was not so, of course, though it is true that Sampson's exhibition of the bull and brief gave rise to the later objections of the legates, and it is also true that Henry's counsel must have been fairly vocal in assaulting the queen's position, since Hall and Cavendish report it so. Still, as was said before, the pretense would no doubt have been kept up as much as possible that they too were interested in defending the bond against the objections that were raised by the legates.

Sanders's version of the public-honesty argument runs thus: "Two obstacles stood in the way of this marriage: one of affinity, which arose from carnal copula between Catherine and Arthur; the other of the righteousness of public honesty, which came sim-

---

[30] Ferdinandus de Loazes, *Solennis atque elegans tractatus in causa matrimonii serenissimorum dominorum Henrici et Catherinae Angliae regum* (Barcelona, 1531), f. 65rv. See Appendix A at n. 58.

[31] *Solennis*, f. 17.

ply from their marriage contract, even if no copula had followed. But in the decree of Julius only the impediment of affinity was relaxed, and no mention was made of the removal of the impediment of the righteousness of public honesty. Because of this, they said, this latter impediment was not removed, and the marriage between Henry and Catherine was illicit and invalid in the eyes of the law."

If Sampson and Bell really did raise this doubt, and raised it in this form, it could be argued that they knew exactly what they were doing. Sampson was aware of Wolsey's version of the argument; we recall that it was he with whom the cardinal first discussed it two years before. But the main thrust of the king's counsel was to prove the consummation of the marriage between Catherine and Arthur, and it would have damaged their case to have admitted as a real possibility that she had emerged from her first marriage still a virgin. Instead they spoke of nonconsummation as a contrary-to-fact hypothesis—*etiamsi nulla copula subsecuta esset*—so that in case her virginity were juridically established they could fall back on the underlying argument. Wolsey, however, was determined to make the meaning explicit in his official articulation of it.

At any rate, the real argument would have to be addressed by the queen's counsel in their defense, since they maintained that there had been no carnal copula. Here is what they said, according to Sanders:

> Let us now come to that last heading, which the opposition believes to contain their most powerful argument.
>
> In the petitions presented to the pope these words were found: "Previously marriage had been contracted *per verba de praesenti* between Lady Catherine and Prince Arthur, Henry's brother." Is not the impediment of the righteousness of public honesty sufficiently set forth by these words, since it arose from the marriage contract alone?
>
> Moreover, the same petitioners go on a little later to say that the "marriage was perhaps consummated by carnal copula." Does not this bring out the impediment of affinity as well, if by chance carnal copula had occurred? For the word "perhaps" was added in order to provide for all possibilities in the marriage, even if carnal copula had by some chance taken place—which in fact it did not.
>
> Since, therefore, the pope understood from what was told him that at most two obstacles stood in the way of a marriage between Catherine and Henry: one, that the female party had been previously married to Arthur,

Henry's brother; the other, that she had perhaps been known by the same
Arthur; the same pope, having understood the whole thing, removed by
his authority the impediment not only of affinity in every meaning of
the word, but also this particular affinity which stood between Henry and
Catherine from the marriage which Catherine had previously contracted
with Arthur, and which she had perhaps consummated by subsequent
copula. Did he not all the more by this very action remove also the impediment of the righteousness of public honesty, which precedes carnal
copula? For if Henry is permitted to marry his brother's wife in spite of
the fact that he may have known her by carnal copula, is he not permitted all the more to marry her if she had only been married and not so
known?[32]

The rhetoric of this composite reply is of course Sanders's, but
its content may be very close to what was actually uttered on the
floor of the courtroom by Fisher or Ligham or other members of
the queen's counsel. One indication that Sanders was not invent-
ing the rebuttals of Catherine's advocates is that the above answer
explains the assertion of the *libellus* that public honesty was explicitly as well as implicitly accounted for in the bull; another is
that when he came to discuss the question of public honesty in his
own name he was oblivious of the point at issue in the legatine
court. He was at pains to show that the impediment of affinity
which Henry alleged to be between him and Catherine did not
exist, but that it did exist between him and Anne Boleyn. Because
there was no consummation of Catherine's first marriage, he said,
there stood between her and Henry only public honesty; but everyone agreed that this impediment was not of divine or natural law
but only ecclesiastical, so that "not even Henry or his advocates
denied that the power of the keys of Peter was sufficient to remove
it. Since, therefore, there was no affinity and since it is agreed that
the impediment of the righteousness of public honesty was satis-
factorily removed by the letter of Pope Julius, nothing now stood
in the way to keep King Henry from being able to marry Catherine
and from being obliged to retain her."[33] Sanders should have realized that there was no such agreement on this last point, from his
own account. He was also mistaken in his previous assumption

32 Sanders, English College MS, ff. 28, 29, 32rv.

33 "Jam vero iustitiae publicae honestatis impedimentum quod solus restat,
cum (ut inter omnes constitit) non diuini aut naturalis, sed tantum Ecclesiastici iuris fuerit, ne Henricus quidem aut aduocati eius negabant potestatem
clauium Petri satis virium ad illud auferendum habuisse. Cum igitur nec affi-

about Henry's acceptance of the purely human character of the law of public honesty. We have seen evidence to the contrary, and shall see more.

In the last two weeks of the trial the court sat three times a week. At the meeting of Wednesday, July 14, the judges first announced an alteration in the second of the articles against the dispensations: Henry's age should read "thirteenth" rather than "twelfth" year. (They neglected to notice that a similar change was necessary in the third article.) Then they introduced two additional articles. The first stated that papal briefs always began the year on December 26, whereas bulls began it on March 25. The second stated the form of contract used in the solemnization of marriage in England: the contracting parties spoke words *de praesenti* to each other, as, "I take you unto my own." The precise purpose of the second article is not clear; but there was some interest in establishing exactly what Arthur and Catherine had spoken to each other when they were married, for Bishop West had been interrogated on the point.[34] No doubt the judges wanted proof that they were fully married *per verba de praesenti*, and not simply engaged *de futuro*.

Witnesses to testify on the additional articles were sworn in immediately. Peter Mates, a Spaniard, Nicholas Rusticus, an Italian, and Thomas Derby, Clerk of the King's Council, were to testify on the first; and Norfolk, Suffolk, Dorset, Shrewsbury, Fitzwalter, Owen, Guildford, and a new witness, Bishop Longland, were to depose on the second. So was Sir Anthony Willoughby, and he was also to testify on the first and second sets of articles. Then, after the judges had expedited other business, Hughes informed them that three elderly ladies, namely, Agnes, widowed Duchess of Norfolk, Mary, Countess of Essex, and Elizabeth, Viscountess of Fitzwalter, were necessary witnesses, but because of ill health could not be compelled to appear in person at the court. The judges therefore appointed two commissioners to swear them in and take

---

nitas ulla fuerit, et impedimentum Justitiae publicae honestatis per Julii pontificis diploma idonee ablatum constet, nihil iam adstabat quominus Catharinam rex Henricus et ducere posset et retinere deberet" (MS f. 47v). The editions are much different.

34 Court Record, ff. 14v–15, 40.

their testimony at more convenient places during the next three days, and Sampson was ordered to be present to see the witnesses received.[35]

Then Hughes notified the judges that various documents pertinent to the case had not yet come to hand. Since therefore that very day, July 14, had been assigned as the term for the proposal of everything in the case, the judges extended it until Friday, July 16.[36] Wolsey, we recall, had summoned Bishop West to come back to London, and the bishop did make an appearance at the Friday session, but it turned out that the court could not yet use his services. Instead, three additional witnesses, William Falk, John Taverner, and John Clamport, were received to testify on the second additional article. Then Hughes informed the judges that not all the witnesses had been examined as yet, and many pertinent documents had not yet arrived. The legates thereupon extended the assigned term to Monday, July 19. A committee headed by John Islip, Abbot of Westminster, a frequent attendant at the trial, was to search various archives on that day (July 16) and the next and report back all helpful documents. Sampson could be present at the search if he so wished.[37]

On Monday the 19th a good many depositions and documents were finally presented. The testimony of the three infirm ladies was handed in. It was noted that Richard Sampson had been declared contumacious for not being present when they were sworn in.[38] John Taylor, Archdeacon of Buckingham, who had been charged with taking the testimony of the other witnesses, appeared in person to present the depositions he had assembled. He had interrogated thirty-four persons, some of them on three occasions, because of the three sets of articles.[39]

Taylor's collection is noticeably incomplete. Some of the witnesses were no doubt left unquestioned because of lack of time. This was probably the case with Thomas Derby, David Owen, and Bishop Longland, who were to be interviewed on the additional articles (third set). It may also have been true for Shrewsbury, who was sworn in before the legates to testify on all three sets, on June 28, July 12, and July 14, respectively, but was questioned only on

35 *Ibid.*, f. 15rv.   36 *Ibid.*, f. 16.
37 *Ibid.*, ff. 16–17.   38 *Ibid.*, ff. 18v, 20v, 54v.
39 *Ibid.*, ff. 23–54v.

the first set. That Taylor was behind in his interviews is shown from Thomas Boleyn's testimony on the first articles. He was received as a witness on July 5, but did not depose until July 15.[40] Anthony Willoughby was to give testimony on the three sets at the same time, but no testimony appears for the second, which contained the main charges against the dispensations.[41] The Earl of Oxford, Lord Great Chamberlain of England, was sworn in on June 28 for the first group of articles, but his testimony does not appear at all in the record for July 19.

Taylor did not say, however, that he submitted the depositions of all the witnesses he had examined; he simply appeared with the depositions of some ("nonnulli") witnesses. At the end of the record, in his 1533 statement of authenticity, Watkins said that he was present at the interrogations and recording of the depositions. He witnessed and heard and put into writing those things, *among others* ("eaque inter cetera respective fieri et reddi vidi et audivi, ac . . . inactitavi et in scriptis redegi"). Clearly, then, there was room for more sins of omission.

Most puzzling and suspicious of all is the case of Bishop Kite of Carlisle. He was received as a witness for the first articles on July 5, was listed as present on July 9, and was sworn in on the second set of articles on July 12, but his deposition is nowhere to be seen. Also of interest is the fact that no testimony appears on the last six articles of the second group. This includes the article on public honesty and the four charges against the brief. The latter were apparently found to be unsatisfactory, since another article on the subject was introduced two sessions later. Three witnesses with expert knowledge were sworn in to testify on it, and the depositions of two of them, Mates and Rusticus, appeared in Taylor's collection on July 19.[42]

The article on public honesty also involved a technical point, this time in canon law. Of the witnesses selected to depose on the set of articles in which it appeared, only one would have any pretense to knowledge on the point. That was, of course, Bishop Kite,

---

[40] *Ibid.*, ff. 23v–25. Shrewsbury's testimony was taken on June 28, the day on which he was received as witness. See LP IV, 5774.1. For Boleyn, see LP IV, 5774.14.

[41] Court Record, ff. 38–40.

[42] *Ibid.*, ff. 51–52. As mentioned above, Derby's report is missing.

whose testimony either was not taken or was suppressed. Warham, however, who had not been received as a witness on these articles, was in fact examined on them (but not, as I mentioned above, on the public-honesty article). It is noteworthy that in the first group of articles it was Taylor's policy to interrogate all the witnesses on all the articles, even those on which the deponents could not be expected to have any knowledge. In such cases, they simply answered that they were not able to testify. In the second set, however, no such care was taken. The witnesses were only interrogated on peace, on Henry's age (but not on the legal implications of Henry's youth specified in articles 2 and 3), on the time of the death of Henry VII, and sometimes on the death of Isabella. Dorset was examined only on the question of Henry's age. Moreover, the questions were not always carefully phrased. For instance, some witnesses were asked simply about the time of the death of one or other of the rulers; Owen was asked whether both died before the solemnization of Henry's marriage; and Norfolk, Warham, and Suffolk were asked whether they died before the contracting of the marriage. (Norfolk and Warham replied that they died before the solemnization, and Suffolk said it was before the contracting).[43]

In the article on public honesty, which was administered on July 9, Wolsey made provision against the possibility that Catherine's first marriage would later prove not to have been consummated. He asserted at the same time, however, that the fact of consummation was at present clearly established. He was referring, at least in part, to the testimony that had been or was being collected from the witnesses sworn in on June 28 and July 5. It was their answers, and the answers of the three noble ladies taken later in July, that were to provide now and in later years the presumptive evidence for consummation in the queen's first marriage. The pertinent articles were the third and fourth. We recall that the fourth, addressed to Henry, has the phrase about consummation removed in the notarial record. But if it had been removed before the witnesses testified on it, Taylor would have been able to rely on the third article, addressed to Catherine, which was left intact.

Most of the pertinent testimony regarded the fact that Catherine and Arthur were seen going to the same bed, or actually in bed

[43] *Ibid.*, ff. 42v–51.

together. But no report was forthcoming, contrary to Wolsey's expectations, of bloodied bedsheets. A good deal was said about Arthur's amusing but feeble bedroom braggadocio on the morning after his wedding night. An example of the use to which it was later put can be seen from *A Glass of the Truth*, a pamphlet printed in September 1532. One of the dialogists says that some witnesses testified that "Prince Arthur did report himself unto them that he had carnally known her; and that at divers times, to some at one time, to some at another, so that his sayings were many times reiterated; which, methinketh, giveth much greater faith, insomuch that it is not to be thought that at all these times he should speak for ostentation and boasting of himself only; for at some time of these it doth appear by attestation of credible folks, whereof some were his servants near about him at that time, that he spake it for mere necessity, demanding and desiring drink incontinently upon his great labors, in the morning very early, to quench his thirst; answering, when the question was asked him, 'Why, sir, and be ye now so dry?' 'Marry, if thou haddest been as often in Spain this night as I have been, I think verily thou wouldest have been much drier.' "[44]

Only two of the witnesses responded to the articles stating that the marriage of Henry and Catherine was against both divine and ecclesiastical law. Archbishop Warham referred the question of divine law to the theologians; he did, however, say that it was his belief that such a marriage was prohibited by both divine and ecclesiastical law, since otherwise there would have been no need for a dispensation from the Apostolic See in the matter. Bishop West asserted, as I mentioned before, that the article was not true in regard to divine law; but he did believe that it was true concerning ecclesiastical law. He also declared that he did not consider the legates to be competent judges in the case, since the queen had appealed it.[45] Bishop Kite's testimony, if he gave it, could hardly have been more unfavorable than this. That West's deposition was submitted and put into the 1533 copy of the record

---

[44] Pocock, II, 414. For the date, see G. R. Elton, *Policy and Police: The Enforcement of the Reformation in the Age of Thomas Cromwell* (Cambridge, 1972), p. 176, who notes that the two editions of 1530 and 1531 in Pollard and Redgrave, *Short-Title Catalogue* 11918 and 11919, are nonexistent. For time of composition and authorship, see below, Chap. 10, n. 7, and Chap. 11, n. 14.

[45] Court Record, ff. 25v–26, 40v–41.

might argue against a hypothesis that Kite's was deliberately suppressed somewhere along the way. But on the other hand, West was no doubt present on July 19 and would have objected if his testimony had not been exhibited.

In addition to being treated in the prelates' depositions, the question of the divine law, like the question of consummation, was probably discussed orally at the trial. Hall states that the whole matter was debated substantially, "so that at the last the divines were all of opinion that the marriage was against the law of God if she were carnally known by the first brother." We know that the truth was not so simple as that, but he agrees with Cavendish in testifying that debate did take place.

After a copy of the depositions had been decreed for Sampson, Abbot Islip appeared in court to report on the search his committee had made. He introduced some documents telling of Henry's age (one correctly put his birth in 1491, but another said 1481), the arrival of Catherine, her marriage to Arthur, and Arthur's death.[46]

The legates then exhibited the Anglo-Spanish treaty of 1503, which arranged the marriage of Henry and Catherine. Wolsey and probably Hughes were familiar with its contents, of course, but apparently Henry's other supporters did not bother to read it very thoroughly. At any rate, in the years to follow, after Wolsey had dropped out of the picture, the document's vital bearing on the question of the queen's virginity was overlooked or forgotten. The treaty in fact stated categorically that Catherine's first marriage had been consummated. It would be another three and a half years before the realization of the treaty's import would dawn on Henry and his advisers. Watkins and Clayburgh did not include anything but the incipit in the copy of the record that they made in the autumn of 1533. But Watkins noted that the text could be found more fully recorded in a copy that he made earlier in the year, that is, February 12, 1533, which was just a month after the treaty had been rediscovered.[47]

Then the legates exhibited a book that Hughes described as containing lawyers' arguments, beginning with the words *Veritatem rerum eam merito*. They also produced the deposition of the

[46] *Ibid.*, ff. 56–58. Cf. LP IV, 5791.
[47] Court Record, f. 58. See above, Chap. 3 at n. 10; below, Chap. 11 at n. 12.

late Richard Fox, Bishop of Winchester. It was taken on April 5–6, 1527, when the prelate was seventy-nine years old, by Richard Wolman, presumably for use in the inquisition that he was to prosecute in the following month. Fox signed it on April 8, much against his will. He said that because he was blind he had no way of being sure what he was signing, and because of the secrecy of the examination he was not permitted to confer with anyone about it. He complied, however, when Wolman informed him that he had an order from the king that would require him to sign.[48]

Then the cardinals introduced two letters of Pope Julius II to Henry VII. The first was dated July 6, 1504; in it the pope apologized for the delay in granting the dispensation, and gave the king the impression that it would be granted immediately. It was this letter that precipitated the actual marriage of Prince Henry to Catherine before the reception of any formal authorization. The second letter, dated February 20, 1505, explained why a dispensation had been already sent to Isabella, and assured the king that his copy was finally being dispatched to him.[49]

All the above documents were exhibited on July 19 in satisfaction of the terms set for such exhibits. Sir Thomas Wriothesley, Garter King-of-Arms, and the southern and northern kings-of-arms testified to the authenticity of the documents in Abbot Islip's process. This done, "the judges by word of mouth exhibited each and all of the things acted, performed, and exhibited in the said cause pertaining to the facts [*quae consistunt in facto*]." They then assigned Wednesday, July 21, for the conclusion of the proceedings, and they ordered Sampson to be present to witness the premises and to see performed the other things that justice demanded.[50]

When the court convened on the 21st, however, the promoter "signified, alleged, and expounded" that after the lapse of the term set for the proposal of everything in the cause pertaining to the facts, the protestation that Henry had made in his youth had come to hand. Since it had an important bearing on the case, he moved that the judges admit it along with an additional article. They did so, stipulating that whatever followed from it would have the

48 Court Record, ff. 58–64.
49 *Ibid.*, ff. 64–66; Pocock, I, 5, 7. See above at n. 8.
50 Court Record, f. 66rv.

full effect of the law. In the new article, they charged that when Henry had reached puberty he had protested against the marriage that he had contracted in his minority with Catherine, and publicly stated that he did not wish to consent to such a marriage or to Catherine as his spouse or wife, by anything that he or anyone else in his name had done or would do. This is a fair summary of the protest, the text of which was also given. It is significant that in making the protest, Henry admitted that he had contracted marriage with Catherine, but insisted that the marriage was invalid because of his age, and said he took this action against it lest it should appear in his mature age to be validated by tacit consent, by mutual habitation, by the giving or receiving of gifts, or by any other means.[51]

In his testimony of two years before, Bishop Fox had said that he supposed that the young Henry had made his protestation at the command of his father, and that the king still wanted Henry to marry Catherine, but that he postponed it because of the matter of her dowry.[52] Warham's testimony differed from Fox's. He stated that before Henry reached the age of puberty Henry VII had asked him for his advice on the matter of the proposed marriage, and he, Warham, had replied that it did not seem honorable or pleasing to God that a brother should marry the wife of his brother. He perceived that the king was not much inclined to the marriage, and he advised him to persuade the prince to protest against it. He believed that Henry made such a protest. In later testimony he said that the king told him that the prince had not yet reached puberty, and Warham replied that if Henry made a protestation it would not be valid because of his minority. Nevertheless he counseled the king to have the prince make such a protest, and then to repeat it on the first or second day after reaching puberty.[53] In fact, Henry made the protest on June 27, 1505, the day before his fourteenth birthday.

After the article was posed and the protestation read, Bishop West identified his signature on the instrument of protest and testified that it was authentic.[54] Bishop Fox testified in 1527 that he thought West or someone else had read the protest in Henry's

51 *Ibid.*, ff. 66v–68.   52 *Ibid.*, ff. 61v–62.
53 *Ibid.*, ff. 26v, 49v.   54 *Ibid.*, f. 68.

name to Catherine at Durham House.[55] But it obviously was not so, and there seems to have been no attempt at the legatine court to establish that Catherine had been apprised of the prince's action.

After West's testimony, the legates extended the time for the conclusion of the case to Friday, July 23. On that day, Campeggio rose to address the court. Cavendish tells us that the king himself had come to Blackfriars "and sat within a gallery against the door of the same that looked unto the judges where they sat, whom he might see and hear speak, to hear what judgment they would give in his suit."[56] The king may have been stationed in the staircase tower at the north end of the upper frater (that is, the Parliament Chamber). The stairs led both to this chamber and to the guest wing to the north, and there were rooms on and over the staircase. There was also a gallery on the western side of the guest wing, which led to the stairs, and the activity in the courtroom might have been visible from there.[57]

Cavendish attributes a long speech to the Italian cardinal, in which he said that the issues at stake were too important to be decided by the legates without consulting the pope, and that he herewith adjourned the court until after the Roman summer holidays. The notarial record, however, contains only the following statement:

When the aforesaid Friday, viz. the 23rd day of the month of July, had come, and the most reverend fathers in Christ, the aforesaid judges and vicegerents, were seated in the above-mentioned place of judgment between the hours of nine and ten in the forenoon, in the presence of us, the undersigned public notaries and witnesses, the aforesaid promoter signified and indicated to them that each and all of the matters pertaining to the facts for the instructing and informing of their minds and consciences had been and were judicially proposed, exhibited, and alleged, and the acts were present before them; and that that Friday had been and was assigned and fixed for the conclusion of this cause. Nevertheless, being attentive to what the most reverend Lord Cardinal Campeggio among other things alleged and affirmed, taking his faith upon the word of a true prelate, that the reaping and harvest vacation had been and was designated to begin each year in the Roman curia, accord-

---

55 *Ibid.*, f. 62rv.

56 Cavendish, p. 89.

57 See E. K. Chambers, *Elizabethan Stage*, II, 489–90. Irwin Smith, *Shakespeare's Blackfriars Playhouse*, p. 105, concludes from Cavendish's report that the Parliament Chamber itself held the gallery in question.

ing to its custom and practice, before the said Friday, and that he and his colleague were bound to follow the rule of the same curia in conducting this cause, the aforesaid most reverend judges in the presence of the proctor for His Royal Majesty and in the face of the queen's contumacy, prorogued and continued the term for the conclusion of the cause, and set it on the first day of October next, and admonished the king's proctor to appear on that day.[58]

Ten days earlier Campeggio had written to Rome of the speed with which the trial was moving, and said that some expected a sentence within ten days. It is evident that Campeggio himself fully expected to hand down a sentence when the time came. His insistence upon Roman procedures was the first independent action that he had taken during the trial. It was the ingenious way that he hit upon for getting round the clause in the legatine commission that empowered one of the legates to proceed to judgment without the other. Wolsey had lost at last and for good.

Four days after the conclusion of the trial, Wolsey was writing to the English envoys in Rome as if the court had not yet adjourned: "Now within one week the days judicial shall expire wherein it is by the law used and appointed to proceed in such causes, and so the course of process must needs of force cease for two months or thereabout."[59] Perhaps some additional time was allowed after the beginning of the harvest vacation to sift the exhibits and verify the records—and to decide what was to go into the official acts. The court clerks gave the assurance at the end of their record that "each and all of these acts were prescribed by the said most reverend fathers."

Campeggio was kept waiting in England for the beginning of October, when the reopening of the trial was scheduled, though after receiving definite word that the case had been advoked to Rome, he repeatedly begged for permission to depart. It was only after the time for the reconvening of the court had passed that the weary diplomat secured his wishes. The king in his anger had not allowed him to see the queen, nor was he now permitted to take his leave of her.[60] As he was waiting to leave the island, he wrote to Rome from Canterbury, on October 7. He said that, since King

58 Court Record, ff. 68v–69.

59 SP VII, 194.

60 Chapuys to Charles, 4 September 1529, SC IV, part 1, 196; 8 October 1529, *ibid.*, p. 273.

Henry was so entirely convinced that his marriage was null and void by divine law, he could not but be pained that the case did not turn out as he had expected.[61]

The recess of the legatine court brought a great change of scene in England. Wolsey disappeared from the action, in disgrace. The story of his fall is so compelling that it has usually diverted attention from the king's great matter. We shall miss him as one of the chief sources of information on the negotiations and events that took place in England; but simultaneously with his departure there appeared on the stage another major *dramatis persona*: Eustace Chapuys of Savoy, Doctor of Both Laws, canon, and former ecclesiastical judge (he had been Official of the Consistory Court of the Diocese of Geneva). He came to England now as the emperor's new ambassador, and on the first of September he sent off the first of his many and infinitely detailed dispatches to his master.

Chapuys was not an insider in the king's affairs; but he had an urbane and ingratiating manner that inspired confidences. There immediately arose in his breast a fierce and unbending loyalty to the queen and her cause, and the information that he assiduously collected on her behalf was usually of the highest reliability—and that not only when it came from her or her supporters; even Henry's partisans, it seems, could not keep themselves from revealing more to him than they should. This was true even of Thomas Cromwell, Wolsey's former factor, who would eventually come forward as the principal agent in the campaign for nullification.

The question of Catherine's virginity was still very much to the fore. No conclusion had been reached in the trial before the legates, and Henry was clearly concerned about the matter, knowing that Catherine had a very good chance of winning her point. About two months after the adjournment of the court, the queen had a conversation with the king one night after dinner (Henry had divorced her from bed but not yet entirely from board). "You wish to help yourself," he told her, "and defend the validity of the dispensation by the fact that you were not known by the prince my brother and that he had nothing to do with you. I am content; but you are not my wife for all that, since the bull did not dispense *super impedimento publicae honestatis*." For that reason, Henry

---

[61] Ehses, p. 134.

said, he would dispute and maintain against the whole world that the dispensation was not sufficient.[62]

This is the closest that Henry would come to admitting the queen's virginity; he had admitted it before, we know, but not since it had become such an important element in this case, unless he had secretly confessed his doubts to the legates. Perhaps he thought that even now there was no real danger in admitting it to the queen, since after all she knew it already; and it gave him pleasure to score a point against her.

We notice that Henry was employing the public-honesty argument in the form that the legates had set forth for use in case the queen really had been a virgin after her first marriage. There had been an elaborate attempt to refute it at the trial, if we are to credit the Sanders account; but Henry had not been present, and perhaps the answers of the queen's advocates had not been fully reported to him or assimilated by him. He would later in all seriousness and sincerity make the outlandish claim that her counsel had been forced to admit consummation in order to escape the argument. At any rate, he was still sufficiently impressed with it to consider using it at Rome.

Chapuys must have been familiar at least with the form that the objection of public honesty presumably took in the promoter's list of doubts, and with the written answer that had been submitted on the queen's side, for he had just sent off to Charles in his previous letter the *libellus* containing the factum and the answers to all fourteen objections.[63] But he had very likely never heard the argument phrased in Henry's way before this time. What did he think of it? "This argument," he says, "would be sufficiently good to use in a dispute against the queen, but among other people it would be found to rest on a one-night's layer of ice."[64]

[62] Chapuys to Charles V, 8 October 1529, Vienna Archives (England, Korrespondenz Karton 4): "Et encoures nagueres devisant vng apres disner avec la Royne yl luy dit, 'Vous vous voules ayder et defendre pour la validité de la dispensation de ce que ne fustes cogneue et n'eust participation avec vous le prince mon frer. J'en suys content. Mays ne pour cella estes vous ma femme, car en la Bulle n'est dispensé *super impedimento publice honestatis*,' et que pour ceste rayson yl vouloit disputer et maintenir contre tout le monde que la dispensation n'estoyt souffizante." Cf. SC IV, part 1, 275.

[63] Letter of 29 September 1529, SC IV, part 1, 258.

[64] "Ce argument estoit asses bon pour disputer contre la Royne, mays entre autres gens yl se trouveroit fondé sus la glace d'une nuyt." (Letter cited in n. 62 above.)

Perhaps the ambassador meant to say that Catherine was very much disturbed by the argument, as if she had not encountered it before, or had not realized its force. Chapuys reassured her, thinking quite honestly that it would not stand up in court. We shall see shortly how the matter of the queen's virginity was regarded in Rome, and what chance Henry's resort to public honesty would have there.

The queen herself soon regained her old confidence in the wisdom of her defense, if she had ever lost it, and some two months later, on St. Andrew's Day (November 30), another after-dinner conversation turned into a dispute, in which Henry made much of the scholarly opinions that he was collecting in his favor, especially those of some of the professors at the University of Paris. Catherine replied that he himself, without the help of his professors, knew perfectly well that his main case against the marriage did not exist, for he had found her to be a virgin when she married him, as he had admitted on more than one occasion. As for professors and scholars, the best of them had already written in her favor, and if she were allowed to collect opinions freely, she had no doubt that she could outnumber him a thousand to one. Henry finally gave it up and left her abruptly, very much disconcerted and downcast by what she had said, and in his discouragement he went to the other wing of the palace, seeking solace from Anne. She, however, gave him a sharp rebuke, and told him that Catherine always won the arguments he picked with her, and that some day he would find her reasoning so convincing that he would go back to her, and Anne would be cast aside.[65] This, of course, is what almost everyone was hoping for.

Henry said nothing more to Catherine about public honesty; he had in the past month received a letter from the pope challenging him to declare himself on Catherine's virginity. It was to leave him literally speechless.

[65] SC IV, part 1, 351–52.

Part Two

THE APPEAL TO ROME

I do refuse you for my judge; and here,
Before you all, appeal unto the Pope,
To bring my whole cause 'fore His Holiness,
And to be judged by him.

I will not tarry; no, nor ever more
Upon this business my appearance make
In any of their courts.

—Shakespeare & Fletcher, HENRY VIII

The Advocation

L ong before the opening of the legatine court, Mendoza had been urging Catherine to send powers of attorney to an imperial agent in Rome. She was willing enough to do so, but she felt that she could not accomplish it without Henry's hearing of it.[1] When she received the summons of May 31, 1529, to appear before the legates, she immediately reported it to her sister-in-law, Margaret of Austria, Governess of the Low Countries, who was, like her, an aunt of Charles V. Catherine wanted her foreign lawyers to be sent back to her (they had already come once before, but had been so harassed that they left almost immediately). Instead, as Mendoza reported (he was now at Margaret's court), it was decided to send, in secret, a notary, who was to instruct the queen to appeal against the very first act of the legates in court, and to send the appeal back to Flanders to be forwarded to Rome.[2]

We saw that Catherine's appeal was drawn up at Baynard's Castle on June 16, two days before she was to make her appearance in court.[3] English notaries were employed to witness the instrument, rather than the surreptitious Flemish emissary. But since the mandate whereby she made over her powers of attorney to Ambassador Mai in Rome had reached Flanders at least as early as June 9, the queen may have had this notary witness a different document of appeal. When Mendoza received it, he sent it off, together with the mandate and supporting letters. It reached Rome

---

[1] SC III, part 2, 878, 882, 885.
[2] SC IV, part 1, 96.
[3] Pocock, II, 609.

on the fifth of July.[4] Mai showed it to the pope immediately, and on the next day Clement informed the English envoys, Benet, Casale, and Vannes, of its reception. Henry's agents pleaded for mature consideration; meanwhile they had intercepted Campeggio's packet in order to delay the news that the legatine trial was under way, hoping that it would end with a sentence in Henry's favor before any action could be taken against it.

The pope gave his assurances that he had done all that he could to hold off advoking the case to Rome. He had been able to put off the imperial demands by saying that the trial was not being held and that the envoys did not have a proper mandate; but now they had a very ample one from the queen, and news had come that matters were moving apace in England. He finally agreed to postpone taking action for a few days, and to ask the emperor's envoys to examine the queen's mandate, which he had not yet read. He would in the meantime try to think up whatever reasons he could for further delay.[5] The Spanish position had, of course, very much improved for other reasons as well. Charles had defeated the French at Landriano and shortly thereafter, on June 29, had come to terms with Clement VII in the Treaty of Barcelona.

On July 9 the English got word that the queen had been declared contumacious, and on the next day the Spanish received a similar report. The end had come. This news, added to what Clement had read in the mandate, made advocation inevitable. The measure was decided upon on July 13, secretly signed by the pope on the next day, and formally passed in Consistory on the 16th.

Catherine's mandate contained more than her powers of attorney for Mai. Besides a copy of the bull and another of the brief, there was a statement by the queen that she had not consummated her marriage with Arthur, and a declaration of all the facts of the case as she knew them. For instance, she admitted that Arthur was indeed past the age of puberty when he married her (and that Henry on the other hand was scarcely twelve years old at the time

[4] SC IV, part 1, 133, 154; Pocock, I, 251. Catherine's mandate is in fact dated May 10, 1529; it appears within another document, dated July 19, 1529, in which Mai appoints two substitute proctors; the whole can be found in the *Extractum registri cause Anglie matrimonialis*, British Museum Add. MS 37154, ff. 7v–15v (Catherine's mandate is on ff. 8–14). See Surtz, "Henry VIII's Great Matter," p. 978, and see above, Chap. 4, n. 2.

[5] Pocock, I, 250–54; LP IV, 5762–64.

of the dispensation); but she insisted that in spite of the circumstance that Arthur had slept in the same bed with her for several nights, she had emerged from the marriage a virgin. The master-stroke was her assertion, borne witness to by the pope in his subsequent letter to the king, that she was so certain of the truth of her virginity and of Henry's knowledge of it that she would rest content with whatever statement the king himself would make upon the matter under oath.[6]

Catherine was undoubtedly convinced of Henry's integrity as a Christian man before his God, in spite of his hypocrisies and rationalizations, but she also was aware of the spur to his conscience —the fact that he had declared her virginity in the past before witnesses. In the same letter in which Chapuys reported Henry's ploy of urging the impediment of public decency, he told of the queen's conviction that the king would never deny that she had not consummated her marriage with Arthur, because he had spoken of it at large a number of times.[7]

The question of the queen's virginity had already been a subject of discussion in Rome, at least among Henry's partisans. We recall that Wolsey had commissioned Gardiner to seek opinions of Staphileus and others on his public-honesty argument. No doubt he did so, and perhaps his response was sufficiently optimistic to induce the cardinal to use it at the legatine court, or to induce John Hughes to include the alternate form of the argument among the doubts derived from the factum. Gardiner, as we have seen, hinted at this latter version of the objection, without developing it, in his refutation of Fisher's book. Staphileus, too, had encountered the argument in this form in one of the *Consilia* of Geminianus, the fifteenth-century canonist, which he had edited two decades before. Here it was argued that a dispensation was surreptitious, and therefore invalid, because affinity was not named in conjunc-

---

6 Ehses, pp. 217, 220, and the dispatches cited in the previous note. Unfortunately, Surtz gives only a sample of the contents of the mandate: "For example, she confesses that Arthur lay with her for several nights but without sexual intercourse (*mecum per aliquot noctes concubuit citra tamen carnalem copulam*)" (*Extractum*, f. 8; Surtz, p. 978). He does not verify the pope's assertion (below at n. 11) that it was in this document that Catherine offered to remain satisfied with Henry's sworn statement.

7 "Et pense que le Roy ne le mettroit en ny, cars plusieurs foys yl l'a dit et propalé." Chapuys to Charles V, 29 September 1529, Vienna, Haus-, Hof- und Staatsarchiv, England, Korrespondenz Karton 4.

tion with public honesty. In addition to citing the admonition of John Andreae, Geminianus remarked that affinity alone could come from illicit copula; but when it came from marital intercourse, the impediment of public honesty was also present and must be mentioned.[8]

But this argument, unlike Wolsey's, assumed that the first marriage had been consummated. Sir Gregory Casale also made use of public honesty upon this assumption, but he made the further assumption, like the author of the *Compendious Annotation*, that the impediment had been imposed by God. His thoughts are contained in a brief in his hand which Bishop Gilbert Burnet discovered in the Cotton Library. Casale's initial objection was that the marriage could and should be annulled because it was contrary to divine and human law: "For divine law forbids the marrying of one's brother's wife, and it is notorious that a brother's wife was married in this instance. As for human law, there are two impediments against this marriage, one of affinity, which, being induced from divine law, is sanctioned with extreme severity, and the other of the righteousness of public honesty, which God has promulgated." He went on to say that according to many scholars and even popes these laws could not be dispensed from. But even granted that a dispensation could be given, it could only be done for grave reasons. He listed some of the usual objections against Julius's bull, and then returned to the weighty objections raised against the possibility of a dispensation. He did not urge them as the sole reason for the invalidity of the dispensation, but he insisted that they should be given due consideration.[9]

Burnet asserts as a fact, though seemingly without evidence, that Casale actually presented his summary to the pope. The date that Burnet's editor, Pocock, assigns to it is May 21, 1529, that is, ten days before Gardiner left Rome to partake in the legatine trial in

---

[8] Dominicus de Sancto Geminiano, *Consilia* no. 33, ed. Ioannes Staphileus (Pavia, 1059 [= 1509]), ff. 20v–21. He also used the outlandish argument that the dispensation was void because it failed to mention that the affinity was in the first genus, even though he admitted that the second and third genera were no longer impediments (f. 20). They had, in fact, been abrogated by Innocent III in 1215. The queen's counsel turned the tables on the king's men by using this thirty-third *consilium* of Geminianus to refute one of the doubts raised at the legatine court. See Appendix A, n. 33.

[9] Burnet, I, 118; IV, 76.

England. If this date is no more than guesswork, we can at least say that Casale composed it after November 1528, since he knew about, and denied the authenticity of, the brief of Julius II; and he no doubt was writing before the university determinations began to come in in the spring of 1530. But if Clement ever saw the essay, we may be sure that he was not impressed by what Casale had to say about the divine laws against the marriage and their indispensability.

We are given the pope's own meditations on the subject of Catherine's virginity in a letter written to Henry the day before Chapuys recorded Henry's threat to appeal to the queen's uncleared public honesty. The pope began his message by disposing of those who believed that "the business pertains to the disposal of divine law," and that one could not safely receive a dispensation from it. He denied the truth of the allegation: the prohibition was one of positive law, and the law was enacted by Pope Innocent.[10] All authorities agreed that a person who was dispensed from this law was safe in his own conscience, "in spite of alleged surreption in the dispensation, which should be tolerated for the sake of avoiding scandal," particularly since, if there was a difference of opinion on the point (that is, whether or not the dispensation was really surreptitious), the law obliged one to follow the course that most favored the marriage.

Clement offered to do away with the difficulties of the dispensation and put Henry's conscience at ease by giving him as many more dispensations as he wished. Even granted for the sake of discussion that the divine law was involved, there was agreement among interpreters of the law that he could dispense from it, given a true cause. "But if it is true, as the queen herself affirms in her mandate, that she was not known by Arthur, and you yourself

---

10 He says Innocent IV but doubtless means Innocent III, whose decree *Deus qui* of 1201 on the law of levirate was incorporated into canon law (CIC X 4.19.9). It allowed the Livonians (Latvians) who had married their brothers' wives before their conversion to stay married, provided that the conditions of the Mosaic code had been fulfilled, that is, that they had married to raise up seed in the name of their childless brothers. The pope forbade such a marriage under any other circumstances. Innocent IV issued no decretal of the sort, and in his commentary on the *Decretals of Gregory IX* he has nothing to say on Innocent III's canon. See e.g. the edition of Lyons, 1525, *Apparatus super quinque libris decretalium*, f. 184v.

know better—she is prepared to stand freely by your oath—there is no doubt that one dispensed in this case is safe in the forum of conscience."[11]

He concluded by returning to the possibility that some untruth had been expressed in the dispensation. If so, he asked, who could maintain, in times when the Turks were threatening, that, in order to avoid such a great danger and scandal, to preserve the peace, and to raise an expedition against the enemy, the pope had not the power to give another dispensation within the marriage itself, which had lasted so long with at least the appearances of marriage?[12]

Obviously, Clement believed that Catherine left her first marriage still a virgin. What would have happened if Henry had responded to the challenge of the queen and confirmed it with his oath, urging at the same time the objection that the bull failed to mention public honesty? The pope's answer, almost certainly, would have been to the point: "If the dispensation was surreptitious, it should be tolerated." He showed himself to be above the quibbles of legal language on this subject.

The letter demonstrates that he objected, at least subconsciously, to the concept that an invalid dispensation should invalidate the marriage that it cleared the way for. As long as there was no error of person or forced consent in the matter, one might well ask why a mere technicality should be given so much weight. Clement's common sense prevailed over canonical precedent in this instance, but perhaps only because Henry's case was very weak and other pressures militated against giving in to his demands. In other circumstances he might have given in, for the juridical practice on which Henry based his appeal was considered quite respectable, and it has persisted to this day. That is to say, Roman Catholic marriage tribunals have the option of granting an annulment on grounds of a defective permit, or on the other hand of following the rule enunciated by Clement, of favoring the marriage and presuming the permit valid unless the contrary can be thoroughly

[11] "Quod si verum est, ut regina ipsa mandato suo affirmat, se ab Arturo non fuisse cognitam, et tu ipse melius nosti, cuius iuramento illa parata est libere stare, nullum est dubium in hoc casu dispensatum in foro conscientiae esse tutum."

[12] Letter of 7 October 1529, in Augustinus Theiner, *Vetera monumenta Hibernorum et Scotorum historiam illustrantia* (Rome, 1864), p. 566.

demonstrated—meaning that the courts can "assume" whatever is necessary to make it valid.[13] They are thus enabled arbitrarily to dissolve or uphold marriages apart from any thought for the quality of the marriage relationship itself and the responsibilities or hardships that the maintenance or dissolution of the union would entail upon the parties involved—though presumably these circumstances would normally be taken into consideration.

The pope was naturally very eager to hear what response Henry would make to his letter. He was to have a long wait. But before the king replied in his own person—nearly a year later—Clement was informed by the English ambassadors of the royal displeasure with the letter, inasmuch as it prejudiced the case by declaring that the law involved was merely human and not divine.

We can gather the response that was made at Rome to this objection from a report submitted to the pope by one of his counselors:

The envoys cannot complain that, in the last brief sent to His Royal Majesty after the case was committed, it was said that marriage is of positive law. It does not say this, if it is well read, but it only says that the law against marrying a dead brother's childless wife is of positive legislation and was introduced by Innocent IV; and it adds that, if it were of divine law, the pope could with good reason dispense from it. The brief was only written with a view to remove the scruple that the king complained about, and not to prejudge the case between him and the queen. This is clear from the fact that it was written to the king alone and not to others. Likewise, when it says that if it was the desire of His Royal Majesty Your Holiness would grant a new dispensation from the impediment, it is as clear as can be that the old dispensation is not thereby presupposed to be valid. Besides, it is obvious that the aforesaid does not prevent an investigation of the reasons given for the dispensation; and if they are proved to be false the dispensation will collapse and the marriage will be invalid. [Or, as another report put it, the letter "creates no obstacle to a sentence of divorce if the dispensation is proved to be surreptitious and invalid."][14]

Since no complaint was forthcoming about what Clement had said concerning Catherine's assertion, he considered it good to hold

---

[13] John T. Noonan, Jr., speaks very well to this subject in *Power to Dissolve: Lawyers and Marriages in the Courts of the Roman Curia* (Cambridge, Mass., 1972), pp. 324–28, 337–38.

[14] Ehses, p. 159; the alternate report can be found in the Vatican Archives, Lettere di principi 14, f. 647 (old number 646).

firm to the article that the queen was never carnally known by Arthur. Salviati reported the pope's feeling in this matter to Campeggio (who was now off on another embassy elsewhere) on June 14, 1530.[15]

About the middle of July 1530, Henry decided at least to give the pope a formal answer. He began his letter by saying that even though he had delayed in responding to the pope's words of October 7, he had not forgotten them. Since their purpose was to enable him, after meditating upon their content, to set his conscience at rest in the matter of his marriage, he could hardly neglect them, or fail to answer them, "after that we had diligently examined and perpended the effects of the same, which we did very diligently, noting, conferring, and resolving everything in them contained, with deep study of mind." He realized that the wrongs that he had suffered from the pope had been caused by the latter's ignorant counselors; but nevertheless Clement himself could not escape some of the blame, for not having provided himself with better advisers.

"Never was there any prince so handled by a pope," he complained, "as Your Holiness hath entreated us." Clement had issued a legatine commission, promising that it should not be revoked, as well as a decretal letter defining the cause; if he had acted justly in granting them, then he had acted unjustly in revoking them. As for the remedies that Clement suggested for his sickness, he distrusted them; and this was his reason for seeking out the advice of every learned man. It was clear from the answers that he had received how much they disagreed with the handful of persons that Clement had consulted on the subject: "Those few men of yours do affirm the prohibition of our marriage to be induct only by the law positive, as Your Holiness hath also written in your letters; but all others say the prohibition to be induct both by the law of God and nature; those men of yours do suggest that now [it] may be dispensed for avoiding of slander; the others utterly do contend that by no mean it is lawful to dispense with that that God and nature hath forbidden."

As a result, Henry continued, "we do separate from our cause the authority of the See Apostolic, which we do perceive to be destitute of that learning whereby it should be directed; and because Your Holiness doth ever profess your ignorance and is wont to speak of other men's mouths, we do confer the sayings of those with the sayings of them that be of the contrary opinion; for to confer the reasons it were too long." The fact is, he said, that not only the universities of Cambridge and Oxford in his own realm but also those of Paris, Orléans, Bourges, and Angers in France, and Bologna in Italy, as well as famous scholars speaking on their own authority, swayed by nothing but their concern for the truth, "do affirm the marriage of the brother with the brother's wife to be contrary to the law of God and nature, and also do pronounce that no dispensation can be lawful nor available to any Christian man in the behalf."[16]

Clement's reaction to Henry's reliance upon the universities can be inferred from his responses to the letter he received at the same time from "the spiritual and temporal lords of England." The latter document was subscribed to by only four bishops, apart from the two archbishops; the king's circuit-riders had collected Wolsey's signature and seal from him in mid-June, when the harassed cardinal was on one of the stages of the journey north to his see of York, and had then moved on to sign up the Earl of Shrewsbury.[17] The letter, which had presumably been written by Henry, or under his supervision, urged the pope to come to a rapid and fitting conclusion in the question of the king's marriage; and by their reference to what the various universities held for true, the undersigned lords left little doubt as to what they thought the conclusion should be.[18]

In one of the briefs occasioned by this letter, the pope told the lords that very few of the university determinations had come to his attention, and those not through the hands of a properly constituted spokesman for the king (he reminded them that it was, after all, Henry's refusal to send his powers of attorney that was holding up the case). Furthermore, the determinations were not

[16] Burnet, IV, 169. The determinations of Bologna and Bourges were obtained on June 10, 1530; Henry's letter was therefore written after hearing of them, and before getting the report of the Padua determination of July 1. Ehses, p. 154, dates it July 13, 1530, the same date as on the letter of the English prelates and lords.

[17] See James Gairdner, *DNB* Wolsey.

[18] Rymer, XIV, 405.

accompanied by the reasons that had led the scholars to their conclusions—they were mere human opinions, unsupported by the
sacred canons and Holy Scripture. On the other hand, the advocates of the opposite view were bringing to him the judgments of
many learned men, whose arguments were drawn not only from
Latin but also from Hebrew sources.[19] This was, equivalently,
Clement's response to Henry's statement that "to confer the reasons it were too long."

In another brief the pontiff informed the same correspondents
that he was not sufficiently moved by the opinions of the four
universities that he had read: "How correct could their conclusions be when they did not hear both sides nor discuss the truth
of the matter? Everyone knows the answer. In addition, the queen's
lawyers maintain that they will be able to produce even more opinions of academies and scholars in their favor than you allege."[20]

The "truth of the matter" was what interested Clement. If
Henry had so carefully "perpended" his letter, why did he make
no answer to the question of Catherine's unconsummated first marriage? If the universities had made their decisions upon the assumption that the marriage had been consummated, whereas in
fact it had not, of what value were they?

Clement did not hesitate to press home the queen's challenge.
Some time before he sent off his replies to the English prelates
and nobles, Jerome Ghinucci, Auditor of the Papal Chamber and
Bishop of Worcester, one of Henry's most faithful and determined
advocates, had reported that "the pope seems always to persevere
in the opinion that the offer of an oath that the queen has made
to Your Majesty gives great justification to her cause." The only
response that the bishop had been able to make was the objection that oaths were not to be taken in cases that did not depend
on the consent of the parties: an annulment could not be effected
by consent. But he had given away the case before this: he had
told the pope that the king could gain nothing from such an oath,
whereas the queen had much to gain thereby.[21]

Somewhat earlier, another pertinent report had come from
Richard Croke, the learned and testy priest who had been busily

[19] Pocock, I, 434 (letter of 27 September 1530).
[20] Ehses, p. 164.
[21] Pocock, II, 11 (letter received on 1 October 1530).

collecting opinions all year in the north of Italy, furiously complaining all the while that the Casale brothers were secretly impeding the king's business (which they were), and becoming even more furious when Henry and his advisers refused to believe him. He told the king that Montini, Campeggio's secretary, was spreading the word far and wide that his master actually had Henry's statement in writing that Catherine had still been a virgin when she married him; and he was alleging further that the king refused to state the truth under oath, after the queen had declared that she would accept whatever he said.[22]

We may well wonder what Ghinucci, Croke, and the others thought of Henry's silence. The answer, I think, can be found in a conversation between Rodrigo Niño, the emperor's ambassador at Venice, and the prothonotary John Casale, on July 11, 1530. Casale reaffirmed that he and his brother Sir Gregory disapproved of what Henry was doing, but he begged Niño to keep it secret (the exchange was duly reported to Croke). Niño then brought up the point that the eleven miserable friars whose opinion constituted the so-called determination of the University of Padua had gone upon the supposition that Catherine had consummated her marriage with Arthur, whereas she had declared to Cardinal Campeggio in the sacrament of confession that it was not true; and this was something that Henry knew better than anyone else. Casale admitted it; he acknowledged that the queen had rested her case on the oath of the king, but said that the king maintained that he had been too much of a child at the time of his own marriage to Catherine to know how to find out for sure if she really were a virgin.[23] He therefore sought to prove that she and Arthur had been together many times in the same bed. Niño asked Casale if it had never happened to him that he had gone to bed a few times with a woman but never had access to her. Casale replied that it had. "Could not, then," the ambassador

---

[22] Letter of 19 October 1530, LP IV, 6694.

[23] "Dixome que assi era que la reyna lo dejava en el jurimento del rey, pero que el rey decia que era tan mochacho que no sabia determinarse en la verdad." Henry was also justifying his silence at this time by pleading amnesia, as is shown in Chapuy's report of 23 August 1530: "The queen says it will be easy to prove quite clearly, for she has several witnesses, and the king himself formerly confessed the fact on several occasions. Even now he will not deny it; he only says he does not remember." SC *Further Supplement*, p. 450.

Croke consulted rabbis at Venice and Francesco Giorgi, The Cabalist Friar of Venice. See Frances Yates "The Occult Philosophy in the Elizabethan Age", p. 31.

pressed on, "the same thing have happened to the Prince of Wales?" He told him of others who had had the same experience, and Casale was unable to make him a reply.[24]

Presumably the pope had not been given any such explanation of Henry's embarrassment, or if he had, he would have assumed that the indications were in favor of Catherine. Certainly the king's sincerity must have been strongly called into question. We should remember that Clement had issued a dispensation at Henry's request allowing him to marry a woman to whom he was related in precisely the same degree of affinity that he alleged between himself and the queen. Lest the pope should forget the point it was brought to his attention in a *consilium* obtained some time during the year 1530.

The theologian or canonist who composed the report said that many persons asserted that Henry was not motivated by scruples of conscience but by a new love. The author assumed that Catherine's marriage with Arthur had been consummated, and pointed out that the affinity stemming from it was legitimate, and duly dispensed by the pope. On the other hand the affinity between Henry and the woman whom he reportedly wanted to marry was not legitimate, but was the result of the king's sinful deeds. It was not honorable for Henry to have obtained a dispensation to marry this woman when the validity of the first marriage was not yet decided; and there was no good reason to put away Catherine and marry the other, since the same impediment existed between them.[25]

Henry's situation was not lost on the champions of the queen, even though they had no knowledge of the dispensations that Henry had procured. Chapuys assured Charles some two years later that even if Henry were free from the queen, he could not marry Anne, because he had had an affair with her sister.[26] The next year, when matters were coming to a head, Dr. Ortiz, the emperor's proctor at Rome, shrewdly observed the same thing that

[24] SC IV, part 1, 656.

[25] Ehses, p. 233. The author said that the fate of the daughters of Henry III should serve as a warning to the king. Apparently Henry VIII had brought up an unhistorical precedent concerning his earlier namesake, and Clement's counselor pointed out that the case had had a bad end (which, however, was equally unhistorical). See *ibid.*, p. 235, n. 1.

[26] Letter of 9 August 1532, Paul Friedmann, *Anne Boleyn*, II, 235–36.

Sanders was to point out in later years, namely, that there was an even closer affinity between Henry and Anne than between him and Catherine, since Catherine did not consummate her first marriage.[27] It is interesting to see that he called the impediment between the king and queen affinity, and not public honesty. This is the modern terminology, and it is a use that Henry and his new archbishop, Cranmer, were to approve of, for a time.

[27] LP VI, 134; Friedmann, II, 235.

CHAPTER EIGHT

Nonconsummation: Pros and Cons

❧✦❧

EARLY IN 1531 Ambassador Mai announced that special *litterae remissoriae* would be granted by the Roman tribunal to enable the statements of witnesses for the queen's side to be collected for presentation at the trial. They were designed especially to gather testimony proving that Catherine's first marriage had not been consummated.

Both Ortiz and Chapuys were impatient at the delay. The move was totally unnecessary, they felt; all that was needed was a declaration that the marriage between Henry and Catherine was not forbidden by an indispensable law, and then it would make no difference what the nature of the queen's relations with Arthur had been. The fact of nonconsummation was not probable in itself, Chapuys said, speaking from a legal point of view; and all the persons who knew anything about it in England had been suborned by the king. The only way to prove it was to build a case around the queen's oath, and to collect witnesses in Spain testifying to her moral integrity, showing that she would rather die than perjure herself. They would thereby vitiate the legal presumptions of the opposition.[1] That is, the presumption of the law would then be on the side of the queen. Chapuys was no doubt referring to the process of compurgation, which was a common means of concluding an inquisition: the accused would deny the charge under oath, and would produce a certain number of witnesses to testify to his good reputation in the matter.

Chapuys finally found four witnesses in England who were will-

[1] LP V, 112, 188, 340, 492. The remissorials were issued on March 13, 1531, and arrived in England for the queen's inspection in June (*ibid.*, 137, 308).

ing to come forward and reveal that Arthur had been impotent. The ambassador hoped to get them accepted in virtue of a secret papal commission that had been sent to him, since no official remissorials had been issued for England. Ortiz reported, however, that the depositions were rejected in Rome because they had not been properly sworn to.[2]

It was otherwise with the Spanish witnesses. Their statements were gathered in fairly good time, and most of them had arrived in Rome by early November, though they were not all assembled until March 1532.[3] But they were not formally presented to the Rota until July 1533, after Henry had taken the law into his own and Thomas Cranmer's hands. The king's delaying tactics at Rome had been so successful that the trial did not begin until four years after advocation, and did not finish until almost a year later. Clement had been moved to issue a stern rebuke to Henry in January 1532 for publicly cohabiting with Anne and showing her marital affection,[4] and in November of the same year he wrote again, threatening him with excommunication if he did not leave her and rejoin Catherine.[5] The pontiff had been alarmed by news of Henry's elevation of Anne to the Marquisate of Pembroke in September and their "honeymoon" journey to Calais in October.[6] In fact, Henry about this time had finally begun to cohabit with Anne in the sexual sense of the word, and she was pregnant before the end of the year. Obviously, Clement's admonitions were having no effect, and would have none. Meanwhile, the preliminaries of the trial continued.

Sometime before the formal presentation in court of the responses to the remissory letters, their contents were summarized and the strengths of the queen's case revealed to the opposition. A similar, though naturally much less circumstantial, document had been presented to the court in late January 1531 by one of Mai's substitutes, who insisted that Henry's party respond to it. It set forth the queen's defense in twenty-five articles, which sought

2 *Ibid.*, 340, 492.

3 *Ibid.*, 516, 866.

4 Clement to Henry, 25 January 1532, Pocock, II, 166–68. The letter was forwarded to Catherine and not delivered to Henry until May (LP V, 1046).

5 Clement to Henry, 15 November 1532, redated 23 December 1532, and published in Flanders, 21 and 23 January 1533, Pocock, II, 378–84.

6 Ehses, pp. 200–201.

to establish: that the original marriage between Arthur and Catherine had been arranged for the purpose of peace; that this marriage had not been consummated, for Arthur, Catherine, and Henry himself had often said as much to trustworthy persons; that, to prevent hostilities over the matter of the dowry, Julius II had given a dispensation to Catherine and Henry to marry, and that they did so with full knowledge of the dispensation; that dissolution of this marriage would provoke Catherine's nephews (Charles V, John III of Portugal, and Ferdinand I of Hungary) to vengeance; and that popes are accustomed to dispense from the impediments of public honesty and the first degree of affinity, and even for brothers and sisters, for the sake of princes and kings.[7]

The later presentation of the queen's case, which took advantage of the remissorial responses, has not yet come to light; but there is extant a rebuttal that was made to it from the king's side. Two copies of this answer exist in the Vatican Archives under the title *English Articles*.[8] The author, single or composite, set forth his objections to Catherine's defense under three headings: (1) whether there was proof for the virginity on which the queen so greatly relied; (2) whether marriage between brother and childless brother's widow was prohibited by positive or divine law, and if it were of divine law whether the Apostolic See could with reason dispense from such a law; and (3) whether the dispensation in question had been given with reason, and whether it was surreptitious.

The first point was then discussed in detail. "The queen seems to use ten arguments," as follows:

1. The marriage with Arthur lasted only five months, and during that time the prince was so weak and of such a delicate complexion that everyone believed him unable to perform the marriage act. *Answer*: "It could be said that" the queen admitted that they had both reached puberty and that they had slept together for several nights. The presumption is that they knew each other

---

[7] Surtz, pp. 984–86, citing the *Extractum registri*, ff. 43–47v. The articles were first submitted, by Alonso Cuevas, on January 23, 1531, and immediately withdrawn for correction; they were resubmitted on January 25; and on the 27th Cuevas accused the opposite party of contumacy in not appearing when cited and in not answering his articles. There also exists a French précis of the articles (LP V, 468). On February 15 Cuevas presented thirteen additional articles for the queen, and five more on March 20 and 22, dealing mainly with the threat of war (Surtz, pp. 989–90, 991). Articles testifying to Catherine's royal blood and exemplary virtue were submitted on October 4 (p. 994).

[8] Printed in Ehses, p. 216.

carnally. Potency is not proved by how one looks or by common opinion, but by other means.

2. Three witnesses heard others say that Arthur admitted the virginity. *Answer*: Hearsay evidence is not probative, nor is first-hand testimony from single witnesses.

3. "The queen is said to prove her virginity from her own assertion, as witnessed by six persons." *Answer*: The witnesses are single; besides, the queen's assertion was extrajudicial and not made under oath.

4. Henry VIII also admitted the virginity. *Answer*: As for the previous argument.

5 and 6. King Ferdinand and Queen Isabella spoke of her virginity. *Answer*: As above; the same response applies to their letters. Also, it was in their interest to speak thus.

7. Henry VII wanted to marry Catherine, and he was not likely to have done so if she had been known by his son Arthur. *Answer*: That this was the king's intention is proved only by hearsay. Because the king was rumored to have wanted to marry her does not mean that she was a virgin, since if the rumor were true he could have desired what was illicit, and then changed his mind.[9]

8 and 9. The inspection of the bedclothes of Arthur and Henry proves the virginity. *Answer*: Witnesses could prove nothing from Arthur's bedclothes unless they had observed all the times that the spouses were together and could have had intercourse. Furthermore, an examination of Henry's bedclothes does not necessarily prove Catherine's virginity, because doctors write that women who have had intercourse a thousand times can use various ploys and medicaments to make every man think that they are virgins; and they say besides that proof from bedclothes is untrustworthy.[10]

10. The bull of dispensation says that the marriage was "perhaps" consummated, and therefore was very much in doubt. *An-*

---

[9] Both sides seemed to assume that a marriage between father- and daughter-in-law would never have been permitted. Cf. Isabella's letter to Estrada, 11 April 1503: she said that such a marriage "would be a very evil thing—one never before seen, and the mere mention of which offends the ears" (SC I, 295). Isabella was horrified at the thought, even though she believed Catherine to be a virgin; but she was probably motivated more by her desire to see her daughter married to the king's son than she was by any thoughts of the incest involved.

[10] We remember that Wolsey alleged that consummation could be proved by Arthur's bedsheets (above, Chap. 3 at n. 10). But no witness could be found at the legatine court to confirm it.

swer: Although *forsan* is sometimes expressive of doubt, it is sometimes also used to state a fact,[11] and that the latter is the meaning of the bull can be gathered from the brief, which was issued on the same day and by the same pope; there it is affirmatively stated that the marriage was consummated. Furthermore, "even if it should be taken as expressing a doubt, it can be said that her virginity could not be deduced from this—quite the contrary, in fact, since the dispensation is requested for affinity."

Clearly, the author accepted the authenticity of the brief. I shall comment on this below, when I discuss his possible identity. On the second topic under discussion, that is, the nature of the law involved and the question of its indispensability, he stated only that he had nothing to say on the subject, "since the doubts themselves need no other demonstration."

On the question of the actual dispensation that was given, he made five observations:

1. The reason alleged (keeping the peace) was frivolous.

2. Some of the rulers had died before the marriage took place.

3. The statement that Henry and Catherine desired to get married would indicate that the pope thought that they were of age, whereas Henry was barely twelve and therefore not able to marry; also, the dispensation would have to remain in suspension until he came of age and got married, which seems to be contrary to law ("alienum a iure").

4. "Fourthly, it could be thought to be surreptitious because even if virginity were proved there remained the impediment of public honesty, which received no mention and was not dispensed from."[12]

5. The article introduced to verify the causes expressed in the dispensation proves nothing, for granted that witnesses said that there was war between Spain and England before 1501, they did not say how long before.

Henry himself had not dared to carry out his threat to Catherine to "dispute and maintain against all the world" that the bull of dispensation was insufficient even if she had been a virgin be-

---

11 He adopts the argument used by the queen's supporters. See Chap. 3 at n. 28 and Appendix A, nn. 73–74.

12 "Quarto posset dubitari an sit surreptitia quia etiam probata virginitate suberat impedimentum publicae honestatis, de quo nulla facta est mentio nec super eo dispensatum est." Ehses, p. 220.

cause of its failure to mention public honesty. To have done so would have come perilously close to admitting her virginity. In July 1531 the king instructed William Benet on the way he was to answer the allegation "which is by the queen and her agents invented," that she was not known by Arthur. He might say first of all, "whether it be so or no," that England was the best place for the truth to be known and tried. Furthermore, for the "certification" of the pope's conscience, "ye will show unto him, which our pleasure is ye do as of yourself, the depositions of the noble men of this our realm, which Dr. Kerne [Edward Carne] hath there exemplified." He was also to say that many other articles might be added which could be proved by "sundry noblemen yet living" concerning Arthur's potency and proof of carnal copula: first, that Arthur strongly solicited other women for carnal copula; second, that he frequently complained that he was not allowed to have intercourse more often with his wife, and manifested his need by showing his erect and inflamed member ("virgam etiam erectam et urentem ostentans"); third, that the queen was thought to have been left pregnant by Arthur, and that therefore Henry VII put off calling Henry Prince of Wales for several months (in case Catherine should bear a child who would inherit the title).[13] This was to be Henry's answer to the pontiff—almost two years after Clement's inquiry—as to what Catherine's status had been when he married her. But some time later he found out a way of insinuating the public-honesty argument without departing from his firm stand. He sent to Carne and Edmund Bonner, Benet's successor in Rome, the *libellus* that the queen's lawyers had submitted to the legatine court in answer to the objections that had been made against the marriage. Henry told his agents that they were to make use of the document to prove the queen's consummation in case the trial should begin.

How could the king have hoped to prove consummation from that politely devastating rebuttal? Let us listen to what he says:

[We] send unto you herewith the copy of a certain book presented afore the legates sitting here in judgment by the late [queen's counsel; in] which be contained divers answers [to the] objections then made against the pope's bulls of dispensation concerning the marriage bet[wixt us] and the said late queen—she consenting [and] assenting that they should be exhib[ited afore the] said legates, as her own counsel doth k[nowledge]

---

and ha[ve for true]. Whereby ye shall well perceive by the answers made to the eighth and ninth argument of that book that the said late queen's counsel and she also were inevitably constrained to confess and knowledge in the said answers that the marriage between Prince Arthur and her was consummate by carnal copulation, or else they must needs have granted that the said bull had been of none effect, as ye may gather of the said eighth and ninth argument and of the answers to them. For in the bull is expressed that the pope dispensed [upon affinity], which springeth not without carnal [copulation], and no mention is made of [the impediment called] justice of public honesty. [Wherefore, if there] were no carnal copulation, by reason where[of he] dispensed upon affinity, then the pope disp[ensed] upon nothing. And so his bull was nothing worth, and consequently for lack of a sufficient dispensation, the marriage was not good, the impediment of justice and of public honesty letting the same.[14]

This is very strange. What did the queen's lawyers say precisely? The eighth article reads, in effect: "Could the dispensation be said to be void because, of the two impediments present, namely, affinity and public honesty, public honesty was not dispensed upon? Or rather is not the contrary true, because both are mentioned explicitly and implicitly, and public honesty is also a necessary consequence?" The ninth article goes thus: "Is the marriage between Arthur and Catherine presumed to have been consummated from their having slept together? Or should it not rather be believed that the marriage was not consummated, and as a result no affinity was contracted and no impediment of divine law stands in the way, since consummation is not proved, and the queen swore an oath that she had never been known by Arthur, and also King Henry confessed the same thing several times?" What Henry did was to take the first parts of the answers to the two objections and treat them as if they were the response to a single objection; that is to say, he simply looked at the *rewording* of the objections and omitted the answers completely. The end product would read thus: "Could the dispensation be said to be void because, of the two impediments present, namely, affinity and public honesty, public honesty was not dispensed upon? Or is not the marriage between Arthur and Catherine presumed to have been consummated from their having slept to-

[14] Record Office SP 1/69, f. 154rv. Cf. SP VII, 359–60, and LP V, 836.4, and see Pocock, II, 495. Gairdner calendars this dispatch among the documents of February 1532.

gether?" With the proper use of ellipsis points the Latin makes sense grammatically.[15] But it makes sense in no other way. Did Henry mistake the meaning of the *libellus* by not recognizing its scholastic and canonistic form? The practice was first to state an objection positively, and give reasons for holding it; then the refutation was presented, with even better reasons to support it. Such incipient dialogues are frequently to be found in the glosses of canon law. It seems clear that Henry was familiar with the convention in general, but he mistook the way that it was applied in the *libellus*. For in spite of the fact that he speaks of the "answers" made to the eighth and ninth arguments, he took the eighth argument as the statement of an objection and the ninth as its answer. There is no suggestion that he was trying to perpetrate a hoax by consciously overlooking the real answers of the queen's counsel, for he sent along the *libellus*, with no caution against keeping it out of the hands of others. And this was not the last time he was to use the argument—he would press it on Archbishop Cranmer, and then would try it on the emperor after he had secured an English annulment.

The author of the *English Articles* ignored Henry's highly unconvincing argument, however, and took up only what the king set forth as the original objection, based on the failure of the bull to dispense specifically from the impediment of public honesty. This may, in fact, have been Henry's intention, and would account for the circumstance that in his letter the king purported to be quoting the objection addressed in the eighth article of the *libellus*, whereas he was substituting the version first suggested and later used by Wolsey, and brought up again by Henry to the queen after the legatine trial—namely, if virginity were proved, the failure to mention public honesty invalidated the dispensation.

In the event, the alleged defect in the bull must have been rejected as unimportant or nonexistent. The bull provided for a dispensation from "any impediment of affinity such as would arise from the foregoing," that is, a previous marriage with Henry's brother that had "perhaps been consummated."

15 "Utrum dispensatio possit dici nulla quia, cum affinitas et publicae honestatis iustitia subessent, non fuit super publicae honestatis impedimento dispensatum ... an praesumatur matrimonium inter serenissimum Arthurum et Catherinam fuisse consummatum ex cohabitatione et thori communione?" See Appendix A.

The fact that the impediment arising from an unconsummated marriage was usually called public honesty and not affinity, and that no mention was made of it in the dispensation when it had been revised at Isabella's request and the "perhaps" inserted, would no doubt have provided a loophole for the pope if he had been determined to invalidate the marriage. But there were authorities, including St. Thomas Aquinas, who considered affinity to begin, at least in a certain form, with the marriage contract.[16] Furthermore, the inclusion of public honesty under affinity was taken for granted in a very important decretal of Innocent III's, the one that put into effect the Fourth Lateran Council's decision to abolish the second and third genera of affinity and to reduce the prohibited degrees of consanguinity and of the first genus of affinity from the seventh to the fourth. In the ordinary gloss of Bernard of Parma, which invariably accompanied the *Decretals*, the question was raised whether public honesty of the second and third genera was also removed thereby. He first answered, typically, in the negative: "It seems not, since he says nothing about it." He then offered arguments to the contrary and concluded in the affirmative. It was, then, similarly assumed that public honesty of the first genus was reduced to the fourth degree. This decretal was alluded to by the queen's lawyers in refuting the form that the objection took at Blackfriars, and it would just as naturally have been used by her advocates in Rome.[17]

It is worth inquiring who the author or principal author of the *English Articles* might have been. We have not much to go on from the text itself, except the fact that the tone is always deferential, at least outwardly, and that the answers are hypothetical and tentative, always beginning with the words "It could be said that . . ." Such a style could, of course, have been adopted by the king's envoys, Carne or Bonner, or the lawyers retained by them in Rome, but a more likely possibility is a member of Clement's own curia, one favorable to Henry's side or at least open-minded, to whom the pope would have given the brief of the queen's case for comment on its weak points.

John Staphileus springs at once to mind. This man, a native of

16 See above, Chap. 1 after n. 28. Scarisbrick, pp. 190–91, discusses some of the proponents of this view.
17 See above, Chap. 7, n. 8, and Appendix A, n. 58.

Dalmatia who since 1512 had been Bishop of Šibenik, or Sebenico, a city on the coast north of Split,[18] was an auditor of the Rota (the English at first thought that he was Dean of the Rota as well). We recall that Wolsey desired Gardiner to consult him about the co-gency of the public-honesty argument, in spite of the cardinal's having just heard that Staphileus in his private interview with the pope had failed to support Wolsey as a legate in the papal commission.[19] He was, in the mind of Ambassador Mai, the author of Henry's whole absurd attempt to annul his marriage.[20] This was not true, of course, but he did support the attempt from early on. Wolsey had met him in France during the summer of 1527,

[18] Staphileus in his prefatory letter to Cardinal Oliver Carafa in his 1509 edition of Geminianus describes himself as "Ioannes Staphileus dalmatinus, utriusque iuris doctor in urbe mane legens" (see above, Chap. 7, n. 8). See P. B. Gams, *Series episcoporum ecclesiae catholicae* (Ratisbon, 1873), p. 419.

[19] Letter of Gardiner and Casale to Wolsey, 13 April 1528, delivered by Fox in person, LP IV, 4167. Surtz, "Henry VIII's Great Matter," p. 828, accepts Wolsey's designation of Staphileus as "The Dean and the Pope's Lieutenant of the Rota" on no better grounds than Wolsey's alleged scrupulosity about using right titles. Yet Wolsey was clearly wrong in considering him the current dean, since, as Surtz himself points out elsewhere, James Simonetta was dean from 1523 to July 17, 1528, and Paul Capisuchi from July 27, 1528, to November 7, 1533 (pp. 959, 1032); and I have not found any other source that names him dean earlier in his career. According to his epitaph in Šibenik, erected by his nephew and successor to the see, he is characterized only as having held a place among the auditors of the Rota ("unum ex Rotae auditoribus locum tenens," Surtz, p. 846, n. 3). It may be that Staphileus acted on occasion as the dean's lieutenant or surrogate, as Simonetta did for Capisuchi; but the term *locum tenens* as applied to Staphileus does not mean "lieutenant" but rather refers to one of the positions occupied by the twelve regular auditors, whose duties were sometimes filled by surrogate auditors. Cf. the entry for Rota Manual 142, in the Vatican Archives Index 1057 (compiled by archivist Hermann Hoberg): "1524–1527 Apr. 12; 1528 Oct. 1–1530 Sept. 9, coram Iohanne Staphileo ep. Sibinicen. locumtenenti (qui deci[di]t ante 1 Oct. 1528) et auditoribus eidem surrogatis, et coram Silvestro Dario." See also Hermann Hoberg, "Die Protokollbücher der Rotanotare von 1464 bis 1517," *Zeitschrift der Savigny-Stiftung für Rechtgeschichte, Kanonistische Abteilung*, 39 (1953), 177–227, esp. 212, for Staphileus's early career as an auditor (on p. 217, an auditor in 1493 is called vice-dean, "Rotae vicedecanus"). Cf. also Hoberg's "Die Amtsdaten der Rotarichter in den Protokollbüchern der Rotanotare von 1464 bis 1566," *Römische Quartalschrift*, 48 (1953), 43–78, esp. 62, 68, 71.

Surtz did not notice Staphileus's edition of Geminianus, but he does analyze another work of the bishop's, *De gratiis expectativis*, an amplification of a compilation by John Baptist Caccialupo, in which it is assumed that matrimonial dispensations can be given for just cause in degrees prohibited by divine law (pp. 842–44).

[20] Mai to Charles V, 4 August 1529, LP IV, 5827 (p. 2609); SC IV, part 1, 159.

and he came to England to investigate the matter; then, at the end of 1527, he set out for Italy, with the intention of convincing the pope of Henry's position. On the way he disputed the question with none other than John Fisher, Bishop of Rochester. Warmed by the memory of the exchange, he wrote to Wolsey afterward that Dr. Marmaduke, who had been present, could tell him with whom the victory had rested. He added that he would have given a small bishopric if only Wolsey and the king had been present to hear the discussion.[21]

But Staphileus was dead. His "seemingly silent death" occurred not long after Gardiner was to have sounded him out on public honesty.[22] His posthumous effect was small: the book that he wrote in support of the king was submitted as evidence during the legatine trial, and, at the same time, Mai was attempting to secure his papers in order to find out his arguments and prepare himself against them.[23]

Henry was not to get another man in court until the appointment of Silvester Darius as an auditor of the Rota shortly before the beginning of the legates' official proceedings in England. Darius left England for Rome on the very day that the legates met to summon the king and queen to appear before them, May 31, 1529.[24] Once arrived, he did yeoman's service for the king in attempting to persuade the pontiff that there were no official actions taking place in England and that there was no intention of coming to the point of passing a sentence—in other words, that there was no reason to honor the queen's appeal.[25] The auditor's zeal on Henry's behalf seems to have slackened after this, for we hear nothing of him again until more than two years later, toward the end of 1531, when he was passing through England on his way to Scotland as apostolic nuncio. He discussed the question of the annulment with Henry, and, as Mai cheerfully retailed the story from

21 Staphileus to Wolsey, from Bologna, 20 January 1528, LP IV, 3820.
22 Ehses, p. 254, gives the date of death as July 27, 1528, though citing Gams, p. 419, who says July 22; the latter date agrees with his epitaph. On July 2, Staphileus was writing from Viterbo about the French bishopric of Dol which had been promised to him but then given to another. See G. Molini, *Documenti di storia italiana* (Florence, 1836–37), II, 69–71; Ehses, p. 253.
23 LP IV, 5768.1.1; see Mai's letter of 4 August 1529.
24 LP V, p. 312.
25 Pocock, I, 244, 264; LP IV, 5766.

Rome, the king ended by insulting him when he saw that he was stoutly defending the preeminence of the Apostolic See. There is some reason to think that Darius was won over to the justice of the queen's side through the influence of the troublesome Nun of Kent, Elizabeth Barton.[26]

What then of Campeggio himself as author of the *Articles*? He was, after all, besides being Bishop of Salisbury, the Protector of England, and he had promised to advance Henry's cause in Rome. Later, when it was all over, the cardinal admitted that if the case had turned on the proofs of virginity contained in the remissorials, he would have had grave doubts about the justice of the queen's case; but since he considered it settled that the marriage was only unlawful by positive law, he had always been certain that she was in the right.[27] He might have been capable of writing this sort of searching examination of the queen's defense, especially since the author of the *Articles* does not try to defend the thesis that the law involved was indispensable—he simply says that the doubt had been raised, which was certainly true. But it is unlikely that Campeggio would have suggested that the testimony of all the witnesses was absolutely unacceptable on grounds of "singularity" (one wonders how the depositions collected on Henry's side would have survived a similarly rigorous application of this test); and particularly one would think Campeggio incapable of the indelicate innuendo that Catherine had falsified her virginity on her wedding night—although legally it was a point that certainly could be made.

Another possibility was the Bishop of Tarbes, cardinal since 1530. And there was, of course, Ghinucci, who had a part in most of the legal maneuvers on Henry's behalf during the long years in which his case was hanging fire. He had never been elevated to cardinal—the imperial cardinals always managed to defeat the king's efforts in that direction, although Clement himself favored it since he wanted to know what Henry was thinking (as if the red hat would make Ghinucci more candid)—but still, as Auditor of the Papal Chamber, he was in an influential position. Further-

---

[26] Ehses, p. 180; LP V, 738, 747; VII, 72.

[27] Ortiz to Charles V, 24 March 1534, Spanish text in SC V, part 1, 89, along with the kind of inaccurate paraphrase that one comes to expect of the editor.

more, after the death in September 1531 of the powerful and an-
tagonistic Cardinal Laurence Pucci, the nemetic Sanctorum Qua-
tuor of the dispatches, Ghinucci fell heir to the office of briefs,
where he was concerned with the granting of indults and bene-
fices.[28]

It was Ghinucci who along with Edward Lee, the future Archbishop of York, examined the original version of the brief of Julius
II in Spain. Since he at that time declared himself willing to stake
his life upon the judgment that it was a forgery, he may seem an
unlikely person to have written the *English Articles*, for the author therein accepts the brief as an authentic document and uses
it to advantage in precisely the way that Catherine had feared, by
pointing out its categorical assumption of the consummation of
her marriage with Arthur. But Ghinucci, as author, could simply
have been making a virtue of necessity, moderating his campaign
against the brief on the grounds that it was not likely to bear fruit.
It would have been in keeping with his unswerving dedication to
the king's cause to use every tool available in defending it.[29]

Another and perhaps even more likely possibility was the greatly
influential Peter Accolti, Cardinal of Ancona, who *was* a former
Dean of the Rota. We remember that it was he whom Wolsey
selected for Gardiner to consult to see if he could rest his conscience on the argument of Henry's ignorance of the dispensation.
That was in 1528. The emperor's ambassador meantime was hoping that he had safely secured the cardinal's services by promising
him the return of his confiscated manuscripts,[30] but he underestimated the effect of large-scale English bribery upon the "Old Man,"
as he was designated by Henry's agents (in contrast to the "Young
Man," the Cardinal of Ravenna, Ancona's nephew Benedict—another well-rewarded agent in His Royal Majesty's service).

[28] LP V, 748.
[29] There is a sad footnote to this story of loyal service: the Parliament of
1534, which verified Henry's annulment and remarriage, deprived not only
Campeggio of the see of Salisbury but also Ghinucci of Worcester—unless,
that is, these prelates should end their deplorable absenteeism and return
within four months to mind their episcopal duties. 25 Henry VIII c. 27, *Statutes*, III, 483–84. But Ghinucci was consoled with the cardinal's hat a year later.
[30] Mai to Charles V, 9 May 1529, SC IV, part 1, 11. He said that Ancona
thanked him with tears in his eyes, saying, "Those manuscripts contain the
key of all my works, and are the soul and life of a man of letters."

In one of their dispatches to England, Gregory Casale and Benet discussed the bishoprics and abbeys that were being arranged for the Accoltis. They went on to give an example of the sort of thing that Ancona was doing for the king, describing the way in which he constantly opposed the imperial supporters. On one occasion, for instance, in the presence of Catherine's advocates, he turned to the pope and asked, "Doth not Your Holiness know that the queen was Prince Arthur's, [the king's] brother's wife?" (he of course meant consummated wife), and said that "if His Holiness would pretend ignorance thereof, he could not do it, for it was notorious. And if His Holiness did not know it before, he said that then he told His Holiness of it; and afterward said constantly to him that His Holiness could not give sentence in the cause."[31]

Casale and Benet in the same letter reported the cardinal's promise that if Henry were to come to Rome and prove that the queen had been known by Arthur, he would not only cast his vote for Henry but would persuade all the others to do likewise. "And, sir," they continued, "because he might see what may be proved *circa carnalem copulam*, we have showed him the attestations that Master Carne brought with him, which as yet he could not peruse, by reason he hath kept his bed this eight days or nine of the gout." Carne's attestations no doubt included not only the lega-tine depositions but also the *libellus* which Henry believed to contain the queen's admission of consummation.

Ancona told the king's men that the matter would be clearer if Henry could prove that, before the marriage contract between him and Catherine was made, there was substantial doubt about whether the dispensation could be granted, and if he could further prove that this doubt might have come to Catherine's attention.[32] The implication of course would be that this was why she insisted on her virginity even at that early date.

Ancona justified the services for which he was being so richly recompensed by saying that everything he did was in accord with his conscience: he really believed in the justice of Henry's case. Yet he admitted that he did not dare to speak his opinion too openly, for then his dealings with the English agents were sure to be uncovered, to the loss of his reputation and the frustration of Henry's whole purpose.[33]

He continued to urge Henry to get on with the case. If he did not send his powers of attorney soon, the cardinal said, it would be difficult to continue delaying the process much longer without appearing to favor the king's cause more than he should. (Carne had in fact had Henry's mandate all along, but he was not to use it unless all else failed.) The king's agents reported still another, more important, reason for apprehension: that since "he could do Your Highness most good in the principal cause, and if he, being so aged, should die before that Your Highness come to the cause, the same should be frustrate of that help that he could do and show in the same."[34]

That was written in July 1532. On Christmas Eve Bonner wrote from Bologna that their fears had come to pass: Ancona was dead.[35]

Could he then have been the compiler of the *Anglici articuli*? The remissory reports were not, of course, officially heard in court until July 1533, but the author must have prepared and submitted the *Articles* a good many months earlier, because he did not make use of the treaty that was struck between Henry VII and Ferdinand and Isabella arranging the match between Henry and Catherine. This instrument stated definitely that Catherine's first marriage had been consummated, a piece of evidence that escaped the notice, or dropped from the memory, of the king's men after the legatine trial. It was only brought to the attention of Henry and his councillors in January 1533 (the Spaniards noticed it more than two years earlier but kept it to themselves). It was seized upon with great commotion and it served as the excuse to precipitate the action that followed, there being now, with Anne's pregnancy, greater urgency than before.[36]

The *English Articles* must therefore have been drawn up sometime before the latter part of February 1533, which was the earliest

---

[33] Casale and Benet to Henry VIII, 29 April 1532, *ibid.*, pp. 252–53.

[34] *Ibid.*, p. 290 (15 July 1532).

[35] LP V, 1658. The cardinal died on December 11. See Surtz, p. 1134.

[36] Bonner back in England wrote to Benet on January 31, 1533, that he had just learned of the treaty (LP VI, 101). For the Spanish correspondence, see LP IV, 6655, 6758. See above, Chap. 3 at n. 10; Chap. 6 at nn. 7, 47; also Chap. 11 below.

that the news of the treaty's discovery could have reached Rome. The author would not have failed to use a document to which the king attached so much importance, or omitted so weighty a rebuttal to Catherine's argument that her parents had asserted her virginity in their letters.

It is then very possible that the *Articles* were drawn up sometime in 1532, and that the Cardinal of Ancona was their author. He is at least the most likely of the several candidates. After his death, his vote in the matter of Henry's marriage was left with his nephew Benedict, who eventually decided not to disclose it. He did, however, give the English ambassadors certain writings (presumably by his uncle) in the king's cause, and it may be that the *Articles* were among them.[37]

[37] Benet to Henry VIII, 11 March 1533, LP VI, 277. Benedict at this time promised to hand over the rest of the writings, which were not at hand (they were in Rome), at a later time. But on May 28, Benet wrote from Rome that the Young Man still had not sent them the rest of his writings, "whereof I have no little marvel" (LP VI, 548). See Surtz, pp. 1135-36.

CHAPTER NINE

The Trial at the Papal Court

SHORTLY after Bonner finally left England for Rome on St. Valentine's Day, 1533 (his departure had been delayed because of consultations over the newly found treaty),[1] Henry wrote to his agents about the fresh arguments that they could use. The pope had recently informed Sir Gregory that the opposing lawyers "agree that the pope in our cause may not dispense without an urgent cause; which opinion His Holiness thinketh much more doth advance the goodness of our matter than the general opinion of the divines and lawyers on our part, which do affirm that the pope may in no wise dispense." Very well, then. The emperor was maintaining that there had been a severe state of war between the rulers of England and Spain at that time. To satisfy the pope that this had not been the case, Henry's agents were to show him that the treaty said these princes were already more friendly with each other than any other rulers in Christendom. The only reasons given for the marriage were the continuation and augmentation of the existing amity, and the virtuous modesty and other qualities of the queen. "In which league is also plainly mentioned and expressed, in two places thereof, that the marriage between our said brother and her was solemnized and perfectly consummate, whereby, and by the depositions of a great number of noble and honorable personages which heretofore by their oath have been examined upon the same, manifestly and plainly appeareth to all indifferent hearers without doubt thereof that the queen was carnally known by our said brother Prince Arthur, and the same dispensation so proceeding without urgent cause to be reputed *invalida*."[2]

1 Chapuys to Charles V, 15 February 1533, LP VI, 160.
2 Pocock, II, 439–40. Henry was still collecting evidence on consummation as

The king's envoys at this time were busy about other things. On the 22d of February a clear triumph was scored: Thomas Cranmer was appointed Archbishop of Canterbury. After this, they labored chiefly for the revocation of the papal briefs against Henry. The long drawn-out business of offering excuses for the king's non-appearance was also continued, until finally, on July 4, 1533, a last declaration was given against his excusator. A few days later word came that Henry had married Anne, and it was determined to let him know that he had incurred the penalties threatened in the briefs.

The trial at last got under way, four years almost to the day after Catherine's appeal had reached Rome.[3] This time it was the king who was held in contempt of court, and it is ironic that the imminent summer vacation again threatened interruption before matters could be brought to a close. As a result only five of the remissory reports were presented.

The Rota examined the whole case, and the current dean, Paul Capisuchi, reported everything in three sessions of the Consistory. Care was taken to have all the cardinals and auditors of the Rota fully informed on all points, because the English were busily urging objections and doubts, and the French cardinals were inclined toward the king's side. There was no need to fear, however; the Consistory duly declared that the prohibition against marrying one's brother's widow was not *de iure divino*.

It was all up for Henry now: a sentence in favor of the queen was inevitable. But then, in the Consistory of July 9, the English exploded a bombshell as unexpected as Campeggio's announcement of adjournment at Blackfriars: they objected that Henry had had witnesses examined when the case was being heard before the legates; their testimony had not been produced at Rome, and the pope could not legitimately pronounce sentence in the case without studying it, and, moreover, without seeing the records of the entire trial that had been held in England.

The bomb could have failed to go off; the Spaniards did their best to defuse it. They pointed out that the queen had reported

---

late as 1534. See the notarial certificate of the testimony of Margaret Clerke touching on the consummation of the marriage of Catherine and Arthur, 31 January 1534, LP VII, 128.

[3] For a Spanish report of the proceedings see LP VI, 808; cf. Carne's letter of 12 July 1533, *ibid.*, 809.

the legatine actions up to the time of her appeal, and they urged that the further proceedings of the court could not legally be admitted to the appeals court. This had been Mai's position from the beginning.[4] In addition, they said that Henry's witnesses could prove nothing against the marriage. Now that the law forbidding it had been declared to be a man-made and positive law rather than a divine mandate, any proofs alleging consummation, Henry's youth, his protest, and the absence of war did not matter. The reason of conserving the peace was valid. The causes brought to light by the remissorial letters would have been sufficient for a dispensation even if the marriage had been forbidden by divine law, which it was not. Even if it could not be absolutely demonstrated that the queen was a virgin at the time of her marriage to Henry, there was no doubt about the consummation of that second union, and it could not be dissolved because of the doubtfully consummated first marriage. Therefore, even if the law were divine, the dispensation was good; Henry had acted on it for many years and had deprived himself of the right of objecting against it.

Here then were all the reasons that the pope himself had urged to Henry almost four years before—the eminently reasonable interpretation of the laws on marriage and dispensation that would have eliminated the curial system of opening and closing loopholes if it had been adopted wholeheartedly. But, as I noted when discussing the pope's letter to Henry, the ecclesiastical courts did in fact have it at their discretion to make use of legal technicalities to invalidate a marriage. Therefore, even though the law in question was declared to be a human one and dispensable by the pope, it would doubtless have been fairly easy for the Rota to find the king's marriage null on the grounds of a faulty license (dispensation), if it had so desired. John Staphileus, one of the auditors of the Rota, had been confident that it could be done, and he unquestionably spoke from experience.

As it was, however, the sympathy as well as the legal opinion of the majority of the curia seemed clearly on the side of the queen. Nevertheless, even though the Spaniards' arguments were doubtless accepted as just, and though it was no doubt admitted also that the pope could legitimately have proceeded to sentence, nothing was done. Instead, in keeping with the policy of delaying the

---

4 Reported in Bryan's letter to Henry VIII, ca. 18 June 1530, Pocock, I, 324.

principal matter, a policy that had been abundantly demonstrated even before the objection about the necessity for the legatine records was brought up, the pope and the cardinals decided to use another method to express their disapproval of the king: all that he had done to the prejudice of the queen was to be revoked *ex officio pastorali.* Two days later, on July 11, in the final Consistory, Clement pronounced a sentence restoring the queen to her original state as Henry's wife, annulling his marriage to Anne and pronouncing all issue illegitimate, and declaring that the king had incurred excommunication and the other penalties designated in the previous briefs. A period of grace and time for repentance was allowed the king, however—and was continually extended, so that Henry managed to live out the remaining thirteen years of his life without a sentence of excommunication ever being put into full effect against him.[5]

According to Carne, even the imperial cardinals admitted that they could not legally proceed without the legatine records; and we have the Cardinal of Jaén's own testimony that the queen's presentation was found to be defective.[6] It might seem surprising that it should have been so. Mai long before had been informed that the records would be required, and began writing for them at least as early as February 1531. Chapuys wrote in reply to say that he could not see that the records were really necessary; it sounded in fact like another of the pope's excuses. Moreover, if Campeggio was unable to get them, no one could.[7]

But somehow Chapuys did secure them, and, after sending off copies on three separate occasions he was chagrined to learn from Mai's by now frantic letters that none of them had arrived. Finally, on October 24, 1531, he sent off a fourth copy, with instructions to the courier to use extreme care and caution. The last letter we have from Mai on the subject is dated 6 November: the records still had not arrived. The last copy that Chapuys sent would not have had time to arrive yet; but in fact it did arrive eventually, and the records, which were subscribed by John Talcarne and

[5] Even Paul III's bull of excommunication was never completely promulgated. See Scarisbrick, p. 361.
[6] LP VI, 809, 940.
[7] LP V, 102, 112. Cf. LP IV, 5866. Gayangos, SC IV, part 1, xx, cites letters of October and November 1530 in which Mai and Chapuys discuss the records, but no such statements appear in the calendar itself.

John Clerk and authenticated by Peter Ligham, Official of the Court of Canterbury, on October 21, 1531, were submitted to the papal court on December 11, as is revealed in the acts of the case recently discovered by Edward Surtz.

However, the records in question turn out to be no more than the materials referred to by the Spaniards on July 9, 1533, that is, the legatine actions up to the time of Catherine's final appeal.[8] As for the rest of the records, the queen's advocates were caught empty-handed. There seems to have been no thought of demanding to see the depositions that Carne had been using to convince the cardinals of the justice of Henry's cause, or of appealing to the testimony of those cardinals who had seen them. Or if these expedients were suggested, they were rejected as unacceptable.

After the pope made his pronouncement of July 11, 1533, *super attentatis*, that is, against Henry's attempted divorce and remarriage, Catherine's advocates proceeded to present the rest of the remissorials, so that the work of the court might be carried on during the vacation, and the expedition of the case urged at the next session.[9]

They were to have no such luck. The adjournment was extended until well into the following year, in spite of Catherine's pleas and all the prodding that her supporters were capable of. Finally, at the end of February, the case was reopened. Bishop Simonetta, Capisuchi's usual surrogate, presented the queen's case in Consistory on February 27, 1534, going through the whole process and the remissorials. They were starting all over again.

Ortiz objected: as from the start, he wanted the question of divine law decided first, and then the need for the remissory matters would be eliminated. It was well known that the point of law had already been determined in the previous year. Henry, in fact, had been informed of the decision, as Ortiz now learned from Simonetta. The king had been told that the verdict must inevitably go against him, and this was why he had rejected the proposal made at Marseilles to hold the court at Calais or some other neutral place.[10]

8 LP V, 421, 437, 488, 491, 516. For the contents of the legatine materials in the *Extractum registri* as reported by Surtz, see above, Chap. 4, nn. 2, 11, 25, 31.
9 LP VI, 808.
10 LP VII, 230, 282, 286.

Nevertheless, the question of divine law was brought up once again in the Consistory of March 4. But by this time some of the cardinals were beginning to share Ortiz's impatience: they had settled these matters the year before, and they resented repeating the deliberations; they felt that it was derogatory of their previous decision. Campeggio especially was of this mind, for as he told Ortiz the day after the final sentence (as we have seen), he believed that the proofs of virginity alleged in the remissorials were inadequate, but he agreed with the emperor's proctor in thinking that they were not necessary.[11] In the end, the cardinals refused to prolong the review and simply referred to their former judgment. There is, by the way, no indication that the demand for the legatine records was ever fulfilled; the responsibility for producing them had been placed upon the king. He was to have presented by October 1 all the processes or writings that he intended to use. It seems likely that Henry did have a carefully censored version of the acts prepared, but that he never sent it. I am speaking of the notarial record that now rests in the Cambridge University Library, which I analyzed above: Nicholas Wootton's testimonial letter at the end bears the same date as the term set for the production of the records, October 1, 1533.[12]

At last—at long last—came the time for sentencing. On March 23, 1534, it was solemnly declared that the marriage between Henry and Catherine "was and is valid and canonical." That was all: no explanations or justifications, no reference to divine law or consummation or dispensation; merely a simple, straightforward declaration vindicating Catherine, at a time when it could no longer help her. At this very moment Parliament was deliberating over the Act of Succession and the other statutes that were to seal off Henry's realm from the universal Church.

The vote of the cardinals present was unanimous, according to Ortiz and Count Cifuentes. Ortiz thought that the French cardinals had purposely stayed away from Rome because they could not in conscience cast their vote against the queen. Charles was informed of those who were to be given rewards for their special services in carrying the matter through. It is pleasant to know that,

[11] See above, Chap. 8 at n. 27.
[12] LP VI, 808. See above, Chap. 4 at n. 2, and below, Chap. 12 at n. 11.

of these beneficiaries of the Empire, Cardinal Farnese, who was to be made pope later in the year, would be satisfied with a gracious letter.[13]

As a postscript, Ortiz noted that a month earlier the pope had allowed a Neapolitan, for a fee of fifteen hundred ducats, to marry the sister of his first wife, by whom he had had four children. According to Ortiz, this in itself would have been enough for a sentence in favor of the queen.[14] It was proof, perhaps he was saying, that the urgent reason in such cases need be nothing more than a handsome stipend.

[13] SC V, part 1, 84; LP VII, 429.
[14] LP VII, 370 (p. 153); Spanish text in SC V, part 1, 90.

Part Three

THE KING'S WAY

Let me not to the marriage of true minds
Admit impediments.

—Shakespeare, SONNETS

CHAPTER TEN

The Search for Academic Approval

We have already observed from a distance, as it were, some of the measures that Henry took in the years after the closing of the legatine court to forward his great matter. At the same time that he was thinking up reasons not to be bound by the summons to Rome, he was trying to influence opinion there in case he should have to obey. While he was toying with the idea of a forceful assertion of the queen's public honesty (see the end of Chapter 6, above), he was planning his campaign to win over scholarly opinion in the academies of Christendom.

It was this latter project that was to occupy him most during the next year or two. The idea of obtaining the support of the learned world began on a local level, and, of course, much earlier than 1529. For example, we have seen the unsuccessful attempt to gain Fisher's approval, and the success that was achieved with Robert Wakefield, the Hebraic specialist; the latter's offer to defend the king's position in all the universities of Christendom is an indication of how naturally the notion would occur.[1] Foreign aid was soon enlisted—Staphileus was invited over from France well before the end of 1527. Already by the beginning of December Wolsey was telling the pope that Henry had consulted many theologians and canonists of the most stunning learning and ability (he is almost comical in the way that he lauds Henry's hordes of experts); all of them had discovered fatal flaws in the bull, and it was asserted by a good many ("a variis multisque ex his doctoribus") that the pope could not dispense at all in the first degree

---

[1] See above, Chap. 1 at n. 12.

of affinity, though Henry himself did not go so far as that. Almost as a proof of the king's moderation on the point, Wolsey inserted into the same packet the request for a new dispensation in that very degree. The allegation of widespread professional support was also incorporated into the drafts of the decretal bulls, which the cardinal also enclosed.[2]

The scruple about the divorce allegedly came from France in the first place, and it was not long before Henry's men were actively trying to win the approval of the University of Paris, which they considered to be the Athens of the academies. A consultation of the Paris theologians was held on October 21, 1528. A vote was taken and a simple majority found for Henry. Dr. Moscosco, a supporter of the queen who was present, denied that the determination had any validity, apart from the fact that the required two-thirds majority was not had; for many of those counted on Henry's side were actually dubious, since they held that the pope could dispense for such a marriage for an urgent cause, but that in their judgment no such urgent cause existed when Julius II allowed the match.[3] It was the next month, we remember, that Henry made his speech at Bridewell, in which he affirmed, according to Hall, that he had asked the opinion of the greatest scholars in Christendom.

The following year, even before the legates had held their first plenary session, Campeggio heard that Henry's agents were back consulting the divines at Paris;[4] and shortly after the trial had recessed Bishop du Bellay of Bayonne reported that Wolsey and the king very much wanted him to collect the opinions of learned men in France.[5] It was in September that Catherine first heard rumors of the plan that Henry had of sending John Stokesley to the University of Paris. Tunstall confirmed the report the next month, and at the end of November Henry was waiting for Stokesley's news. Meanwhile Chapuys had already received information that some of the Parisian doctors were absolutely convinced that the marriage was good and indissoluble, and that no amount of pressure from either King Francis or King Henry would be able

2 Wolsey to Gregory Casale, 5 December 1527, Burnet, IV, 20–21, 26, 29–30.
3 SC III, part 2, 829–30.
4 Letter of 4 June 1529, Ehses, p. 99.
5 Letter of 23 August 1529, LP IV, 5862.

to persuade the university to declare otherwise. Catherine had been strengthened by this news when, a little later, she boldly confronted Henry's prediction of Parisian support with the assertion that a fair poll of learned opinion would come out overwhelmingly in her favor.[6]

It was about this time that Thomas Cranmer appeared on the scene. The story is told by John Foxe, the martyrologist, who drew in part at least on the report of Ralph Morice, later Cranmer's secretary, that it was Cranmer who, in the late summer of 1529, first suggested the idea of canvassing the universities. The account cannot be altogether true, since, as we have seen, the University of Paris had long been the object of Henry's attentions. Perhaps Cranmer suggested extending the net. But more important was the reason he allegedly gave for the project, according to Foxe: if the king could be sufficiently assured of the invalidity of the marriage, he could "proceed to a final sentence" (presumably by having it annulled in a local ecclesiastical court), and there would be no need for an appeal to Rome. Henry was delighted with Cranmer's ideas and had him compose a treatise on the marriage; he also approved of Cranmer's suggestion to commit the question to the universities of Oxford and Cambridge. Cranmer was no doubt the "marvellous and serious wise man" who was encouraging Henry at this time, of whom the Earl of Wiltshire (Anne's father), in the company of Cranmer, was to inform Charles V. This man had told the king that he would not be considered pious but rather impious if he transgressed his Master's law for the sake of a servant (that is, the pope).[7]

---

6 SC IV, part 1, 238, 305, 351–52. See above, Chap. 6 at n. 65.

7 LP IV, 6111 (p. 2729). For Foxe, see *Acts and Monuments*, 4th ed. (London, n.d.), VIII, 7–9. G. R. Elton, *Policy and Police*, p. 178, finds the first public statement of the "local solution" (the "private" origin of which I here attribute, as likely, to Cranmer in 1529) in *A Glass of the Truth*, which appeared in September 1532: Parliament should find a way to instruct the metropolitans of the realm to conclude the affair, "their unjust oath to the pope notwithstanding" (Pocock, II, 418–19). Elton associates the solution with the new policy of Thomas Cromwell, which triumphed in May and June 1532, after Sir Thomas More resigned as chancellor; and he dates the actual composition of the *Glass of the Truth* statement before Archbishop Warham's death on August 23, 1532, on the grounds that both metropolitans would not be referred to if one were dead (pp. 176, 179). But it may have been the prospect of a pliable new metropolitan like Cranmer that inspired the statement; see the next chapter below. Warham had been sounded out on the plan of a local

Cranmer, perhaps as Wiltshire's chaplain, joined him on his embassy to the emperor at the beginning of 1530. But before departing, Cranmer took the book that he had composed to Cambridge, and had some success in winning several of the learned doctors to his view. Later on, when Henry's letters were read to a general assembly of two hundred of the doctors, M.A.'s, and B.A.'s, it was voted that the king should be answered by "indifferent men," not including therefore "all such as had allowed Dr. Cranmer's book, inasmuch as already they had declared their opinion."[8]

Henry had a difficult time of it in Oxford and Cambridge. Apart from any question of the rightness or wrongness of his position, or of the motives that were known or suspected to be behind his desire for the annulment, he seriously underestimated the intelligence of the recipients of his letters. What were these scholars to think when he wrote that the greatest clerks in Christendom both at home and abroad had affirmed and subscribed to the opinion "that it is against the divine and natural law to marry the wife of one's brother deceased without children"?[9] They knew as well as Catherine that this was not true.

Finally, after much bullying, in early March, an allegedly universal vote was secured at Cambridge affirming it to be "more probable" than not that it was against the divine law to marry one's brother's wife who had been carnally known. A month later a similar statement was obtained at Oxford.

These determinations were almost worse than nothing, but they would have to do. The universities had carefully avoided saying that such a marriage was against natural law, and that the pope could not dispense from it. Far less did they specify that the ban

---

trial in 1531 and had refused to go along with it; and in February 1532 Norfolk tried unsuccessfully to get support for the idea that the case should be tried in the temporal jurisdiction. See Mortimer Levine, "Henry VIII's Use of His Spiritual and Temporal Jurisdictions in His Great Causes of Matrimony, Legitimacy, and Succession," *Historical Journal*, 10 (1967), 3–10, esp. 3–4.

[8] Gardiner to Henry VIII, February 1530, Burnet, IV, 130. Jasper Ridley, *Thomas Cranmer*, p. 27, conjectures that Cranmer's personal appearance at Cambridge took place before his meeting with Henry. On Cranmer "the wise man," see Ridley, p. 30 and n.

[9] Letter to Cambridge, 16 February 1530, LP IV, 6218. The determinations are collected in *Dodd's Church History of England*, ed. M. A. Tierney, I (London, 1839), 369–78, except for that of Ferrara, for which see Rymer, XIV, 397.

included a virginal widow as well as one who had consummated her first marriage.

They would have to produce better results abroad. It must have been disconcerting for Henry to hear from Bishop Ghinucci, writing early in February 1530, that there were no universities of theologians in Italy at all; and that, furthermore, he did not think it wise to attempt to get the opinions of individual theologians while the emperor was in the vicinity. But within a fortnight Richard Croke was to write that they had gone ahead and begun to collect signatures.[10] By mid-year it was the turn of the Signory at Venice to be disconcerted: when the incensed Spanish ambassador presented them with a determination of some friars adorned with the official seal of the University of Padua, they could only reply that they had not known that there was a college of divines at Padua.[11]

Henry had specific instructions for his agents: they were to try to get the theologians to say that the law was divine and indispensable, and the canon lawyers to say simply that it was divine, if they would not admit indispensability; they were also to declare the brief a forgery and the bull inadequate by reason of Henry's nonage and his protestation.[12]

The king's conviction that the theologians were the hard-line supporters of the Levitical degrees and the canonists the laxists was no doubt qualified when he heard the reports of the voting at the University of Angers on May 7. The faculty of theology had come to the discouraging conclusion that such a marriage was not against either divine or natural law, even when the first marriage had been consummated. The faculty of canon and civil law, however, had decided that an indispensable divine and natural law stood in the way—when, that is, the first marriage had been consummated. Though he had no liking for the rider at the end of the latter determination, Henry gratefully accepted it, and hoped that word of the former would not be spread abroad.

Opinions similar to that of the Angers Law School came in from

10 LP IV, 6205 (p. 2785), 6229.

11 LP IV, 6514. Surtz, "Henry VIII's Great Matter," surprisingly does not deal with these doubts about the existence of a theological college at Padua, but rather makes it clear that such a college did indeed exist, and he quotes from its records (pp. 58–61, 68–69, 95–97).

12 Pocock, I, 296–97 (delivered to Croke by Ghinucci).

the law faculty at Paris on May 23 (by a simple majority) and from the theology faculty at Bourges on June 10. Both these decisions stated that the prohibition was indispensable when consummation had occurred, but did not specify the kind of law involved.

But none of these decisions came up to the earliest continental determination, that of the University of Orléans, which had been delivered on April 5. The faculty there had declared that such marriages were against the divine law and that the law did not admit of dispensation. They did not mention consummation. An even better decision was handed out by some divines of the theological college of the University of Bologna on June 10, the same date as the Bourges determination. Here it was declared that the law was both divine and natural, and indispensable. Other similarly impeccable declarations were received from the Parisian theologians on July 2, again by a simple majority, and, more than two months later, from Toulouse (September 17) and Ferrara (September 24). The Padua determination (July 1) was flawed, like that of Orléans, only by the failure to mention natural law.

Henry was disturbed when he learned of the defect in the Padua decision and sent back instructions to try to have it redone in the form used by the Bologna theologians—though if possible with a more eloquent preface. But the king's agents were no more able to get a new determination out of the friars than was the emperor's man, who sought to have them specify that consummation was necessary, if they would not retract their first statement or declare the king's marriage indissoluble. They were already in too much trouble with the Signory to want any more.[13] We recall that when Rodrigo Niño was speaking with John Casale he asserted, without contradiction from Casale, that the Padua friars had specified that the law named by them as indispensable presupposed that the first marriage had been consummated. This was the received doctrine on the subject of affinity, and it would have been unusual to affirm that public honesty (the sole existing impediment where no consummation had occurred) came under as severe a prohibition.

The need for consummation was given special attention by the lawyers at Bologna,[14] and doubtless this point was an important

13 LP IV, 6581, 6591, 6633.
14 LP IV, 6633.

reason for their failure to issue a satisfactory determination to match that of their theological coresidents.

We must remember that all during the last part of 1529 and the first half of 1530 Henry was stewing over the answer that he should make to Pope Clement's claim that no divine law was involved in his case, especially if Catherine's first marriage had not been consummated—which she left up to Henry to declare. By the time he had finally determined to reply to the pope's letter of October 7, 1529, both of the English and five of the foreign university decisions had come in, and five of these seven pronouncements insisted on the necessity of consummation.

If, therefore, Henry had had the nerve to carry out his threat to urge the public-honesty defect in the bull (and it could be argued that he did so indirectly a couple of years later, as a backstop to an argument for consummation), there was no serious danger that he would push it to the extent of irrevocably proving Catherine's virginity unless he was absolutely guaranteed of Clement's favorable reaction—which he knew from the pope's letter of October 7, 1529, was by no means the case.

Clement there indicated his belief that Catherine had indeed been dispensed from public honesty. He further suggested that, in the event that the dispensation were shown to be faulty, the proper course would be simply to grant a new dispensation and validate the marriage retroactively. Such a *sanatio in radice* could not, of course, be effected without Henry's renewed consent to the marriage. But his refusal to give consent would demonstrate his lack of good will in the matter.

If the king had gone ahead with his threat and if the pope had accepted the queen's public honesty as an invalidating cause, Henry could simply have proceeded to marry Anne. He would be secure in his own opinion that affinity came from marriage, not from coitus; and he would hope that the nature of his relationship with Anne would never come to the attention of his former canonical and theological supporters. But, on the other hand, if the pope did not accept the public-honesty argument, the king would have been left with a virgin bride on his hands, so to speak. He would then have to seek public support for his personal view that the indispensable divine law covered even the quasi-affinity of public honesty. And he would have to achieve this without bringing up the embarrassing question of whether it also covered affinity *ex coitu illicito*. But the latter question would inevitably arise in the widespread debate on the nature of affinity that would have followed; it did in fact arise, in any case. Therefore if the traditional view were to prevail against Henry's bribery and high-pressured cajolery, he would lose on both fronts. Not only would his former supporters in the indispensable school of thought be unable to give him any help in breaking away from Catherine, because she was not related to him by affinity, but they would, furthermore, have to forbid his marriage to Anne under any circumstance, because she was related to him in an inviolable degree of affinity.

Such, then, was the substance of Henry's meditations in the summer of 1530. As we saw, he decided for the moment to ignore what the pope had to say about his knowledge of the queen's virginity, or lack of it. Instead, he simply contested the pontiff's assertion that scholarly opinion denied the existence of a divine law in the matter.

At the end of November 1530 Chapuys reported that the eight continental determinations had been handed over to Archbishop Warham. For some unexplained reason the ninth determination, that of Ferrara, was never utilized, even though the perfection of its formulation was matched only by those of the University of Toulouse and of the Bolognese and Parisian theologians.

The pronouncements were likely to be printed, Chapuys said, and so they were, at once. At the end of January 1531 the report came that the pope had read them in a text printed in English, and that he was highly displeased by what he saw. Some months later a more substantial edition came off the press, in which the determinations in their original Latin were followed by a lengthy white paper, also in Latin, which justified the king's position. Thus Clement's complaint that the university decisions were unaccompanied by reasons from Holy Scripture and the sacred canons would now be groundless. The king's treatise, however, had actually been composed by John Stokesley, Edward Fox, and the Italian Franciscan Nicholas de Burgo in the autumn of 1529, long before any of the university determinations had been secured,[15] and it remained to be seen how cogent were the reasons it pro-

---

[15] LP IV 6738, and V, 68; Pocock, II, 396 (see above, Chap. 6 at n. 44); LP VIII, 1054; A. F. Pollard, *DNB* Stokesley.

vided. John Fisher started composing an answer immediately, and Ortiz, in Rome, had already received and read by the middle of July 1531 his rebuttal to the first chapters. The doctor summarized the king's book by saying that it used rhetoric rather than reason, and that it cited many authors for him who were really against him.[16]

Fisher finished his long treatise by November, and Chapuys sent it off at once. At the same time the translators of the king's Latin book, including Sir Thomas Elyot and Cranmer, completed their task of rendering the work into English. Cranmer had also made some additions and alterations. The result was issued as *The Determinations of the Most Famous and Most Excellent Universities of Italy and France That It Is So Unlawful for a Man to Marry His Brother's Wife That the Pope Hath No Power to Dispense Therewith.*[17] The book was circulated throughout the realm forthwith, and was no doubt bestowed upon likely readers free of charge.

The *Determinations* treatise contained some of the usual arguments proving the Levitical prohibitions to be absolute moral laws, but it set them forth in a very simple-minded and homiletic style. It avoided the real difficulties against Henry's position and sought to give an impression of unanimous support from the learned and saintly voices of the past. Here, for example, is what the composite author had to say about the bearing of carnal copula upon these divine laws of Leviticus:

Among all, there is one thing that I would have thee, gentle indifferent reader, specially to mark, which divers of these holy and approved doctors do hold also, that the brother cannot marry a woman that is but only handfast unto his brother, and if he do the marriage cannot stand by help of any dispensation, and that all such marriages must needs be utterly broken, lest carnal persons should apply their minds and be encouraged by such beastly examples to do likewise.

We are given the names and explicit opinions of only two of these divers previously quoted doctors, namely, Nicholas of Lyre and Hugh of St. Victor. Nicholas allegedly held that Adonijah had violated the Levitical law in desiring to marry Abishag, the girl that David in his old age had used as a bedwarmer and had left

16 LP V, 342, 378.
17 LP V, 546.

"a clean virgin." The gentle indifferent reader was to assume, of course, with Lyre, that she had been David's wife.

As for Hugh of St. Victor, he was quoted as saying that though an unconsummated marriage was not symbolic of the union between God and his Church, it did symbolize the union between God and the soul; therefore it was a true marriage: "For true marriage is before any fleshly meddling, and marriage may be holy without any such thing; it should doubtless not be so fruitful if such meddling were not, but marriage is much cleaner if no such thing be in it."

"Wherefore," according to Hugh, "the very, true, perfect, and full marriage is the same company, conversation, and living together, the which is consecrate by the league or bond of spousage or promise that one doth make to the other, when both of them by their free and willing promise do make themselves debtors the one to the other, and do willingly bind themselves by covenant that from henceforth the one will never depart from the other," and so on. In other words, since carnal coupling did not give rise to the essence of marriage, its absence made no difference. "And therefore this only consent and agreement of their minds is thought to uphold and continue this unpartable conversation and living together, and this consent was ordained for this cause, that this company of the one with the other, the which was begun between them by this consent and agreement, should not be suffered to be broken at any time as long as they were both alive."

That is (let us take an example at random), the contract of marriage that had passed between Anne Boleyn and the secret husband whom Henry and Wolsey had sought to divorce from her by a papal decree could only be dissolved by his or her death. But Henry's scholars could not have been expected to know about such particulars.

The authors went on to make explicit their contention that public honesty was included under the prohibitions of Leviticus: "So that now, reader, as thou hast seen by these two authors, it is plain and open that not only the first degree of consanguinity and affinity but also the first degree wherein marriage is forbidden for a justice grounded only upon a certain common honesty and comeliness is forbidden by the law of God in the Levitical, and cannot be dispensed withal by men."

As proof that this was so, the reader was referred to Pope Alexander III, who preferred to let a certain resident of the city of "Papi" named "Henry" be forsworn than to allow him to carry out an oath that he had made, namely, that he would arrange a marriage between his youngest son and the girl who had been betrothed to his now deceased eldest son. The pope told the local bishop: "Because that it is written in the Levitical that the brother cannot have the brother's spouse, we command thee that thou suffer not this foresaid Henry to fulfill his purpose, and that thou compel him by the order of the Church to do penance for his unlawful oath." (We saw above when discussing Alexander's decretal that the elder brother had not died, but had been excluded by consanguinity. Bishop West pointed out this fact in refuting the arguments of the *Compendious Annotation*.)[18]

The king's book concluded the argument thus:

Wherefore, seeing that these things be thought true to so many and so discreet authors [that is, the three just cited, and the divers unnamed others who were quoted before on different matters] that it is not lawful for a man to marry his brother's spouse, how much more unlawful ought we to think this thing that a man should marry his brother's widow with whom his brother had had carnally ado, and that he should uncover the privities of her which before is one flesh with his brother, not only by the bond of marriage itself with the other brother but also by reason of carnal commission and meddling with the same?[19]

The readers were of course meant to think that Catherine fitted this latter description and that the foregoing was simply a buildup to this *a fortiori* conclusion.[20] If it also served by the by to convince anyone who might have had a sneaking and unjust suspicion that Catherine's first marriage had not been consummated, so much the better.

How persuasive would such argumentation have been? Upon an unlearned and undiscriminating audience its effect might have been quite overwhelming, but let us see what the Bishop of Rochester thought of it. He considered it essential to dissect the king's book paragraph by paragraph and expose every sophism and fal-

[18] See above, Chap. 3 at n. 26.

[19] *Determinations*, chap. 4, ff. 90–93. A copy is in the Granville Library, no. 1224.

[20] This *a fortiori* argument was made in the treatise beginning *Queritur* in Lambeth Palace Library MS 2342, ff. 84–108 (f. 80).

lacy of its "most learned authors" to the light of his scholarship
and his relentless irony. His commentary on the passage just cited[21]
will give us a taste of his method:

As for their next note of warning, that no dispensation can allow the
marriage of a brother's spouse who is still a virgin, they contend that this
was the opinion of some of the previously named authors and especially
Lyranus and Hugh of St. Victor. But unless my memory violently deceives
me, no one mentioned before this asserts that the pope can in no way
dispense in such a case. Therefore here too they [the authors of the king's
book] are to be accused of attempting to obfuscate the truth in a matter
of extreme importance.

Furthermore, he said, Nicholas of Lyre said nothing to confirm
their contention. In the first place he was speaking of the father's,
not the brother's spouse (Fisher therefore conceded Lyre's interpretation of Abishag as David's wife). He goes on:

Certainly he was well enough aware of and often affirmed that the brother's spouse, even a wife who was carnally known by the brother, could be
married by another brother if he died without children, and that this
was not only not fobidden but commanded in the Law. They will, therefore, never demonstrate what they have promised, namely, that Lyranus
had passed to the opinion that the pope cannot give a dispensation allowing a brother's wife untouched by him to marry a surviving brother.

And Hugh of St. Victor? They departed a long way from the
truth in quoting him as they did, Fisher asserted. They had to
stitch together a patchwork of texts taken from different places
and in the wrong order: the first part was from the middle of the
third chapter of Hugh's treatise, the second from the beginning of
the same chapter, the third again from the latter part, and the
fourth from the end of the fourth chapter. "But, what is even more
unbecoming to the integrity of such great men, they lost sight of

21 *Iohannis episcopi Roffensis responsum ad libellum impressum Londini
1530*, London, British Museum MS Arundel 151, ff. 266v–268. The whole work
is analyzed in Edward Surtz, *The Works and Days of John Fisher*, p. 362. The
king's book is dated April 1530, meaning 1531. See Burnet, IV, 136 n. 30. For
some reason the new year is begun after April, a practice that is also followed
in the Orléans determination of April 5, which is dated 1529; that of Angers
on May 7 is dated 1530, as are all the later ones. A copy of the Latin version
of the book, titled *Gravissimae ... totius Italiae et Galliae academiarum censurae ...*, is to be found in the Granville Library, no. 1251.

those words which make an utter shambles of their opinion."[22]
For, toward the beginning of the fourth chapter, Hugh distinguished between the law of nature and the law of Moses. The first
forbade marriage only between parents and children; the second
added several other degrees, whether because of natural decorum
or for the increase of modesty. " 'From then on,' he says, 'a prohibition made it illicit to do what nature had allowed.' " So, Fisher
added, one could conclude from this that the marriage of a brother's childless widow was forbidden neither by nature nor by the
Mosaic law, since it was not contained even in the Levitical prohibitions. "Certainly one's opinion of these most learned men could
not remain unaffected when they close their eyes to such clear statements."

"But they say," the bishop continued, "that Hugh maintains that
there is true marriage where no bodily intercourse has followed.
So do I. But what will they gather from that? That there can be no
papal dispensation allowing a dead husband's brother to marry
his wife? It is certain that there is no dialectic by which they will
make good that inference." For, he said, Hugh did not deny the
possibility of a dispensation when the first marriage had been consummated, much less when it had not been consummated.[23]

As for the decretal letter of Alexander III, Fisher pointed out
that it concerned a man whose vow was illicit because he bound
himself to act against the canons that set up the impediment of
public honesty. For so doing, the pope ordered him punished for

22 Cf. what he says earlier about their citations from St. Thomas: "If they
had read over what he replied to the third objection in the same question, they
would have strangled themselves" (f. 259).

23 Hugh of St. Victor, *De sacramentis* 2.11: *De sacramento coniugii*, chaps.
3–4, ed. Migne, *Patrologia latina*, CLXXVI, cols. 481–85. Fisher was accurate in
his analysis of Hugh, who does not discuss the possibility of dispensations at
all, even in the sixth degree, when he cites several canons imposing the impediments of consanguinity and affinity on various degrees (chaps. 15–16). But in
the fourth chapter he does advocate allowing the legitimacy of children born of
parents who unknowingly entered into forbidden marriages. He excepts brother-sister matches and similar unions, where ignorance could not be pleaded as an
excuse, and where shame would forbid it. He does not discuss the law of levirate.
The king's book quoted some of these sentiments a bit earlier, but omitted the
key sentence about the Mosaic law forbidding what had been allowed by nature. See above, p. 12, for Fisher's conclusion that the Levitical ban applied only
to the wife of a living brother.

his unlawful vow and forbade the marriage. There was certainly nothing said about a dispensation having been sought and denied. If Pope Alexander did not wish to dispense, did it mean that he could not? This kind of reasoning would get those *doctissimi* nowhere. Fisher accepted without comment their assumption that the elder brother in the case had died, and simply refuted their conclusion:

It is not, as they contend, because of the former union of the flesh that such marriages are forbidden. For we have often exploded this view before, showing both from Scripture and the writings of authorities that no fleshly unity remains when one of the partners has died; even if the dead husband were brought back to life he would have no claim upon the surviving woman, unless they renewed their nuptials and entered another marriage.

Odd as this argument may sound to us, it had been widely used and accepted by ecclesiastical writers of the past.

Fisher did not bring up the point that it was the general opinion in the Middle Ages that the Levitical degrees were held to be indispensable (except in a case like Henry's, however, where the law of levirate applied); it would have been a gratuitous gift of an advantage to his enemies. Moreover, he cannot be blamed for failing to realize or admit that Pope Alexander considered the impediment of public honesty to be indissoluble. As we saw, the canon was not accepted or utilized for this purpose but rather it was utilized for the purpose of condemning unlawful oaths, as Fisher explained.[24]

Fisher's reply to the *Determinations* was circulated in manuscript but was never printed. The response made by Thomas Abel, called *The Unconquered Truth*, did see print, however, and it will be instructive to compare his approach with Fisher's. Abel was Queen Catherine's chaplain and one of her counsel, a brave and determined priest who had given the quietus to Henry's scheme to trick Charles V into sending to England the original version of Julius II's brief. Listen to his reply to the king's authors on the subject we have been examining, that is, their contention that public honesty in the Levitical degrees was a God-imposed impediment:

[24] See above, Chap. 3 at n. 22.

Here ye may see how openly and without all shamefastness they lie. They bid you mark which divers of the holy and approbate doctors do hold that the brother cannot marry a woman that is but only handfast to his brother after his death (thus they must understand it), and if a man do, the marriage cannot stand by help of any dispensation. First, these persons have brought no doctor that this doth affirm, and there is neither Master Lyre nor Hugh de Sancto Victore that doth say that the pope cannot dispense with a man that he may marry that woman which was only but handfast to his brother, after his brother's death. Hugo de Sancto Victore in all his long process that these persons bring in hath not a word of the pope's power and dispensation, nor Master Lyre in this case. Moreover, it is evident that it is but only forbidden by the law of the Church that a man may not marry his brother's spouse after the death of his brother. There is no Scripture nor doctor saying that such marriage is forbidden by the Levitical law; nor again there is no doctor that doth say that the pope cannot dispense in this case. You may see what persons be these. They care not how falsely they say. They be not ashamed to speak against all reason and learning.

As for Alexander III, "the pope doth not always dispense where he may dispense." Moreover, when they say that the pope cited Leviticus as prohibiting a brother from marrying his brother's spouse, "I answer that it is not forbidden in the Levitical law that a man shall not marry his brother's spouse; nor there is no manner of mention made of any such marriage.[25] And so ye may see that all that cure they bring is not for their false purpose."

In their conclusion "they continue in their customable lying. For they say that many discreet authors have judged that it is forbidden in the Levitical law that a man shall not marry his brother's spouse, and that such a marriage is so unlawful that the pope cannot dispense upon it. This, ye see, is manifestly false, for there is no discreet author that so saith, and if there be any authors that so judge why do not these persons bring them in? But they say very falsely, for there be no discreet authors that so judge and say."

Abel continues his almost incantatory denunciation of "these false persons and their false sayings" for applying their *a fortiori* argument to the queen, and he goes on to strike a further blow:

But I will show you a very truth, which is this: The Queen's Grace that now is was a maiden when Her Grace was married last, and in witness and record that this is true, Her Grace hath sworn and testified upon a

---

25 On Alexander III's use of "spouse" rather than "wife" in his quotation of Scripture, see above, Chap. 3, n. 20.

book and received the Blessed Sacrament of the altar that she was a maiden when Her Grace was last married. Wherefore the determinations of the faculty of divinity and the canon of the University of Paris, though that they be false, yet they make nothing against this matrimony, nor the determinations of both the faculties of law of the University of Angew nor the determination of divinity of the University of Biturs [Bourges]. For these have determined on this wise, that if there were passed between the husband and the wife carnal copulation, that then the brother may not marry his brother's widow, nor the pope cannot dispense upon such marriage. So now, though the determinations of these universities be false as be all the other, yet these rehearsed help nothing the pestilent and malicious purpose of these pestilent persons, forasmuch as the Queen's Grace was a maiden when she was last married.[26]

Little wonder that Abel would suffer imprisonment and death after so vehemently—and accurately—giving the lie to his king.[27]

There were several attempts to refute Abel's treatise, but none of them ventured to respond to his remarks on public honesty. One of them, a book of six hundred pages in the hand of Thomas Derby, Clerk of the King's Council, started out bravely enough by speaking of the great number of authorities who "avow to be unlawful to any man to marry his brother's wife, specially known afore carnally by his brother, which is dead." But just a few pages later the author summarized his conclusions, which presupposed carnal knowledge in the first marriage: he denied that God "commanded or put at liberty the brother german to marry with his brother german's wife, known by him before, though he left her without issue." He affirmed that "the Levitical law forbidding that the brother shall not marry the brother's wife, if the said brother which is dead had carnal knowledge of her, is indispensable by any man's power or authority."[28]

A second treatise, containing close to five hundred pages, skirted the issue altogether.[29] Another refutation, which is no more than a

26 Thomas Abel, *Invicta veritas* ("Lüneburg," 1532), sig. N-N iiv. See below, Chap. 11, n. 14, for James Gairdner's doubts about Lüneburg.

27 Abel and two other priests, Richard Featherstone and Edward Powell, the surviving nonepiscopal members of the queen's legatine counsel, according to Rastell's list (Ridley had died in 1536, having conformed to the Act of Supremacy), were executed on July 30, 1540. They were beatified in 1886, and though they were not among the forty English martyrs canonized by Pope Paul VI in 1971, one day their turn will undoubtedly come.

28 Record Office SP 1/60, ff. 4, 7v, 8rv. Cf. LP V, 1.1.

29 Record Office SP 1/61; LP V, 1.2. See also the short treatise in Pocock, I, 517–18.

three-page draft, started with reflections on the Levitical law. The author observed that Leviticus did not specify whether the first brother had had children or not, and did not even state whether or not he had had carnal knowledge of his wife. What it did speak of was the wife's turpitude, that is, fleshly unity with her husband. This presumably came from carnal copula, and would be the same whether there were children or not, unless one were to say that a man and his wife were one flesh only if they had children. But since the sacred text made no mention of carnal copula, then either the unity of flesh came from the matrimonial consent alone, or else the divine law presumed that a man's wife, by the very fact that she was a wife, was carnally known by him. For the purposes of his argument, the author did not consider it necessary to decide between these alternatives—it was enough that Abel would be forced to choose one of them.[30] But if Abel were to choose the reading according to which the wife was carnally known, then he would be able to exempt Catherine from the law, since he maintained that Catherine had had no carnal knowledge of Arthur.

Another point-by-point refutation of the king's book is to be found in a lengthy treatise by Jerome Novati, the Milanese canonist who served as Catherine's advocate in Rome, and who in September 1533 became an auditor of the Rota. Of the work's thirteen theses, Novati devotes almost nine-tenths of his discussion to the first: namely, that "the pope can, in a particular instance, dispense in such a case, even without reason, and more so with reason, and even more so because the queen was a virgin [*regina non fuit cognita*]."[31]

---

[30] Record Office SP 6/9, f. 44rv. On f. 45 he went on to speak of Deuteronomy. Gairdner in LP V, 1.3, mistakenly included SP 6/9, ff. 41–43, as part of this treatise, whereas these leaves are a fragment of another treatise; see below, Chap. 13, n. 10.

[31] See Surtz, "Henry VIII's Great Matter," pp. 668, 671–76, and 695, n. 11. Novati's work is titled *De legitimo serenissimae Catharinae de Castiglia de Arragonia reginae Angliae matrimonio conclusiones XIII*, and consists "of some 338 folios"; it exists in the Vatican Library, MS Lat. 5639. Novati deals with the determinations and the treatise that follows in the king's book on ff. 241–275. I have not seen the work, and unfortunately Surtz does not describe what Novati has to say on the subject of the queen's virginity. Surtz dates the work between 1532 and 1534.

CHAPTER ELEVEN

Further Efforts Toward Consummation

Henry's public and private theology in his guileful little homily had not, as we have seen, passed the inspection of his critics unscathed. But even before Fisher's reply was finished and smuggled abroad, the king's campaign of self-justification had run into trouble. On April 2, 1531, Chapuys reported a meeting of Parliament at which the chancellor, Sir Thomas More, first read in the House of Lords, by the king's command, a complaint stating that there were some who said that Henry pursued his great matter for the love of another woman, and not for conscience's sake; but this, the chancellor proclaimed, was definitely not the case. Brian Tuke then read the determinations of the universities, and when he had finished, John Longland, Bishop of Lincoln and Henry's confessor, and John Stokesley, the new Bishop of London, delivered speeches in favor of the king's position.

Absent from the gathering were the three prelates who were considered to be the queen's chief supporters: Tunstall (now bishop of Durham), Warham, and Fisher. It seems that Fisher was recovering from poison administered by a well-meaning but unappreciated supporter of the king. It was hoped that other sympathizers of the queen would be too timid to make their views heard. But Henry Standish, Bishop of St. Asaph, and John Clerk, Bishop of Bath and Wells, who like the three above-named prelates were members of the queen's original battery of lawyers and theologians, began to make objections. If they were not altogether fearless men they had at least some moral courage remaining to them. The Duke of Norfolk, Anne's uncle, knowing (according to Chapuys) that Lincoln and London would get the worst of the debate, interrupted. Someone then asked More what he thought, and he said simply that he had often spoken his mind on the matter to the king. The whole business was thus left up in the air.

Then a delegation went down to Commons for a repeat performance, except that this time the chancellor added that the king wished them to be thus advertised of this matter so that when they returned home they might inform their neighbors of the truth. Longland and Stokesley seem to have been able to go through their mission unimpeded. They took it upon their consciences with great ceremony that the king's marriage was more than illegal, and Stokesley described at length the impartiality and authority of the determinations. However, though the bishops met with no opposition this time, they also met with no support.[1]

What objections would Clerk and Standish have raised to the determinations of the universities? Would any of them have denied the presumption that the queen had consummated her first marriage? We do not know for sure, of course, but we do know that Henry was very fearful of this objection at the time. On the last day of May 1531 the king sent a group of councillors to pay an evening visit to the queen at Greenwich. The dignitaries were "mostly reluctant persecutors," especially Edward Lee and Stephen Gardiner, who were soon to take over the sees of York and Winchester, both of which had been vacated by Wolsey's death. They set about their business with some embarrassment, with Lee first telling the queen that since she had had bodily knowledge of Prince Arthur, she should firmly believe that her marriage with the king was detestable and abominable before God and man. Catherine replied that there had been no such bodily knowledge between her and the prince, and that this was not the time to discuss it. Bishop Longland took over then and pressed the point: there was no use denying her copula with Arthur, for there were solemn and evident proofs to the contrary.

Catherine answered that all such proofs were falsified; she knew the truth better than anyone in the world, and if proof were needed she could produce abundant evidence apart from her oath, which would expose as lies all contentions to the contrary. Gardiner broke in at this point, and said that the presumption of the law would be enough to prove consummation, since she and the prince had

[1] LP V, 171 (pp. 83–84).

lived and slept together for some time. Catherine answered that she did not proceed by cavil and presumption, but only according to the exact truth; and as for his presumptions and his laws, he could go and ventilate them at Rome with the others.[2] (At Rome Ortiz later received a full report of Catherine's encounter with her adversaries. He was ecstatic: "Another St. Catherine disputing with the doctors!" he exclaimed, convinced that the Holy Ghost had inspired her and spoke through her. He rushed off with his letter to show it to the pope and the cardinals. They were so profoundly impressed with her responses that they thought they should be published.)[3]

As Catherine's crestfallen visitors departed, Dr. Lee was overheard to remark that all the trouble taken by the king in this matter had gone for nothing, since the queen asserted so positively that she had not been known by Arthur.[4] A few weeks later the remissorial letters, designed chiefly to gather testimony of Catherine's virginity, secretly arrived in England for the queen's approval.

Then, on July 11, 1531, Henry made his final break from Catherine, sneaking out early one morning with his train without even bidding her farewell. He was never to see her again.

Later, when the queen had made some solicitous inquiries after the king, he finally sent off a reply, drafted with the help of his council, rebuking her obstinacy in swearing that she had never consummated her marriage with Arthur, and in preaching it to the whole world. But he would establish the contrary by good witnesses; and that being so, it was certain that the pope's dispensation for their marriage could not be valid. This had already been proved to all the world. She would do better therefore to spend her time in looking for witnesses to prove her alleged virginity than in addressing herself to the world or to him.[5] He could not have known that Chapuys had just sent off his report on the remissorials, recommending improvements in the questions designed to prove lack of consummation; or that the ambassador had even

[2] Chapuys, LP V, 287 (pp. 134–37); see also Garrett Mattingly, *Catherine of Aragon*, p. 240.

[3] Ortiz to Charles V, 19 July 1531, LP V, 342.

[4] LP V, 287 (p. 138).

[5] Chapuys, 31 July 1531, LP V, 361 (p. 167).

taken the testimony of a handful of witnesses alleging Arthur's impotency.

Henry was so worried over the defects in the university determinations that he decided to attempt to remedy them, despite the fact that he had spent the better part of a year in a second campaign among the academies, with discouraging results. He had been trying to get support for his thesis that the pope could not lawfully cite him to Rome; finally, in June 1531, he received two favorable responses, from the University of Orléans and from the lawyers of Paris; he was to get no more. Nevertheless he sent Edward Fox to Paris to persuade the university to make good the contention of the white paper that Fox had helped to write: that is, to declare that even if the first marriage had not been consummated the pope could not legitimately allow the second, because verbal consent, not carnal connection, constituted the essence of marriage. It was evident to Chapuys that the king undertook this mission because he knew for certain that Catherine was a virgin and, what was more, that it could be proved.

Fox returned toward the end of August, having labored with the utmost diligence to no effect. Before the next month was out he was off again for the same purpose of having public honesty declared a divine law.[6] This last assault on the academies was destined for total failure. Another way would have to be found.

Henry's dream was to be able to go ahead with an ecclesiastical trial in England without bothering about the pope or his Roman court. But who would preside over such a trial? Wolsey would have done it—he would have done anything to get back into his master's favor—and if his legatine authority had gone out of fashion, Henry could easily have designated a domicile in the Province of York or the Diocese of Winchester and thus come under the cardinal's jurisdiction. But the king was too late—Wolsey was dead. The other archbishop, Warham, timid though he had always been, absolutely refused.

Henry then offered the see of York to his cousin, the learned Reginald Pole, who had reluctantly participated in the drive to secure the support of the University of Paris.[7] This man (later

---

[6] LP V, 401, 432.
[7] See his letter to the king describing the difficulties encountered, 7 July 1530, Pocock I, 563.

Cardinal Archbishop of Canterbury under Queen Mary) might easily be thought by some to have a better right to the throne than Henry, especially now that the king had made everyone so aware of the importance of a legitimate pedigree. For he was the grandson of George, Duke of Clarence, younger brother of Henry's grandfather Edward IV. If Edward's marriage to Elizabeth Woodville were to be regarded as invalid because of precontract and witchcraft, as Richard III's Parliament had proclaimed, his children, including Henry's mother, would be illegitimate. As for Henry VII, he had his personal claim only from the bastard Beaufort line.

Pole candidly let Henry know that he did not at all agree with his purpose and sent him a treatise, apparently meant for his eyes alone, setting forth his views on the subject. Cranmer, who read it, described it to Anne's father as having so much wit and eloquence that if it were made known to the common people they would be irrevocably convinced that the king was in the wrong. The purpose of the treatise was to urge Henry to commit his case to the pope's decision (Cranmer thought that Pole "lacketh much judgment" herein). As for the law of God in the matter, the king could just as easily justify the opposite view if he so pleased. The universities, Pole said, often came to their decisions for sensual rather than rational motives; he could draw on his own experience at Paris to bear witness to the trouble it had taken to win them over to the king's side. Henry now stood, his cousin warned, on the brink of the water, but there was still a chance of saving himself; one step further, however, and all his honor would be drowned.[8]

Henry next approached Edward Lee, his almoner, who had done him even better service in working for the divorce than his cousin. Lee agreed to take on the post, but after he was installed as Archbishop of York on October 20, 1531, he changed his mind about the advisability of effecting the divorce.

This left the king in the doldrums. Almost a year was to pass before he could see a way out. His frustrated inactivity came to an end when the octogenarian Archbishop Warham died on August 22, 1532. Henry pondered for a while on his replacement, and then made his decision. On October 1 he sent Nicholas Haw-

---

[8] Cranmer to Wiltshire, 13 June 1531, LP V, App. 10.

kins to relieve Thomas Cranmer of his post as ambassador to the emperor. Henry allegedly had said upon first hearing of him that Cranmer had the right sow by the ear; now he would have to renew his hold. The embassy had been a broadening experience for Cranmer. While he was attending on the emperor at Ratisbon, his fellow envoy Sir Thomas Elyot wrote of the exhilarating state of the clergy of Nuremberg: all the priests had for wives the fairest women of the town.[9] Cranmer had meditated for a long time upon the ins and outs of virginity and marriage in the king's case; and if the evidence that he joined Elyot, Sampson, and others in shifting his support to Catherine is unconvincing, he was at least won over to the views of the German reformers in another respect and took to heart the fruit of their reasoning by marrying the niece of Osiander's wife. When he heard the astounding news of his appointment to the see of Canterbury, however, he felt obliged to hide her and dissimulate her existence, if he was to accept the appointment. He had married once before, in the days before his ordination to the priesthood, and it had cost him a fellowship at Cambridge.[10]

On the anniversary of Edward Lee's consecration as Archbishop of York, Cranmer wrote to Henry to report on Charles's crusade against the infidel and the ravages that his troops had inflicted upon the Christian countryside on the way to Vienna. Then he added an ominous note. He had seen comets day after day, and others had seen a blue cross above the moon and a flaming horse's head and a burning sword in the sky: "What strange things these tokens do signify to come hereafter, God knoweth, for they do not lightly appear, but against some great mutation. And it hath not been seen, as I suppose, that so many comets have appeared in so short a time."[11] He felt that the world was big with destiny. In a few days he would learn that he himself was destined to play a major role in earthshaking events.

The world was not to be alone in showing signs of pregnancy. Anne Boleyn had finally resigned the ultimate favor to the amorous advances of the king, after tantalizing him for years with her

[9] LP V, 869.

[10] See Jasper Ridley, *Thomas Cranmer*, pp. 16–20, on his first wife, and pp. 42–45 on his alleged shift to Catherine's position.

[11] LP V, 1449.

refusals. In due time she conceived a child—Queen Elizabeth that was to be—and as soon as her state was discovered she and Henry were secretly joined in wedlock. The marriage, which may have been nothing more at this point than a contract *per verba de praesenti*, took place sometime around January 25, 1533 (as official sources gave out later), shortly after the reluctant archbishop-elect had returned to England.

Chapuys reported, a month later, the rumor that Cranmer himself had married the couple. The ambassador was willing to credit it, or at least he believed it very probable that if he had not already solemnized the spousals he had promised to do so. If he had in fact done so, he added, Henry had taken the best means to prevent him from changing his mind, as Lee had done, once he was raised to his dignity.

About the same time that Henry and Anne privately ratified their already consummated union, the king's men adverted to the wording of the original treaty between the powers of England and Spain arranging the marriage of Henry and Catherine. The discovery was received like a divine revelation: here at last was absolute and irrefutable evidence that the marriage between Catherine and Arthur had been consummated.[12] If the queen in her speeches and Reginald Pole in his treatise had appealed to the authority of Henry VII and Ferdinand and their councils to verify the validity of the dispensation, Henry would also appeal to their authority to prove that Catherine's virginity had given way to her first husband's embraces before he departed from this life.

The king accordingly commanded his chief councillors to assemble a group of scholars, both clerical and lay. They were asked to deliberate upon a proposition that was asserted to be the received opinion of all theologians, namely, that if Catherine's first marriage had been consummated, the second was null and void. For proof of consummation Henry cited not only the presumption of the law but also the affirmation of Henry VII and Ferdinand in the treaty of 1503. He exhibited to the committee a copy that had been notarized and certified as authentic by John Clerk, Bishop of Bath, an avowed supporter of the queen. When the learned company saw it, they agreed with the king's conclusions,

12 See above, Chap. 8 at n. 36.

and declared that it only remained for him to initiate judicial proceedings by the authority of the Archbishop of Canterbury. Cranmer's appointment had not yet been approved by Rome, but Henry with good reason felt confident that the pope would concede him this favor, and then he would have only to wait for the official bulls to arrive to be able to achieve his desire according to form.

Meanwhile, as Chapuys wrote on February 23 (as it happened, the day after Cranmer's appointment had been ratified in Rome), Henry was putting great pressure on Lee, Cranmer, Stokesley, Gardiner, Longland, and many others, Italians as well as Englishmen, to sign a document that would apparently have given their full authorization to the proceedings that he intended. No pressure was necessary for Cranmer—he even begged the privilege of being allowed to sign. Stokesley and Longland, too, seemingly made little trouble about it, for Chapuys mentioned only Lee and Gardiner as still holding out.

Catherine was greatly disturbed by these recent events. Chapuys assured her that the treaty really proved nothing at all; but, no doubt because of the fuss that Henry was making over it, she was afraid that now the whole world would think that she had sworn a false oath at the hands of Cardinal Campeggio.[13]

Chapuys was right, of course; the written and oral testimony of Ferdinand and Isabella's real views, which Catherine's supporters had collected in Rome, was sufficient to undercut Henry's claims for the treaty. One letter in particular was devastating. Ferdinand had written to de Rojas, his ambassador to the pope, that even though the treaty stated that the marriage had been consummated, "the truth is that it was not consummated, and that the said princess our daughter remained as intact as before she was married, and this is very certain and well known where she is." But, he explained, because of the English people's habit of raising doubts and scruples, the lawyers in England thought it good to state in the dispensation that the marriage had been consummated, "in spite of the fact that the princess our daughter remained intact, and, though she and Prince Arthur waked together [*se velaron*], they did not consummate the marriage." The letter was obligingly

13 LP VI, 142 (p. 65), 152, 160 (p. 74), 180.

published by "Philalethes Hyperboreus" at Antwerp in July 1533, in a treatise written in response to *A Glass of the Truth*.[14]

The brief of Julius II had been issued prematurely for the consolation of the dying Queen Isabella, as Mai had pointed out to Clement years earlier.[15] Obviously, she would not have derived any consolation from the assumption that her daughter had lost her virginity in her first marriage. Long before this, Isabella and her husband had been careful to find out the truth of the matter, and she had used the fact of nonconsummation as a selling point in negotiating the marriage of Catherine to young Henry.[16] It is usually assumed, therefore, as I mentioned earlier, that Isabella must have insisted that the papal dispensation assert her daughter's true condition. In the face of such a request, coupled with the English insistence that consummation had taken place, Rome compromised by inserting the *forsan*, thereby treating the consummation as merely conjectural.

In early March 1533, Parliament passed the Act in Restraint of Appeals to Rome, thereby giving a theoretical justification to the plan of concluding the annulment case. This statute, which was organized by Cromwell, had the incidental effect of giving the king control of all ecclesiastical jurisdiction.

In anticipation of Cranmer's appointment, Henry ordered a reconvening of the Convocation of the Province of Canterbury. It opened on March 26, 1533, at St. Paul's Church, with Bishop

---

[14] Letter of 23 August 1503, given in the original Spanish in the *Parasceve* (Introduction) to the never written *Anticatoptrum* (Anti-Glass, i.e. Reverse Mirror); see Pocock, II, 426. The author's pseudonym means "Lover of the Truth from the North." Some thought him to be Vives; others conjectured Cochlaeus. The surreptitious printing of the work was arranged in Antwerp by William Peto, English Provincial of the Observant Franciscans. James Gairdner, *DNB* Peto, concludes that the imprint of Lüneburg, 250 miles to the east of Antwerp and seemingly without a printing press, is fictitious. It has often been assumed that Peto himself was the author; but Stephen Vaughan, Cromwell's friend in Antwerp, who knew of Peto's publishing effort, believed that Fisher was the author. Whoever he was, he seems to have known personally the author of *A Glass*, whom he calls Catoptropaeus ("Glasser"), and describes as "a great rabbi in the royal court" (pp. 422–24). He thus assumes him to be single and not composite, which perhaps tells against G. R. Elton's suggestion, *Policy and Police*, pp. 176–77, that Henry VIII himself had a hand in the book's composition. See above, Chap. 6 at n. 44 and Chap 10, n. 7.

[15] Report of 7 April 1529, SC III, part 2, 973.

[16] Letters of 16 June 1502 and 11 April 1503, SC I, 271, 302.

Stokesley of London as temporary president. When describing the events of the Convocation some months later, Stokesley recalled how unpopular the cause of the divorce had become, and said that its opponents hated him as almost its only patron.[17] He displayed several volumes of depositions taken in the matter of the king's marriage, together with a copy of the treaty of 1503, and began to read the university determinations, but was interrupted by the question whether they should be debating the problem of the marriage against the pope's command. Stokesley put down the scruple by showing them a brief from the pope in which he urged everyone to speak his mind. (A convocation of this sort, however, was hardly what Clement had intended.)

At the second meeting of the Convocation two days later, the Bishop of London began again with the reading of the determinations: those of Paris, Orléans, Bologna, Padua, Bourges, and Toulouse. He omitted, if the record is accurate, the sentence of the lawyers of Angers, and perhaps that of the Parisian lawyers as well, since it, like the Angers statement, insisted that the first marriage must have been consummated. But so did the determination of the University of Bourges. It is perhaps not unfair to think that when Stokesley came to the telling phrase he gave it no special emphasis.

When he had finished the readings, he said that he wished to pose to the assembled prelates the question as it had been formulated by the theologians of Paris, since it contained, he assured them, the substance of all the other determinations. (The question deliberated upon at Paris was this: "Would a marriage with the widow of one's brother deceased without children be so prohibited that it could not be allowed by a dispensation of the supreme pontiff for a Christian man to marry the widow of his brother and retain her as his wife?")

Some of the prelates and clergy wanted time to think, and the meeting was adjourned until four in the afternoon. Stokesley then read what he said was the Parisian version of the question, but he phrased it thus: "Are marriages with the widows of brothers deceased without children so prohibited by natural as well as di-

17 For the records of the proceedings see Pocock, II, 442ff. For Stokesley's remarks, see below, Chap. 14, n. 18.

vine law that the supreme pontiff could not grant a dispensation for such marriages already contracted or to be contracted?" In this way he made it seem that the affirmative answer given by the Paris divines was categorical and did not allow the possibility that the levirate practice was still open to, or even incumbent upon, Jews who had not yet accepted Jesus as their Messiah.

After a certain amount of disputation, three bishops, namely Stokesley himself, Longland, and Standish—the latter had finally come out openly for Henry (the queen had suspected his sincerity before, though perhaps not altogether justly)—along with thirty-six abbots and priors, responded that they agreed with the determinations of the universities.

The next day, March 29, the matter was disputed further, and six abbots said that they would agree to the determination if there were added the words, "if the said widow had previously had carnal knowledge of the deceased brother."

The game was up. The question of consummation would have to be formally discussed.

By now, however, Cranmer's bulls had arrived, and he was installed as archbishop on March 30. The next day the bulls were exhibited to Stokesley, Gardiner, and Longland, and Convocation was recessed until the following day, when Cranmer officially assumed command. When he appeared in the chapter house, he did nothing more than make "divers communications." Presumably, he sounded out the king's supporters on how to proceed—that is, on how best to surmount the obstacle of the queen's alleged virginity. It was decided to divide and conquer. The canonists would be asked to decide whether there was sufficient proof for the consummation of Catherine's first marriage, and the theologians would decide on the nature of the prohibition against the second marriage, granted that the first had been consummated. There was no attempt made to argue the position taken by Stokesley in the king's white paper, which Cranmer had translated, that the indispensable divine law did not depend on consummation but only on the marriage contract. We shall see that Cranmer had just written a treatise for the king defending this view, but he doubtless realized that it could not find favor with the clergy at large.

The archbishop decided to treat in Convocation first the theological question, and on the following day he convened the theologians of the lower house to hear opinions on the question, "Would it be lawful to marry the wife of one's brother, who was known by him, after he has died without children, and [if not], is the prohibition against it a divine law indispensable by the pope?" Of the twenty-three members present, fourteen agreed that the case in question was against divine law and indispensable; seven disagreed; one did not know; and one said that there was a divine and moral law against it, but that it could be dispensed from. This latter view was a very common one at the time; it was the position of Cardinal Cajetan, and lay behind the opinion of those who believed that the pope could dispense only for an adequate reason. It would not have been lawful for him, in other words, simply to lift the ban altogether.

The canonists of the lower house were then consulted as to whether in their opinion it was sufficiently proved from all the evidence before them that carnal intercourse had taken place between Arthur and Catherine. The speaker and all the members of the house presented the answer of the canonists to Bishop Stokesley on April 3: they determined that such consummation was sufficiently proved, and stated their answer "with one voice and the consent of all, except for some protestations from among them; all of which was to be exhibited in the presence of the very reverend Archbishop of Canterbury in the upper house."

Of the attending prelates in the upper house, only three were canonists: Gardiner and John Voysey, Bishop of Exeter (another of Catherine's former counselors), who agreed with the (almost) unanimous vote of the lower-chamber lawyers, and John Clerk, who disagreed. That was on April 4; on the 5th, a spokesman from the king appeared before the body and demanded an answer from the entire Convocation, and required that the records of their proceedings be published. The time for discussion was past.

The theologians therefore were asked whether such a marriage was forbidden by an indispensable divine law. The votes, including the 197 cast by proxy, numbered 253 in the affirmative, with 19 in the negative. Only five bishops were in attendance, including Fisher. The latter, through some oversight, was not listed as present, but his name appears among those who participated personally in the balloting. He and George de Athequa, Bishop of Llandaff, voted against the king's position. Athequa was the not very forceful Spaniard who had been Queen Catherine's confessor; it was his misfortune later to be imprisoned, having been captured in attempting to flee the country.

The bishops who voted in favor were Stokesley, Longland, and Standish; in addition Stokesley and Longland had the proxies of five other bishops between them—including, surprisingly, Nicholas West of Ely (who was on his death-bed) and Laurence Campeggio of Salisbury. Among the lower clergy the king could count as his supporters Robert Wakefield, Richard Croke, and Edward Fox. Among those holding for the queen were Robert Shorton, Richard Featherstone, and Edward Powell.

It was then the turn of the canonists, who voted 41 to 6 that consummation was sufficiently proved. The vote of the bishops was as before, with Gardiner adding the names of three others for whom he was proctor, including Jerome Ghinucci of Worcester. In the lower house, Peter Ligham voted in the negative; on the other side were Richard Wolman and John Bell, as well as Thomas Bedell, former secretary of Archbishop Warham, and now Clerk of the King's Council. He was to play a prominent role in the great matter in the near future. Another canonist who voted in the affirmative was Polydore Vergil. He was typical of the timid soul who threw in with the king against his conscience. Perhaps he salved it at the time by holding, with Campeggio, that Catherine's virginity could not be proved before the law; and since he was numbered among the canonists, he was not required to pronounce upon the law itself. But when he passed judgment upon the marriage in his history of England (in a passage he did not dare to publish during Henry's lifetime), he maintained that the marriage was good not only because it was allowed by the law of levirate but also because Catherine testified that her first marriage had not been consummated.[18]

The Northern Convocation voted on the same two questions, but not until the 13th of May, by which time Cranmer had already begun the trial of the marriage at Dunstable. The names of the participants in the York Convocation are not given; it was Archbishop Lee's duty to preside over it, though we know from Cha-

[18] *Anglica historia*, ed. Denys Hay, Camden Society, 3d series, no. 74 (London, 1950), p. 149. See my *Divine Providence*, p. 106, n. 84, and *Traditio* 23: 308, n. 119.

puys that Stokesley went up from London to present the king's case, and that he was manfully opposed by Cuthbert Tunstall, his predecessor in the see of London, and now Bishop of Durham. The final vote of the theologians and canonists was 49 to 2 and 47 or 48 to 2, respectively, in favor of the king—a substantial improvement in the relations of the more important members of the English Church with their Supreme Head.[19]

19 Wilkins, III, 765; LP VI, 653.

CHAPTER TWELVE

Annulment and Ratification

❧❦

Not long after the votes of the Southern Convocation had been hastened to a satisfactory conclusion, Henry had a conversation with Chapuys, in which he let the imperial ambassador know that God and his conscience were on very good terms. Chapuys did his best to disturb the king's happy state. He offered to show him the names and letters of the scholars of the University of Paris who had supported the queen. Henry was not interested, and changed the subject. The subject emerged again, however, and the question of Catherine's virginity came up: "When I urged," Chapuys says, "that he had oftentimes confessed that the queen was a virgin, and he could not deny it, he admitted it, saying it was spoken in jest —as a man jesting and feasting says many things which are not true. And when he had said this, as if he had won a very great victory or discovered some great subtlety for gaining his purpose, he began to crow, telling me, 'Now have I paid you off? What more would you have?' "

Discouraged but not overcome by the king's stubborn high spirits, Chapuys began to discuss the legatine trial. Henry contended in response that it was illegal to appeal to a court out of the kingdom; he did not force Catherine to come to England—Arthur had summoned her, with whom she had consummated marriage.[1] If Henry was still not prepared to swear that Catherine had left her virginity with Arthur, at least he would now state it. For he had, as we shall see, been comforted once more by the reasonings of "a marvellous and serious wise man."

[1] LP VI, 351 (pp. 164–66).

Before the end of April, Henry and Catherine were cited to appear before Cranmer at the priory of Dunstable for another *ex officio* inquisition on the validity of their marriage.[2] But this time it would end in a sentence. Henry dutifully empowered a proctor, namely, Dr. John Bell, who appeared at the first plenary session on May 10, 1533; but Catherine, who was being lodged not far from Dunstable, at Ampthill, refused to take any notice of it, much to Cranmer's relief: on the 12th he wrote to the king that he had declared her *contumax* and could therefore proceed with more deliberate speed than he had thought possible.[3] He was to say in his final sentencing that "the divine presence took the place of the most serene Lady Catherine, who was absent out of contumacy."

Meanwhile Chapuys had displayed powers of attorney from Charles to appeal and protest anything done against the queen and to present papal letters to preserve her rights. He demanded that he be allowed to discharge his commission. Henry asked him to confer with his council, which he did on May 7. The ambassador delivered a long discourse in Latin, explaining how the universities had been corrupted; even so, he said, the University of Paris held that if Catherine had not consummated her marriage with Arthur, her second marriage was licit, and he gave them innumerable reasons (so he wrote to Charles) to prove that she had not been known by Arthur. He was answered by Dr. Fox, who said that the king had been moved by the Holy Ghost and his own great learning to the conclusion that he could not retain Catherine as his wife.

It was clearly felt that this was not an adequate answer, and Chapuys was summoned by the council some days later to be given a more satisfactory reply. The ambassador took the occasion to inquire about the particulars of Henry's marriage to Anne. Norfolk could not enlighten him, since he had not been present and had not been informed of them. Chapuys warned him that this acting "under the chimney" would make the whole world all the more suspicious of the marriage.[4]

2 In his sentence, Cranmer termed the trial a "causa inquisitionis de et super viribus matrimonii ... coram nobis in iudicio ex officio nostro mero." Rymer, XIV, 468.

3 LP VI, 491 (p. 179), 465 (p. 207), 470.

4 LP VI, 465 (pp. 208–9), 508.

In the meantime, the Dunstable inquisition was moving apace. The record of the process survives,[5] as do other accounts, so that we can form a good idea of what took place. Cranmer wrote later that Bishop Longland was his assistant at the trial, though the recorders made no mention of him, whether as assessor or promoter. Among the king's counsel were Bishop Gardiner, Dr. Hughes, and Thomas Bedell.[6] When Cranmer called for a representative of the king, Dr. Bell came forward and read a protestation (the text of which is not given), and thereupon exhibited his proctorial papers. The archbishop then asked if anyone wished to appear for Catherine. When no one responded, Thomas Legh was interrogated on the citation that he had delivered to her. He answered that she had refused to come, saying that "her matter dependeth at Rome." She made this statement in the hearing of Sir Francis Bryan (Anne Boleyn's cousin), Robert Shorton, and numerous others who were attending upon her. Cranmer then asked again three or four times in a loud voice whether anyone wished to appear for her. Since the time appointed for her appearance was between the hours of nine and eleven in the morning, he waited until the bell struck eleven before declaring her contumacious. Then, as at the legatine trial, he introduced articles detailing the crime of which Henry and Catherine were defamed.[7]

Rather than address Henry and Catherine directly, as did Cardinals Wolsey and Campeggio, Cranmer referred to the royal couple in the third person. Only four of his articles survive, since they were not recorded in the acts, but the pattern seems to have been nearly the same as before. The first article stated that Catherine married Arthur and consummated the union with carnal copula. The next stated that Henry and Arthur were brothers, and the third detailed the marriage of Henry and Catherine. There must have followed one or more articles stating that such a marriage was forbidden and was an open scandal. The final surviving article specified that both Henry and Catherine were residents of Cranmer's province of Canterbury, and therefore came under his jurisdiction.[8]

---

[5] British Museum MS Arundel 151, ff. 342–352v. Cited below as Dunstable Record.

[6] Cranmer to Nicholas Hawkins, 17 June 1533, *Works of Thomas Cranmer* (Cambridge, 1844–46), II, 244.

[7] Dunstable Record, ff. 343–344v.

[8] Pocock, II, 481–82.

In the legatine court, Henry was required to respond to the articles under oath. We recall that in the notarial record of that trial compiled later in 1533 the clause specifying consummation of Catherine's first marriage had been deleted. If the deletion was made before Henry gave his testimony at the 1529 trial, he would have been saved the embarrassment of committing himself on the point. If it was made later, its purpose could only have been to prevent a reader of the document from realizing that the king had unknowingly complied with Catherine's challenge, which was on its way to the pope at the time he was testifying, of accepting his sworn word in the matter. We shall see shortly that this latter supposition is probably the correct one, and that it was not until after the Dunstable trial, when the legatine record was being prepared to be sent to Rome, that the passage was deleted. In any case, it was a clumsy deception, since a space was left to indicate where the missing passage had been.

At the Dunstable trial, it was not Henry but Bell who was ordered to respond to the articles under oath, when so required. At the 1527 trial, Bell had been able to report back Henry's assertion that consummation had occurred in Catherine's first marriage. But that was before reflection had given him a delicate conscience on the point. As we shall see, Cranmer had recently provided Henry with a method of affirming Catherine's consummation of the marriage without denying her physical virginity when she entered upon her second marriage. But probably the king was still not willing to run the risk of perjuring himself, even when thus fortified. As it was, no one but Cranmer knew what reply Bell made. When he appeared with his responses two court-days later, on Friday, May 16, he first declared that the protestation he had entered before assuming Henry's proxy was still in effect. Then he delivered the responses to Cranmer, who read them silently, as was evident ("ut tunc videbatur"); and then, as the legates had done, he simply asserted that Bell referred to an apostolic dispensation. Bell did not make his answers in consultation with Henry, nor did he reply under oath, according to the report that Thomas Bedell sent to Cromwell on the last day of the trial. Bedell thought that Henry would be interested to see what answers his proctor had made to the articles.[9]

---

[9] Dunstable Record, ff. 344v, 348v; Bedell to Cromwell, Pocock, II, 476.

To return to the events of May 10: after delivering the articles to Bell, Cranmer asked William Clayburgh and Richard Watkins for the record and depositions of the legatine court. They expressed their willingness to comply, but first they entered a protestation. Then they produced a book containing all the depositions, and also a leather bag containing "all the acts, muniments, processes, and exhibits had and made before the said lord legates," and they declared under oath that everything done and submitted at the trial was therein contained, "with no substantial addition or subtraction that would change the substance of the factum." After adding to the exhibits a transumpt sealed by Archbishop Lee of York (perhaps a statement on the inauthenticity of the brief of Julius II), Cranmer adjourned the court until the following Monday, May 12.[10]

On that day Cranmer was able to declare Catherine truly and manifestly contumacious, upon obtaining the depositions of Bryan and two others (Thomas Vaux and James Gage) who had witnessed her refusal of the citation. Then arrangements were made for depositions to be taken in the principal matter from Agnes, widowed Duchess of Norfolk, who had also testified for the legatine court, and Lady Jane Guildford. Cranmer announced that it had been reported to him that the two ladies were unable to make the journey to Dunstable, because of old age and ill health, and therefore he handed down a special commission to secure their testimony on the following Wednesday at the parish church of Lambeth, where Bell was to witness their oaths.[11]

On Friday, May 16, Watkins appeared with the depositions of the two ladies, and, like Bell after him, he first referred to the conditions of his protestation, which put him under the threat of excommunication, before delivering them to the judge. When Bell had turned in his answers and Cranmer had read them, the archbishop asked him whether he had a copy of the dispensation. He replied that one could be found among the exhibits submitted by Clayburgh and Watkins. The court clerks, John Hering and Thomas Argall, listed at this point other documents that Cranmer found in the leather bag apart from the dispensation. One item

[10] Dunstable Record, ff. 344v–346.

[11] Dunstable Record, ff. 346v–348; cf. Bedell, in Pocock, II, 473; Cranmer to Henry, LP VI, 470.

in particular is of interest to us: "Responsiones euisdem regie maiestatis facte dictis articulis."[12] Since Henry's responses were included among the complete acts and exhibits of the legatine court, Watkins and Clayburgh must have deliberately omitted to include them in the copy they made later that year, which concluded with Nicholas Wootton's testimonial of October 1, 1533.[13] And if Henry did respond to the question of the consummation of Catherine's first marriage, then the answer that Dr. Bell provided would doubtless have corresponded to it.

Cranmer continued the trial until the following day, Saturday, May 17. When the court reconvened, he asked Bell if he had anything further to submit, since that was the day assigned for exhibiting all the evidence. He also asked if anyone else had anything to reveal or exhibit for Catherine. This can be taken as an indication that the same favor was extended to the supporters of the queen in the legatine trial, where she had also been declared absent through contumacy. That is, when the promoter, Dr. Hughes, according to my reconstruction of the events, proposed the doubts arising from the factum, the legates must have asked for comments or rebuttals from both the king's proctor and anyone who wished to speak for the queen, and we have seen that *libelli* were judicially exhibited on the queen's behalf.

Bell responded in the negative, and no one appeared for the queen. Then Cranmer introduced the determinations of Oxford and the continental universities, the report of the Canterbury Convocation, and the *consilia* and opinions of a good number of theologians and canonists, most of them Italians, who were listed by name.[14]

Not all of these documents were favorable to a divorce, or at least not so favorable as Henry wished. Some months later, when Cromwell asked for the material exhibited at the court, Thomas

12 Dunstable Record, ff. 348–349v.

13 See above, Chap. 4 at n. 2, and Chap. 9 at n. 12.

14 Dunstable Record, ff. 350v–351v. In his letter to Cromwell on May 10, Bedell requested that these documents be sent to Dunstable as quickly as possible. They also needed a copy of Henry's protestation, which the chancellor (Audley) had in his keeping at that time (Pocock, II, 473). There is no indication that the protestation ever arrived. Clayburgh and Watkins later secured possession of it, however, for it appears in their single-volume record of the legatine trial.

Bedell sent everything off to him with the warning to sort it out
carefully before sending any of the documents abroad: "For some
of them make not best for the purpose and leaneth much to this
point, *Quod papa ex causa possit dispensare contra ius divinum*,"
that is, that given a reason the pope could grant dispensations
from divine law.[15]

Friday, May 23, the day after Ascension Thursday, which was
the first subsequent free day in the Church calendar, was named
as the time for the final sentence. On that day, Cranmer first announced that several muniments, writings, and exhibits had been
produced and exhibited to prove the content of the articles (that
is, to verify the facts and the charge that the marriage was illicit
and invalid), and since the last session other relevant documents
had come to hand, which he proceeded to introduce. They were
the report of the York Convocation and the determination of the
University of Cambridge. Then the archbishop asked if anyone
had anything to say, and repeatedly demanded if anyone had or
knew anything to prevent him from handing down his sentence
in the case. No one responded, again much to his relief, for he
had expressed his fear that Catherine or her friends or counsel
would appear in court before he gave sentence, and the process
would thereby be greatly impeded. The king's counsel at the trial
were uncertain of what steps should be taken if an objection were
to be placed against handing down the verdict.[16]

In his formal declaration, he said that he had reviewed all the
evidence, including the answers that King Henry himself had
made to the articles put to him (presumably his deposition submitted to the legatine court), and also the depositions of many
noblemen, the determinations of the principal academies in practically the whole of Christendom, the opinions of both Convocations, and the treaty made between Henry VII and Ferdinand. He
then pronounced the marriage null and void from the beginning,
because, according to the arguments he had seen, it was prohibited
by divine law.[17] We notice that Henry must have stopped insisting on the natural-law qualification. Cranmer claimed to be act-

---

[15] Bedell to Cromwell, 1 September 1533, Pocock, II, 509.
[16] Dunstable Record, f. 352rv; Cranmer to Cromwell, 17 May 1533, *Works*,
II, 242.
[17] Rymer, XIV, 468–69.

ing as legate of the Apostolic See,[18] but he made no reference to the pope's power of dispensation, either to confirm it or to deny it, and had no comment to make on the actual bull of dispensation of Julius II. But a month later Cranmer summarized his action in these terms: "I gave final sentence therein, how that it was indispensable for the pope to license any such marriage."[19] In the next chapter we shall discuss the reasoning upon which the archbishop based his judgment.

Thomas Bedell wrote to Cromwell on the day the trial ended that he trusted that the sentence as given was more to his liking than the original form, and indicated that it was he who had altered it (at least I take this to be the meaning of Bedell's coy comment that Cromwell would know who it was that had bettered it).[20]

That same day Cranmer wrote to Henry to inform him of the sentence and to discuss further action. Specifically, the king had asked him to have the royal council arrange a procuracy to set in motion validation proceedings for Henry's marriage to Anne, and the archbishop told him that he had complied. He realized that there was need for haste since Anne's coronation was set for the first of June.[21]

As soon as Henry received word of the sentence of annulment, he may have taken the precaution of repeating his pact of marriage with Anne, and of having the union solemnized once again, if indeed it had ever been solemnized before. The king was naturally concerned about the legal validity of his second marriage. Even though he was convinced *in foro interno* that his first union was null and that therefore he had been free to contract a second, nevertheless he would not have been considered free in the external forum to enter another marriage until the first was officially declared void. (Cranmer was in the same situation: his German bride was not validly married to him, because of the canons governing priestly celibacy.) At all events, Henry insisted upon another trial *de viribus matrimonii*. This time, however, there could

---

[18] Every archbishop by his office was a *legatus natus* rather than a specially appointed *legatus a latere*, like Wolsey.
[19] Cranmer to Hawkins (n. 6 above), p. 245.
[20] Pocock, II, 476.
[21] Cranmer to Hawkins, p. 244.

not be an inquisition, since there was not the requisite ill report about the marriage but on the contrary only the best opinion of it throughout the land. It was necessary therefore for the king and his new queen to initiate the proceedings themselves.

Accordingly, the royal couple empowered a proctor (probably Bell again) to petition the archbishop for a judgment on their marriage. The trial took place in a "well-known high gallery" in Lambeth Palace near London. Under the prescribed form in such a case, the presiding judge did not present articles to the couple, but rather their proctor submitted a *libellus*, or as Cranmer termed it, a summary of allegation, to the judge. The proctor then petitioned for a sentence or judicial decree fortifying and strengthening the marriage and bringing it to the public notice with all the effect of the law.

Cranmer complied and delivered sentence on Wednesday, May 28. He found that the details of the true, pure, and legitimate marriage *per verba de praesenti* as set forth in the proctor's *summaria allegationis* were verified. That being so, acting according to the counsel of certain legal experts to whom he had communicated the question, he declared that the marriage had been validly contracted and solemnized, and that the couple were regarded as man and wife in the public estimation, and he added to the union the protection of his pastoral and judicial authority.[22]

Bishop Stokesley later conjectured the nature of Cranmer's action at Lambeth. He spoke first of the decisions of the theologians and canonists of the Canterbury Convocation. Then, "with the trust of his own learning and of others besides, I suppose that My Lord of Canterbury did give sentence of divorce of the first marriage and so proceeded *ex abundanti* [beyond that was required] to the approbation of this *etiam per sententiam, posteaquam id quod unicum videbatur obstare prius connubium, lata super eo divortii sententia, sustulerat*"; that is, he confirmed, also by a judicial sentence, the king's second marriage, once he had removed what seemed to be the only impediment, namely, the previous marriage, by having handed down a sentence of annulment upon it. The bishop may have assumed that Cranmer effected a *sanatio in radice*, that is, a retroactive validation of a previously invalid

22 Rymer, XIV, 470–71.

union; or, perhaps more likely, that he was announcing the validity of a marriage contracted during annulment proceedings, when one of the parties was still legally married to someone else. According to canon law, such a second marriage was considered retroactively valid once the first marriage was declared null.[23] It may be that such was the interpretation even though the annulment proceedings during which Henry and Anne married were not the same as those that resulted in the annulment, and even though Cranmer in his sentence of validation on May 28 made no mention of Henry's first marriage in his sentence; he did not in fact mention any of the impediments that we discussed earlier (I shall try to sound out his mind on them later, when the time comes to discuss the annulment of Henry's marriage with Anne). Nevertheless, the possibility remains that Cranmer was referring to a recontracting and resolemnization that took place after the sentence of divorce. When he wrote several weeks later to his successor at the emperor's court, Nicholas Hawkins, he denied that he himself had married Henry and Anne, and he made it clear that he had not fully investigated the circumstances of their original marriage. Even at the time of writing (June 17) he was not sure of the date on which the marriage had taken place—it was sometime around the last feast of St. Paul (that is, January 25), as well appeared from Anne's being now somewhat big with child (as if it followed that they had necessarily gone through the forms of marriage before she became pregnant). "I myself knew not thereof a fortnight after it was done," he asserted. "And many other things be also reported of me, which be mere lies and tales."[24]

[23] Stokesley to Bedell, 4 January 1534, Record Office SP 1/82, f. 12 (LP VII, 15); see above, Chap. 2, n. 4. On *sanatio*, see Kelly, *Traditio*, 23: 283 n. 51. As Richard H. Helmholz, "Marriage Litigation in Medieval England," University of California Ph.D. dissertation (Berkeley, 1970), pp. 31–32, reports, "By far the most common matrimonial case in the medieval Church courts was the action to establish a marriage," not to nullify marriage. "Some of the actions of marriage were brought for particular and special reasons. Two people were anxious to get married, but common rumor had it that they were barred by consanguinity, or that one had another spouse still living. An action of marriage, begun by either party and uncontested by the other, was a way of creating the publicity to end such gossip and to permit them to live together in peace." Cf. Helmholz's work in revised form under the same title (Cambridge, 1974), pp. 25–26, where most of the above is omitted.

[24] Cranmer to Hawkins, p. 246.

On July 5, Henry sent two couriers to Rome, after hearing that his excusator had been refused. They carried, as far as Chapuys could make out, the by now well-worn determinations of the universities, the sentence of Archbishop Cranmer, and an appeal to a general council against the exclusion of the excusator.[25] Well before their arrival, however, the pope would have pronounced his own sentence against Cranmer's and Henry's actions.

The day after his messengers left for Rome, the king sent off instructions and documents, including perhaps the records of the Dunstable trial,[26] to Nicholas Hawkins, his envoy to the emperor. Hawkins was to stress particularly the authority of the determinations, pointing out that Bologna declared in his favor even though it was in papal territory; the pope had shown himself to be partial, and, since an ecumenical council once decreed that all trials should be held in the places where the cases first arose, the Archbishop of Canterbury was within his rights in giving sentence.

Hawkins was to provide Charles with whatever other arguments might prove helpful, as, for example, all the proofs that were received to establish consummation in the first marriage of the ex-queen. One of the proofs of consummation that was sent along was none other than the *libellus* that had been submitted to the legatine court by the queen's lawyers,[27] which Henry had sent to Carne in Rome some time before. It was accompanied by the identical outlandish argument, namely: in combating the eighth and ninth objections, which urged that the bull was defective because it failed to dispense upon public honesty, the defense counsel and the queen herself were forced into declaring that the marriage had indeed been consummated.

As before, the argument was designed to cut both ways. If Charles dismissed the admission of consummation, as he would have to if he took the trouble to reread the *libellus* (it was, after all, not new to him, since Chapuys had sent him a copy of it four years before), the objection of public honesty would still stand— unless, of course, the emperor accepted the real answer that the

25 LP VI, 805.

26 LP VI, 775.4. On May 30, Henry had requested notarized copies of the sentences of May 23 and May 28. Cranmer complied, and Henry gave notice of his reception of the two decrees on June 6. Rymer, XIV, 465–72.

27 The king sent the original document, which is extant in the Vienna Archives. It is reproduced in Appendix A.

queen's counsel had made to it in the *libellus*, which Henry had overlooked.[28]

To this argument was added another, one that relied on the doctrine that the pope could not dispense if the first marriage had been consummated; it addressed itself to the brief rather than the bull, since the brief stated the fact of consummation categorically. To make the argument work it was necessary, of course, to assume that the brief was genuine, as did the Cardinal of Ancona or whoever it was who compiled the *English Articles* in Rome. The king reasoned as follows: "In the brief, whereof ye receive here a copy (the original whereof is in the emperor's custody), it is expressed that narration was made to the pope of the said carnal copulation, and that supplication was made to the pope to dispense upon affinity so contracted. If the said narration or suggestion were true, then Prince Arthur knew the said late queen carnally, by reason whereof the marriage betwixt the King's Grace and her is not good and never was good by the prohibition of the law of God forbidding the brother surviving to marry his dead brother's wife by him carnally known. And if the said narration or suggestion was false, then the said brief is and was of none effect, for a rescript obtained upon a false suggestion is of no force." The same was said to apply to the bull, of which the *forsan* qualification was conveniently forgotten.[29]

The argument was not that the documents were invalid because they dispensed upon affinity instead of public honesty (if Catherine truly had not consummated her first marriage); rather, they were invalid because the assertion of consummation was false. This was the reverse of an earlier argument sent to the emperor, which asserted that Catherine and her parents falsely suggested to the pope that she was still a virgin (hence the wording "perhaps consummated") because they were afraid that the pope would think the dispensation beyond his powers if she were not. The brief, according to this earlier argument, was simply a clumsy forgery concocted a generation later, which attempted to cover over the lie that was evident in the bull.[30]

[28] See above, Chap. 8 at n. 14.

[29] Pocock, II, 495–96; LP VI, 775. Hawkins received his instructions on July 18, 1533, along with a copy of the brief of Julius II—an indication that the above arguments were really sent (LP VI, 855).

[30] LP IV, 5156.4 (p. 2267).

Henry had good reason for wanting to justify himself to Charles. The last thing he wanted was the war that Chapuys was secretly urging; it had been reported to the emperor how precarious the king's situation was: he had only one castle in London (the Tower), and only a hundred archers in his guard. Any other protection had to come from his barons.[31] Chapuys was very circumstantial in describing the disaffection of these barons from the king. But for the present at least, Charles was willing to keep the quarrel on the level of verbal disputation; his forces were already scattered enough as it was, and he was not eager to have yet another front to worry about.

A month or so after the dispatch to the emperor's court had been sent, the order went out once more to collect documents justifying the divorce. At the end of September Gardiner, accompanied by Bonner and Vannes, was sent into France with "a bag full of writings." They were officially envoys to the pope, who was now in France consulting with King Francis,[32] but no doubt the records were meant as much for Francis's eyes as for the pope's. On October 1, Wootton, acting as Official of London, put his seal of approval on Clayburgh and Watkins and the volume of legatine acts that they had just compiled. That date, which marked the beginning of the autumn juridical season, had been set by the papal Consistory for the king's exhibition of the legatine records. Henry doubtless meant this copy for that purpose, and was perhaps constrained to keep it in England until after the harvest vacation in order to have it formally authenticated in an ecclesiastical court. But it seems that the king eventually changed his mind and decided not to send it after all.

At the beginning of the next year a priest was assigned to gather together all the tracts he could find in favor of Henry's divorce and take them to Germany,[33] where, it seems, another stab was to be made at obtaining Lutheran support for the king's actions. At the same time, Henry began the task of securing the approval of his own people. He reassembled his "Reformation Parliament," which met on January 15, 1534. He facilitated his undertaking by countermanding the attendance of those who were likely to oppose

31 LP VI, App. 7.
32 LP VI, 1090, 1164, 1331.
33 SC V, part 1, 25–26.

him, for example, Archbishop Lee, Bishops Fisher and Tunstall, and Lord Darcy. Fisher ignored the order, and in March he was convicted of treason, allegedly for refusing to reveal what the Nun of Kent had told him. His name and that of More were both removed from the bill of attainder (which otherwise would have meant execution without a trial) when More insisted upon the right to defend himself before the Lords, but the lesson was not lost upon other would-be opponents of the king's desires, and within a few days the Act of Succession was passed. On March 30 proclamation was made of Henry's divorce from Catherine and marriage to Anne, and the same day the Archbishop of Canterbury was empowered to receive the oaths of the king's subjects agreeing to the act. On April 4, the members of Parliament were required to sign the new statute—a device, Chapuys wrote, designed to make them confirm the iniquity of the ordinances.[34]

The terms of the Act of Succession should be looked at in detail. The first article began by recalling the great strife that had occurred in the past because of conflicting claims to the crown. Therefore it was thought essential to nullify and declare against God's laws the marriage between the king and Lady Catherine, who had formerly been the lawful wife of Prince Arthur, and "by him was carnally known, as doth duly appear by sufficient proof in a lawful process had and made before Thomas by the sufferance of God now Archbishop of Canterbury." The archbishop's separation of the couple was therefore to be pronounced valid.[35] The chief thrust of the Dunstable proceedings, then, was seen to be the establishing of consummation in Catherine's first marriage.

The Parliament also sought the ratification of the lawful marriage between Henry and Queen Anne, according to the just judgment of the said archbishop, "whose grounds of judgment have been confirmed as well by the whole clergy of this realm in both the Convocations and by both the universities thereof as by the universities of Bologna, Padua, Paris, Orléans, Toulouse, Angers, and divers others [viz. Bourges and Ferrara], and also by the private writings of many right excellent well learned men."

Henry's final campaign for university and clergy support was the easiest of all. He had had no success at all in finding approval

---

[34] LP VII, 373, 390, 392, 434.
[35] 25 Henry VIII c. 22, *Statutes*, III, 471–72.

for the opinion that coitus was not the determining factor in the acquisition of scripturally prohibited affinity; he would therefore not be so foolhardy as to submit his marriage with Anne to their scrutiny, but would simply claim that their previous approval automatically authorized it. There had, in fact, been some attempts to have the English clergy, or at least their chief spokesmen, declare that they had specifically approved the king's second marriage. But the support was not unanimous. Bishop Stokesley, for one, had objected to signing the statement that Bedell sent him, for, as he said, "to my remembrance, the clergy did not entreat expressly, by name, of this marriage, but only of the invalidity of the first marriage, and that by the discussion of two conclusions whereupon that wholly rested, that one appertaining to the learning of theologians and that other of the lawyers; the which the clergy of both the provinces, every part for that appertained to their learnings, thought to be true." He described what he supposed to be the subsequent actions of the Archbishop of Canterbury (cited above). "Wherefore," he continued, "if I should have subscribed to this point after your form, viz. that the clergy of both these provinces determined this marriage to be good whereof by name they spoke no word, I should seem to subscribe more of affection, not only this but others heretofore, than of known or supposed truth, and so bring my learning and conscience in this matter in less estimation." He therefore sent back the form with alterations that would make it acceptable to him.[36]

The second article of the act stated that "many inconveniences" had arisen from marrying within the degrees forbidden by God's laws—"that is to say, the son to marry the mother or the stepmother, the brother the sister, the father his son's daughter or his daughter's daughter, or the son to marry the daughter of his father precreate and borne by his stepmother, or the son to marry his aunt, being his father's or mother's sister, or to marry his uncle's wife, or the father to marry his son's wife, or the brother to marry his brother's wife, or any man to marry his wife's daughter or his wife's son's daughter or his wife's daughter's daughter or his wife's sister." (The Levitical qualification to the last degree, "while his wife is still alive," was prudently omitted.) Although these mar-

<hr>

[36] Letter of 4 January 1534, Record Office SP 1/82, f. 12 (LP VII, 15).

riages "be plainly prohibit and detested by the laws of God," yet they had occasionally been allowed "under colors of dispensations by man's power," notwithstanding the fact that no man had power to dispense with God's laws, as all the clergy of the realm "and the most part of all the famous universities of Christendom and we also do affirm and think." Therefore any annulments that had been made of any such forbidden marriages (e.g., of brother and brother's wife) were hereby confirmed, and the issue declared illegitimate; and—this is the third article—all others so married were to be separated by ecclesiastical sentence.

The fourth article proclaimed that the issue of King Henry and Queen Anne were the lawful issue and heirs to the crown. Princess Mary was not mentioned; if she was automatically illegitimated by the above provision, the point was not stressed.[37] The next five articles gave details of the proclamation of the act, the penalties of treason to be incurred for opposing it, and the oath to be sworn affirming it. The tenth article was a rider to the second, apparently an afterthought inserted by the heavy royal hand, but incongruously placed at the end. It read: "Provided always that the article in this act contained, concerning prohibitions of marriages within the degrees afore mentioned in this act, shall always be taken, interpreted, and expounded of such marriages where marriages were solemnized and carnal knowledge was had."

The qualification was not phrased as tightly as Henry could have wished; both solemnization and consummation were said to be requisite, though Henry was secretly secure in the opinion that solemnization, or simply a *de praesenti* contract without ceremony, was enough. He did not dare to insist on receiving public approbation of this view: it had met with too much opposition before, and to urge it now might have wrecked the whole Act of Succession or at least aroused unwelcome suspicions. As it was, some obstinate minds could allege that this codicil revalidated his marriage to Catherine or at least left it in doubt, since consummation in her first marriage had not really been proved. No

[37] Mortimer Levine, "Henry VIII's Use of His Spiritual and Temporal Jurisdictions," pp. 5–7, argues that Henry and others probably believed that the Act bastardized Mary, but that Cromwell may deliberately have left the point ambiguous in case another legitimate heir should be required in the future. But Levine does not advert to the clause of illegitimation in the second article.

matter. Hanging, drawing, and quartering would take care of such cavilers, if they should put their opinions in writing. The important thing was that extramarital affairs were not elevated to the dignity of the divinely protected Levitical unions, and so his marriage with Anne was safeguarded; it was as clear as day that she was not his wife's sister.

The other point continued to worry the king, however, and seven or eight weeks after the bill had been approved, he sent a commission headed by Archbishop Lee and Bishop Tunstall, two of the stalwarts who had not been allowed to take their seats in Parliament, to Catherine to persuade her to submit to the Act of Succession. It was the second such delegation to attempt this mission, and this time they were to hint that she would be subject to the death penalty if she refused. Their bluff was called when she said that she would welcome it, provided it were done in public (as was required by the law).

The prelates' report was sent to the king on May 21, and it is instructive to see what his threats could do to the resolution of two moderately conscientious servants of God.

Lee told Catherine, among other things, that "carnal knowledge, which is the great key of the matter, is sufficiently proved in the law, as also some that were of her counsel do avow." Perhaps he made a halfhearted gesture to the miserable Tunstall at this point, for he was at one time a member of her counsel. In reply Catherine "utterly denied that ever carnal knowledge was had between her and Prince Arthur, and that she would never confess the contrary; and with loud voice when mention was made of this point she said they lied falsely that so said."

To the archbishop's next point, that once carnal knowledge was proved a divorce was made between her and the king, "she answered that she is not bound to stand to that divorce made by My Lord of Canterbury, whom she called a shadow." The pope had declared in her favor, and that was all that counted. Catherine also asserted that all of her counsel had always told her that her cause was a just one, and Bishop Tunstall was constrained to reply that the matter upon which they had been consulted before the legates was dependent only on the validity of the bull and the brief. (This was not altogether true, as we know.) Since that time, he said, the question of divine law had arisen, and it was declared by the universities—one of them in Bologna, the pope's own city—that when carnal knowledge had been had in the first marriage the pope could not dispense upon the second.

In fact, the bishop went on, speaking no doubt by rote, the pope had once agreed that if Henry would send a proctor to Marseilles, he would declare in his favor, because his cause was just and good. This was in accord with the decretal bull sent with Campeggio to England, "whereof the effect was, that if marriage and carnal knowledge was had betwixt Prince Arthur and her, the legates should pronounce for the divorce. According whereunto, proofs were brought in before the legates, and also since, before the Convocations of this realm and the bishops of Canterbury, and by them allowed and approved as sufficient and lawful."

Tunstall's description of the content of the decretal bull is not to be taken as an accurate report; the drafts did not say anything about the judgment's hanging upon proof of consummation. That this was the case in fact cannot be doubted, but it need not have been made explicit in the bull; it would have been taken for granted.

The bishop ended his harangue of the ex-queen by saying that it plainly followed from all this (a logical leap was necessary, one that Catherine could not make) that the sentence recently given by the pope was not valid, because it declared good a dispensation that he did not have the power to make; "therefore I had now changed my former opinion and exhorted her to do the semblable and to forbear to usurp any more the name of a queen."[38]

The queen, however, refused, probably much to Tunstall's secret relief and satisfaction.

[38] Pocock, II, 569.

CHAPTER THIRTEEN

Cranmer and the King's Conscience

Much of what I have said about Henry's thoughts on what constituted the incestuous unions interdicted by God's law has been conjectured from certain inescapable implications of the facts of the case. Let us pursue the matter a bit further to see if it is possible to come closer to the king's mind.

I have tried to show how essential it was for Henry to bring public honesty within the scope of divine law. There had been some attempts on the part of his advisers to do this, but none of them was truly satisfactory, and in fact the case put in the king's book was a shoddy piece of deception aimed at the masses. Henry had to have the point justified to his own conscience. The question was, who could do it to his satisfaction? The obvious answer was the Archbishop of Canterbury.

Why did Henry choose Cranmer for this exalted post? The idea did not come out of the blue. Was it only because he was a family chaplain of the Boleyns? Or because the suggestion to try the case in a local ecclesiastical court on the basis of the university determinations had come from him? Or because the king saw in him a man who could be molded or bullied into doing what he was told without much heed for the kind of conscientious scruple that plagued Henry himself? Or could it have been that Henry unburdened his conscience to him, perhaps upon some indication in his words that he would be able to dissolve those scruples or help him void them without painful consequences? He must have found that the man possessed a mind like his own—that he had, in fact, concocted a solution similar to the one that he himself had been brewing.

When Cranmer finally returned home to England in January 1533 from Italy, where he had received the king's summons, he was still stunned by the plans Henry had for him. He was to be the agent by which the king was to be freed from the incestuous toils that tortured him. He had often told the king how righteous his beliefs in the matter were, and how justified he would be in acting according to them, even though the judgment of the world might not be in total agreement. Therefore, while he was awaiting the formal approbation of his appointment from Rome, the new archbishop was to busy himself in setting down on paper all those reasons and authoritative statements which had led him to the conclusions that Henry had found so consoling in times past.

Cranmer complied, and no doubt finished his treatise in good time. It can be dated from the fact that he took advantage not only of the university determinations but also of the Anglo-Spanish treaty, which must have been rediscovered around the time when he returned to England. He entitled his work *Twelve Articles by Which It Is Right Plainly Demonstrated That a Divorce Must Necessarily Be Made Between Henry VIII, the Most Unconquered King of England, and the Most Serene Catherine.*[1] The book was not intended for the vulgar eye, and therefore was not committed to the printer, though it could have stood up much better against the slings and arrows of the opposition than most of what had been published before this time—especially the white paper that he had helped to translate. To have spread the treatise abroad would have raised unhealthy suspicions about Henry's relations with Catherine, and also about the possibility that Cranmer had prejudged the case. It was instead given to a special secretary, whose Italian hand had been employed in the past in analyzing the foreign theologians who had pronounced for or against the king on the question of the pope's dispensing power. The scribe made two copies that survive, one "handsomely bound in gilt edges and velvet cover, being the original binding in which it was presented to the king," and the other the personal copy of the archbishop-elect, inscribed to "Thomas of Canterbury."[2]

---

[1] *Articuli duodecim quibus plane admodum demonstratur divortium inter Henricum octavum Angliae regem invictissimum et serenissimam Catherinam necessario esse faciendum.* Text in Pocock, I, 334–99.

[2] LP VI, 530. Henry Jenkyns, *The Remains of Thomas Cranmer*, I (Oxford, 1833), viii, note t, states that the inscription on the flyleaf, "Thomas Cantu-

The work had two main objectives: the first, to show that un-consummated marriages fall under the indispensable ban of the Levitical degrees, and therefore that Henry's marriage should be annulled whether Catherine had come to him a virgin or not; the second, to prove that in spite of all appearances to the contrary, Catherine really had consummated her marriage with Arthur. It might be thought that the latter point made no real difference, given the author's conclusion that consummation added no further binding force to the law. But it will soon appear that consummation did make a difference, not in the internal forum of conscience, btu in the external forum of ecclesiastical law.

In the first article the author attempted to demonstrate that the natural and divine impediment of affinity was induced only by the marriage contract. (In other words, the real impediment of affinity was none other than the impediment usually known as public honesty.) He was well aware of the common opinion that affinity proceeded from licit and even illicit intercourse, but he would show that he had reason and authority on his side. First of all, he said, it was clear from Scripture, from the Fathers (among whom he included the popes), and from reason itself that the kind of affinity banned by natural and divine law must come either from the marriage contract alone, or from the contract followed by intercourse, and never from intercourse alone.

He appealed to Nicholas of Lyre's interpretation of the fate that befell Adonijah when he wanted Abishag. No doubt Cranmer had not seen Fisher's refutation of the *Determinations* on this point, since Fisher's work had not been printed. "The prohibition against incestuous marriage," Cranmer continued, "refers specifically not to carnal copula but to the marriage contract and regards that alone; this is what God forbids and prohibits, as borne witness to by Scripture: 'And a man shall not take the wife [*uxor*] of his father,'" that is, the stepmother, whether carnally known or not. The fact of the matter was, he contended, that the turpitude spoken of in Leviticus came neither from intercourse nor from the marriage bond, but from daring to contravene a natural and

---

arien'," as in Cranmer's hand, but Gairdner denies it. It cannot be proved absolutely that Cranmer was the author; it is only very likely. But if he did not write it, at least he must have read it and been familiar with its arguments.

divine prohibition. There was no turpitude per se—Cain was allowed to marry his sister, and God conceded to the Hebrews the right of marrying a brother's wife.[3]

(It is evident that the subsequent revocation of permission to marry one's sister—and according to Cranmer, one's brother's wife as well—would constitute a *divine* prohibition against further use of the practice, but Cranmer did not pause to show how it was a natural prohibition as well. This point was the subject of his twelfth article, but when he came to it, he said that there was no need to prove it, for it had been abundantly demonstrated by the determinations of the universities and in many treatises.[4] His own earlier book, which he took himself or sent to Cambridge at the end of 1529, was of course one such treatise.)

Going further in pursuit of his first article, he said that just as true and perfect marriage came from the marriage contract alone, so too it was with affinity. He appealed to canon law and cited Popes Gregory the Great and Julian on the matter of espousals,[5] and attempted to prove from the writings of the commentators that the canons implied an affinity imposed by divine and natural law only for espousals *de praesenti* and not *de futuro*. When coming to speak of affinity in a formal way, he cited the definition of civil law: "Affinity is a propinquity arising from nuptials." There was, he confessed, another definition—namely, "Affinity is a propinquity arising from carnal copula"—and though admittedly almost the whole body, hand and foot, of theologians and canonists accepted this definition, there were some who held for the other, and he urged that they be heard. He cited Thomas Aquinas, Peter of La Palu, William of Paris, Torquemada, and others, and showed the difficulty of holding the more common opinion. Thus, Innocent IV and Antoninus of Florence said that if a man penetrated his wife but no semen flowed, the matrimony was not consummated and no affinity was contracted. Cardinal Zabarella, on the other hand, said that if a man emitted seed on the surface of the pudenda and some of it flowed inside, the marriage was consummated and affinity arose; he gave the example of

---

[3] *Articuli duodecim*, pp. 336–41.
[4] *Ibid.*, p. 399.
[5] *Ibid.*, p. 342, citing the forged decretals discussed above, Chap. 1 at 11.

a Frenchman who actually begot a child on his wife in this way—
her vagina had been too tight to admit him, and so the conception
took place with her hymen intact.[6]

Again, Innocent III held that simple "pollution" on the surface
of the wife's privities caused affinity, even though no seed entered
the chamber. But Thomas and Albert the Great said that unless
there were a mixing of the man's seed with the wife's within the
chamber there would be no affinity and no consummation. (Thus
Thomas held for both sides, for he was quoted above as saying
that "marriage causes affinity not only by reason of carnal copula,
but also by reason of the conjugal society, by which marriage has
also its natural aspect; therefore affinity will be induced from the
very contract of marriage itself, *per verba de praesenti,* before in
tercourse takes place." Thomas then would not say that there was
no affinity before the mixing of the seeds.) Many took an opposing
view, Cranmer continued, for they declared that only the male
seed was necessary for affinity, since it alone sufficed for generation. This was the common medical opinion, he said, but Hostiensis (Henry of Susa, Cardinal of Ostia) and others disagreed.
One could easily see, he concluded, that once a solid scriptural
foundation had been laid aside, how diverse were the opinions
of men, and as a result no one could tell how it was that affinity
arose.[7]

What was to be said, he asked, about the kinsmen and in-laws
of Jesus and his mother? Perhaps Sacred Scripture was wrong in
designating them as such! No, there was true affinity contracted
between Mary and Joseph's relatives, and between Joseph and
Mary's relatives, so that when Joseph died his brother could not
have married Mary. He went on to speak with much eloquence
on the subject of the Holy Family. Jesus himself, he said, was
called Joseph's son because of a singular and most perfect degree
of affinity.[8]

How then was one to explain the universal opinion that affinity
also arose from intercourse? Even the lawyers who followed Sacred
Scripture in defining affinity as proceeding from marriage contradicted the definition in their law, where affinity was said to come

6 *Ibid.,* pp. 342–44.
7 *Ibid.,* pp. 343, 344–45.
8 *Ibid.,* pp. 345–47.

from concubinage. The answer lay, he asserted, in the nature of legal proof and the needs of the external forum, as opposed to those of the internal forum, that is, one's conscience before God. There was nothing that could more easily prove the substance of marriage and its effect of affinity than carnal copula. Therefore there was enacted into law, both canon and civil, the notion that affinity arose from intercourse. It was, however, a purely human law, not binding in conscience, except insofar as obedience was required according to the sanctions of pontifical law.

Therefore, he continued, if someone were to promise marriage, even *de praesenti*, simply out of a desire to seduce a girl, but were lacking all internal consent, and if intercourse should follow, there would be no marriage *in foro Dei*, because consent was necessary; but in the forum of the Church marriage would be considered to exist, by the decree of Innocent III; and according to the canon of Gregory IX the same was true even of a promise *de futuro*, because, as Pope Alexander specified in another decretal, the consent *de praesenti* was presumed to have been given. Moreover, if such a person should contract a true marriage later, with real internal consent, he would be compelled by the judgment of the Church to leave the woman to whom he was genuinely married in the eyes of God and to return to the girl he had seduced.

The theologians and lawyers, Cranmer went on, extended the rule even further and declared that affinity also arose from intercourse when no contract of marriage had preceded, so that decency and honesty might be preserved in the external forum. As a result, exterior decency, as Panormitanus rightly remarked, was given more attention in the contracting of marriage than the truth of the matter. Cardinal Zabarella, following what Cranmer called the beautiful deduction of Hostiensis, went to the extreme of saying that this kind of affinity occurred even if the woman were unwilling or asleep, and Pope Innocent and others asserted that even unnatural carnal commerce gave rise to it.

There was, then, ultimately no contradiction between the two views of affinity. "Whenever the pronouncements of the Fathers, theologians, and doctors of canon and civil law affirm that affinity arises from carnal copula, they are always to be interpreted as referring to an impediment in the external forum, and one that is sanctioned by human law alone; when, however, they say that the affinity arises from the nuptial contract, they are to be understood as speaking of the *forum Dei* and of the effects of divine and natural law."[9]

Cranmer concluded his discussion of the first article by saying rather pointedly that decrees of the Fathers were binding only as long as necessity made them profitable to the universal Church. He then moved to the second article, in which he desired to show that the essence of marriage consisted only in the conjugal pact and not in carnal copula. This was not difficult to prove, since it was agreed on all hands; the union of Mary and Joseph provided the prime argument. He was simply working up to an argument that had been urged rather shabbily in the *Determinations* booklet: namely (to use the phraseology of Cranmer's third article), "A husband and his wife become one mind and one flesh by the conjugal pact alone, with God as the principal agent." A marriage contract therefore was not like other contracts because God himself intervened and made it indissoluble. Cranmer confessed that the laws of the Church said that husband and wife became one flesh by sexual intercourse, but this was based on a legal fiction: that is, they were to become two in one flesh by reason of their offspring. The Church necessarily made use of legal presumptions and fictions in order to make decisions in cases of doubt, or simply by way of convention. The fiction in this case was even extended to fornication, so that a man was said to become one flesh even with a prostitute. But the divine law had no need of such fictions since it regarded only the naked and open truth.[10]

It was, he maintained, only the bond of marriage that was indissoluble, not the act of intercourse. "Why is it then," he asked, "that almost all professors of pontifical law, relying solely on the sayings of men, gratuitously affirm, against the truth of the Gospel, that an unconsummated marriage can be dissolved by the authority of the Roman pontiff, in spite of the protest to the contrary of all theologians and even some canonists—as if it were in

9 *Ibid.*, pp. 347–52.

10 *Ibid.*, pp. 352–74. A somewhat similar argument is to be found in a fragment of a treatise in the Record Office, SP 6/9, ff. 41–43. These folios comprise the eleventh article of the treatise: "An uxor viri defuncti sine liberis sit censenda fuisse una caro cum illo, quamvis ipsa neget sese ab illo carnaliter cognita."

the power of man to root out the Gospel and the faith of Christ, especially when it is sanctioned by pontifical law that a second consummated marriage is not to be preferred to a first marriage not yet consummated, since by the bonds of the first marriage, as Panormitanus says, each spouse has the right to the other, and we do not doubt that the second marriage can in no way be made in prejudice of the law to the other one already contracted?"[11]

This monumental question could have pulled Cranmer into deep water with his lord and master. Would not such a stand as his primate was taking jeopardize his recently contracted and consummated marriage to Anne Boleyn? Or had not Henry told Cranmer about Anne's earlier clandestine marriage? I shall return to this question later. We recall that a similar case for the indispensability of *de praesenti* marriage contracts had been made in the *Determinations* treatise. There was in fact an even stronger tradition for this position than for the indispensability of the Levitical degrees.[12]

In setting forth his arguments against the possibility of this sort of divorce, Cranmer declared himself to be especially shocked by the views of Cardinal Cajetan (Thomas de Vio, General of the Dominicans, who in 1531 had advised Clement that Henry's marriage with Catherine was good).[13] Cajetan not only abandoned his fellow theologians and joined the canonists in saying that the pope could dissolve a nonconsummated marriage, but went so far as to say that he could dissolve a consummated marriage, even one between Christians, for the mere reason of conjugal discord and to

---

[11] *Articuli duodecim*, p. 380. See below, Chap. 15 at n. 26, for the decree that Cranmer was citing.

[12] See above, Chap. 10 at n. 19. John T. Noonan, Jr., *Power to Dissolve*, pp. 129–35, rehearses the tradition denying the pope the power to dissolve nonconsummated marriages, and also shows that popes during the fifteenth and sixteenth centuries did in fact effect such dissolutions, though the practice was not widely known. Clement VII's dispensation allowing Henry to marry any woman in spite of a previous unconsummated marriage (above, Chap. 2 at n. 25) can be added to Noonan's list of precedents; and his hypothesis that papal assumption of the power predated Martin V (1417–31) is verified by the report of the Avignon curialist Giles Bellemère in 1392, during the reign of the first Clement VII. As we saw above (Intro., n. 8), Cardinal Zalva of Pamplona listed nonconsummated marriage as one of the divine laws upon which the pope had power to grant dispensations.

[13] See Kelly, *Traditio*, 23: 308, n. 119.

avoid adultery and murder; and he declared further that it was allowable to a Christian to divorce his wife on grounds of fornication (that is, adultery) and to remarry.[14]

Here was a theologian after Henry's own heart. Why, he might have asked, had not Cajetan's *quodlibet* been pointed out to him before? If only the king could get this most respected of Thomists on his side, he could then attempt to win the pope over to the cardinal's eminently reasonable and practical—and hitherto unsuspected—views on the permissibility of divorce when good reasons urged it.

It has long been thought that Henry made such an attempt to persuade Cajetan of the justice of his position. The evidence cited is a letter to the king from the cardinal under date of January 27, 1534, in which he reviewed the theology of the case. But the opening words of the letter show quite clearly that it was unsolicited:

I rejoice over what has been told me, that Your Majesty has been moved to break asunder your old marriage and marry a new wife not by Your Highness's authority but by the documents of Sacred Scripture, and that you profess to know that your actions are legitimate not merely from putting your belief in doctors, but also from relying on the acumen of your own insight, and your own intelligence. We ought surely to thank God for adorning our age with a king who is a theologian; and therefore I thought it would not be beyond the realm of Christian charity to beg you, most learned king, to deign to read and weigh what I have written below, and to compare it with those things which motivate Your Majesty's intellect.

Cajetan then set forth his reasons for thinking that the scriptural foundations upon which Henry's opinion was based were not valid; specifically, he said, it could be shown from other texts and from history that the prohibition against marrying one's brother's wife presupposed that both brothers were still alive. He concluded:

If these considerations, most learned king, seem to be true and sufficient, what has been done should be corrected. But if they are judged to be insufficient, I beg that their deficiencies be pointed out. For I am confident that by the bounty of God's grace one who begins will finish the task.

---

14 *Articuli duodecim*, p. 381, citing Cajetan, "In quodlibetis, q. 9, in materia de matrimonio." One day Cranmer himself, also a theologian rather than a canonist, would come to have opinions even more radical than Cajetan's. See below, Epilogue.

If, however, these considerations are thought to be probable, I beseech the Defender of the Faith to act like a man caught between the probabilities of one side and another. For Your Majesty very well knows what must be done in cases of doubt, as it is set forth by the divine law of Deuteronomy 17, for taking action when doubts occur. Finally, if these reasons are false, deign, most learned prince, to refute them, for I stand ready to learn and change my opinion. Remove, I beg of you, this scandal to so many Christians in Europe, a scandal not only to the common people but also to the religious and learned. But remove it by making evident the justice of what has been done, so that scandal be not given but taken back. For I offer myself to be the herald of Your Highness's justice.[15]

We do not know if Henry was even tempted to reply to the cardinal. He had been made secure in his own conscience by a theologian whom he valued far more highly than the Dominican Cardinal-Bishop of Gaeta.

But to return to Cranmer's treatise: he went on to develop his seemingly hard line against divorce. The Church, he said, could not dissolve marriage. It could, however, take away the right or obligation of intercourse; for example, if a man should sin with the kinswoman of his wife, he would be forbidden by the statute of the Church to have further relations with his wife because of the affinity thus contracted. It was not even true that the Church could dissolve a marriage if one of the spouses were to take the vows of a religious order. But, Cranmer suddenly insisted, the marriage would be dissolved nevertheless in such a case—not by the Church, or by the pope, but by God himself, just as He dis-

---

[15] British Museum Additional MS 29547, f. 6. The letter is cited in Rinaldi, *Annales ecclesiastici*, A.D. 1534, nos. 1–2. Cf. LP VII, 110, where Gairdner seems to interpret the letter as completely favorable to Henry. In citing Deuteronomy 17 the cardinal seems to be hinting gently that Henry should let the papal court decide the matter. The chapter reads, in part: "If thou perceive that there be among you a hard and doubtful matter in judgment . . . and thou see that the words of the judges within thy gates do vary, arise and go up to the place which the Lord thy God shall choose, and thou shalt come to the priests of the Levitical race, that shall be at that time: and thou shalt ask of them, and they shall show thee the truth of the judgment. And thou shalt do whatsoever they shall say, that preside in the place which the Lord shall choose, and what they shall teach thee according to his law. And thou shalt follow their sentence; neither shalt thou decline to the right hand nor to the left hand. But he that will be proud, and refuse to obey the commandment of the priest who ministereth at that time to the Lord thy God, and the decree of the judge, that man shall die." Of course, Henry could reply that God's priest had given judgment, the priest whom he himself, as Supreme Head, had chosen to rule his Church (and whom the Bishop of Rome had also approved).

solved marriages of infidels according to the so-called Pauline privilege. Furthermore, as in cases of Pauline privilege, even consummated marriages could be nullified, when one of the spouses entered religion. For, as he had already demonstrated, consummation added nothing to the essence of marriage.[16]

By this line of argumentation, Cranmer succeeded in giving a theological basis to the highly dubious and revolutionary expedient that had been toyed with by both Henry and the pope some years before, of packing Catherine off to a nunnery and then licensing Henry to remarry, in spite of his unquestionably consummated present marriage. Her consent was necessary, unfortunately, and though it was hardly likely to be forthcoming in the future, it would be good for Henry to have this convincing justification at his fingertips in case the opportunity should present itself.

The fourth and fifth articles of the treatise, which asserted that carnal copula gave rise to a marriage impediment of affinity that was binding only by the law of the Church, followed directly from the foregoing. True incest existed, Cranmer said, only in the degrees forbidden by divine and natural law, and only here were to be found true and perfect consanguinity and affinity. The affinity arising solely from sexual intercourse impeded marriage only by ecclesiastical statute, "and the transgressors of this statute do not commit incest properly so called, but only a certain crime of disobedience in offending against the Church. The Roman pontiff therefore can easily relax this kind of disobedience (which could only be called incest metaphorically) with the grant of a dispensation—which is something he cannot do with true incest." The affinity therefore "which comes from illicit coitus with the sister or daughter or mother of one's wife," whether before or after the marriage, raised no impediment by natural or divine law, but impeded the contracting of marriage, and dissolved marriages already (invalidly) contracted, by human law alone, and this law was subject to dispensation by the Church.[17]

If Cranmer was not aware of Anne's early marriage, clearly he had knowledge of Henry's illicit relations with Anne's sister (and with her mother, if such there had been) and of the dispensation Henry had received from the pope for the affinity thus contracted.

16 *Articuli duodecim*, pp. 382–86.
17 *Ibid.*, pp. 387–92.

It is clear, too, that the archbishop was relying on the papal dispensation when he approved Henry's marriage at the end of May. For the protest that he made before taking the oath of allegiance to the pope did not reject the pontiff's authority; it merely stated his intention of not binding himself to do anything against God's law, or against the king or realm of England or its laws and prerogatives, and left himself free to reform religion in whatever ways he might think necessary.[18]

In arguing that it was affinity and not public honesty that arose from the marriage contract, and in quoting with approval the opinion of Anthony of Budrio (ca. 1338–1408) that illicit intercourse gave rise not to affinity but to public honesty,[19] Cranmer was urging a very sensible reform in canonical practice, one that returned to the original ecclesiastical tradition. It was finally adopted by the Roman Church, but not until the new *Code of Canon Law* was issued in 1917. In England, divinely prohibited affinity was divorced from illicit copula in 1534, but, as we shall see, was reunited to it in 1536; and it remained so defined until 1861.

With the sixth article Cranmer began the second part of his work, which he dispatched in a few pages. Carnal copula, he admitted, rendered a marriage consummated, but this consummation was only an accidental perfection, since, as he had established earlier, it had nothing to do with the essence of marriage. With this as a preface, he proceeded to the important seventh article: "Marriage can be consummated with carnal copula even without the wife's loss of her irrecoverable virginity."[20]

The truth had come out at last. Henry had confessed to this marvellous and serious wise man all the details of that first night in bed with his new queen, after she had been despoiled of her adornments, which were not those of another man's former wife, but of a virgin bride. The memory of it still haunted him, even after all the long years that had passed. She had often insisted beforehand that her marriage with Arthur had never been consummated, and he believed her. He believed her even more that night. She had obviously never been touched. He was awkward about it, and when, finally, with a great struggle, he had brought it off, she was bleeding. Henry remembered the blood on the sheets

---

[18] Wilkins, III, 757.   [19] *Articuli duodecim*, p. 390.
[20] *Ibid.*, pp. 393–94.

very well, as did the servants of the chamber, perhaps some of them the very same who had failed to find any blood years before, after each of the six or seven nights that Catherine had spent together with Arthur. They all recalled it well enough to swear to it when the remissorial letters were sent around a generation later.

Henry believed for long after that Catherine had come to him a virgin and had yielded him her maidenhead. There had been no reason to question it. But then, when the great doubts came about his marriage, when the terrifying words of Leviticus struck home to him and he feared that he had violated the law of God and had invited divine punishment upon himself, he learned that the queen's virginity might make all the difference in the world in the proof of his sinful state. He was furious to hear that even Wolsey was hesitant on that score, and wrote him a letter of rebuke. The cardinal's servile response straightened out the truth of the affair: someone had revealed the king's scruple to the queen. She had undoubtedly received learned advice on how to defend herself—Dr. Sampson said that "the queen was very stiff and obstinate, affirming that your brother did never know her carnally and that she desired counsel as well of your subjects as of strangers." This is why Wolsey suggested to Sampson that if it were really true that she had never been known by Arthur they could use the argument of public honesty.[21]

It was true that the matter had come to the queen's attention; four days before Wolsey's letter was written Henry himself had told her that they were living in mortal sin by being married to each other. More importantly, the Spanish ambassador had found out about the matter a month and a half earlier, when Wolsey first convened his formal inquisition.[22]

Wolsey's argument might be very good, but where did this leave Henry's conviction that he had violated the divine law? It was agreed shortly after this time to attack the bull of dispensation rather than to question the pope's power in granting the dispensation, but Henry had by no means abandoned his conviction, and he felt it strengthen when he saw the great difficulty there would be in getting the bull declared inadequate.

[21] Letter of 1 July 1527, Record Office SP 1/42 (SP I, 195; LP IV, 3217); see above, Chap. 1 at n. 24.

[22] Mendoza's letter of 18 May 1527 reported it to Charles, SC III, part 2, 193–94; see also his letter of 13 July, *ibid.*, p. 276.

He certainly believed that illicit intercourse could not give rise to the prohibited relationship of Leviticus, because it seemed so right that he should marry Anne. It was also clear as crystal to him, the more he thought about it, that consummation made no difference to the divine interdict. This was why Henry was so grateful to find that Cranmer shared this view.

And yet (that terrible conscience of his) there was a persistent doubt: it was so generally held that consummation was necessary —he had only to remember the crashing failure of his attempt to find university support for his view. Could he be wrong? If so, that could only mean that Catherine had not come to him a virgin, in spite of all signs to the contrary. Perhaps Dr. Cranmer could suggest a remedy for his dilemma. It must have been, therefore, this need to minister to the king's conscience that was the chief reason for Cranmer, after proving that consummation was not necessary, to set about establishing that consummation had actually occurred, in a treatise that only the king would read.

There were, Cranmer said, following the Dominican theologian Peter of La Palu, three ways in which a woman's virginity could be lost: (1) when a man broke into her pudendal chamber with her consent, and neither of them emitted seed; (2) when she emitted seed without the man's entering in or emitting seed; and (3) when the man emitted seed without breaking in, and somehow she received it into her chamber, even though no seed came from her. Sometimes pregnancy could result in this last way (there was that Frenchman's wife that Cardinal Zabarella knew about), which could not happen unless the woman's virginity were lost.[23] If, therefore, a bride were to admit her husband to lie with her, and he only polluted her (the ugly word was the technical canonical term) by spilling his seed in the vicinity of her pudenda, then, in spite of the fact that her physical virginity was not irrecuperably lost—her hymen would remain unbroken and no seed would have issued from her—the marriage would nevertheless have been consummated and affinity induced. He proved this from the canons of the popes and the commentaries of the learned Cardinal Torquemada. The gloss to the decretal *Iuvenis* of Pope Eugenius III

---

[23] As so often happens in clinical discussions of this sort, the normal course of things is lost sight of in the midst of the pathologies and abnormalities. Surely the "fourth way," in which both parties "emitted seed" after penetration, deserved a mention.

rightly observed, he said, that the action of the spouses in this situation was performed not only with marital affection but also with the desire and effort to enter into the *pudoris claustra*. Such an action, therefore, just as it would induce affinity and prevent them from marrying anyone else,[24] would also consummate the marriage.

He thereupon proceeded to the eighth article: "That the most serene Catherine was left a virgin by Prince Arthur, we do not affirm." He drew light from the Hebrew words for virgin. No girl could be called *halma* unless she was a young virgin completely whole, never touched by a man in any way, or polluted, and about whose pudicity and integrity there was no doubt and no suspicion. The word *nahara* would be more appropriate for Catherine after she had been widowed of Arthur, for it meant simply "young woman," whether carnally known or not.

In the ninth article, he asserted: "That the most serene Catherine was corrupted [another ugly technical term] by the same illustrious Prince Arthur and the marriage consummated we do not doubt, because of the many circumstances that attest to it and create a very strong presumption." For, he explained, there was no one who did not know that at that time Arthur was sufficiently mature and potent, and Catherine ready and able to receive a man. Cyprian said that the mere being in bed together was enough to declare the woman wholly corrupted. Furthermore, when Arthur died Catherine was taken care of by some very noble women who wondered whether she were pregnant; and since she objected nothing to the contrary, it was surely to be presumed that she had come to Henry already corrupted—especially since the depositions of many of the most noble persons in the realm attested to those circumstances which proved from all sides by a violent presumption that the marriage had been consummated. The same was explicitly stated in the treaty signed by the rulers of the two countries, and also in the brief obtained on Catherine's supplication from the Roman pontiff to remove the impediment of affinity.

He assumed here and in the next article that Catherine herself had written to the pope for the dispensation, even though the document, like the bull, named Henry also as a petitioner (and of

---

[24] He should have qualified this assertion by saying that it was human and not divine law that was in question here.

course Henry and his supporters consistently denied that he knew anything about the request). The fact that Cranmer took for granted the authenticity of the brief in a private treatise meant only for the king's eyes is an indication that this was now also Henry's view, or indeed that it had been his secret opinion—or fear—all along.

The tenth article stated that Catherine's oath could not overcome the strong presumption to the contrary; and the penultimate article, that no judge could legally accept such an oath from her.[25]

This treatise by Cranmer was the final assurance that Henry needed to make himself sure of the man he had chosen to be archbishop; he did not resort to the crude device that was reported to Chapuys of having him officiate at his marriage to Anne Boleyn. And it was also the final assurance that he needed for his own peace of mind. Now he could and would have his way.

In addition to the steps actually taken by Archbishop Cranmer in annulling the king's first marriage, Henry also thought of having him issue a formal statement on the consummation of Catherine's first marriage which would relieve the king of any obligation to declare his mind on the subject. Cranmer first drafted in his own hand the following declaration:

From the declarations of witnesses of the greatest nobility, which are also confirmed by the wording of the treaty concluded between the most illustrious and powerful princes, parents of the most serene Royal Majesty and the most noble Lady Catherine, and corroborated by the supportive evidence of other allegations, it seems to us to be established, by canonical and legitimate probability, that the illustrious Prince Arthur had carnal knowledge of the aforesaid most noble Lady Catherine, and that no judge whatever should pronounce otherwise upon this kind of testimony, but rather, after considering exhibits of this sort, should necessarily incline his mind to move in accord with our opinion, to the extent indeed that the unsupported oath of the queen be not permitted by the laws to be received as evidence for a divergent conclusion. This indeed is our judgment and opinion.

Henry, apparently not satisfied with this draft, tried to work out another phrasing. His first attempt was: "We indeed, striving to exonerate both our conscience and that of our king *as much as in us* [deleted] as occasion offers, in order that we might investigate the pure truth of this matter . . ." Leaving that unfinished, he tried

[25] *Articuli duodecim*, pp. 394–98. For the twelfth article, see above, at n. 4.

again: "We indeed striving to act upon these things which could exonerate both our conscience and that of our king, and, ultimately, bending our efforts [according to] the precept of God, it seems evident to us that it is established by canonical and legitimate probability, upon seeing the testimony of the most noble persons brought forth beforehand in court . . ." He also wanted to include some mention of the queen's *libellus*, which, as I have shown before, he erroneously believed to contain an admission of consummation. After a false start, he arrived at the following: "And, added to this, the confession of the *instrument* [deleted] brief judicially exhibited for the defense of the said Lady Catherine by her proctor."[26]

Another version of Cranmer's statement in a different hand has him say that, because of the testimony "very recently aired in this matrimonial and divortial cause between the most illustrious and powerful king, our lord, and the most serene Lady Catherine, the pretended queen, along with other supportive evidence pertaining to the cause, we deem, declare, attest, and judge that it was shown to our tribunal and is strongly to be presumed" that carnal copula occurred between Arthur and Catherine.[27] This wording indicates that the plan of having the archbishop issue a statement on consummation was hit upon shortly after the Dunstable trial, when Henry once again got out the queen's *libellus* to send it off to the emperor. The idea was abandoned, as far as we can tell, no doubt because of a fear that it would raise too much curiosity as to why the king needed to have his conscience exonerated.

[26] Record Office SP 1/65, f. 13 (LP V, 6.5). The document is reproduced in Appendix B. It should not be necessary to labor over the point that Henry was referring to a legal brief, not the brief of Julius II. The latter was exhibited judicially not for Catherine's defense but for Henry's justification.

[27] Record Office SP 1/65, f. 15 (LP V, 6.6).

Part Four

AFTERMATH

By my troth and maidenhead,
I would not be a queen.
—Shakespeare & Fletcher, HENRY VIII

CHAPTER FOURTEEN

The Second Annulment

᚛᚛᚛

AFTER THE Act of Succession had been passed, Henry was at last free to live with Anne in peace. There was, however, one overwhelming difficulty: some months after the legislation had been forced through Parliament he had begun to tire of her. As the time wore on he came to meditate more and more upon the marriage that he had struggled so long to effect.

The birth of a daughter in September 1533 had been a heavy blow—Henry had been confident beyond measure that it would be a boy. But it took the miscarriages that followed to set him twisting and turning again along the well-worn wrinkles of that part of his brain which calculated divine displeasure. Was his marriage to Anne, he asked himself, just as immoral as his union with Catherine, or (God forbid) even more so?

Any doubts about the first marriage which might have lingered on in the contrived corridors of Henry's mind were laid to rest when Catherine of Aragon died at the beginning of 1536. Henry held a ball in honor of the event—ostensibly he was celebrating the end of the threat of war from the emperor, but his relief may have been more general. Catherine was bad for his conscience.

But what was he to do about his other wife? A few days after Catherine's death, Henry, like a man going to confession ("comme en confession"), confided to someone at his court the great secret that "he had entered into this marriage seduced and constrained by witchcraft, and for this reason he believed that he was able to take another wife," and he gave his confidant to understand that he desired to do so. God had proved the invalidity of the marriage by refusing to grant him any male children. Chapuys could hardly believe his ears when it was reported to him, but he had it on good authority.[1]

A couple of years before, Chapuys had taken a grim satisfaction in Anne's delivery of Elizabeth. The sex of the child had been a great reproach, he said, to the physicians, astrologers, sorcerers, and sorceresses who had promised with such assurance that it would be a boy.[2] The ambassador had been astonished at what reliance the king placed upon that kind of nonsense beforehand, but surely, he thought, he had learned his lesson. Now it appeared that his superstitiousness was incurable, only this time he was using his dark beliefs to very good effect—once again, he was making out a case of nullity for himself, now based on lack of free consent. What an infinitely resourceful instrument his conscience was! Still, why not? Richard III's Parliament had leveled the same charge of witchcraft against Henry's grandmother Elizabeth Woodville and her mother in winning the affections of his grandfather Edward IV, and it had worked well enough, at least for a time. Another precedent was to be had in what was undoubtedly the most sensational witchcraft trial in English history, that of Eleanor Cobham, Duchess of Gloucester, in 1441. One of the accusations made by Henry Chichele, Archbishop of Canterbury, in the *ex officio* inquisition against her was that she had won the heart and hand of her husband, the Duke Humphrey, by the sorcery and witchcraft of Margery Jourdemayne; and one of the lesser known effects of the trial was the annulment of their marriage.[3]

In February 1536, Chapuys reported the last miscarriage of the Concubine, as he liked to call Anne. He said that when Henry came to visit her he scarcely spoke a word, except to say that "he saw clearly that God did not wish to give him any male children."[4] Anne had good reason to feel apprehensive. Within a short time Cromwell had gathered together evidence of some rather unlikely adulteries between Anne and a few of her intimates and crowned the whole case with a charge of incest between her and her brother. All this was considered treasonous, on the basis that it endangered

---

[1] Chapuys to Charles V, 29 January 1536, Paul Friedmann, *Anne Boleyn*, II, 202–3.

[2] LP VI, 1112.

[3] For these episodes and other examples of suspected witchcraft plots against Henry's predecessors, see my forthcoming "English Kings and the Fear of Sorcery," *Mediaeval Studies*, 39 (1977).

[4] Letter of 25 February 1536, LP X, 351 (p. 134).

the king—for example, it made him sick when he heard about it; also, it involved a plot against his life. The proof of the latter charge was a report that the queen had told one of her friends that she would marry him after the king died.

There were other things, too. She had told her sister-in-law that Henry was practically impotent—he had "neither vigor nor virtue" in bed. (When Chapuys saw fit to express his doubts to the emperor about Jane Seymour's virginity, he added that Henry would perhaps be happy to be so far relieved of the trouble he might otherwise have, considering the Concubine's report of him; and it would also give him a good excuse to rid himself of her when he wearied of her.)[5] Henry's difficulties as a lover may have been an important element in his inconstancy. For him the great pleasure seems to have been in the hunt rather than in the kill. Perhaps his embarrassment inevitably produced in him a suspicion that his partner despised him for his lack of virility. It is likely that his suspicions were justified in Anne's case, and that her delinquency in this matter was in reality the most serious charge against her and the fundamental cause of her downfall.

On the day that Anne was arrested, Chapuys reported that he had found out a few days before by good authority that even if the adultery had not been discovered, Henry was already set on abandoning her; for he had found witnesses to testify that nine years earlier a marriage had been contracted and consummated fully (*charnellement*) between her and Henry Percy. He went on to say that the king would have revealed his intention sooner if it had not been for some of his council, who argued that he could not divorce the Concubine without tacitly affirming not only the validity of his first marriage but also—and this was what he feared most —the authority of the pope.[6]

It is not altogether clear why an annulment on these grounds would constitute a tacit approval of the pope's authority; was it simply because the papal supporters had held for the invalidity of the marriage to Anne all along? Their reason, of course, was that he had been validly married to Catherine at the time he

5 LP X, 901, 908.

6 Letter of 2 May 1536, Vienna, Haus-, Hof- und Staatsarchiv, England Korrespondenz Karton 7 (LP X, 782). Anne could not have married Percy in 1527, since Percy married Mary Talbot in 1524. Perhaps they meant nine years before she married the king, viz. early 1524.

remarried, and they might have ridiculed any other excuse for annulment as a mere subterfuge. But Chapuys himself had told Cromwell, a month before Anne's arrest, that His Majesty's present marriage was null for a number of obvious reasons. He was no doubt being sincere, for he privately expressed his hope that Henry would be delivered soon from such an abominable and more than incestuous marriage.[7] No doubt he was thinking primarily, apart from Henry's marriage to Catherine, of the affinity that arose from his affair with Anne's sister. This latter impediment was reportedly resorted to in the ecclesiastical nullification process, and it figured in the parliamentary verification of the decree of nullity. For, incredible as it may seem to us, and no doubt also to his contemporaries, Henry decided to go ahead and get an official divorce (that is, annulment), in spite of Anne's almost certain conviction and speedy execution, and in spite of the fears that had been raised about the effect of such a divorce upon the status of his first marriage and the authority of the pope. His reason was that he—most unnatural of fathers—wished to swell the ranks of his officially illegitimate children by adding Elizabeth to Mary and Henry Fitzroy, in order to make way for his future issue, or, failing that, to settle the succession on young Henry.

Cranmer therefore convened, *ex officio suo mero sive nobili*, another springtime *inquisitio versus regem et reginam de et super viribus et valore sive nullitate matrimonii inter ipsos contracti, solemnizati, et consummati*. The trial was held in "a certain low chapel" of Lambeth Palace, apparently simultaneously with the treason trials. The acts of the court do not survive, so far as is known, except for Cranmer's own account of the final day, May 17, 1536, when he pronounced sentence.[8] This was two days after the end of Anne's trial for treason, in which she had been sentenced to death, and two days before the sentence was executed. It was also almost exactly three years after the trial in which he had solemnly proclaimed her marriage to Henry to be good. Just two weeks earlier, on the day after Anne's arrest, Cranmer had written to Henry: "I am in such a perplexity that my mind is clean amazed. For I never had better opinion in woman than I had in her, which

7 Letter of 1 April 1536, LP X, 601.

8 Wilkins, III, 803–4. The Latin description of the trial cited above is a combination of Cranmer's two references to it.

maketh me to think that she should not be culpable. And again, I think Your Highness would not have gone so far, except she had surely been culpable."[9]

The change in the archbishop's attitude to the king's second marriage came swiftly, for he must have summoned Henry and Anne to appear at his inquisition only a short time after writing the above letter. Whether either of them appeared in person is not known. At the end of the trial, which "was in progress for some time and at that time was still pending undecided," both were represented by proctors, Anne by Nicholas Wootton and John Barbour, and Henry once more by Richard Sampson, dean of his chapel (in a few weeks he would become Bishop of Chichester). Cromwell and Chancellor Audley were also there, and Thomas Bedell and John Tregonwell were among the counsel for the king. Also present as witnesses were Richard Gwent, Edmund Bonner, and Thomas Legh.[10]

Chapuys heard conflicting accounts of what had happened, from not very reliable sources. One informant said that the archbishop declared Elizabeth illegitimate by finding that her father was Henry Norris, one of Anne's convicted accomplices, and not the king. Others reported that the child's illegitimacy followed from the prelate's annulment of her parents' marriage on grounds of Henry's previous connection with Mary Boleyn.[11] Charles Wriothesley, however, another contemporary, said that it was proved at the court in which Henry received his annulment that a secret contract had been made between Anne and Henry Percy, and that it was for this reason that she was declared never to have been the lawful queen.[12]

[9] Cranmer to Henry, 3 May 1536, *Works*, II, 324 (LP X, 792).
[10] Wilkins, III, 803.
[11] Chapuys to Granvelle, 19 May 1536, LP X, 909.
[12] *A Chronicle of England During the Reigns of the Tudors*, ed. W. D. Hamilton (London, 1875), pp. 40–41. Professor Mortimer Levine has reminded me that Wriothesley's assertion that Anne was declared never to have been lawful queen is contradicted by the second Act of Succession. There Catherine of Aragon is referred to as "late Princess Dowager," and Anne Boleyn is called "late Queen Anne," the invalidity of her marriage notwithstanding. Professor Levine concludes from this that "the Parliament of 1536 seems to have inadvertently followed Sir Thomas More and implied that Anne was queen by statute and not by marriage." If this was the case, then we ought also to find another example of inadvertence in Cranmer's sentence, cited below, when he refers simply to "Queen Anne," without the qualification of "pretensed."

It was never officially revealed what the grounds for the annulment were. In his decree of nullity of May 17, an official copy of which was signed on June 10, introduced to the Convocation on the 21st, and subscribed by both houses on the 28th of the same month, Cranmer did not specify the reasons, any more than he did in his earlier decree ratifying the marriage or in his sentence annulling the king's first marriage. He simply said that the articles that raised objections to Henry and Anne's marriage (in the manner that we have seen in previous trials) were sufficiently proved. He repeated, however, only the introduction to the articles and not their content, saying instead: "We wish these articles to be considered as inserted and totally repeated at this point, so far as it is expedient."[13] Furthermore, he did not, as in the Dunstable sentence, list the evidence on which he had based his conclusion; rather, he merely noted that "nothing effectual or sufficient had been or was offered, alleged, deduced, or proved on the part or for the part of the same most illustrious and powerful lord, our king, and the most serene lady, Queen Anne, which would vitiate or in any way weaken such proof" as he had for the articles. That being the case, he declared that "the said marriage had been altogether and entirely null, invalid, and void."[14]

An official explanation of what happened was given in the new Act of Succession that was passed by the Parliament which began to sit on June 8. The legislators began their prepared text by apologizing for the previous Act of Succession, for they had thought in their consciences that the king's marriage with Lady Anne had been "pure, sincere, perfect, and good," and in fact it was so "reputed, accepted, and taken in the realm." But "now of late God of his infinite goodness, from whom no secret things can be hid, hath caused to be brought to light evident and open knowledge . . . of certain just, true, and lawful impediments, unknown at the making of the said acts, and sithen that time confessed by the said Lady Anne before the most reverend father in God, Thomas, Archbishop of Canterbury, Metropolitan and Primate of all England, sitting judicially for the same, by the which plainly appeareth that the said marriage between Your Grace and the said Lady Anne was

[13] "Quos quidem articulos pro hic insertis et totaliter repetitis, quatenus expedit, haberi volumus."
[14] Wilkins, III, 803, 804.

never good nor consonant to the laws, but utterly void and of none effect."

They went on to repeat much of the section of the previous act condemning the king's first marriage to Catherine of Aragon, but with an important difference: the testimony of the universities and other authorities had originally been introduced in such a way as to lend approval to the marriage between Henry and Anne; now it was brought to bear solely upon the unlawfulness of the first union. Catherine's consummation of marriage with Prince Arthur had been duly proved in the archbishop's court, it was repeated, but now her issue, along with Anne's, was specifically declared illegitimate; the issue of Queen Jane was to be the lawful heir; and, failing such, Henry was empowered to name an heir of his own choosing.

The prohibitions of Leviticus were renewed, again because of the many "inconveniences" caused by their violation, but the trailer at the end of the old act limiting the affinity to solemnized and consummated marriages was omitted. Now consummation was specified for each wife, but not solemnity; and a new rule added affinity *ex coitu illicito* to the ban: "It is to be understood that if it chance any man to know carnally any woman, that then all and singular persons being in any degree of consanguinity or affinity as is above written, to any of the parties so carnally offending shall be deemed and adjudged to be within the cases and limits of the said prohibitions of marriage."[15]

Could it be that Henry had had second thoughts about the view that he and his primate had held against almost the entire learned world, which made affinity depend on the marriage contract and not carnal copula? If so, he would now realize that God was punishing him for entering into the very same kind of incestuous union that he thought he had had with Catherine. But the corollary of this was that there had been no incest at all in his marriage with Catherine. For, unless he continued to accept Cranmer's very specious and unconvincing reasons for believing Catherine's first marriage to have been consummated, at the same time that he rejected his really very weighty reasons for basing affinity upon marriage rather than intercourse, this conclusion would have been inescap-

[15] 28 Henry VIII c. 7, *Statutes*, III, 655.

able. Certainly, Henry was not beyond this kind of escapism. The same may be true of Cranmer, for, as we shall see, in later years he would actively propound the notion that the divinely sanctioned affinity was induced both by licit marriage and by illicit copula. But that was more than a decade in the future, after Henry's son Edward VI had succeeded to the throne, and after the archbishop's ideas on marriage in general had matured drastically.

Since the new Act of Succession still insisted on Catherine's consummation, we must conclude that some sort of rationalization had taken place, if we assume that the act faithfully represented Henry's thinking. But this is by no means a necessary assumption. In the past, indeed in the first Act of Succession itself, Henry had allowed it to be proclaimed that consummation was a necessary condition for the divinely prohibited degrees when he clearly did not believe it himself. Similarly, he could have arranged for the new statement (viz., that carnal copula determined the boundaries of divine affinity) not believing it himself but thinking that to the world at large this would be the most credible and acceptable reason for invalidity. Another possibility is that he really had come to believe the statement but was doubtful of Catherine's inclusion under it, and for that reason sought to assure himself of the continuing invalidity of his first marriage by resurrecting the old argument that public honesty was not mentioned in the dispensation. However personally dishonorable the revelation of a connection with Anne's sister would be (he knew it was no secret anyway), and however insincere he might appear for having knowingly entered into the same kind of union as that over which he had manifested such conscientious horror, it was no doubt the reason that would be least apt to revive sentiments in favor of his first marriage and of the authority of the pope. But this allusion to his fornicatory affinity was not made at all directly but was buried within the rhetoric of the act, to be unearthed only by the most demanding and industrious of minds, whereas the marriage with Anne was explicitly said to have been annulled because of "certain just, true, and lawful impediments" previously unknown to Parliament, and presumably unknown to everyone but Anne. Henry's amour with her sister Mary would not fall under this category.

Was there any truth to this parliamentary declaration? If it was no more than a typically pompous overstatement of "indenture English," there would be a certain poetic justice in the fact that the words have been taken literally to confirm the story that Anne was really Henry's daughter, the reasoning being that if all of Henry's known impediments are eliminated from the small number of possible obstacles to marriage, direct consanguinity is left to be included among the "certain unknown impediments" that Anne could have revealed.[16] We may safely ignore this possibility, but some others need another look. It will be evident from the decree annulling Henry's marriage to Anne of Cleves that it is not at all unlikely that several impediments were urged also in the case of Anne Boleyn. Even Henry's alleged constraint by witchcraft may have been dressed up in a form presentable to a semipublic inquisition of the sort that was held at Lambeth. It is not inconceivable that such an excuse would be acceptable to Cranmer, for, although he would as time went on come to propose some extremely radical changes in the laws on marriage, he would retain the traditional idea that impotency or frigidity induced by witchcraft was a legitimate impediment to marriage (see the Epilogue, below).

As I said above, we do not know whether Anne confessed hitherto unknown impediments to the archbishop when he was presiding over the inquisition that ended on May 17, though we do know that she was not present on the day of sentence. We also know that on May 16, Cranmer was admitted to her presence in the Tower as her confessor, and apparently he left her with her hopes pathetically raised: she believed that the execution would be stayed and she would be permitted to retire to a nunnery.[17] From this, it has been suggested that Cranmer led her to think that her life would

---

16 See David Lewis's translation of the Sanders-Rishton *Rise and Growth of the Anglican Schism* (London, 1877), pp. xl–xlvi. Admittedly, the fact that Anne was Henry's daughter would have been a fairly well kept secret, but Lewis does not explain how it could be known to Anne and not to Henry. Professor Levine writes me: "Sanders's story that Anne was born of a liaison between Henry and Lady Elizabeth during Sir Thomas Boleyn's 'absence of two years in France on the king's affairs' is not only incredible but also impossible. Boleyn's only extended stay in France was as ambassador from early 1519 to early 1520, which rules out David Lewis's theory that Anne was born in 1510 or early 1511; 1507 or earlier as Anne's birthyear would make the liaison take place in Henry VII's reign, which would be rather unlikely." For evidence of an earlier birthyear for Anne, following Friedmann (1502 or 1503) and J. H. Round (1501), see Edward E. Lowinsky, "A Music Book for Anne Boleyn," *Florilegium historiale: Essays Presented to Wallace K. Ferguson* (Toronto, 1971), pp. 160–235, esp. 185–86 and 228, n. 71. Professor Levine favors 1501 or even 1499.

17 LP X, 890.

be spared if she would consent to an annulment, and that he induced her to grant powers of attorney to the proctors who represented her at the hearing on May 17. These proctors, it is reasoned,
could then have revealed the impediments in her name, in answer
to the articles which Cranmer raised against the marriage on the
basis of what she and others had told him, so that the statement of
Parliament would be fundamentally accurate. One of the weak-
nesses of this supposition is that it rests on the assumption that the
whole inquisition began and ended in the single morning session of
May 17. Cranmer's account of that day in court, as well as the
precedent of the other inquisitions we have examined, suggests
that this was not the case. In Cranmer's instrument of June 10, he
stated that on May 17 between the hours of nine and eleven in the
morning (the standard formula for the opening of the session—it
did not mean that the session lasted only two hours), he was sitting
judicially in the inquisition process, which "aliquandiu vertebatur
et adtunc pendebat indecisim." There had been a mature, exact,
and diligent examination and discussion of the process and its
merits, and Henry and Anne now appeared through their proctors
to demand sentence. In the sentence itself, after first invoking
Christ and having, as he said, only God himself before his eyes, he
asserted that he had reviewed the whole and entire process of the
trial and acted with the counsel of the legal experts to whom he
had communicated the matter. To be sure, much of his statement
simply reflects the use of traditional formulas, but he doubtless
would not have used them in this way if the trial had not taken
several days. It is highly likely, therefore, that Anne made some
kind of a response to the articles before she was sentenced to death
in the treason trial on May 15.

Before delivering his sentence of annulment, Cranmer stated
that he was proceeding "on the basis of some true, just, and legitimate causes recently [iam nuper] brought to our attention." He
may have been referring to a confession of hitherto unknown impediments, and of course it is also possible that she made the confession not in her first response to the articles but after she was
condemned to death.

We must ask, then, what information, what details of her former
life hitherto unknown to the archbishop could Anne have revealed
to him that would have constituted impediments to her marriage

with Henry. First of all, there was her precontract *de praesenti*, which Henry sought to have Pope Clement dissolve. As I pointed out earlier, Cranmer could not have known of the precontract when he wrote his treatise for Henry, since he maintained that there was no practical way to dissolve such a marriage—unless, of course, her secret husband had died in the meantime or had entered a religious order. (Anne's own plan of entering into religion would have dissolved whichever of her marriages was the valid one, according to Cranmer's theology in the *Twelve Articles,* but that is hardly what was called for at the moment; it was her death that was called for, and that, when it took place, decisively divorced her from whomever she was canonically married to.) In Cranmer's view, the discovery of the precontract would have been sufficient grounds for the dissolution of the marriage; only one diriment impediment was necessary, and there can be no doubt that he tried his best to find such an impediment. He was clearly telling the truth in admitting in his many recantations before his execution under Queen Mary that he had sometimes been forced to put his name to policies and acts that were against his conscience (his signing of the second Act of Succession would be one example, if he had not yet changed his views on the purely positive-law nature of affinity *ex coitu illicito*); but he thereby proved that he, like the king, did indeed have a conscience. His original reaction to the questioning of the king's present marriage may have been the same as Bishop Stokesley's, when, a few days before Anne's arrest, someone came to him and asked if he thought that the king could leave her; Stokesley answered that he would express himself on the subject to no one but the king, but that he would like to know the royal inclination beforehand.[18] Bishop Fisher had been ex-

18 Chapuys to Charles V, 29 April 1536, LP X, 752. Chapuys considered Stokesley to have been the principal cause and instrument of the first divorce, and this was indeed Stokesley's own estimate of his role. In the letter from Stokesley to Bedell cited above (Chap. 12 at nn. 23 and 36), in which Stokesley refused to say that the clergy had approved the marriage of Henry and Anne, he complained that he was being calumniated by those who said he was being two-faced and not well affected in this *causa animi,* that is, the matter of the king's conscience. For he had promoted it in countless assemblies throughout almost the entire world, "not to mention that I recovered it when it had already fallen to the ground from the hands of the legates and was thereafter despaired of and wept over. For you yourself are a witness of what [I achieved] among our neighbors at St. Paul's: no one on either side [did] more, and, to speak with your

ecuted only the year before for holding just such an opinion as
the king now seemed to want. Once Cranmer knew what was required of him, however, he attempted to justify it as best he could.
It was only natural.

What else of interest could Anne have revealed to her extraordinary confessor? Let us reflect more deeply on her precontract *per
verba de praesenti*. Is it likely that the young Anne Boleyn would
have married a man secretly and not consummated the union? It
is true that she held off Henry for close to six years, but that was
precisely because she could not be sure of marrying him. The king
must have interrogated Anne in 1527 in order to ascertain the
impediments that stood in the way of meeting her demand to be
made queen. It is not probable that she would have admitted to
anything, such as a consummated precontract, that would have
uncovered an irremovable barrier to her ambition.

A secretly consummated marriage is just the sort of thing that
could have been known to Anne, and unknown to others, which
she could have confessed to Cranmer. The precontract alone would
have sufficed for the archbishop, given his theology, but the consummation would have mattered to Henry because he had rejected
this part of Cranmer's theology and relied on the papal dispensation he had received.

The day before her "confession," Anne had been convicted of
the incredible charge of having committed incestuous adultery.
Would it have given her any satisfaction to reveal now a long-kept
secret that might have prevented Henry from ever starting on his
long and frustrating effort to divorce Catherine? One thing we can
be fairly sure of: Anne's conscience was not so scrupulously tender
as Henry's, and if she possessed such a secret it is not likely that it
would ever have disturbed her equanimity of soul as she awaited
her ascension to the throne at the side of her royal lover.

If Anne made such a confession, it would not have come as a

---

good pardon, no one as much. All who were fighting against the cause hated
me as though I were the cause's only patron; and nevertheless, even they, at
least some of them, [are those] who now enjoy the fruit of my patronage." Record Office SP 1/82, f. 13 (cf. LP VII, 15). In the letter cited above, Chapuys said
that even though Stokesley was the principal agent of the first annulment, the
bishop now heartily repented of his action, and would willingly promote the
divorce from the Concubine, since she and her race were such abominable
Lutherans.

surprise to Henry. He would have believed anything of her now, and in fact it was precisely this that he would have wanted most to hear from her and that Cranmer would have been instructed to ply from her.

In all of this, Henry Percy's alleged partnership in Anne's contract is of importance. We must keep in mind what Chapuys said earlier: Henry had determined to divorce Anne not because of evidence of a contract with Percy—he knew all along that there had been a contract, if not with Percy then with someone else—but because witnesses had turned up who said that Anne had consummated her contract with Percy.

Cromwell, it seems, assembled the charges of adultery and treason and then abandoned the trail of the precontract, thinking it would not be needed any longer. But when he learned that the marriage would still have to be annulled, he took it up again, and sent out a friend of Percy's to ask the earl himself about it. The latter wrote to the secretary under date of May 13, just two days before the end of the treason trial and four days before sentence was given in the marriage inquisition. He said:

This shall be to signify to you that I perceive by Sir Raynald Carnaby that there is supposed a precontract between the queen and me; whereupon [i.e., upon such a supposed precontract] I was not only heretofore [in 1532] examined upon my oath before the Archbishops of Canterbury and York, but also received the blessed sacrament upon the same before the Duke of Norfolk and other the King's Highness's council learned in the spiritual law; assuring you, Mr. Secretary, by the said oath and blessed body, which afore I received and hereafter intend to receive, that the same may be to my damnation if ever there were any contract or promise of marriage between her and me.[19]

Let us try to piece together the history of Percy's relationship with Anne. In 1522, when Anne had not long been returned from France, she and young Henry Percy, a page in Cardinal Wolsey's household, fell in love. Both had already been spoken for, however. For the last two years Anne had been destined for Sir James Butler; and Percy for the last six years, from about the time that he was fourteen years old, had been engaged to Mary Talbot, daughter of the Earl of Shrewsbury.[20] Both Anne and Percy wanted to be

19 Percy to Cromwell, Burnet, VI, 167.
20 LP II, 1935.

released and allowed to marry, but there was no hearing of it. Wolsey, at the king's command, broke up the affair, calling in old Northumberland, Percy's father, to bring his son into line. It has been thought that Anne's undying hatred for Wolsey was born at this time.[21]

Around the beginning of 1524 Percy married his destined bride, Mary, but it was an unhappy union almost from the start. Finally, in 1532, after he had abstained from her for more than two years, he told her (so she said) that he did so because long before he married her he had promised himself to Anne.[22] Mary saw this as an opportunity to escape from the marriage, and wrote to her father about it. Her letter was passed on to Norfolk, who gave it to Anne; and Anne, Chapuys said, showed it to Henry VIII himself and insisted upon a public investigation. She denied everything, publicly at least. Privately, she and Henry may have connived at keeping it secret, if this was the contract she had previously admitted to the king and Wolsey. At her request, therefore, Percy was sent for and examined. Whatever the truth was, he denied any such contract to the council, and solemnly repeated his denial at the king's command before the Archbishops of Canterbury and York. No doubt his answer had been directed—by Anne, or Henry, or both. Chapuys remarked, "Either he had been suborned, or it was through fear that he denied having contracted marriage with the said lady, even though the contrary be evident to many."[23]

If he had made such a contract, its revelation would perhaps have done no serious damage to Anne's prospects in the eyes of the world, since it could be dissolved, at least according to the liberal school of canonists that had the ear of the pope; Henry had already taken the precaution privately of obtaining a divorce-clause of this sort in Clement VII's general dispensation, and, if necessary, a specific decree could be arranged. But if Percy had made and consummated the contract, there would have been only one way of dissolving it, and Henry would not have to go far to find an occasion for it. The withholding of information so vital

[21] See James Gairdner, *DNB* Anne; Cavendish, pp. 29–35.

[22] "Cars long temps avant qu'il la print, il avoit promise dame Anne," Chapuys to Charles V, 28 June 1532, Vienna, Haus-, Hof- und Staatsarchiv, England Korrespondenz Karton 4; cf. Friedmann, I, 159–61.

[23] "Ou pour subornacion ou crainte, nya entierement avoir contracte marriage avec la dit dame, combien que la contraire soit manifeste a pluseurs."

to his interests could easily be sanctioned by the penalty reserved for traitors. If such were the facts, then, and if Percy did deny them in 1532, he felt no inclination to admit his perjury four years later, but chose rather to repeat it in just as sacrilegious a manner, even though the truth might now gain him the royal favor.

The fateful events of mid-May 1536 can be reconstructed as follows. On May 9 order was given for a grand jury to be empaneled on the next day. Indictments were handed down against Anne and her alleged associates on May 10, accusing Anne of "holding cheap the most excellent and most noble matrimony between her and the king," and giving herself to adultery. On May 12, Norris, Weston, Brereton, and Smeaton were found guilty by the petty jury. On the same day, the Duke of Norfolk was appointed for the occasion Lord High Steward of England in the trial of his niece and nephew, Anne and George Boleyn.[24]

Meanwhile, Archbishop Cranmer's inquisition was also probably under way, and he would be busy assembling evidence to prove the content of the articles of accusation, which, to say the least, held cheap the marriage between Anne and Henry. Cromwell sent Sir Raynald Carnaby to Henry Percy at Newington Green in Islington to get an admission of the marriage contract, and we have seen the denial that Percy sent on Saturday, May 13. Also on Saturday, various mandates were issued in preparation for the appearance of the Boleyns on Monday to be tried by their peers, among them Henry Percy, Earl of Northumberland. Perhaps Percy participated in Anne's overthrow because he resented her having made him testify about the precontract. When he appeared on May 15 to be one of her judges, in spite of her strong protestations of innocence, he joined the others in finding her guilty and condemning her to death. But when the time came to pass upon her brother, Percy departed, "because of a sudden weakness of his body."[25]

The next day Anne's old friend and protégé Thomas Cranmer appeared in her cell to hear her confession. He had not been in England when Percy was questioned about his precontract in June

24 LP X, 848, 876; Appendix to Wriothesley's *Chronicle* (n. 12 above), pp. 215–16.
25 "Praefato comite Northumbriae propter subitaneam debilitatem corporis sui tantummodo excepto et absente," Wriothesley, pp. 223–24.

1532—Archbishop Warham still held the see of Canterbury and Cranmer was with the emperor. Warham died two months later and Cranmer was soon summoned, but by the time he reached England the affair was half a year old and talk about it had died down. Doubtless he had heard nothing of the matter before, and now he asked her to tell him all about it.

It has been conjectured that Anne confessed to having married Percy whether it was true or not, in order to save her life. But it is fairly certain, as I showed in Chapter 2, that she had been married to someone before she fell in with the king. She may simply have confessed the engagement and marriage that Henry and Wolsey referred to in the dispensation they drafted in 1527; they were no secret, at least to Henry. If it was not Percy that she was married to, she may have lied now and said that it was, in order to fall in the better with the evidence against her at the inquisition. For according to the canonical procedure cited in the 1540 act of Parliament doing away with the impediment of precontract (yes, it would come to that), the assertion by one of the parties that such a contract had taken place was not enough to prove it; if the other party denied it, two witnesses were necessary.[26] And since witnesses were reportedly available to testify to a consummated contract with Percy, Anne's testimony would further support the existence of that union.

Let us assume that only a nonconsummated marriage could be proved—the one, specifically, that Henry had in mind when he petitioned for a dispensation from the pope. Cranmer, we know, did not believe such a dispensation possible, but others did, including Henry, who had acted upon it when he married Anne. The question then arises as to the legal status in 1536 of papal dispensations in England. In the Parliament of 1534, an act had been passed forbidding further dispensations from Rome, but nothing was said about dispensations already received.[27] But in the Parliament convened in the month after the Boleyn trials, another act was passed which declared all papal dispensations void from the beginning. That is to say, Parliament did not invalidate previously valid dispensations, but simply explained that they were never valid in the first place. If Cranmer shared this opinion, he could

26 32 Henry VIII c. 38, *Statutes*, III, 792.
27 25 Henry VIII c. 21, *ibid.*, p. 465.

have declared the king's marriage to be void on the grounds that none of the impediments mentioned in Clement VII's dispensations of 1527 and 1528 had been validly removed. The act of Parliament went on to grant a general validation or *sanatio in radice* to all marriages contracted and solemnized before November 3, 1534, except where there was a "divorce or separation had by the ecclesiastical laws of this realm." Thus Anne's marriage to Henry was exempted, and Cranmer could have relied on the positive-law impediments which the invalid papal bulls had failed to remove, including Henry's affinity in the first degree arising from illicit copula with Anne's sister. The parliamentary act further exempted from the general validation all marriages "prohibited by God's laws, [as] limited and declared in the act made in this present Parliament for the establishment of the king's succession, or otherwise by Holy Scripture."[28] This, of course, was a reference to Henry's first-degree affinity, which almost all authorities, with the exception of Henry and Cranmer, had held to be of the same rank as affinity contracted within marriage, as specified now in the 1536 Act of Succession.

It was necessary to take this public stand on affinity, because the circumstances of Henry's impediment and the papal dispensation that he had received for it were known. Only the year before, in fact, Reginald Pole had addressed the king in his treatise on the *Defense of the Unity of the Church* and rebuked him for seeking to divorce Catherine because she was his brother's wife while at the same time trying to get a dispensation to marry the sister of his one-time concubine; and he said further that the dispensation had been granted, but on condition that it was first established that the pope did not have power to dispense in the former case. If perhaps Pole did not send his book to Henry until after hearing of Anne's execution, he had shown it to others, and the king no doubt suspected that his enemies had heard of the dispensation; after all, it was his chief opponent, the late Bishop of Rome, who had granted it.

Let us consider briefly the other impediments named in the invalid papal dispensation. As indicated above, a nonconsummated *de praesenti* precontract would now be considered to have stood in the way of the marriage, even in the eyes of those who held that

[28] 28 Henry VIII c. 16, *ibid.*, p. 672.

it was possible for such contracts to be dissolved. There might have been some basis for spiritual kinship, but none for legal, and a valid case could hardly have been made for consanguinity. It would be rather difficult to prove that Henry was Anne's second or third cousin when he was really only her seventh or eighth. As for public honesty, it would stand as an impediment if it could be proved that a former fiancé or husband of Anne's was Henry's third cousin. If it could be established that Percy had been so involved with Anne, a herald could simply be brought in to testify that he and the king were unquestionably third cousins—without adding that arcane quibble about Percy's being "once removed." Even if Percy's contract to Anne were to be considered invalid by reason of their previous spousals to other mates, the impediment of public honesty would still have arisen. If he had consummated his love for Anne, whether with or without a contract, whether before or after such a contract, and whether the contract was valid or invalid, the impediment of affinity *ex coitu licito sive illicito* would instantly have seized upon all his male relatives through the fourth degree. If a contract had been made, by the way, Percy may not have been deliberately perjuring himself when he denied it, but only employing mental reservation or equivocation. It is likely that he remained engaged to Mary Talbot during his whole relationship with Anne, and even if he and Anne did go through the forms of marriage he may have thought that there was no contract in a legally binding or valid sense. If so, he would have mentioned to Mary the precontract after eight years of marriage to her only as a reason for keeping his distance from her. The law in force at the time, however, was that a contract *de praesenti* automatically dissolved spousals *de futuro*.[29]

29 See Cranmer, *Articuli duodecim*, Pocock, I, 342; and West, 2 Ely, f. 117 (Lambeth MS 2341, f. 160). Cranmer and West gave the same reason, that a greater bond prevailed over a lesser. West, dealing with Henry's secret protestation against his spousals, pointed out that spousals could be dissolved lawfully only by a judgment of the Church (that is, if the other party did not wish to back out), or by entering into a *de praesenti* contract. He quoted the chapter *Adolescens* of Gregory IX in the title *De sponsalibus et matrimoniis*, CIC X 4.1.32, according to which a youth who was engaged *de futuro* to one girl and later married another *de praesenti* was judged to be validly married to the second, even though he tried without succeeding to have carnal intercourse with his original fiancée.

From all this it seems possible that Cranmer may have based his decision on several undispensed impediments when he pronounced the marriage of Henry and Anne null and void on May 17.

On the same day, perhaps at the very time that Cranmer was handing down his sentence, Anne witnessed, from her cell in the Tower, the execution of her brother and the other four convicted accomplices.[30] She was to die on May 18, and on that day she went to confession again, presumably to Archbishop Cranmer, and received Holy Communion, after which she affirmed to the lady in charge of her, upon the damnation of her soul, that she had never been unfaithful to the king. She considered herself well prepared for death, and to her great disappointment her execution was postponed until the next day. On the morning of the 19th she received the Eucharist once more, and declared her innocence once more to Sir William Kingston, the Keeper of the Tower. At nine o'clock she was beheaded.[31]

There is no indication that Cranmer was present at the execution. But we do know something of his activity on that day, for he issued under date of May 19 a dispensation, signed by his own hand, permitting Henry to marry Jane Seymour, in spite of their being related "in the third and third degrees of affinity."[32] So that if Percy's relationship with Henry had not been so scrupulously defined as being "in the fourth and fifth degrees," we are assured by this decree that the king's metropolitan was able to bring strict standards to bear upon such computations when the need arose. The decree also shows that both Cranmer and Henry were still observing the purely ecclesiastical laws on marriage impediments. But how, we might well ask, could Jane Seymour be related in the third degree of affinity to Henry? She was certainly not the second cousin of either Catherine or Anne. They *were* related through Edward I (so was everyone else, it seems); Catherine of Aragon was her sixth cousin thrice removed and Anne Boleyn her eighth with one remove. No, what it meant was that Jane was the second cousin of one of Henry's former mistresses or casual bedfellows. Cranmer then was releasing him from the impediment

---

30 Chapuys to Charles V, writing 17 May 1536, LP X, 908 (p. 379).
31 *Ibid.*, 19 May (p. 380); Kingston to Cromwell, LP X, 902, 910.
32 LP X, 915. See D. S. Chambers, *Faculty Office Registers*, p. xxiv.

that he preferred to call public honesty, but which was known in the law as affinity *ex coitu illicito*; thus he was preserving his Supreme Head from committing a sin of metaphorical incest.

On May 20, Henry and Jane were formally betrothed, and they married with somewhat indecent haste before the month was out. For it seems that she too, like Anne, had kept Henry waiting. It was a happy match, since Jane died before Henry could tire of her, as Chapuys assumed he would. But perhaps we should not be so cynical. By all accounts she was a very good woman, loved not only by Henry but by the people as well; and in giving Henry a male heir, she removed what had been the chief sign of God's disfavor in his previous unions.

CHAPTER FIFTEEN

The Third Annulment

Henry's next marriage was a disaster. Plain Anne of Cleves, suggested as a bride because a North European alliance was considered advantageous at the time, found in Henry a reluctant husband, and, by his own admission, an impossible lover. His mind began to race and his eye to roam as soon as he saw her. He reluctantly went through with the marriage, but soon afterward another annulment was in the offing, and another marriage.

The fortunate intended spouse was Catherine Howard, Anne Boleyn's first cousin. As in 1527, Henry took steps to overcome the impediments to the new match before the old one was disposed of, and, as before, he got caught in the crossfire. But it made small difference now, since he was calling the shots.

Henry married Anne in January 1540. A few days after Parliament opened on April 12, Cromwell was created Earl of Essex, as if in reward for arranging the match; but Henry was already thinking up ways to dissolve it. On June 10, Cromwell was accused of treason by the Duke of Norfolk, and he was immediately arrested and imprisoned in the Tower. A bill of attainder against him was introduced on June 17 and concluded on the 29th. On July 2, a bill reducing marriage impediments was read in the House of Lords. It had obviously been designed, at least in part, to prepare the king's way to Catherine. After the reading, it was given to Cranmer, Tunstall, Gardiner, and the new Bishop of Rochester, Nicholas Heath, for examination and correction. It is not known what changes, if any, the prelates made in the document. At any rate, they did not spend much time on it, for it was passed by the unanimous vote of the Lords on the next day, and by July 5 it had received the approval of the Commons. In one of its provisions, the act stated, in suitably unctuous forensic cant, that in times past it had been possible to break up a long-standing solemnized and consummated marriage, even when children had been born to it, by means of applying to the usurped power of the Bishop of Rome, upon the pretense of a former contract made but not consummated, proved by two witnesses, even though there had been no objection or mention of it at the time of the marriage. To correct this abuse, it was decreed that all marriages contracted and consummated after July 1, 1540, were to be considered valid and indissoluble, notwithstanding any unconsummated contracts that might have been made beforehand.[1] The language of the statute sounds so like a description of his own exploitation of legal technicalities in attempting to break up his marriages to Catherine of Aragon, Anne Boleyn, and Anne of Cleves that it seems incredible to think that Henry's good sense failed him and permitted attention to be called to himself in this way. But he must have been so secure in his convictions, new as they were, that he did not give a moment's thought to any unflattering reflections that the wording of the act might cast on him.

It has been assumed that, like her cousin Anne Boleyn, Catherine Howard had informed Henry that she had made one or two contracts of marriage in the past, and that Henry therefore decided not to dissolve in particular whichever of Catherine's contracts was the binding one, but to eliminate the impedimental nature of all *de praesenti* contracts in general. If so, perhaps he got the idea from the dispensation that Clement VII had given him, permitting him to marry any woman in spite of her having entered into a nonconsummated marriage. Or perhaps he had asked Cranmer to grant such a divorce for Catherine, and the archbishop had replied that he did not believe that he had the power to do so, since it involved a contract *de praesenti*. Henry could find his views on this point by consulting his *Twelve Articles*.[2] The king might then have decided to use his prerogative as Supreme Head to

---

[1] 32 Henry VIII c. 38, *Statutes*, III, 792; *Journals of the House of Lords*, I, 128–52.

[2] It had also been the opinion of the authors of the *Determinations* treatise. Two of them, Bishops Edward Fox and John Stokesley, were dead by 1540. The third, Nicholas de Burgo, had returned to Italy some time before. See above, Chap. 13 at n. 12.

override his primate. The wording of the act was so vague, perhaps by Cranmer's doing, that Cranmer might in conscience have been able to give his assent to it, by interpreting it to refer only to pre-contracts *de futuro,* while Henry could take it to include *de praesenti* precontracts as well. But it was clearly meant to refer only to the latter, since, as we have seen before, a *de futuro* contract did not impede one from validly entering into a *de praesenti* marriage. More likely, then, Cranmer would have rated this as another of those times that he was forced to sign his name to a policy that went against his conscience; unless, indeed, he had already changed his mind on the matter.

The assumption that the act on precontracts was designed to clear Catherine Howard from a previous matrimonial bond may be true. It is certain that she needed such a divorce. On the other hand, it is possible, and probably more likely, that she kept her earlier marriage skirmishes to herself. In either case, we shall see that the act had a definite bearing on Henry's past as well as hers, and was meant to serve as a way of demonstrating himself *divorced* from Anne of Cleves in case his *annulment* should be impugned.

There was another element in the act on precontracts that was undoubtedly aimed at an impediment between the king and his new bride. Catherine easily fell outside the limits of sacred affinity but well within the bounds of the ecclesiastically imposed degrees. And Henry therefore took care of this problem as well by effecting a general abrogation of the law. The statute declared that it was for the sake of lucre that "other prohibitions than God's law admitteth" were added, "as in kindred or affinity between cousin germans and so to fourth and fourth degree, [or] carnal knowledge of any of the same kin or affinity." The result of all this was that "no marriage could be so knit and bounden but it should lie in either of the parties' power and arbiter, casting away the fear of God, by means and compasses to prove a precontract, a kindred, an alliance [i.e., causing public honesty or affinity-from-marriage], or a carnal knowledge to defeat the same," and so enter into a new marriage, and "live all the days of their lives in detestable adultery to the utter destruction of their own souls and the provocations of the terrible wrath of God upon the places where such abominations were suffered and used." Therefore, it concluded, "no person of what estate, degree, or condition soever he or she be

shall after the said first day of the month of July aforesaid be admitted in any of the spiritual courts within this the king's realm
or any of His Grace's other lands and dominions to any process,
plea, or allegation contrary to this foresaid act."[3] Five days after
the aforesaid date of limitation, and one day after the act was
concluded, the Lords and Commons asked Henry to have his marriage tried by the clergy in a joint convocation of both provinces.
On the ninth of the same month the said clergy, in apparent contradiction to the act of Parliament, declared the marriage null on
the basis of a contract that Anne had made in the past.

In fact, however, they avoided violating the letter of the new
law, since the act provided that no marriage contracted and consummated after July 1 could be dissolved on grounds of a precontract; Henry's marriage had been contracted well before that time,
and he maintained that it had never been consummated; furthermore, he claimed that he had raised doubts about the precontract
before he went through with the marriage. But the process was
certainly against the spirit of the law, since the ecclesiastical sentence of annulment specifically stated that a precontract *de praesenti* invalidated any subsequent marriage. Cranmer had a hand
in drawing up the sentence, though Gardiner was in charge of
building the case against the marriage, and both these prelates were
joined by the other clergy in pronouncing it.

Thus Cranmer was able to repair, partially at least, the damage
he had done to his conscience in helping to repeal what he believed
was an unrepealable divine law. After Henry's death, as we shall
see, the archbishop would consent to repeal the repeal—and not,
as it might seem, further to assuage his guilt, since by this time he
approved of divorce in cases not only of nonconsummated marriages but of consummated ones as well. As for Gardiner, he may
have been in a similar quandary, if he believed as Cranmer did
in his *Twelve Articles*. But if he agreed with Henry in thinking

[3] For the record, it should be said that the excuse of consanguinity or affinity
was only rarely pleaded in annulment cases of the time, as is shown by Helmholz, *Marriage Litigation in Medieval England* (Cambridge, 1974), pp. 77–87
(cf. his diss., pp. 71–81), from records before 1500. As for precontract, it is instructive to look at Cranmer's Faculty Office registers from 1534 on. In the first
two years five such contracts were validated, and only four in the next three
years. In 1540 there was none, with the possible exception of that between Anne
of Cleves and Francis of Lorraine, as will be shown below. See D. S. Chambers,
Faculty Office Registers, p. xxxvi.

that indissolubility of marriage, according to divine law, began not with the marriage contract but with the consummation of marriage, then he would have little or no scruple in helping Henry to take advantage of the man-made law on precontracts to rid himself of an old wife and to repeal the law in order to make the dissolution stick or to secure a new wife.

Just how long the plan for the annulment trial had been in preparation is not clear. Chapuys was on assignment away from England at this time, and we miss his valuable reports. Bishop Gardiner, the leader of the opposition to Cromwell,[4] and Thomas Wriothesley, one of the king's principal secretaries, were at work on it in June, for on June 30 Cromwell wrote an abject letter to the king answering the leading questions that Gardiner and Wriothesley had formulated. For instance, he said that the king had inquired about the marriage covenants that had been made between Anne and a son of the Duke of Lorraine, and had been told that they were only spousals. The king had said several times that he did not want to marry her, and that, after he had gone through with it, he never knew her carnally.[5]

The process was set in motion, as we saw, on July 6, when the king's permission was sought and received to put the marriage to trial. The request was initiated by Audley, Cranmer, Tunstall, Norfolk, Suffolk, and Southampton, who told the other lords in Parliament of the great troubles caused in the past by dubious titles of succession, and expressed their concern over the king's present marriage. They were the commissioners who had arranged the union, and it occurred to their memory that some difficulties arose at the time, of which several still remained. It was apparent to them that certain impediments existed, on account of which they very much doubted the validity of the marriage, and they wished to consult Parliament on what was to be done. It was decided to ask the king to let the matter be put to the judgment of the clergy. The king complied, expressing his conviction of the learning, honesty, and piety of the clergy, and the justice, equity, and truth of what they would decide. When so requested, he said in addition, with God as his witness, he would testify and conceal

---

[4] See G. R. Elton, *Political History: Principles and Practice* (Cambridge, 1970), pp. 147–49, and "Thomas Cromwell's Decline and Fall" (1951), reprinted in *Studies in Tudor and Stuart Politics and Government*, I, 189–230.

[5] LP XV, 821, 823 (Burnet, IV, 424).

nothing that would contribute to the truth of the marriage and its circumstances.[6]

Canonically speaking, both husband and wife needed to be notified and cited to any action impugning or testing their marriage in court, but their consent to the action was not required. An instance action could be brought by a third person (for example, by someone who claimed to be clandestinely married to one of the spouses); or the judge himself could proceed *ex officio*, whether merely on the basis of public infamy, as in Henry's previous annulment trials, or entirely or partly at the instigation (promotion) of specific accusers. To cite the commission given on December 20, 1535, by Stephen Gardiner, Bishop of Winchester, to Dr. Edmund Steward to act as his vicar general and official (that is, judge) of his consistory: he could proceed "ad alicuius partis procurationem, promotionem, sive instantiam, etiam ex officio mero, mixto, vel promoto."[7]

The present action was, of course, "promoted" by the six commissioners. And if Henry's views of the new formalities between Church and Crown in England had demanded in 1533 that Cranmer should seek license in suitably humble terms from the king to proceed *ex officio mero*, such permission was no doubt all the more called for under the circumstances of 1540. Queen Anne was also consulted, and she too consented to the process.

On the next day, July 7, the double Convocation met at the chapter house of St. Peter's Church, Westminster. Among the prelates attending were the two archbishops, Cranmer and Lee, and twelve bishops. The upper house was much diminished, because of the recent enforced retirement of the abbots and priors. Cranmer, who presided, explained the purpose of the gathering, and Richard Gwent, prolocutor of the lower house, presented the king's commission. Bishop Gardiner then explained "the species or parts of the causes of invalidity in an illuminating oration." This speech corresponds to the *libellus allegationis* which he must have presented, consisting of a summary of the facts of the matter, from which he derived objections supported by legal arguments. Con-

6 *Journals of the House of Lords*, I, 153.

7 *Registra Stephani Gardiner et Iohannis Poynet, episcoporum wintoniensium*, ed. Herbert Chitty, Canterbury and York Society no. 37 (Oxford, 1930), p. 50.

vocation decreed that a committee should study all the various proofs establishing the facts ("omnia et singula probationum genera quae in facto consistunt"). The committee was composed of Archbishops Cranmer and Lee, Bishops Bonner (who succeeded to the see of London after Stokesley's death), Tunstall, Gardiner, and Bell (now Bishop of Worcester), and eight members of the lower house, including Richard Gwent. The committee designated five of their number, Tunstall, Gardiner, Gwent, Thomas Thirlby (Bishop-designate of the new diocese of Westminster), and Richard Layton (Dean of York), to take the depositions of witnesses. Cranmer then adjourned the Convocation until the next day, a Thursday, between the hours of six and eight in the morning.[8]

Meanwhile, on Wednesday afternoon witnesses were examined and their depositions were exhibited before Convocation at the Thursday morning session, along with other pertinent public instruments. Among those supposedly examined on the afternoon of July 7 were Lord Cobham and Thomas Wriothesley, though Cobham's deposition is dated July 6, and is in Wriothesley's hand. The other public instruments mentioned included Henry's own deposition, Cromwell's answers, and reports on the investigations made concerning the espousals between Anne and the son of the Duke of Lorraine.[9]

One of the depositions was signed by the six commissioners who had handled the negotiations for the marriage, including therefore Cranmer and Tunstall, though these two prelates were not mentioned as among the witnesses sworn in on July 7—perhaps because they were members of the present investigating committee. The statement of the commissioners dealt only with the question of Anne's previous espousals. In 1539 they had instructed Nicholas Wootton (who since 1538 had been in charge of Cranmer's faculty office)[10] to insist that the matter be clarified. He had done so, but to no effect, as they found out when Anne arrived in

---

[8] Wilkins, III, 851–52. On Thirlby, see LP *Addenda* 1457, which rules out the interpretation placed on LP XV, 737, that Richard Sampson became Bishop of Westminster on May 30, 1540.

[9] All of the documents used at the trial are contained in the notarial record of the proceedings certified by Richard Watkins, Anthony Hughes, and Thomas Argall, British Museum MS Harley 1061, summarized in LP XV, 861.2. See also LP XV, 850.10.

[10] Chambers, *Faculty Office Registers*, p. xxv.

England. When Henry inquired about the point, the ambassadors from Cleves could produce no document concerning the espousals, "but only by words made a light matter of it, saying it was done in their minority, and had never after taken any effect." Henry was most unwilling to have the marriage proceed, but the ambassadors persuaded him to do so, and promised to produce proof in the near future that the espousals had been dissolved. Subsequent to the marriage the ambassadors did send "a writing for a discharge," but it was not in authentic form, and far from clarifying the matter, it made it all the more confused, "couching the words of that sort that the espousals by them spoken of to have been made long ago may be taken for espousals not only *de futuro*, but also *de praesenti*." The condition upon which the king entered the marriage therefore was not fulfilled, and apparently could not be fulfilled.[11] It is noteworthy that the commissioners did not definitely decide that the precontract was *de praesenti*; it was enough for their purposes that the possibility existed.

The commissioners were unquestionably justified in reaching this conclusion. According to records produced at the Convocation, the ambassadors, Hogesteden and Olisleger, declared on January 5, 1540, that when Anne and Francis, the eldest son of the Duke of Lorraine, were still under the age of puberty, they were pledged to contract marriage as soon as they reached marriageable age, according to the terms of the agreement made between their parents. The ambassadors themselves had read the said agreement, and they had furthermore been present when Henry de Groff, ambassador of the Duke of Gueldres, who had arranged the agreement, declared it to be null and void. Hogesteden and Olisleger then promised, if at all possible, to produce authentic copies both of the said agreement and of the manner of the said denunciation within the space of the next three months.[12]

The ambassadors did not fulfill their promise to send a copy of the marriage agreement, but they did send a notarized statement that on February 26, 1540, they had investigated the Cleves archives and found the following report. On February 15, 1535, Henry "de Chroiff" proposed several things concerning the affairs

---

[11] John Strype, *Ecclesiastical Memorials*, I, part 2 (Oxford, 1822), 452–53.

[12] MS Harley 1061, f. 13rv. Gairdner and Brodie speak of two agreements, having misread "dictorum" as "duorum."

between Duke Charles of Gueldres and the Dukes of Lorraine and Cleves, and especially concerning the business of the spousals between the children of the latter two dukes. Among other things he announced and declared that the spousals were off ("der hilich aff sy"), or as Hogesteden and Olisleger paraphrased it, they were not going to take their course ("sponsalia illa progressum suum non habitura"), for which Duke Charles was very sorry, both because of what he had done and what he was about to do in the matter. A few pages further in the same archival record, it was reported that Elbert Palland, the Marshall of Cleves, on commission from the Duke of Cleves had spoken further with Duke Charles, and reported to his own duke's counselors on April 17, 1535, that Charles knew for sure that the first spousals ("die irste hilick") of Anne "aff wer," that is, "fore inania vel progressum suum non habitura."[13]

This was all that Henry had been able to get from Cleves. The ambassadors would not or could not supply a copy of the marriage agreement, which may have specified that a *de praesenti* contract was made between Anne and Francis, even before they had reached puberty. Henry himself, we recall, had long ago made such a contract, according to the specifications of the Anglo-Spanish treaty of 1503. In such a case, the marriage would be considered to be an engagement *de futuro* until the parties reached puberty, when it would take on its *de praesenti* force, upon evidence that the original consent had been maintained and not repudiated. At any rate, according to the ambassadors the agreement had been that Anne and Francis would marry as soon as they reached the legal age; and they gave the impression that the contract had been broken off before this age was reached. But the only evidence they could subsequently produce that the marriage plans had been interrupted was the report of the Duke of Gueldres's disappointment on hearing the match was off. Furthermore, the report came in 1535, almost eight years after Anne's twelfth birthday, which was the canonical age of marriage for a girl.[14] Henry must have been delighted.

Henry's own deposition made no mention of the precontract, but dwelled on his disappointment at Anne's lack of beauty; his

13 *Ibid.*, ff. 14v–15v.
14 *Glossa ordinaria*, CIC X 4.2.2, at the word "canonibus."

desire to find means to break off the marriage; his lack of consent when he married her; and his inability to consummate the marriage. He declared that "if she brought maidenhood with her," he did not take it from her by true carnal copulation.[15]

It would appear from Henry's account that he tried to consummate the marriage and failed. Although Cranmer had attempted in his *Twelve Articles* to prove to him that such an effort was more than sufficient to prove consummation when it had been a question of Henry's brother Arthur and his wife—even their being in bed together would constitute proof, he said—there is some indication that Henry was not altogether convinced in his conscience that Cranmer had proved his point. But Henry certainly did allow and encourage such legal presumptions when they were being urged against Catherine. Henry was also at pains to establish that Anne was not a virgin when she married him. Perhaps he wished to set forth the possibility that her previous contract had been consummated, thereby rendering it absolutely indissoluble. He may also have wished to counteract any contrary conclusions that might have resulted from an inspection of her present condition. We know that such an inspection had been arranged, or at least meditated upon.[16]

We recall that in the case of Catherine of Aragon, Henry had said he was too much of a boy to know how to tell whether she was a virgin or not. Now that he was older, he felt that he had more experience in the matter, but it seems that he was still not altogether sure. He told Cromwell, "I have felt her belly and her breasts, and thereby, as I can judge, she should be no maid."[17] Similarly, he told Sir Thomas Hennage that "plainly he mistrusted her to be no maid, by reason of the looseness of her breasts, and other tokens"; and Anthony Denny quoted the king as saying that "she was not as she was reported, but had her breasts so slack and other parts of body in such sort that His Highness somewhat suspected her virginity."[18] These witnesses went on to report that Anne's physical condition and doubtful virginity made it all the more impossible for the king to effect copula, for she provoked no sexual desire in him. The king's physician, Dr. Butts, said that

[15] Burnet, IV, 430.
[17] Burnet, IV, 427.
[16] LP XV, 821.4.
[18] Strype, I, part 2, 458–59.

Henry had revealed to him that he had had two nocturnal emissions since he had been married, which reassured him of his potency: he "thought himself able to do the act with other but not with her."[19] If Henry had been better read in the opinions of the schools, he could have alleged the impediment of impotency through demonic witchcraft, for St. Thomas Aquinas and others stated that it was characterized by frigidity toward one's wife but not toward other women.[20]

At the Thursday morning session of the court, four more lawyers from the lower house were added to the general committee, including John Tregonwell and John Hughes. Then, after the session had been under way "for no little time," Cranmer continued the Convocation until three o'clock in the afternoon. At that time, presumably after the committee made its report, the members of the Convocation unanimously asserted that the proofs they had seen were sufficient to show that there had never been a marriage between Henry and Anne, and that he was free to marry elsewhere, as was Anne, as long as the divine law permitted it. The committee was charged with the task of composing a testimonial or certificatory letter on this matter to the king. The Convocation was then continued until eight o'clock on the next day, Friday, July 9. We are not told what was done at this session beyond "mature consultation upon everything that concerned the said cause." It was then recessed until three in the afternoon. It reconvened for more mature consultation, and then the trial was concluded.

In the past when trials were held in convocation, it was the practice for the presiding archbishop, as metropolitan of the province, to give sentence in his name alone, with the other bishops present, though not the lower clergy, named as assessors (*assidentes*). This can be seen in the processes held before the Convocation of Canterbury as recorded in the register of Cranmer's predecessor of a century earlier, Henry Chichele. In the case of a double convocation, it would no doubt have been proper for both metropolitans to issue the sentence. On this occasion, however, the certificatory letter was prepared for all the clergy to

---

19 *Ibid.*, p. 461.
20 See Thomas, *Commentary on the Sentences*, 4.34.1.3; cf. H. A. Kelly, *The Devil, Demonology, and Witchcraft*, rev. ed. (New York, 1974), p. 62.

sign, and was now so signed, to serve as the judgment or decree of the entire Convocation.

In the letter, which was addressed to Henry, the clergy stated first that, according to their findings, Anne's previous contract impeded her marriage to the king and rendered it ambiguous and confused. Because Henry had been so insistent that a declaration be made about it, such a declaration could be considered to have been a condition necessary for the validity of the marriage. The condition was not fulfilled, for the king was falsely told that the matter had been investigated and that all had been resolved. Even if this expectation of the king's had not constituted a precondition, the unexplained precontract left the marriage up in the air (*in suspenso*); and if the precontract were *de praesenti*, which was likely, the marriage would be void. It was therefore rightly held suspect.

Furthermore, the king did not have "an internal, pure, perfect, and integral consent," and there had also been a misrepresentation of the lady's person, in order that she could be brought to these shores with her real qualities unknown. The solemnization of the union, which followed directly after, was forced upon the extremely reluctant and unwilling king "by very great, very grave, urgent, and pressing causes which could understandably constrain a person to act against his desire and inclination."

Also, carnal copula did not take place between the king and Lady Anne, nor could it licitly do so (a nice touch—even if it had taken place it would not have consummated the marriage, which was invalid to begin with). Finally, they were afraid that aspersions would be made in the future against the issue of the marriage, if it were allowed to stand, because the undeclared contract might be brought up. Therefore, claiming to follow ecclesiastical precedent, they declared the marriage null and void; and, in accord with their previous decision, they pronounced Henry free to marry any other person not prohibited by divine law, and, in spite of their fears over Anne's precontract, they extended the same freedom to her.[21]

[21] Wilkins, III, 852–55. Burnet, IV, 431–39, and SP I, 629–33, give the letter of sentence along with the names of the signers. For earlier trials before convocation, see *Chichele Register*, vol. III, and my article "English Kings and the Fear of Sorcery," n. 64.

When the members of Parliament approved this judgment shortly afterward, they were being more forthright than the clergy in admitting that Anne could remarry, in the light of the action they had taken in making precontracts voidable.[22] If they had had confidence in their action, they could have acknowledged that she could even validly remarry King Henry, in the unlikely event that his free consent were forthcoming, and in that event they need not have feared any aspersions against the marriage.

Henry later described the sequence of events to John Clerk, Bishop of Bath and Wells, and Nicholas Wootton, who had been sent to Cleves to apprise the duke, Anne's brother, of the trial that was to be held in the matter of the king's marriage. "After due proof of the fact, and mature deliberation how to apply the truth of learning thereunto," the king recounted, a sentence was given on Friday and announced to both houses of Parliament on Saturday. On the same day it was made known to Anne, who, "confessing the integrity of her body, agreed willingly to the determination of the clergy."[23]

According to Henry, then, Anne vindicated her virginity, and he was willing enough to believe her. But in the above-cited act of Parliament, which was introduced on Monday, July 12, Anne was reported to have declared only "that she remaineth not carnally known of the King's Highness's body."

It is not obvious at first sight why Henry, the clergy, and Parliament were so insistent that the king had not consummated his marriage to Anne, since they also insisted that the marriage was not valid in the first place. The full significance of the point appears in a document containing a justification of the annulment. Presumably Clerk was to use it in speaking with the Duke of Cleves, since it contains corrections in his hand. The condition upon which the king entered the marriage, that is, the clearing up of the precontract, was first described at length: Henry was unwilling to marry the spouse or wife of another man. Then it was stated with a twist to the truth that after the wedding, while

---

22 32 Henry VIII c. 25, *Statutes*, III, 781–82; cf. n. 1 above.

23 Henry to Clerk and Wootton, ca. 24 July 1540, SP VIII, 404–5. According to the *Journals of the House of Lords*, I, 154, Gardiner read the sentence first in Latin and then translated it in English, and explained some of the causes upon which it was based.

the king was waiting for the condition to be fulfilled, he deliberately abstained from carnal copula, in order not to "implicate" himself. For he knew that the Gospel saying "What God hath joined together, let no man put asunder" applied only to marriages that had been consummated, "as ye do know." After the day fixed for the fulfillment of the condition was past, the question was committed to the clergy, who judged him free of his marriage bond. It was essential to waste no time in coming to this decision, for it was feared that the son of the Duke of Lorraine would later allege his precontract, and if it were verified, the marriage of Anne to Henry would be nullified by the laws of the Bishop of Rome, even though children were born to it—"which the Bishop of Rome, being mortal enemy to the king and the realm, would soon have given ear hereunto, to slander the succession of this realm."[24] Finally, it was pointed out that "matrimony nonconsummate is under the disposition of the Church, as ye do know, so that the Church thereof may dispose, upon grounds, that it shall not bind, but be at liberty, as ye know, *per ingressum religionis* [that is, by entry into a religious order]; so that a contrary law to that that the Bishop of Rome useth may be made, that the second matrimony, consummate, shall take away from the first, not consummate; as the Bishops of Rome themselves, diverse times, when it made for their purpose, have judged: cap. *Licet, De sponsa duorum*."[25] The canon referred to is that of Pope Alexander III, who legislated that spousals *de praesenti* were not dissolved by a subsequent marriage, even one consummated by carnal copula. At the end of his decretal letter, however, the pope admitted that others held a different view, and that an opposite judgment had at times been made by certain of his predecessors.[26]

[24] Actually it had been reported that, on the contrary, the pope had been asked by the papists to dispense Anne from her earlier contract in order to make her marriage to Henry valid. George Cobham was told this by "Palant the younger," a knight in Anne's train. For some reason Palant believed this action of the papists to be against the laws of God, and he feared that if the king knew about it he would not enter the marriage for any worldly good. Cobham's deposition, as was noted above, was dated on the day before it was supposed to have been taken. Furthermore, his report of Palant's words, which were underlined in the Hatfield manuscript (see LP XV, 850.10), was omitted from the acts of the trial, MS Harley 1061, f. 7.

[25] SP I, 635–37; LP XV, 909.

[26] CIC X 4.4.3. Cranmer at one time referred to this decretal as expressive of an inviolable divine law. See above, Chap. 13 at n. 11.

Henry therefore clearly intended, by his act on precontracts, that the marriage he was to contract and consummate with Catherine Howard after July 1, 1540, would dissolve the marriage he had contracted but not consummated with Anne of Cleves, if the case for its nullity were impugned.

After approving of Henry's annulment from Anne of Cleves, Parliament requested him to marry again. He did so on July 28, 1540, again acting with majestic instancy. There is no record of spousals *de futuro* preceding the union.

The new Queen Catherine had committed many indiscretions, and she carried on similarly after marrying the king. Her deeds caught up with her after she had been married for a year, and in the investigations that followed more than enough evidence was uncovered for yet another annulment. Catherine had clearly been engaged to marry Francis Dereham, and they called each other husband and wife, and Dereham confessed that he had frequently lain with her. Their contract therefore had been consummated. Catherine denied that she had ever consented to be Dereham's wife—perhaps she was denying a contract *de praesenti*. But even spousals *de futuro* when followed by intercourse were considered sufficient, since, as Cranmer had correctly stated to Henry in his *Twelve Articles*, consent *de praesenti* was presumed in law. But the king did not want the precontract business brought up. Perhaps he thought it would not be good for his reputation; besides, it was sufficient to have her condemned of treason, for there was no offspring to worry about, as there was in the case of Anne Boleyn.

The king, however, could not get any admission of adultery after Catherine married him, so he had to rest content with a violent presumption to that effect. In fact, as Gairdner rightly points out, Catherine had been committing adultery (or, one should rather say, bigamy) not with Dereham but with the king, since her consummated marriage to Dereham had been established.[27]

The bill of attainder passed against Catherine in February 1542 stated that Henry had married Catherine thinking her to be chaste, whereas in fact she had lived a vicious life beforehand and continued it afterward. This was sufficiently heinous to condemn her

---

[27] James Gairdner, *DNB* Catherine.

to death for high treason. In order that adequate precautions might be taken for the future, it was ordered that any lightness of conduct in a queen was to be revealed to the king, and it was declared that an unchaste woman who married the king would be guilty of high treason, as would anyone who concealed such unchastity; and incontinence of or with a queen was similarly to be considered an act of high treason.[28]

Henry had accepted Catherine of Aragon as a virgin when he married her; but on reflection two decades later, he thought that he might have been mistaken, though he would not swear to it. Presumably he took Anne Boleyn, too, to be a virgin, but was no doubt willing to admit the contrary if, as Chapuys alleged, witnesses came forward to testify that she had consummated her marriage to Henry Percy. He had no reason to question Jane Seymour's virginity, but he did find signs of its lack in Anne of Cleves. He may or may not have accepted her assertion of the integrity of her body, but after his experience with Catherine Howard he must have realized that the tokens of maidenhood and its loss were very fallible indeed. In marrying his sixth wife, Catherine Parr, his worries on this score were over, for if she brought no maidenhood with her, she could have decently left it with one of her two former husbands.

In the foregoing attempt to fathom King Henry's conscience in the matter of his marriages, I have attempted to show not only a consistent concern on the king's part to justify himself before God, but also a remarkable consistency in his views. When he first became convinced that God was punishing him for his marriage to his brother's wife, he affirmed or at least let it be affirmed in his name at Wolsey's inquisition in 1527 that Catherine had consummated her marriage with Arthur. But when he realized the vital bearing that this factor had upon his case, he could not bring himself to assert it under oath in the future, for he knew, or feared, that it was not true. And though he encouraged a presumptive case to be made for it, he went on to convince himself that she was forbidden him even if she had not had carnal knowledge of Arthur. The marriage contract itself, he felt, was sufficient. Henry thereby elevated the impediment of public honesty, which arose

[28] 33 Henry VIII c. 21, *Statutes*, III, 857.

from such a contract, to the level of divine affinity, and he demoted affinity *ex coitu illicito* to a purely human terrain. In addition, he agreed with the pope that a nonconsummated marriage, such as Catherine had had with Arthur and Anne Boleyn had supposedly had with Henry Percy, could be dissolved by human authority. His marriage to Catherine was therefore null from the beginning; a dispensation could be had for the affinity between him and Anne; and Anne could be divorced from her husband.

The Henrician shift of the criterion for in-law incest, from sexual congress (with or without marriage) to the matrimonial contract (with or without sex), had both Scripture and common sense to recommend it. But if the traditional view was too strong for the king to overcome publicly, there is, at the same time, no compelling reason to suppose that he ever abandoned his own view in the forum of his conscience. Even when the time came to annul his marriage to Anne Boleyn, he did not necessarily recede from his view on affinity *ex coitu illicito*. Though he found it politic to restore its divine status in the 1536 Act of Succession, he need not himself have relied on this view to find his marriage void, since there were other grounds of nullity at hand. The most certain of these grounds, of course, was this same degree of affinity arising from his carnal knowledge of Mary Boleyn, regarded not as divine law but as the result of a man-made statute requiring ecclesiastical dispensation. For the 1536 Parliament nullified Henry's marriage, in effect, by voiding all papal dispensations in England and specifically exempting from revalidation all marriages that had been annulled in the English ecclesiastical courts.

In his subsequent marriages, we no longer hear of any fear of the divine displeasure. He did raise the question whether his marriage to Anne of Cleves were bigamous because of a previous marriage on her part, but this was a question of human, not divine, law. He proved this at the time of his annulment from Anne of Cleves by doing away with marriage as an impediment to another marriage, so long as the second marriage was consummated and the first was not. Thus he demonstrated his consistency with the position he had taken earlier. In the marriage with Catherine Howard, the bigamy was on the divine level, as it may in fact have been in the marriage with Anne Boleyn, if she was indissolubly united by intercourse to her first husband. But the problem was resolved before God's wrath could express itself, unless it had done so in his fifth queen's failure to conceive a child of him. As for his last marriage, the only dispensation he received was one that he could have arranged to do without, that is, the right to marry at any time or place before any celebrant, without the reading of banns.[29] The king's fears about offending God through an unholy alliance had been put to rest.

[29] Dispensation issued on July 10, 1543, signed by Nicholas Wootton, LP XVIII, part 1, 854.

Epilogue

THE YEAR after Henry died, Parliament, presumably under the guidance of Archbishop Cranmer, saw to it that the provision of the statute of 1540 making precontracts voidable was repealed. The reason given was a very logical one: the new law had encouraged breach of contract. Therefore, henceforward, if a precontract (*de praesenti* understood) were proved, the judge must command that the said precontract be carried out, with solemnization and consummation of the marriage.[1]

Nothing was said about the indissolubility of precontracts, or indeed of consummated marriages, nor was it declared whether divinely prohibited affinity came only from marrying (Cranmer's original view), or from copula (so the 1536 Act of Succession, still in force), or from both (as in the 1534 Act), or from either. We are able to acquire a good idea of the archbishop's current views, however, from the proposals made by a commission established to reform canon law, appointed by Edward VI, with Cranmer himself in charge of drawing up its conclusions. The most startling innovation in the section on marriage was that absolute divorce of perfectly valid unions, consummated as well as unconsummated, was to be allowed as a matter of course. When, for instance, one of the spouses was convicted of adultery, the other might enter a new marriage; for Christ himself had said so. But the innocent party should still be urged to be reconciled to the guilty spouse.[2]

---

[1] 2–3 Edward VI c. 23, *Statutes*, IV, 68. The bill was introduced on November 29, 1548, committed *ad ingrossandum* on December 4, and concluded on January 21, 1549, by the assent of all the Lords, with only two exceptions.

[2] *Reformatio legum ecclesiasticarum* (London, 1640), p. 49.

Cranmer, in other words, had come fully abreast of Cardinal Cajetan and even overtaken him, having allied himself with the more liberal school of Lutheran theologians. Divorce was also to be allowed in cases of desertion, and also when one of the spouses had been long absent (if a husband were to show up later and have a good excuse, his wife must return to him; if not, he must be thrown into prison for life and allowed no access to his former wife). Finally, it was also to be allowed if one of the partners should attempt to kill the other, or be excessively brutal.

As for the impediments to marriage, if one of the spouses were unable to perform the conjugal act because of some bodily defect or because of witchcraft, and this condition were unknown to the other, the marriage would be null; but if there were sufficient knowledge and free consent, the union might take place, "since no injury can be done to those who are willing." A mistaken conviction about the condition of the partner (that is, whether free or slave) would also invalidate marriage, as would force or fear. All these points agreed with the old canons; not so with spiritual kinship, which was no longer to be an impediment.

Furthermore, no persons forbidden by divine law were to marry. For otherwise "our realm and the churches in it would be contaminated with incest, and the persons who were so defiled with these nefarious unions would necessarily incur the great wrath of God." Persons forbidden marriage were not only those listed in Leviticus, but also all persons like them; therefore, since one could not marry one's daughter or granddaughter, so too a great-granddaughter and more remote descendants were forbidden; just as nephews might not marry aunts, so too uncles might not marry nieces, great-nieces, great-great-nieces, and so on. Simply stated, everyone in the direct line was out of the running, and in the collateral line all degrees touching the first. The same was true of affinity, which "proceeds from the union of men and women," and was found "not only in legitimate marriages but also in the illicit union of bodies." (Note that the marriages are not specified as consummated.) Just so, as a son should not marry his mother, neither could he have his father's concubine; as the father should not marry his son's wife, so too he must abstain from the woman his son had abused; and the same reason that prohibited the mother from being united to the husband of her daughter banned her from the man who had forced her daughter. (The picture is clear regarding the invalidity of Henry's marriage to Anne Boleyn, even though the example of a woman being forbidden the man who has had her sister or mother was not explicitly given.) The ban also extended beyond the frontier of death: just as it was a horrible crime to violate the wife of one's father, brother, or uncle while he was alive, so too marriage with her after his death was equally abominable. The violation of these laws was to be punished with life imprisonment.[3]

When Queen Mary ascended the throne, Parliament duly declared the marriage between Henry VIII and Catherine of Aragon valid; it had received the consent of everyone involved, and of the best and most notable men of learning in all Christendom, and had so continued for twenty years. (Parliament was not yet ready to refer to the pope's role in all this.) Then afterward "the malicious and perverse affections of some, a very few persons," had smuggled a scruple into Her Majesty's father's conscience, and by corrupt means obtained the apparent support of various universities. There was no mention of the legatine court or of the effort to get an annulment from Rome. Cranmer's judgment of annulment was condemned; it had been based "partly upon his own unadvised judgment of the Scripture, joining therewith the pretended testimonies of the said universities, and partly upon the bare and most untrue conjectures, gathered and admitted by him upon matters of no strength or effect." Parliament therefore proceeded to repeal the 1534 Act of Succession (which Henry had already repealed) and as much of the 1536 act as declared Mary illegitimate and the marriage of her parents unlawful.[4]

After the queen married her cousin Philip II of Spain, she took her Parliament a long step further in the direction of the old traditions. All statutes passed against the Apostolic See of Rome were revoked. Included in the repeal was another part of the 1536 Act of Succession, namely, the prohibition to marry within the degrees named in it. Repealed too was the 1540 act concerning precon-

---

[3] *Ibid.*, pp. 40–47, 55.

[4] 1 Mary session 2 (1553) c. 1, *Statutes*, IV, 200. Mortimer Levine, "Henry VIII's Use of His Spiritual and Temporal Jurisdictions," p. 9, notes that Mary's Parliament in so acting assumed for itself jurisdiction in a matrimonial cause.

tracts and degrees of kinship, part of which had already been
stricken out under Edward VI, and it was requested that all the
marriages that had been made since 1540 which might be invalid
because contracted within the prohibited degrees of consanguinity,
affinity, spiritual kinship, or by reason of public honesty, "or for
any other cause prohibited by the canons only," might be validated and the children born of them declared legitimate. Cardinal
Pole complied with this request by granting a general dispensation, with the condition, however, that those who knowingly or
maliciously entered into such marriages in defiance of the canons
must be absolved of excommunication and of the guilt of incest,
or sacrilege.[5]

The first act of Elizabeth's first Parliament restored to the crown
its ancient jurisdiction and abolished all foreign power repugnant
to it; that is, it revived the "good laws" made by Henry VIII,
which had been enforced until they were abrogated by Her Highness's sister. Since, however, it would be going too far to say that
all the laws repealed by Mary were good laws, Mary's law of repeal was repealed in such a way that all the laws she had repealed
by it were to remain repealed unless otherwise provided.

The 1536 Act of Succession, which declared Elizabeth illegitimate, was thus left in limbo. Seemingly the fact was overlooked
that, since Mary had carefully avoided repealing that part of the
act, the queen's bastardy was still on the books. The 1540 act as
emended under Edward VI was resurrected, meaning therefore
that no impediments of consanguinity or affinity were to be recognized outside the Levitical degrees. The degrees were not named
but divine affinity was no doubt understood in the 1540 statute to
be induced only by intercourse, and anyone who cared to run
through the degrees in his mind would be forced to the conclusion
that for all its precautions Parliament had managed to declare its
sovereign illegitimate once again.[6]

What Elizabeth's personal views on the Levitical degrees were
is not known, though it is noteworthy that she toyed with the idea

[5] 1 & 2 Philip and Mary c. 8, *Statutes*, IV, 246–50.
[6] 1 Elizabeth I c. 1, *Statutes*, IV, 350–51. Levine, p. 9, points out that Elizabeth's Parliament in recognizing her title gave prominent place to the Act of
Succession of 1544, which restored both Mary and Elizabeth to their proper
places in succession but not in blood, and only vaguely mentioned her descent
from the blood royal of England.

of marrying her brother-in-law, Philip II of Spain, with no apparent qualms of conscience.

Cranmer's suggested reformation of canon law was not adopted as such; the canons on divorce were completely ignored, but in 1563 the Archbishop of Canterbury, Matthew Parker, who had been on the reform commission, issued an admonition giving a table of prohibited degrees much like that advocated by Cranmer, and declared that marriages made within these degrees were in violation of the laws of God and the realm; affinity was said to arise "as well by unlawful company of man and woman as by lawful marriage."[7] (Once again, marital affinity was not said to require consummation.) Thus, to the thoughtful observer, the queen's illegitimacy was made still more explicit. Furthermore, in 1571, John Foxe published, with the archbishop's license, the whole report of the commission under title of *The Reformation of the Ecclesiastical Laws*.

In the same year that Archbishop Parker had promulgated his decree specifying the Levitical degrees and declaring them inviolable, the Council of Trent proclaimed that the Church could grant dispensations for some of the Levitical degrees; the dispensable degrees were not specified, and in the course of time since Trent almost every relationship between man and woman by blood or marriage, except the ultimate sacred bond between parent and child, has been exempted from or declared exemptible. Even brother-sister unions have been allowed to stand by the Church of Rome, and the same could in theory be done for marriages contracted between a grandparent and grandchild.[8]

Meanwhile, in the Church of England, Archbishop Parker's table of prohibited degrees was incorporated into the Book of Common Prayer, and it remains there to the present, a tribute and a relic to a conscientious king's terror of incest. Furthermore, the table received statutory recognition for hundreds of years.

Until the Marriage Act of 1835, however, a marriage within the

---

[7] G. H. Joyce, *Christian Marriage*, p. 556. Kelly, *Traditio*, 23: 271.

[8] For the history of this progressive relaxation, see my essay "Kinship, Incest, and the Dictates of Law," pp. 69–78. On brother-sister marriages, see p. 75. It is Cardinal Pietro Gasparri, the chief architect of the 1917 *Code of Canon Law*, who asserts that such marriages are allowed, and he cites one example from the curial archives to which he had access. See his *Tractatus canonicus de matrimonio*, rev. ed. (Rome, 1932), I, 133, 432–33.

prohibited degrees was not considered void from the beginning, as under the old canon law. Rather, it was considered voidable— that is, valid until and unless pronounced invalid by an ecclesiastical court, provided the judgment came during the lifetime of both parties. The Act of 1835 made such marriages void from the beginning.[9]

The courts and Parliament have greatly whittled down the forbidden degrees of affinity in the past century or so. In 1861 it was established that "carnal connection without an actual and legal marriage does not constitute affinity."[10] In 1907, the Deceased Wife's Sister's Marriage Act exempted the degree exempted by the Book of Leviticus itself, and the Deceased Brother's Widow's Marriage Act of 1921, in defiance of Henry VIII's scruples, opened up the privilege, if not the duty, of the law of levirate to all men, whether their deceased brothers had had children or not. In 1931, nieces and aunts of one's deceased wife were made available, as well as the widows of one's uncles and nephews. Curiously, the act did not explicitly make the corresponding males available to women: on paper, they were still forbidden their former mates' uncles and nephews, and the widowers of their nieces and aunts. Implicitly, however, they were included, as a little reflection will show: if a man may marry, for instance, the niece of his deceased wife, then it follows that the niece may also marry him, her aunt's widower. The Act of 1949 made the inference explicit, and added other exemptions. Once a man's wife was dead, he could marry the sister of his mother-in-law or father-in-law, or the widow of his nephew, and a widow could marry the brother of her father- or mother-in-law, and a woman could marry her niece's widower. The act also, for the first time in post-Henrician parliamentary law, specified the prohibited degrees. The following marriages were forbidden (arranged by canonical computation):[11]

A. Direct consanguinity:
    1st degree: parent/child
    2d degree: grandparent/grandchild

---

[9] *Halsbury's Statutes of England*, 2d ed., vol. 28 (Continuation Vol., 1948–49, London, 1951), p. 654.

[10] *Wing v. Taylor (falsely calling herself Wing)*, cited by Lord Simonds, *Halsbury's Laws of England*, 3d ed., vol. 19 (London, 1957), p. 783, note a.

[11] *Ibid.*, p. 782, notes r and s, p. 783, note e; *Halsbury's Statutes* (n. 9 above), pp. 654–55, 722–23.

B. Collateral consanguinity:
  1st & 1st degree: brother/sister
  1st & 2d degree: uncle/niece or nephew/aunt

C. Direct affinity:
  1st degree: *a*) parent-in-law/child-in-law
        b) stepparent/stepchild
  2d degree: *a*) grandparent-in-law/grandchild-in-law
        b) stepgrandparent/stepgrandchild

D. Collateral affinity (while first spouse is alive):
  1st & 1st degree: brother-in-law/sister-in-law
  1st & 2d degree: uncle-in-law/niece-in-law
          or nephew-in-law/aunt-in-law

E. Legal kinship: adopter/adopted

Finally, the Marriage Act of 1960 eliminated Section D above, thereby allowing a man to marry his sister-in-law, aunt-in-law, or niece-in-law, even though his first wife is not dead but only divorced. Furthermore, if Herod and his brother Philip were alive at this day and in good standing in the Church of England, no John the Baptist from the ranks of the clergy would be entitled, "it seems," to refuse Herod Communion, simply because of his marriage to Herodias.[12] On the other hand, it is never allowable to marry direct affines like mothers-in-law or daughters-in-law or stepdaughters, or to marry adopted daughters, nor is it permitted for marriage to exist between blood relatives in the first degree mixed with the second (that is, the third degree by civil computation). Thus, in the summer of 1971, a resident of Southampton, aged twenty-four, married his niece, aged twenty, and accordingly the couple were haled into court for a violation of the Marriage Act, and their marriage was declared null.[13] It was a marriage that even Cardinal Torquemada would have considered allowable for an adequate cause, but the neo-Levitical laws of the British Parliament admit of no dispensation.

[12] *Halsbury's Statutes of England*, 3d ed., vol. 17 (London, 1970), p. 109.
[13] *The Times* (London), 16 July 1971 (p. 3) and 29 July (p. 4). The young man in question expressed his intention of marrying in Denmark after a fortnight's residence, but it is considered that such a marriage would still not be recognized in Britain, for the couple would not be regarded as legal residents of Denmark after so short a domicile.

Appendixes

The Queen's Libellus

Factum and Responses to Fourteen Objections Against Julius II's Bull of Dispensation. Presented by the Counsel of Catherine of Aragon to Cardinals Campeggio and Wolsey at the Legatine Court of 1529.

[Vienna: Haus-, Hof- und Staatsarchiv, England, Varia Karton 2. Abbreviations have been silently expanded, except in the citations.]

FACTUM

Henricus .vij. Angliae Rex filios duos masculos Arcturum Primogenitum et Henricum Serenissimum nunc Angliae Regem habens Clarissimam Dominam Catherinam Illustrium Hispaniarum Regum filiam Arcturo iam puberi matrimonio copulauit post cuius obitum sine liberis tractatum fuit de nuptijs inter dictam Catherinam et Henricum nunc Regem Anglie contrahendis, et obstantibus impedimentis affinitatis et publicae honestatis iusticiae contracta inter eos fuerunt sponsalia sub conditione si papa dispensaret, et ideo à sede apostolica in forma infrascripta dispensatio impetrata fuit cuius virtute Serenissimus Henricus et Illustrissima Catherina per verba de presenti sponsalia contraxerunt. Henricus Rex tunc erat impubes Et post biennium in pubertatis principio aduersus sic contracta sponsalia ignorante regina reclamauit protestando se a contractis sponsalibus disentire et nolle Dominam Catherinam in vxorem ducere nec se vnquam eam in uxorem ducendi animum habuisse, mortuo postmodum Henrico .vij. predictus Serenissimus Henricus .viij. successit in Regnum, qui cum matura etas eum ad matrimonium prouocaret Cum eadem Illustrissima Domina Catherina matrimonium sollemniter in forma ecclesie contraxit et carnali coppula cum prolis susceptione matrimonium consumauit ex quo nata est et viuit Clarissima Domina Maria

DISPENSATIONIS TENOR

[Julius II's Bull of Dispensation follows, here omitted]

EX FACTO HEC DUBIA ORIUNTUR

P⁰ An ducere relictam fratris sine liberis defuncti sit diuina lege prohibitum ex aduerso dicitur sic Levi. .18 et 20.[1] nos contrarium, tum quia tale preceptum non est morale nam non obligauit semper et ad semper Gen: 38:[2] c. 1.35: q: pᵃ.[3] et per consequens talis prohibitio est euacuata nec hodie ligat nisi tantum ex ecclesie constitutione ut

---

[1] Leviticus 18 and 20.
[2] Genesis 38.
[3] The first chapter of the first Quaestio in Causa 35. CIC Gratian 2.35.1.1.

per Thom: *Sup.* pᵃ. 2ᵉ: q: 104:[4] tum quia etiam mortuo fratre sine liberis precipitur superstiti fratri sub pena ut relictam fratris sine liberis defuncti uxorem ducat Deut: 25:[5] ca pᵒ: 35: q: pᵃ. Gen: 38:[6] in his tamen est aduertendum an predictis obstet quod tale preceptum fuit in figura institutum: c: *olim:* 8: q: pᵃ.[7] et quod si aliquando deus Concessit id fuit dispensatione et ex causa neccessitatis factum: c: pᵒ: §. *his ita:* 35: q: pᵃ.[8]

2⁰ Presupposito quod Casus sit Jure diuino prohibitus An Papa ex potestate absoluta vel ordinaria dispensare potuerit Et an talis dispensatio etiam si sit ficta sine Causa saltim in foro contentioso sustineatur de quibus pro et Contra in: 4⁰: *Sent:* d: 40: *cum seq:*[9] in c: fi: *de diuor:*[10] in c: *litteras de restitu: spol:*[11] et in c: *que in ecclesiarum de Const:*[12] et per sumistas in eorum summis/

3⁰ An Dispensatio viribus careat presuposito etiam quod dispensationis tempore nullus verisimilis ineat belli timor quasi quod sine causa vere subsistente sit facta arg: c: *Tali:* 1: q: 7:[13] et not: per Inno: in c: *Innotuit de elect:*[14] abb: et doc: in c: *Cum olim de re iud:*[15] et vana iudicatur suspitio que non fundatur in causa de presenti iuxta not: in L: pᵃ. ff: et C. *de trans:*[16] in L: *qui cum tutoribus* et L: *Cum hi:* §. *sed cum lis* ff: eo.[17] An uero talis ratio pacis conseruande iustam dispensandi causam inducat saltim in Regibus propter maius periculum quod ex illorum discordia Christiane Reipublice euenire solet arg: c: *vbi periculum de electio.* in vj⁰ .[18] Et ne Regi dispensationem

---

[4] Thomas Aquinas, *Summa theologiae* 1–2.104. The scribe erroneously refers to the Supplement to the *Summa*.

[5] Deuteronomy 25.

[6] See notes 3 and 2 above, respectively.

[7] Chapter *Olim*, Causa 8, Quaestio prima. CIC Gratian 2.8.1.8. Gives a spiritual interpretation of the law of levirate of Deuteronomy 25.

[8] Paragraph *His ita* of Gratian's introduction to Quaestio 1 of Causa 35. CIC Gratian 2.35.1.§2.

[9] The arguments for and against in Peter Lombard's *Sentences*, Distinction 40 and following.

[10] The final chapter of the title *De divortiis.* CIC X 4.19.9.

[11] Chapter *Litteras* of the title *De restitutione spoliatorum.* CIC X 2.13.13.

[12] Chapter *Quae in ecclesiarum* in the title *De constitutionibus.* CIC X 1.2.7.

[13] Chapter *Tali.* CIC Gratian 2.1.7.17.

[14] What is noted by Innocent in the chapter *Innotuit* of the title *De electione et electi potestate.* CIC X 1.6.20.

[15] The Abbot of Palermo (Nicholas Tudeschi) and other doctors commenting on the chapter *Cum olim* of the title *De sententia et re iudicata.* CIC X 2.27.12.

[16] In chapter (i.e. *lex*) 1 of the title *De transactionibus.* Justinian Digest (= ff) 2.15.1 and Code 2.4.1.

[17] In the chapter *Qui cum tutoribus* and in the paragraph *Si cum lis* in the chapter *Cum hi* of the same title. Justinian Digest 2.15.8.9, 20. "Eo" (= eodem) seems to be in a different hand, which we may call Hand B.

[18] Chapter *Ubi periculum* of the title *De electione et electi potestate.* CIC Sextus 1.6.3.

petenti que pluribus alijs concessa sit fieret iniuria L. pᵃ. §. *permit-*
titur ff. *de aq: quo: et est:*[19] Et propter inimicitie dubium quod ante
affinitatem Bone memorie Arcturi militabat ar: not: per glo: in c:
.§. *affinitates* 35. q. 7.[20] Et ad tollendum lites que
post diuortium ob iminentem dotis et iocalium restitutionem oriri
poterant iuxta not: per glo: et abb: in Rubrica *de doti: et dot: post*
diuor: rest:[21] maxime cum propter damnum non obstante papa intel-
ligitur vsus potestatis plenitudine et quia alias actus esset nullus iux:
not: per Paul. *de cast:*[22] in L. *si testamento* C: *de testa:*[23] et not: mod:
in L: quoque C: *de test: milit:*[24] Et papa ex alijs causis asserat se mo-
tum/

4⁰ An dispensatio sit inualida quia in ea narratur pro parte Serenissimi
Henrici suplicatum fuisse et de mandato non constat iux: not: per
abb: in c: *innotuit de elec:*[25] ar: c: *nonnulli de rescrip:*[26] in c: fi:
de procur: in vi⁰.[27] et mandatum non presumitur ut not: Bal: in L:
ij: C: *si ex fal: instr:*[28] Cum ex contrario videatur affirmari posse
quod potuerit per coniunctam personam impetrari d: c: *nonnulli*[29]
maxime per patrem ar: L: *patri:* ff: *de mino:*[30] iuncta L: iij. §. *Si*
emancipatus de bon: pos: con: tab:[31] Et in litteris dicatur pro parte
Henrici supplicatum quod saltim in aduersarium transfert onus probandi per not: in Cleᵃ. pᵃ: *de proba:*[32] et Gem: Con. 33:[33] et quia

---

[19] Chapter 1, paragraph *Permittitur* of the title *De aqua cottidiana et aestiva.*
Justinian Digest 43.20.41.

[20] Referring to an unnamed chapter of CIC Gratian 2.35.7. Only the gloss
of the second chapter of this seventh question has a paragraph *Affinitatis* (not
Affinitates), but it does not seem relevant.

[21] As noted by the gloss and by the Abbot of Palermo on the rubric to the
title *De donationibus inter virum et uxorem et de dote post divortium resti-*
tuenda. CIC X 4.20.

[22] Chapter by Paulus in the title *De castrensi peculio.* Justinian Digest
49.17.20.

[23] Chapter *Miles si testamentum* of the title *De testamento militis.* Justinian
Digest 29.1.35 (the reference to the Code for this and the next law is a mistake).

[24] Chapter by Modestinus of the title *De testamento militis.* Justinian Digest
29.1.32.

[25] The Abbot of Palermo on the chapter *Innotuit* of the title *De electione*
et electi potestate. CIC X 1.6.20.

[26] Chapter *Nonnulli* in the title *De rescriptis.* CIC X 1.3.28.

[27] The final chapter in the title *De procuratoribus.* CIC Sextus 1.19.9.

[28] Baldo degli Ubaldi's commentary on chapter 2 of the title *Si ex falsis in-*
strumentis vel testimoniis iudicatum sit. Justinian Code 7.58.2.

[29] Chapter *Nonnulli* noted above (n. 26).

[30] Chapter *Patri* of the title *De minoribus vigintiquinque annis.* Justinian
Digest 4.4.27.

[31] Chapter 3, paragraph *Si emancipatus* in the title *De bonorum possessione*
contra tabulas. Justinian Digest 37.4.3.5.

[32] The first chapter of the title *De probationibus.* CIC Clementinae 2.7.1.

[33] Geminianus (Dominic of San Gimignano), *Consilia*, no. 33, ed. John Staphileus (Pavia, 1509), f. 20 rv. Geminianus is dealing with a case of false repre-

filius sciens rem gestam per patrem consentire videtur L: *dotem* ff: *sol: ma:*[34] L: *sed ea que in patris* ff: *de spon:*[35] Et Henricus factus iam pubes videtur ratum habuisse c: p⁰: *de spon:* in vj⁰:[36] maxime etiam contrahendo post dispensationem obtentam in facie ecclesie Et quia impetratio tendit ad libertatem filij arg: not: per doc: in L: i: C: *de precib: imp: off:*/[37]

5⁰ An Dispensatio dicatur surreptitia quia Concupiscientia ad matrimonium contrahendum et ad pacem conseruandam in dispensatione expressa in eo qui erat impubes esse non poterat ar: L: pᵃ. C: *de fil: mon:*[38] §. *preterea* inst: *quib: non est permis: fac: test:*[39] An vero contrarium possit affirmari quia Henricus Rex licet tempore dispensationis esset impubes erat tamen proximus pubertati. §. *pupillus* inst: *de inutil: stip:*[40] L: *apud celsum de dol: mal: exep:*[41] Et per not: in L: *Donatarium* C: *de acq: pos:*[42] et in c: p⁰: et ij: *de desp: impub:* in 6⁰:[43] et in c: *puberes*   [44] et c: *Juuenis de spon:*[45] et in c: fi: *de eo qui cogno: Cons: vxo: sue*/[46]

---

sentation. He disallows the decretal of Pope Clement V (cited above in n. 32), which assumes the truth of all petitions made to the pope, because in this instance there is definite proof to the contrary. The petitioner not only did not officially represent the lady in question, but also he lied to the pope in saying that she wished to marry when in fact she had protested her determination not to do so. (I wish to thank Professor Stephan Kuttner for first suggesting that the *libellus* reference was to Geminianus.)

[34] Chapter *Dotem* of the title *Soluto matrimonio dos quemadmodum petatur.* Justinian Digest 24.3.37.

[35] Chapter *Sed quae patris* in the title *De sponsalibus.* Justinian Digest 23.1.12.

[36] The first chapter of the title *De sponsalibus et matrimoniis.* CIC Sextus 4.1.1.

[37] Commentary of the doctors on chapter 1 of the title *De precibus imperatori offerendis: et de quibus rebus supplicare liceat vel non.* Justinian Code 1.19.1.

[38] Chapter 1 probably of the title *De filiofamilias minore.* Justinian Code 2.22.1.

[39] Paragraph *Praeterea* of the title *Quibus non est permissum facere testamentum.* Justinian Institutes 2.12.1.

[40] Paragraph *Pupillus* of the title *De inutilibus stipulationibus.* Justinian Institutes 3.20.9.

[41] Chapter *Apud Celsum* of the title *De doli, mali, et metus exceptione.* Justinian Digest 44.4.4.

[42] Chapter *Donatarum* in the title *De acquirenda et retinenda possessione.* Justinian Code 7.32.3.

[43] The first and second chapters of the title *De desponsatione impuberum.* CIC Sextus 4.2.1, 2. This apparently is a mistake: the title in Sextus has only one chapter, and the similar title in Gregory has fourteen. The blank following *puberes* seems to indicate the writer's uncertainty.

[44] Chapter *Puberes* in the title *De desponsatione impuberum.* CIC X 4.2.3.

[45] Chapter *Iuvenis* of the title *De sponsalibus et matrimoniis.* CIC X 4.1.3.

[46] The final chapter of the title *De eo qui cognovit consanguineam uxoris suae.* CIC X 4.13.11.

6º Vtrum per protestationem factam ab Henrico in Jnitio pubertatis et dispensatio et sponsalia antea contracta viribus careant iux: not: per host: et doc: in c: *de illis de desp: impub:*[47] in quo dicitur nobis suffragari secundum matrimonium et quod per tractatatum et coppulam fuit a protestatione recessum in c: *tua* et c: *Juuenis* ——— ij: et c: *ad id quod de spon:*[48] in c: *per tuas de cond: ap:*[49] et que in c: *sollicitudinem de ap:*[50] Et quia protestatio Regina ignorante cum alijs de quibus in .§. *morte* et in c: *Cum Marthae. de const:*[51]

7º An si reperiatur quod Serenissimus Henricus dispensationi renuntiauit matrimonium subsequens sit nullum quia semel extinctum etc[?] L: *qui res .§.   aream* ff: *de solu:*[52] An vero econtra propter Regine preiuditium ar: not: in L: *fi:* ff: *de pac:*[53] in L: *nemo pro socio*[54] maxime post vsum ad not: in c: *ad apostolicam de regul:*[55] Et satis sit quod remaneat Contrahendi habilitas quo ad reginam ar: L: *si Comunem* ff: *que ser: amitt.*[56]

8º Vtrum dispensatio possit dici nulla quia Cum affinitas et publice honestatis iusticie impedimento subessent non fuit super publice honestatis impedimento dispensatum iux: not: per glo: Jo. And. super *arbore affinitatis* post prin:[57] An vero Contrarium quia tacito et expresse uidetur ficta [*sic*] de vtroque impedimento mentio in dispensatione et quia   in neccessariam consequentiam ad ea que late abb: et doc: in c: *non debet de cons: et affi:*[58]

9º An presumatur matrimonium inter Serenissimos Arcturum et Catherinam fuisse Consumatum ex cohabitatione et Thori Comunione ad

[47] Hostiensis (Henry of Susa, Cardinal of Ostia) and other doctors on the chapter *De illis* of the title *De desponsatione impuberum.* CIC X 4.2.7.

[48] Chapters *Tua, Iuvenis,* and *Ad id quod* of the title *De sponsalibus et matrimoniis.* CIC X 4.1.26, 3, 21. The reference to 'ij' is doubtful. The author also seems to be in doubt. Perhaps he is referring to chapter 2, *Praeterea,* which specifies that spousals *de futuro* are dissolved if the two parties agree to it.

[49] Chapter *Per tuas* in the title *De conditionibus appositis in desponsatione vel in aliis contractibus.* CIC X 4.5.6.

[50] Chapter *Sollicitudinem* in the title *De appellationibus, recusationibus et relationibus.* CIC X 2.28.54.

[51] Chapter *Cum M.* in the title *De constitutionibus.* CIC X 1.2.9. The indication "§ *Morte*" probably refers to Justinian Digest 17.2.65.9–11.

[52] Paragraph *Aream* of the chapter *Qui res* of the title *De solutionibus et liberationibus.* Justinian Digest 46.3.98.8.

[53] Chapter *Fideiussoris* of the title *De pactis.* Justinian Digest 2.14.23.

[54] Chapter *Nemo* in the title *Pro socio.* Justinian Digest 17.2.35.

[55] Chapter *Ad apostolicam* in the title *De regularibus et transeuntibus ad religionem.* CIC X 3.31.16.

[56] Chapter *Si communem* in the title *Quemadmodum servitutes amittantur.* Justinian Digest 8.6.10.

[57] The gloss of John Andreae on the *Arbor affinitatis,* after the beginning. See above, Chapter 6 at n. 7.

[58] Comment by the Abbot of Palermo and other doctors on the chapter *Non debet* in the title *De consanguinitate et affinitate.* CIC X 4.14.8.

not in c: *litteras de presu:*[59] An vero potius credendum sit matrimonium non fuisse inter eos Consumatum et per consequens affinitatem non esse contractum nec impedimentum prohibitionis diuine
obstare c: *lex diuine* 27: q: 2:[60] tum quia Consumatio non probatur
et Regina iure Iurando asserit se nunquam fuisse ab Arcturo cognitam ex not: in c: p⁰: *de frig: et male:*[61] tum quia Serenissimus Henricus id pluries est confessus iuxta ea quae haben. in auct. *Sed rem
necesse.* C. *de donat. an nup.*[62] et in c: *is qui de spons.*[63]

10⁰ Moveri potest et dubium An sponsalia contracta inter prefatos Henricum et Reginam tenuerint Cum dispensatum fuerit non super
sponsalibus sed super matrimonio contrahendo que dificultas tolletur
ar: *tex*: in L: *tutor*: ff: *de sponsa:*[64] et quod fuit matrimonium contractum

11⁰ Vtrum quia tempore dispensationis obtente Henricus erat inhabilis
ad matrimonium contrahendum quia erat impubes c: *puberes de
desp: imp:*[65] dispensatio sit inefficax licet factus maior matrimonium
contraxerit arg: c: *si eo tempore de rescrip*: in vj⁰:[66] An vero satis
sit fuisse habilem quo ad effectum tollendi impedimentum affinitatis
de quo agebatur vel quod habilitas exequtionis tempore existens
sufficiat ar: c: *et cui* _____ *Cum vulg: de preb*: in 6⁰:[67] et in c: *eam
te. de rescrip:*[68]

12⁰ Vtrum ex eo matrimonium sit inualidum quia tempore quo Contractum fuit dispensationis causa cessabat vz. Conseruatio pacis inter
Serenissimum Henricum vij: et ferdinandum Hispaniarum Regem
et Reginam Elisabet nam ante matrimonium contractum Henricus
et Elisabet fuerunt diem functi arg: c: *Cum cessante de ap:*[69] An
vero matrimonium sustineatur quia semel fuit impedimentum subla-
tum et sic affectus erat consumatus ex not: in L: *titia* .§. *imperator*

---

[59] Chapter *Litteras* of the title *De praesumptionibus.* CIC X 2.23.14.

[60] Chapter *Lex divinae.* CIC Gratian 2.27.2.18.

[61] The first chapter of the title *De frigidis et maleficiatis et impotentia coeundi.* CIC X 4.15.1.

[62] Justinian, Authentic Constitutions 7.9.2, as summarized in the paragraph
Sed iam necesse after the chapter *Si constante* of the title *De donationibus ante
nuptias, vel propter nuptias, et sponsalitiis.* Justinian Code 5.3.19. See, for example, *Corpus iuris civilis* (Amsterdam and Lyons, 1664), pp. 187–88.

[63] Chapter *Is qui* of the title *De sponsalibus et matrimoniis.* CIC X 4.1.30.

[64] Chapter *Tutor* of the title *De sponsalibus.* Justinian Digest 23.1.15: "Scias
tamen, quod de nuptiis tractamus et ad sponsalia pertinere."

[65] Chapter *Puberes* of the title *De desponsatione impuberum.* CIC X 4.2.3.

[66] Chapter *Si eo tempore* of the title *De rescriptis.* CIC Sextus 1.3.9.

[67] Chapter *Et cui* (Hand B) in an unnamed source, and chapter *Cum vulg.*
in the title *De prebendis* of Sextus (no such chapter exists).

[68] Chapter *Eam te* in the title *De rescriptis.* CIC X 1.3.7.

[69] Chapter *Cum cessante* in the title *De appellationibus, recusationibus, et
relationibus.* CIC X 2.28.60.

de leg: ij:[70] et talis causa licet etiam fuerit finalis satis est ex duabus finalibus alteram remanere .§. *affinitatis* instit: *de nup*:[71] L: *si neutri de prin*: C *red*:[72]

13⁰ An constito quod Regina fuerit ab Arcturo Carnaliter cognita An ex eo dispensatio sit inualida quia non firmiter sed sub dubio forsan id expositum sit ar: c: *super litteris de rescrip*:[73] An vero contrarium sit dicendum ex not: in c: *nisi*. versic *forsan ex humilitate de* [74] et per Paul: in L: *mutus* ff: *de procu*:[75]

14⁰ Vtrum dispensatio etiam ex falsa causa Concessa valeat vel sustineri debeat ratione vitandi scandali iux: not: in c: *quia circa* et in c: *quod dilectio de Consang: et affin*:[76]

---

[70] Paragraph *Imperator* in the chapter *Titia* of the title *De legatis et fideicommissis* 2. Justinian Digest 3.1.87.3.

[71] Paragraph *Adfinitatis* of the title *De nuptiis*. Justinian Institutes 1.10.6.

[72] Chapter *Si neutri de prin.* of the title *Red.* (faulty reference to the Justinian Code).

[73] Chapter *Super litteris* in the title *De rescriptis*. CIC X 1.3.20.

[74] From what is noted in the chapter *Nisi* on the line (versiculum) "forsan ex humilitate" in the title *De renuntiatione*. CIC X 1.9.10. Probably refers to the line "Quod si forsan humilitatis causa," etc. The reference should be to a line later in the same chapter, "et forsitan non cuius libet," on which the *Glossa ordinaria* comments, "Istud forsitan non videtur poni dubitative, sed affirmative." The words "versic." and "humilitate" were added by Hand B.

[75] Paulus in the chapter *Mutus* of the title *De procuratoribus et defensoribus*. Justinian Digest 3.3.43.

[76] Chapters *Quia circa* and *Quod dilectio* of the title *De consanguinitate et affinitate*. CIC X 4.14.6, 3.

Statement of Archbishop Cranmer

on Proof of Consumation in Catherine of Aragon's First Marriage.
[Public Record Office SP 1/65, ff. 14, 16.]

Cranmer's hand (f. 13):

Ex attestationibus testium nobilissimarum personarum, scriptura etiam tractatus inter illustrissimos et potentissimos Principes, serenissimae Regiae ~~mag~~ maiestatis et ~~Ch~~ Clarissimae Dominae Catherinae parentes conclusi confirmatis, atque aliarum allegationum adminiculis corroboratis, videtur nobis canonica et legittima fide constare illustrem Principem Arthurum clarissimam dominam Catherinam praedictam carnaliter cognouisse, nec debere iudicem quemcumque ex huiusmodi productis aliter pronunciare, sed oportere eum huiusmodi exhibita considerantem motum animi sui in nostram opinionem inclinare, adeo quidem vt solum Reginae iusiurandum in diuersam partem per leges admittere non liceat. Ita quidem sentimus et opinamur.

Henry VIII's hand (f. 13):

> elaborantes vt et consientias nostras ~~exhonoremus~~
> regisque nostri exhonoremus

Nos quidem~~quantum in nobis~~ prout occasio datur vt sinceritatem huius facti investigaremur

---

                in his
Nos quidem∧elaborantes que et consientias nostras Regisque nostri ex-
                    Denique   enitentes
honorare possint preceptumque∧Dei mientes∧/ perspectum nobis videtur

canonica / et legittima fide constare visis attestationibus testium nobilis-
                           per antea
simarum personarum in iuditio∧prolatis

             instrumento   Regine
accedente etiam∧confessione per∧procuratorem exhi
                 bevis brevis
accedente etiam confessione∧ instrumenti iudicialiter pro defensione.

Dicte Domine Chaterine a procuratore eiusdem suo exhibiti

(Continued overleaf)

Another hand (f. 15):

Visis attestationibus clarissimorum virorum ac nonnullarum personarum aliarum In hac causa Matrimoniali et diuorcij nuperrime Inter illustrissimum et potentissimum Regem Dominum Nostrum et Serenissimam Dominam Keterinam / Reginam pretensam Ventulata Vna cum alijs Adminiculis facientibus ad causam opinamur Dicimus Attestamur et Arbitramur Iudicio nostro ostensum~esse~ ~et~ ~violenter~ ac violenter presumendum Carnalem copulam Inter Arthurum et Dictam Dominam Catherinam tunc temporis principem et principissam Interuenisse Maxime cum Simull vt vir et vxor cohabitabant et pernoctabant ac Invicem sese Maritali tractabant affeccione

Works Cited

References in parentheses after the entries are to chapter and note; for example, "9.8" means "cited above in Chapter 9, note 8."

I. MANUSCRIPTS

CAMBRIDGE

Cambridge University Library

Dd 13.26: Court Record of the legatine trial. (4–6 *passim*; 12 after 8)
Ff 5.25: John Fisher, *Licitum fuisse matrimonium*. (5.16–17)

LONDON

British Library at the British Museum

Additional 4622: *A Compendious Annotation*. (3.18)
Additional 29547: Cardinal Cajetan to Henry VIII. (13.15)
Additional 37154: *Extractum registri cause Anglie matrimonialis coram R.P.D. Paulo Capisuccho*. (4.2, 11, 25, 31; 7.4, 6; 8.7; 9.8)
Arundel 151: John Fisher, *Responsum ad libellum impressum Londini 1530*. (Intro. 11–12; 10.21)
———: Dunstable Court Record. (12.5–16)
Cotton Vitellius B xii: Drafts of the decretal bull. (3.4)
———: Documents of the legatine court. (3.34; 4.11, 14)
Harley 1061: Record of the Cleves trial. (15.9, 12–13, 24)

Lambeth Palace Library

2341: Treatises by Nicholas West, Bishop of Ely. (3.18–33; 6.23; 14.29)
2342: Treatises by John Fisher and others. (6.23; 10.20)

Public Record Office

SP 1 Folio C.1: *Acta iudicialia*, trial of 1527. (1.5–20)
SP 1/42: Letter of John Fisher, 1527. (4.21)
———: Letter of Cardinal Wolsey, 1 July 1527. (13.21)
SP 1/54: List of exhibits at the legatine court. (3.18; 4.22; 5.12, 18; 6.24)
———: Stephen Gardiner, *Liber contra Roffensis orationem*. (5.18–24)
SP 1/60: Thomas Derby, Response to Thomas Abel. (10.28)
SP 1/61: Anonymous response to Thomas Abel. (10.29)

SP 1/65: Cranmer's statement. (4.30; 13.26–27; App. B)
SP 1/69: Henry VIII to Carne and Bonner, 1532. (8.14)
SP 1/82: Letter of John Stokesley, 4 January 1534. (12.23, 36; 14.18)
SP 6/9: Treatises on Leviticus. (10.30; 13.10)

Westminster Archives, Archbishop's House

MS 1: Response to the Bishop of Ely. (3.18–32)

ROME

Corsini Palace Library

244 (36 D2): Annotated dispensation of Clement VII, 1527. (2.5)

Venerable English College Archives

Edited MS of Nicholas Sanders's *De origine ac progressu schismatis anglicani*. (2.18–19; 6.17, 26, 32)

VATICAN CITY

Vatican Archives

AA Arm. I–XVIII, 3265: Draft of the decretal bull. (3.4)
Index 1057: Index to Rota manuals. (8.19)
Lettere di principi 14: Legatine commission. (6.23)
————: Report to Clement VII. (7.14)

Vatican Library

Lat. 2345: Giles Bellemère, *Consilia*. (Intro. 8; 13.12)
Lat. 5639: *Hieronymi Novati Mediolanensis de legitimo serenissimae Catharinae de Castiglia de Arragonia reginae Angliae matrimonio conclusiones* XIII. (10.31)
Ross. 832: Giles Bellemère, *Super Decretales*. (Intro. 7)

VIENNA

Haus-, Hof- und Staatsarchiv

England, Korrespondenz Karton 4: Letter of Chapuys, 8 October 1529. (3.14; 6.62, 64; 7.7)
————: Letter of Chapuys, 28 June 1532. (14.22–23)
England, Varia Karton 2: The queen's *libellus*. (1.16; 3.30; 4.30; 6.5, 30; 7.8; 8.15, 17; 12.27; 13.26; App. A)

II. PRIMARY PRINTED WORKS

(Old printed books and pamphlets, more recently printed editions
of manuscripts and collections of documents, calendars,
extracts, registers, etc.)

Abel, Thomas. *Invicta veritas*. Pseudo-Lüneburg, 1532. (10.26)
Andreae, John. *Declaratio arboris affinitatis*. In *Corpus iuris canonici*, vol. 1, cols. 1433–36. (6.27; App. A.57)

————. *In primum-sextum Decretalium librum novella commentaria.* 6 vols. Venice, 1581. Vols. 1–5 reprinted Turin, 1963. (Intro. 8)

Aquinas, Thomas. *Commentum in quattuor libros Sententiarum magistri Petri Lombardi. Opera omnia,* vols. 6–7. Parma, 1856–58. (15.20)

————. *Summa theologiae. Opera omnia,* vols. 1–4. Parma, 1852–54. (App. A.4)

Boniface VIII. *Liber sextus decretalium.* In *Corpus iuris canonici,* vol. 2. (6.15; App. A *passim*)

Burnet, Gilbert. *The History of the Reformation of the Church of England.* Edited by Nicholas Pocock. 7 vols. Oxford, 1865. (*passim*)

Calendar of Letters, Dispatches, and State Papers Relating to the Negotiations between England and Spain. Edited by G. A. Bergenroth, P. de Gayangos, et al. 13 vols. and *Supplement* to vols. 1–2. London, 1862–1954. *Further Supplement* (1513–42). Edited by Garrett Mattingly. 1940. (*passim*)

Calendar of State Papers and Manuscripts Relating to English Affairs Existing in the Archives and Collections of Venice. Edited by Rawdon Brown. Vol. 4. London, 1871. (4.23)

Cavendish, George. *The Life and Death of Cardinal Wolsey.* Edited by Richard S. Sylvester. Early English Text Society, no. 243. London, 1958. (4.17, 26, 28; 5.9; 6.56–57; 14.21)

Chambers, D. S. *Faculty Office Registers, 1534–1549.* Oxford, 1966. (1.2; 5.1; 14.32; 15.3, 10)

Clement V. *Constitutiones clementinae.* In *Corpus iuris canonici,* vol. 2. (4.6–7; App. A.32)

Codex iuris canonici. Rome, 1917. (13 after 19; Epil. 8)

Corpus iuris canonici. Edited by Emil Friedberg. 2 vols. Leipzig, 1879–81. Reprinted Graz, 1959. *Glossa ordinaria* in the edition of Lyons, 1606 (*passim*)

Cranmer, Thomas. *Articuli duodecim quibus plane admodum demonstratur divortium inter Henricum octavum Angliae regem invictissimum et serenissimam Catherinam necessario esse faciendum.* In Pocock, I, 334–99. (13.1–25; 14.29)

————. *The Works of Thomas Cranmer, Archbishop of Canterbury, Martyr, 1556.* Edited by J. E. Cox. 2 vols. Parker Society Publications, nos. 12, 24. Cambridge, 1844–46. (12.6, 16, 21, 24)

The Determinations of the Most Famous and Most Excellent Universities of Italy and France That It Is So Unlawful for a Man to Marry His Brother's Wife That the Pope Hath No Power to Dispense Therewith. [November 1531.] Granville no. 1224. (10 at 17, 19)

Durantis, William. *Speculum iuris.* Venice, 1585. (1.3; 5.3; 6.3)

Ehses, Stephan. *Römische Dokumente zur Geschichte der Ehescheidung Heinrichs VIII von England.* Paderborn, 1893. (*passim*)

Emden, A. B. *A Biographical Register of the University of Oxford to A.D. 1500.* Oxford, 1957–59. (Intro. 8)

————. *A Biographical Register of the University of Oxford, A.D. 1501–1540.* Oxford, 1974. (4.12)

Fiddes, Richard. *The Life of Cardinal Wolsey.* London, 1724. (3.10)

Foscarari, Giles. *Der Ordo iudiciarius des Aegidius de Fuscarariis.* Edited by Ludwig Wahrmund. Quellen zur Geschichte des römisch-canonischen Prozesses im Mittelalter, ser. 3, no. 1. Innsbruck, 1916. Reprinted Aalen, 1962. (6.3)

Foxe, John. *Acts and Monuments.* 4th ed. London, n.d. (10.7)

Gams, P. B. *Series episcoporum ecclesiae catholicae.* Ratisbon, 1873. (8.18, 22)

Gasparri, Pietro. *Tractatus canonicus de matrimonio.* Rev. ed. 2 vols. Rome, 1932. (Epil. 8)

Geminianus (Dominic of San Gimignano). *Consilia.* Edited by John Staphileus. Pavia, 1509. (7.8; 8.19; App. A.33)

A Glass of the Truth. [September 1532.] In Pocock, II, 385–421. (6.44; 10.7; 11.14)

Gratian of Bologna. *Concordia discordantium canonum (Decretum).* In *Corpus iuris canonici,* vol. 1. (1.28; 13.5; App. A *passim*)

Gravissimae atque exactissimae illustrissimarum totius Italiae et Galliae academiarum censurae, efficacissimis etiam quorundam doctissimorum virorum argumentationibus explicitae, de veritate illius propositionis, videlicet quod ducere relictam fratris mortui sine liberis ita sit de iure divino et naturali prohibitum, ut nullus pontifex super huiusmodi matrimoniis contractis sive contrahendis dispensare possit. London, April 1530 [= 1531]. Granville no. 1251 (10.21)

Gregory IX. *Decretales* (X). In *Corpus iuris canonici,* vol. 2 (*passim*)

Hall, Edward. *Chronicle.* Edited by Henry Ellis. London, 1809. (3.16; 4.26)

Halsbury's Laws of England. 3d ed. Vol. 19. London, 1957. (Epil. 10–11)

Halsbury's Statutes of England. 2d ed. Vol. 28, Continuation Volume, 1948–49. London, 1951. (Epil. 9, 11). 3d ed. Vol. 17. London, 1970. (Epil. 12)

Herbert, Edward (Baron Herbert of Cherbury). *The Life and Reign of King Henry VIII.* London, 1649. (4 at 2)

Hugh of St. Victor. *De sacramentis christianae fidei.* Reprint of J. P. Migne. In *Patrologia latina,* vol. 176, cols. 173–617. Paris, 1880. (10.23)

Innocent IV. *Apparatus super quinque libris Decretalium.* Lyons, 1525. (7.10)

Journals of the House of Lords. Vol. 1. N.p., n.d. (15.1, 6, 23)

Justinian. *Corpus iuris civilis* (Authentic Constitutions, Code, Digest, Institutes). Amsterdam and Lyons, 1664. (App. A.62). Edited by Paulus Krueger, Theodore Mommsen, et al. Eds. 6–16. 3 vols. Berlin, 1954. Vol. 1, ed. 21. Berlin, 1970. (App. A *passim*)

Latham, R. E. *Revised Medieval Latin Word List from British and Irish Sources.* London, 1965. (4.13)

Letters and Papers, Foreign and Domestic, of the Reign of Henry VIII. Edited by J. S. Brewer, James Gairdner, and R. H. Brodie. Vols. 2–21. London, 1864–1910. Vol. 1, 2d ed., 1920. *Addenda,* vol. 1, 1929–32. Whole series reprinted with corrections, Vaduz, 1965. (*passim*)

Letters and Papers Illustrative of the Reigns of Richard III and Henry VII. Edited by James Gairdner. 2 vols. Rolls Series, no. 24. London, 1861–63. (6.14)

Loazes, Ferdinand de. *Solennis atque elegans tractatus in causa matrimonii serenissimorum dominorum Henrici et Catherinae Angliae regum.* Barcelona, 5 June 1531. (6.30–31)

Molini, Giuseppe. *Documenti di storia italiana.* 2 vols. Florence, 1836–37. (8.22)

Panormitanus (Nicholas Tudeschi, Abbot of Palermo). *Commentaria … in primum-quintum Decretalium librum.* 9 vols. Venice, 1591–1618. (3.31; App. A.15, 21, 25, 58)

Parasceve. Pseudo-Lüneburg, July 1533. In Pocock, II, 422–32. (11.14)

Pocock, Nicholas. *Records of the Reformation: The Divorce, 1527–1533.* 2 vols. Oxford, 1870. (*passim*)

Pollard, A. W., and Redgrave, G. R. *A Short-Title Catalogue of Books Printed in England, Scotland, and Ireland and of English Books Printed Abroad, 1475–1640.* London, 1926. (6.44)

Reformatio legum ecclesiasticarum. Edited by John Foxe. London, 1640. (Epil. 2–3, after 7)

Register of Henry Chichele, Archbishop of Canterbury, 1414–1443. Edited by E. F. Jacob. 4 vols. Canterbury and York Society, nos. 42, 45–47. Oxford, 1937–47. (1.11; 2.16; 15 after 20)

Registra Stephani Gardiner et Iohannis Poynet, episcoporum wintoniensium. Edited by Herbert Chitty. Canterbury and York Society, no. 37. Oxford, 1930. (15.7)

Registrum Hamonis de Hethe diocesis roffensis, A.D. 1319–1357. Edited by Charles Johnson. Canterbury and York Society. Oxford, 1948 (6.20)

Rinaldi, Odorico, continuator of Caesar Baronius. *Annales ecclesiastici.* Edited by G. D. Mansi. 38 vols. Lucca, 1728–59. Edited by A. Theiner (abridged). 37 vols. Bar-le-Duc. 1864–83. (13.15)

Rymer, Thomas. *Foedera, conventiones, litterae, et cuiusque generis acta publica inter reges Angliae et alios quosvis imperatores, reges, pontifices, principes, vel communitates.* Citations are to the 2d ed., 20 vols., London, 1726–35, as given in the 3d ed., The Hague, 1739–45. (*passim*)

Sanders, Nicholas. *De origine ac progressu schismatis anglicani.* Revised by Edward Rishton. Cologne, 1585. 2d ed. further revised anonymously. Rome, 1586. (2.18; 6.33)

Scotus, John Duns. *In quartum librum Sententiarum.* In *Opera omnia.* Paris, 1891–95. (Intro. 8)

Staphileus, John. *Tractatus de gratiis expectativis ac aliis litteris gratiae et iustitiae, olim bonae memoriae Iohannis Staphilei episcopi Sibenicensis sacri palatii apostolici causarum auditoris.* Venice, 1590 (8.19)

——— (ed.) See Geminianus.

State Papers: King Henry VIII. 11 vols. London, 1830–52. (*passim*)

Statutes of the Realm. 11 vols. London, 1810–28. Reprinted 1963. (*passim*)

Stefani, F., et al. *I diarii di Marino Sanuto.* Vol. 51. Venice, 1898. (4.23, 29)

Strype, John. *Ecclesiastical Memorials.* 3 vols. Oxford, 1820–40. (15.11, 18)

Tancred of Bologna. *Ordo iudiciarius.* Edited by Friedrich Bergmann. In *Pilii, Tancredi, Gratiae libri de iudiciorum ordine.* Göttingen, 1842. (6.3)

Theiner, Augustinus. *Vetera monumenta Hibernorum et Scotorum historiam illustrantia.* Rome, 1864. (7.12)

Tierney, M. A. *Dodd's Church History of England.* Vol. 1. London, 1839. (10.9)

Ubaldi, Baldo degli. *Commentaria in Corpus iuris civilis.* 9 vols. Venice, 1572. (App. A.28)

Vergil, Polydore. *The Anglica historia of Polydore Vergil, A.D. 1485–1537.* Edited by Denys Hay. Camden Society, ser. 3, no. 74. London, 1950. (11.18)

"Vie du bienheureux martyr Jean Fisher." Edited by F. van Ortroy. *Analecta bollandiana,* 10 (1891), 121–365; 12 (1893), 97–287. (4.1; 6.22)

[Vives, Luis.] *Non esse neque divino neque naturae iure prohibitum quin summus pontifex dispensare possit ut frater demortui sine liberis fratris uxorem legitimo matrimonio sibi possit adiungere, adversus aliquot academiarum censuras tumultuaria ac perbrevis apologia sive confutatio.* Pseudo-Lüneburg, September 1532. Granville no. 1234. (Intro. 14)

Wakefield, Robert. *Kotser codicis R. Wakfeldi quo, praeter ecclesiae sacrosanctae decretum, probatur coniugium cum fratria carnaliter cognita illicitum, omnino inhibitum, interdictumque esse, tum naturae iure, tum iure divino, legeque evangelica atque consuetudine catholica ecclesiae orthodoxae.* N.p., n.d. [ca. 1534]. Granville no. 1252. (1.29–31)

———. *Syntagma de hebraeorum codicum incorruptione.* N.p., n.d. [ca. 1534]. Granville no. 1226. (1.29, 31)

Wilkins, David. *Concilia Magnae Britanniae et Hiberniae.* 4 vols. London, 1737. (*passim*)

Wriothesley, Charles. *A Chronicle of England during the Reigns of the Tudors.* Edited by W. D. Hamilton. London, 1875. (14.12, 24–25)

III. SECONDARY SOURCES

Barnard, F. P. "The Kinship of Henry VIII and His Wives." *Miscellanea genealogica et heraldica,* ser. 5, vol. 3 (1918–19), pp. 194–96. (2.11)

Bowker, Margaret. *An Episcopal Court Book for the Diocese of Lincoln, 1514–1520.* Lincoln Record Society, no. 61. Lincoln, 1967. (1.1)

Brundage, James A. "Concubinage and Marriage in Medieval Canon Law." *Journal of Medieval History,* 1 (1975), 1–17. (Intro. 17)

Chambers, E. K. *The Elizabethan Stage.* 4 vols. Oxford, 1923. (4.3; 6.57)

Chrimes, S. B. "A Tycoon among the Tudors." *Times Literary Supplement,* 6 December 1974, p. 1392. (Intro. 2)

Dauvillier, Jean. *Le mariage dans le droit classique de l'église.* Paris, 1933. (3.22)

Dictionnaire de droit canonique. Edited by R. Naz. 7 vols. Paris, 1924–65. (1.1, 4)

Elton, G. R. *Policy and Police: The Enforcement of the Reformation in the Age of Thomas Cromwell.* Cambridge, 1972. (6.44; 10.7; 11.14)

———. *Political History: Principles and Practice.* Cambridge, 1970. (15.4)

———. *Studies in Tudor and Stuart Politics and Government.* 2 vols. Cambridge, 1974. (Intro. 2; 15.4)

Friedmann, Paul. *Anne Boleyn.* 2 vols. London, 1884. (2.13; 7.26–27; 14.1, 22)

Gairdner, James. Articles in *DNB* on Anne Boleyn (14.21), Catherine Howard (15.27), William Peto (11.14), and Thomas Wolsey (7.17)

———. "The Draft Dispensation for Henry VIII's Marriage with Anne Boleyn." *EHR,* 5 (1890), 544–50. (2.10)

———. "New Lights on the Divorce of Henry VIII." *EHR,* 11 (1896), 673–702; 12 (1897), 1–16, 237–53. (2.2, 6; 3.13)

Gilles, Henri. "Gilles Bellemère et le tribunal de la Rote à la fin du XIVe siècle." *Mélanges d'archéologie et d'histoire,* 67 (1955), 281–319. (Intro. 8)

Hay, Denys. *Polydore Vergil.* Oxford, 1952. (5.7)

Helmholz, Richard H. "Marriage Litigation in Medieval England." Ph.D. dissertation, University of California, Berkeley, 1970. Revised and published under the same title in Cambridge Studies in Legal History. Cambridge, 1974. (12.23; 15.3)

Hoberg, Hermann. "Die Amtsdaten der Rotarichter in den Protokollbüchern der Rotanotare von 1464 bis 1566." *Römische Quartalschrift,* 48 (1953), 48–78. (8.19)

———. "Die Protokollbücher der Rotanotare von 1464 bis 1517." *Zeitschrift der Savigny-Stiftung für Rechtgeschichte, Kanonistische Abteilung,* 39 (1953), 177–227. (8.19)

Janelle, Pierre. *L'Angleterre catholique à la veille du schisme.* Paris, 1935. (5.18)

———. *Obedience in Church and State: Three Political Tracts by Stephen Gardiner.* Cambridge, 1930. (5.18)

Jenkyns, Henry. *The Remains of Thomas Cranmer, D.D., Archbishop of Canterbury.* Vol. 1. Oxford, 1833. (13.2)

Joyce, George Hayward. *Christian Marriage.* 2d ed. London, 1948. (Epil. 7)

Kelly, H. A. "Canonical Implications of Richard III's Plan to Marry His Niece." *Traditio,* 23 (1967), 269–311. (Intro. 6, 14–15; 1.12; 2.19; 11.18; 12.23; 13.13; Epil. 7)

————. "Clandestine Marriage and Chaucer's *Troilus.*" *Viator,* 4 (1973), 435–57. (Intro. 4)

————. *The Devil, Demonology, and Witchcraft.* Rev. ed. New York, 1974. (15.20)

————. *Divine Providence in the England of Shakespeare's Histories.* Cambridge, Mass., 1970. (3.16; 11.18)

————. "English Kings and the Fear of Sorcery." Forthcoming in *Mediaeval Studies,* 39 (1977). (1.1; 4.6; 14.3)

————. "Kinship, Incest, and the Dictates of Law." *American Journal of Jurisprudence,* 14 (1969), 69–78 (1.27; 2.16; Epil. 8)

————. *Love and Marriage in the Age of Chaucer.* Ithaca, 1975. (Intro. 4, 17; 2.13)

Levine, Mortimer. "Henry VIII's Use of His Spiritual and Temporal Jurisdictions in His Great Causes of Matrimony, Legitimacy, and Succession." *Historical Journal,* 10 (1967), 3–10. (10.7; 12.37; Epil. 4, 6)

————. *Tudor Dynastic Problems, 1460–1571.* Historical Problems: Studies and Documents, no. 21. London, 1973. (Intro. 1)

Lewis, David. Introduction to his translation of Nicholas Sanders and Edward Rishton, *The Rise and Growth of the Anglican Schism.* London, 1877. (14.16)

Lowinsky, Edward E. "A Music Book for Anne Boleyn." In *Florilegium historiale: Essays Presented to Wallace K. Ferguson,* pp. 160–235. Toronto, 1971. (14.16)

Mattingly, Garrett. *Catherine of Aragon.* Boston, 1941. Reprinted London, 1950. (Intro. at 2; 3.17; 4.18, 20; 11.2)

Moore, Cecil. *Memoir of the Father of Black Letter Collectors (John Moore, Bishop of Ely).* London, 1885. (4.2)

Morris, Colin. "A Consistory Court in the Middle Ages." *Journal of Ecclesiastical History,* 14 (1963), 150–59. (1.1)

Noonan, John T., Jr. *Power to Dissolve: Lawyers and Marriages in the Courts of the Roman Curia.* Cambridge, Mass., 1972. (7.13; 13.12)

Parmiter, Geoffrey de C. *The King's Great Matter: A Study of Anglo-Papal Relations, 1527–1534.* London, 1967. (Intro. 3)

Paul, John E. *Catherine of Aragon and Her Friends.* London, 1966. (5.7)

Pollard, A. F. Article on John Stokesley, *DNB.* (10.15)

Ridley, Jasper. *Nicholas Ridley.* London, 1957. (5.7)

————. *Thomas Cranmer.* Oxford, 1962. (2.19; 10.8; 11.10)

Scarisbrick, J. J. *Henry VIII.* London, 1968. (Intro. at 2, 15; 1.23, 25; 2.6; 6.29; 8.16; 9.5)

Sheehan, Michael M. "The Formation and Stability of Marriage in Fourteenth-Century England: Evidence of an Ely Register." *Mediaeval Studies,* 33 (1971), 228–63. (Intro. 4)

Smith, Irwin. *Shakespeare's Blackfriars Theatre: Its History and Its Design.* New York, 1964. (4.3; 6.57)

Smith, Lacey Baldwin. *Henry VIII: The Mask of Royalty.* London, 1971. (Intro. 1)

Surtz, Edward. "Henry VIII's Great Matter in Italy: An Introduction to Representative Italians in the King's Divorce, Mainly 1527–1535." Xerox University Microfilms, Monograph Series, no. LD00025. Ann Arbor, 1975. (4.2, 11, 25, 31; 7.4, 6; 8.7, 19, 35, 37; 9.8; 10.11, 31)

——. *The Works and Days of John Fisher*. Cambridge, Mass., 1967. (5.16; 10.21)

Thurston, Herbert. "The Canon Law of the Divorce." *EHR*, 19 (1904), 632–45. (3.4)

Woodcock, Brian L. *Medieval Ecclesiastical Courts in the Diocese of Canterbury*. Oxford, 1952. (1.1)

Index

Index

Only early authors are included below; for later sources and authorities, see the notations after each entry in Works Cited, pp. 299–307. The following abbreviations are used:

B.C.L.	Bachelor of Civil Law	D.Cn.C.L.	Doctor of Canon and Civil
B.Cn.C.L.	Bachelor of Canon and		Law
	Civil Law	D.Th.	Doctor of Theology
B.Th.	Bachelor of Theology	M.A.	Master of Arts
D.Cn.L.	Doctor of Canon Law	O.P.	Order of Preachers
D.C.L.	Doctor of Civil Law		(Dominicans)

Abel, Thomas, M.A., chaplain to Catherine of Aragon (d. 1540), 186–89, cf. 67. *See also* attainder

Abishag, 181–82, 184, 224

academics, consultation of, 29, 59–60, 66, 131, 142–44, 173–79, 209–10, 223. *See also* determinations

Accolti, Benedict, Bishop of Ravenna and Cardinal (the Young Man), 160–61, 163

Accolti, Peter, former Dean of Rota, Bishop of Ancona and Cardinal (the Old Man), 56, 160–63, 215

Acton (Hatton), John, O.P., D.Th., 8, 9n

Adonijah, 181–82, 224

advocation to Rome, 128, 136, 149

affinity:
between Henry VIII: and all his wives, 43, 259; and Catherine of Aragon, *see* Catherine of Aragon, consummation, Henry VIII, Julius II, *and* public honesty; and Anne Boleyn, *see* Boleyn, Mary; and Jane Seymour, 250–60; and Catherine Howard, 261, 263
degrees of, 5–7, 47–48, 284–85, cf. 44–46, *see also* Leviticus; dispensations for, 6–15, 22, 47–48, 232, 256–57, 263–64, 282, 283, *see also* Boleyn (Anne), dispensations, *and* Julius II; and divine law, 1–2, 6–16, 24, 26, 28, 29, 30, 33–37, 43, 47–48, 58, 66–67, 68–69, 74, 82–83, 91, 97, 105–6, 107, 110, 113, 123, 124, 138–39, 141, 142, 143, 150, 152, 159, 164, 165–66, 168–69, 173–74, 176–80, 183, 185, 186, 187–88, 189, 194, 199–203, 210–11, 215, 218–21, 233, 235, 236n, 247–48, 257,

263, 277, 279, 280–81, 282–83, 285, *see also* determinations, divine law, Julius II, *and* public honesty
from coitus, 16, 33–34, 225–27, 247–48, 257–58; from either coitus or marriage, 225–28, 248, 279, 280, 283; from illicit coitus, before marriage, 16, 34–35, 46–49, 50, 146, 180, 220, 227, 232, 235, 247–48, 257, 260, 277, 279, after marriage (= supervening), 48, 231, eliminated, 233, 284; from marital coitus, 27, 86, 146, 279; from marriage contract, 33–34, 52, 146–47, 156, 179, 219, 224–33, 247–48, 279; from marriage dubiously consummated, 117–18, cf. 166; from solemnization and consummation of marriage, 219, 247, 279
history of, 5–14, 33–34, 107, 138n, 139; inclusive of public honesty, 115–16; joined with public honesty, *see* public honesty; rarely pleaded in annulment cases, 264n; second and third genera of, 138n, 156; "Tree of Affinity," 114

Albert the Great (Count von Bollstädt), O.P., St., theologian, Bishop of Ratisbon (d. 1280), 226

Alemanni (Alamandi), Bernard, D.C.L., Bishop of Condom (d. 1401), 8, 9n

Alexander III, Pope (1159–81), 44n, 105, 227 (ref. to CIC X 4.5.3), 274, cf. 229; and divine status of public honesty in *Ad audientiam*, 67–71, 183, 185–86, 187. *See also Decretals of Gregory IX*

Alexander V, Pope (1409–10), 10

Alexander VI, Pope (1492–1503), 10, 14

Ancona, Cardinal of (Anconitane), *see* Accolti, Peter

Andreae, John, of Bologna, D.Cn.C.L. (d. 1348): on dispensability of divine law of Leviticus, 7–10, 13; on public honesty, 107, 114–15, 138, 293

Angers, 143, 177–78, 187–88, 217. *See also* determinations

Anne of Cleves, Queen of England: descended from Edward I, 43, 259; precontract with Francis of Lorraine, 264, 265, 267–69, 272–73, 277; physical appearance of, 261, 269–70; and virginity, 270, 273, 276; marriage to Henry VIII, 261, 265–66, 267–68, 270, 272, 273–74; marriage not consummated, 14n, 261, 270–71, 272–75; agrees to trial, 266; marriage annulled, 4, 249, 264, 265–72; declared free to remarry (notwithstanding her precontract), 272–73; marriage dissolved if not annulled, 14n, 263, 265, 273–75

annulment: distinguished from divorce, 16, 16n; of marriage of Humphrey, Duke of Gloucester, 242; of marriage of Louis XII, 14n; of three of Henry VIII's marriages, summarized, 4, 262, 276–77; processes of, *see* trials; validity of marriages contracted during annulment proceedings, 40, 213

Anthony of Budrio, 233

Anticatoptrum, 198n

Antoninus, O.P., St., Auditor of Rota, Archbishop of Florence (d. 1459), 225

Antwerp, 198

appeal, to pope, *see* Catherine of Aragon *and* Parliament; from pope to general council, 214

Aquinas, St. Thomas, O.P. (d. 1274), 34, 106, 156, 185n, 225–26, 271, cf. 230

archdeacons, as judges, *see* jurisdiction

Argall, Thomas, 208, 267n

Armagnac, Bernard, Count of, 8, 9n

Arthur Tudor, Prince of Wales: marriage to Catherine of Aragon (Nov. 1501), 1, 24, 103–4, 106, *see also* Catherine of Aragon; solemnization of marriage, 90–91, 119; and consummation stated or debated, *see* consummation; alleged admission of consummation, 61, 122–23, *see also* depositions; alleged denial of consummation, 150, 151; potency or impotency, 148–49, 150–51, 153, 192–93; frailty, 150–51; death (Apr. 1502), 61, 103–4, 124

Arundell, Thomas (gentleman of Wolsey's privy chamber), 112n

Athequa, George de, Bishop of Llandaff (resigned 1537), 79, 201–2

attainder: of Elizabeth Barton, John Fisher, and Thomas Abel, 217, cf. 188n, 251–52; of Cromwell, 261; of Catherine Howard, 275–76. *See also* treason *and* trials (secular)

Audley, Sir Thomas, Lord Chancellor, 209n, 245, 265–66, 267–68

Augustine, St., Archbishop of Canterbury, 6

banns of marriage, dispensed, 278

Barbour, John, 245, 250

Barlow, John, 40–41

Barton, Elizabeth, Nun of Kent, 159, 217

Baynard's Castle, 78–79, 86, 88, 135

Beaufort, bastard line of, 194

Beaufort, Edmund, 2d Duke of Somerset (d. 1455), 45–46

Beaufort, Edmund, self-styled 4th Duke of Somerset (d. 1471), 45–46

Beaufort, Eleanor, 45–46

Beaufort, John, Duke of Somerset (d. 1444), 10, 45–46

Beaufort, John, Earl of Somerset (d. 1410), 9–10, 45–46

Beaufort, Margaret, Countess of Richmond, mother of Henry VII, 10, 194

Beaufort, Margaret, Countess of Somerset, *see* Holland

Bedell (Bedyll), Thomas, B.C.L., secretary to Warham (1516–32), Clerk of King's Council in 1532, Archdeacon of Cleveland, etc. (d. 1537), 202, 206–7, 209–10, 211, 213n, 218, 245, 251n

Bedford, Jacquetta, Duchess of, 43

bedsheets, proof from, 61, 122, 151, 233–34, cf. 159

Bell, John, D.Cn.C.L., Dean of the Arches in 1517, Archdeacon of Gloucester in 1518, Bishop of Worcester in 1539, resigned 1543 (d. 1556): Henry VIII's proctor at Westminster trial (1527), 25, 29–30, 102, 114; and Robert Wakefield, 37n; Henry's proctor at legatine court (1529), 79, 114, 117; Henry's proctor at Dunstable trial (May 1533) and perhaps at Lambeth gallery trial (late May), 205–9, 212; submitted treatise or brief for Henry to legatine court, 113; present at Cleves trial, 267

Bellay, John du, Bishop of Bayonne, 65–66, 75, 84–85, 92, 174

Bellemère, Giles, D.Cn.C.L., Bishop of Avignon (d. 1407), 8, 9n, 229n

Benet, William, D.C.L., Archdeacon of Dorset, present at Westminster trial in 1527 (d. Dec. 1533), Henry's envoy to pope, 153, 160–61, 162n, 163n

Bernard of Parma, *see Glossa ordinaria*

betrothal (= spousals *de futuro*, contract *de futuro*): and Anne Boleyn, 44, 49–52, 253–54, 256, 257–58; and Anne of Cleves, 265, 267–69; between Catherine of Aragon and Prince Henry, 103–4, 108, 111, 114; between Henry VIII and Jane Seymour, 260; creates public honesty, 34, 44, 49–52; dissolution of, 50, 107, 258, 293n, cf. 263; followed by coitus creates marriage, 275; marriage before the age of puberty regarded as, 105, 126, 269; none between Henry VIII and Catherine Howard, 275; null before age of seven, 44, 49

bigamy, 40, 275, 277–78, cf. 213, 213n. *See also* precontract (impediment)

Blackfriars, 77, 79, 127. *See also* legatine court

Blanche of Navarre, 11

Blount, William, Lord Mountjoy, 94–95
Boleyn, Anne, Queen of England:
  before 1527: descended from Edward I,
    43, 259; birth of, 249n; Henry VIII sug-
    gested as father, 47, 249; relatives of,
    see Bryan, *and the Boleyns and Howards*;
    to marry Sir James Butler, 44, 253; rela-
    tions with Henry Percy and her supposed
    first marriage, 16, 44–46, 49–51, 243,
    245, 252–56, 258, 276; hated Wolsey, 254;
    loved by Henry VIII, 1–2, 33; considered
    a virgin by Henry, 276, cf. 252–53
  1527: revealed to Wolsey as king's in-
    tended wife, 38; impediments between
    her and Henry, 16–17, 34–35, 38–53, 146–
    47, 174, 182, 213, 229, 232, 241–42, 243–
    44, 245–59, 277, 281
  1529: fears Henry will return to Cath-
    erine, 131
  1532: and investigation of precontract
    with Percy (June), 5, 253, 254–55, 255–
    56; given Marquisate of Pembroke
    (Sept.), 149; allows Henry her bed, 149,
    195–96; "honeymoon" to Calais (Oct.),
    149; pregnant with Elizabeth, 149, 162,
    195–96, 213
  1533: marries Henry, 165, 196, 205, 211–
    13, 229, 237; marriage validated in court
    (28 May), 211–13; coronation (1 June),
    211; pope declares marriage null and
    issue illegitimate, 167, 168; birth of
    daughter, 241–42, cf. 275
  1534: marriage ratified in Parliament,
    160n, 217–19, cf. 246
  1536: and Lutheranism, 252n; Henry's
    disaffection, 241–42; miscarriages, 241–
    42; allegedly treasonous acts, 242–43;
    arrest (2 May), 244, 251; summoned by
    Cranmer to inquisition, 245; treason
    trial, 244, 250, 252, 255, 256; sentenced
    to death (15 May), 250; admissions to
    Cranmer, in confession (16 and 18 May)
    and in court, 246, 249–50, 252–53, 255–
    56, 259; conscience, 252; marriage an-
    nulled (17 May), 4, 213, 246, 250, 259,
    262; grounds for annulment, 245–59,
    281, cf. 277; still called queen, 245n,
    246; executed (19 May), 251, 257, 259,
    cf. 244; annulment confirmed by Par-
    liament and daughter declared illegiti-
    mate, 246–49, cf. 242, 245, 256, 277,
    282, 283
Boleyn, George, Anne's brother (Viscount
    Rochford toward end of 1529), 242, 255,
    256, 259, cf. 250, 252
Boleyn, Mary, Anne's sister and Henry's
    mistress, 16–17, 34–35, 44n, 47–48, 146–
    47, 219–20, 232, 244–45, 248, 257, 277,
    281
Boleyn, Sir Thomas, Viscount Rochford,
    Earl of Wiltshire and Ormond in 1529,
    Anne's father (d. 1439), 101, 112, 121,
    175–76, 194, 249n
Bologna, 143, 162, 178–79, 180, 199, 214,
    217, 220. *See also* Andreae, Clerk, deter-
    minations, Gratian, Peter of Ancarano,
    and Tancred

Boniface VIII, Pope (1294–1303), *Liber
    sextus decretalium*: 1.3. *De rescriptis*,
    chap. 9, *Si eo tempore*, 294; 1.6. *De
    electione et electi potestate*, chap. 3,
    Ubi periculum, 290; 1.19. *De procura-
    toribus*, chap. 9, *Procurator*, 291; 4.1.
    De sponsalibus et matrimoniis, chap. 1,
    Ex sponsalibus, 50n; 4.2. *De desponsa-
    tione impuberum*, chap. 1, *Si infantes*,
    105n
Bonner, Edmund, D.C.L., chaplain to Wol-
    sey, Bishop of London in 1540 (d. 1569),
    153, 156, 162, 164, 245, 267
Book of Common Prayer, 283
Bourges, 143, 178, 188, 199, 217. *See also*
    determinations
Brandon, Charles, Duke of Suffolk, 101,
    112, 119, 122, 265–66, 267–68
Brereton, Sir William, 255, 259
Bridewell, 64, 77, 78, 81, 86n, 174
brother-sister marriage, 33n, 225, 283, 285
Bryan, Sir Francis, 166n, 206, 208
Burgo, Nicholas de, D.Th., co-author of
    Determinations treatise in 1529, 180, 262n
Burnet, Gilbert, Bishop of Salisbury
    (d. 1715), 76, 138
Butler, Sir James, 44, 253
Butler, Sir Piers, Earl of Ormond, 44
Butts, William, M.D., 270

Cain, 225
Cajetan, Cardinal (Thomas de Vio, O.P.,
    Bishop of Gaeta, d. Aug. 1534), 201,
    229–31, 280
Cambridge, 143, 175–77, 210, 217, 225.
    See also determinations
Campeggio, Laurence, former Auditor of
    Rota, Bishop of Salisbury and Cardinal
    (d. 1539): before the legatine trial, 57n,
    59–62, 64, 66, 82n, 84, 86n, 145, 221;
    after opening court, 3, 77, 78, 81, 85,
    86, 86n, 92, 112, 114, 174, 197, *see also*
    legatine court *and* Wolsey; adjourns
    court, 127–28, 165, cf. 78; and legatine
    records, 68n, 167; promise to Henry VIII,
    96; and Henry's stand on Catherine's
    virginity, 95–96, 145; after leaving En-
    gland, 142, 160n, 202, cf. 68n; and
    English Articles, 159; and papal trial,
    95–96, 159, 169, 202
canonistic dialogue, 155–56
canonists (includes "civilians," i.e. those
    with degrees in civil law), 3, 7, 11, 12–13,
    16, 29, 33, 35, 51, 70, 177–80, 187–88,
    200–203, 209, 225–29, 230n, 254
canonization trials, 3
canon law, *see Code of Canon Law and
    Corpus iuris canonici*
Canterbury: Archbishops of, *see* Augustine,
    Chichele, Cranmer, Parker, Pole, War-
    ham; Convocation of, *see* Convocation;
    Court of, *see* Ligham
Capisuchi, Paul, Dean of Rota until becom-
    ing Bishop of Nicastro in Nov. 1533,
    157n, 165, 168, cf. *Extractum registri*
Carew, Mr. (William Carey), m. Mary
    Boleyn (d. 1528), 44n

Carnaby, Sir Raynald, 253, 255
Carne, Sir Edward, D.C.L. (d. 1561),
 Henry VIII's excusator in Rome, 153,
 156, 161, 162, 165, 167, 168, 214, cf. 143,
 173
Casale, Sir Gregory, 40, 113n, 138–39, 145,
 157n, 160–61, 164, 174n
Casale, John, 96, 145–46, 178
Catherine of Aragon, Queen of England:
 before 1527: descended from Edward I,
 43, 259, cf. 150n; arrival in England,
 124, 204; marriage to Arthur, 1, 24, 68,
 90–91, 103–4, 106, 115, 119, 124, 165,
 204, 206, 217, 247–48, 277; in bed with
 Arthur, 61, 122–23, 137, 144–45, 151, 197;
 suspected of being pregnant, 61–62, 153,
 236; charged of consummation, 30,
 150, 151, 233; dowry disputed, 106, 126,
 150; betrothed to Henry before dispensation is sought (1503), 103–4, cf. 108,
 111, 114; to be dispensed from public
 honesty and affinity, 103, 115, cf. 16, 70;
 dispensed by Julius II, 2, 25, 30, 31,
 103–5, 125; marries Henry, aged 13, *per
 verba de praesenti* (1504), 58, 103–4,
 cf. 26, 28, 111, 125, 126, 269; does not
 know of Henry's protestation against
 marriage (1505), 103, 105, 126–27; still
 called wife by Henry, 105; marriage
 solemnized (1509), 1–2, 54–55, 91,
 104–5, 122, 206, cf. 111; marriage consummated, 24, 104, 151, 166, 233–35;
 virginity until that time accepted and
 admitted by Henry, 30, 95–96, 107, 137,
 145n, 150, 151, 233–35, 276; children
 and miscarriages, 32–33, 53, 104, *see also*
 Mary I; possibly spiritual kin to Anne
 Boleyn, 52–53
 1527: not officially notified of Westminster inquisition, 3, 23, 234; hears of
 it and receives counsel, 31, 82–83, 234;
 suspects Wolsey, 21, 23, cf. 81; consummation of first marriage charged at Westminster and admitted by Henry, 24–25,
 27, 30, 109, 276, cf. 33, 35–37; denies
 consummation, 31, 234, cf. 30, 74, 107;
 former patron of Wakefield and Pace, 35;
 marriage impedes Henry's papal dispensation, 40–42
 1528: marriage impugned at Rome,
 54–59; Wolsey not certain of consummation, 56–57, 96, cf. 29–32, 234; marriage defended by Bishop West, 67–74,
 115–16, 183, 258n; intended defense
 against the legates, 60–62, cf. 73, 98, 123,
 151n; visited by legates (24 Oct.), 59,
 86n; urged to enter a convent, 14n, 59,
 63, 232; visited by Henry (25 Oct.), 59–
 60; counsel appointed for her (26 Oct.),
 60, 62–63, 73, 82, 82n, 85, 190, 220,
 see also Athequa, Clerk, Fisher, Standish,
 Tunstall, Vives, Voysey, Warham, *and*
 West; confession of virginity to Campeggio, 60, 86, cf. 145; her revelation of
 papal brief and protest against its admission of consummation (7 Nov.), 61–65,
 67; virginity discussed in Rome, 137–39;
 urged to send mandate of procuracy to
 Rome, 135
 1529: sends mandate dated 10 May,
 135, 136n; mandate contains denial of
 consummation and offer to accept Henry's sworn statement, 136–37, 139–40,
 144–45, 207; cited to legatine court
 (1 June), 78, 135; appeals to Rome
 (16 June), 73–74, 78–79, 86, 135; declares
 virginity to Campeggio under oath, 60n,
 86, 107, 197, cf. 148, 187–88, 202, 237;
 appearances in court (18 and 21 June),
 79–80, 81, 84–87; her proctor at court,
 80; counsel at court, 72, 81–82, 84, 87–88,
 92–94, 96–99, 102–3, 108–9, 109–10,
 112–13, 114, 117–18, 130, 153–54, 188n,
 209, 214, 238, *see also* Abel, Clerk,
 Featherstone, Fisher, Ligham, Powell,
 Ridley, Standish, Tunstall, Warham,
 West, cf. Gwent, Shorton, *and* Talcarne;
 defense of virginity and reference to
 public honesty, 85–87; declared contumacious (21 June–5 July), 87, 89, 90,
 92–93, 94, 95, 101, 128; final appeal
 (21 or 24 June), 88, 88n, cf. 165–66,
 168; objections addressed to her *in
 absentia* (25 June), 90–92; consummation of first marriage discussed, 74,
 90–91, 93–94, 95–98, 99, 107, 108, 109,
 111, 114–18, 122–23, 124, 130, 153–55,
 214–15, 238, cf. 103; visited by cardinals
 at Bridewell or Greenwich, 86n; said to
 have approved *libellus* on the bull, 103,
 109, 153–54, 238, *see also libellus*,
 queen's; other *libelli* submitted for her,
 68n, 112–13, 114, 209; her mandate and
 appeal arrive in Rome (5 July), 135–36,
 165; Rome hears of her being declared
 contumacious (9–10 July), 136; trial
 advoked (16 July), 136; not allowed to
 see Campeggio after legatine court, 128;
 hears of Henry's canvassing of the University of Paris (Sept.), 174; debate with
 Henry on public honesty (Oct.), 129–31,
 137, 139, 140, 152–53, 155, 173, 179;
 her challenge to accept Henry's oath on
 virginity reported to Henry by the pope,
 131, 137n, 139–40, 141–42, 144–45, 153,
 179, 180; pope's views on her virginity,
 139–42, 144, 146; appeal to academic
 support (Nov.), 131, 144, 175
 1530: Henry's current thoughts on her
 virginity, 145–46, 179–80, 270, 276, cf.
 193; her virginity and the university
 determinations, 145, 176–79, 193,
 199–200
 1531–33: consummation of first marriage debated at Rome, 146–47, 148–57,
 159, 160, 161, 162–63
 1531: Chapuys on defending her virginity, 148; legatine records sent to
 Rome, 76n, 165–68; and the *Determinations* treatise (pub. Apr. and Nov.),
 181–83, 193, cf. 200; defended in Fisher's *Responsum*, 12, 181, 183–86, 190,
 224; denies consummation to Henry's
 councillors (31 May), 191–92; defended

in Loazes's book (pub. 5 June), 115–16;
sees remissorial letters (June), 148n,
192; Henry leaves her for good (July),
192; is rebuked by Henry, 192–93
  1532: pope orders Henry to rejoin her
(Jan. and Nov.), 149; defended by Abel,
186–88
  1533: and rediscovery of treaty, 165,
196–98; consummation proved in Cranmer's *Twelve Articles*, 224, 233, 235–37,
247, 270; consummation affirmed and
marriage impugned by king's councillors
and both convocations, 196–97, 198–203,
212; Henry asserts consummation, 204,
cf. 207; cited to Dunstable, 205, 206, 208;
alleges her trial at Rome, 206; undefended at Dunstable, 209; marriage
annulled by Cranmer (23 May), 4, 210–
11, 212, 213, 214n, 217, 220, 246, 281,
cf. 262; defended in Novati's treatise,
189; defended by Philalethes Hyperboreus (July), 197–98; trial proceeds at
Rome (4 July), 165; alleged proof of consummation sent abroad, 214–15; marriage
declared at Rome not contrary to divine
law, 165, 166, 168–69; restored to Henry
by papal decree (11 July), 167, 168;
trial at Rome adjourned, 165–68
  1534: trial at Rome reopened (Feb.),
168; question of consummation avoided,
169; marriage approved by papal court
(23 March), 169; annulment ratified by
Parliament (March–April), 160n, 217–
20; daughter illegitimated, 219, 219n;
refuses to submit, denies consummation,
220–21; called Princess Dowager, 245n
  1536: death, 241; consummation and
annulment again declared by Parliament,
247–48
  1553: marriage declared good by Parliament, 281
Catoptropaeus, 198n
Cavendish, George, 75, 81–82, 83, 84, 85–
86, 87, 88, 93–94, 109, 116, 124, 127,
254n
celibacy, priestly, 9n, 17n, 211; cf. religious
vows
Chapuys, Eustace, D.Cn.C.L., imperial
ambassador in England:
  correspondence: of 1529, 64n, 103,
129–31, 137, 139, 174–75; of 1530, 145n,
180; of 1531, 148–49, 167, 181, 190–91,
192–93; of 1532, 146, 254; of 1533, 164,
196, 197, 202–3, 204, 205, 214, 216, 237,
242; of 1534, 217; of 1536, 241–42, 243,
244, 245, 251, 252n, 260
  background, 129; reports arrival in
England (1 Sept. 1529), 129; misinter-
prets Catherine's protestation of 1528,
64n; sends the queen's *libellus* to
Charles, 103, 130; reaction to Henry's
public-honesty argument, 130–31, 137;
informs Catherine of Parisian support,
174–75; on proof of queen's virginity
(1531), 145n, 148, cf. 137; collects
depositions of Arthur's impotency, 148–
49, 192–93; sends legatine records to

Rome, 167; sends Fisher's *Responsum*
to Rome, 181; reports on investigation of
the Percy precontract (28 June 1532),
254; not aware of Henry's dispensation
to marry Anne, 146; reports on Henry's
marriage to Anne (1533), 196, 205, 237;
reassures Catherine about treaty, 197;
disputes with Henry, 204; officially protests actions against Catherine, 205; encourages Charles to war on England, 216;
on Elizabeth's birth, 242; on Henry's
suspicion of witchcraft (1536), 241–42;
on Stokesley's role and repentance, 251n,
252n; on Henry's lack of virility and
Jane Seymour, 243, 260; unable to learn
grounds of Anne Boleyn's annulment,
245; absent from England in 1540, 265
Charles, Emperor, King of Spain: nephew
of Catherine of Aragon, 15, 150; early
relations with England, 21, 77; ambassadors to England, *see* Mendoza *and*
Chapuys; ambassadors and agents in
Rome, *see* Cifuentes, Mai, Muscetula,
and Ortiz; agents in Venice, 15, *see
also* Niño; informed of Westminster
inquisition (1527), 234; army captures
Rome, 29n; warns Henry against questioning marriage, 66; sends copies of
brief to England (1528), 63–64; defeats
French at Landriano, Treaty of Barcelona with Clement VII (June 1529),
136; English embassies to, 103, 155, 175–
76, 194–95, 213, 214–15, 238; crusades
(1532), 195; unwilling to war with
England (1533), 216; to reward cardinals
for their vote (1534), 169–70; his threat
of war ends with Catherine's death, 241
Charles VIII, King of France, 14n
Chichele, Henry, Archbishop of Canterbury
(1414–43), 26n, 242, 271
Cifuentes, Count, 169
citra, meaning of, 80, 80n, cf. 26, 137n
civil (Roman) law, 6, 72, 99, 177, 225, 227,
285, cf. canonists *and see* Appendix A
Clamport, John, 120
clandestine marriage, 5, 17n, 49–51, 229,
266, cf. 196, 205; defined, 16, 44, 44n;
see also Percy *and* precontract
Clarence, George Plantagenet, Duke of,
194
Clarence, Thomas of Lancaster, Duke of
(d. 1421), 9–10
Clayburgh (Claiborough, Claybroke), William, D.Cn.C.L., prothonotary of Chancery, Archdeacon of Worcester in 1531
(d. 1534): clerk of Westminster trial
(1527), 23, 24n, 88, 113–14; clerk of
legatine court (1529), 3, 75, 80, 114, cf.
95, 112, 127; submitted *libellus* to
legates, 113; submitted legatine records
to Dunstable court (1533), 208; compiled a one-volume legatine record
(authenticated 1 Oct. 1533), 3–4, 75–
76, 79, 80, 91, 113, 124, 209, 216
Clement V, Pope (1305–14), *Constitutiones clementinae*: 2.1. *De iudiciis*,
chap. 2, *Dispendiosam*, 78; 2.7. *De pro-*

bationibus, chap. 1, *Litteris*, 291, 292n; 5.11. *De verborum significatione*, chap. 2, *Saepe*, 78

Clement VI, Pope (1342–52), 46n

Clement VII (Robert of Geneva), Pope (at Avignon, 1378–94), 8, 9n, 229n

Clement VII (Giulio de' Medici), Pope (1523–34):

1527: in Castel Saint' Angelo during sack of Rome, 29n, cf. 38; asked by Henry for dispensation, 38–53, 174, 251; asked for a protestation, 39, 41; grants Henry dispensation (Dec.), 41–43, 51–52, 53, 229n, 257–58, cf. 254, 262; and suggestion that Henry remarry before annulment, 40

1528: at Orvieto, 52, 54; has read Henry's book on the marriage, 113; knows of Henry's passion for Anne, 52; grants new dispensation (13 Apr.), 52–53, 55, 257–58; grants legatine commission (13 Apr. and 8 June), 3, 55, 59, 77–78, 89–90, 92, cf. 157; advised by the English on decretal bull, 54–55, 57–58, 66–67, 173–74; grants decretal bull (June), 59, 65, 142, cf. 221; his pollicitation to Henry not to revoke the legatine trial (July), 113n, 142

1529: treaty with Charles V (29 June), 136; policy of delaying the case, 136, 166–67; advokes trial, 136; letter to Henry tells of Catherine's offer to accept king's oath (7 Oct.), 131, 137, 139–41, 153, 166, 179–80; offers new dispensation for Henry's present marriage, 139, 141; and public honesty, 138–40, 179; reliance on Catherine's virginity, 141–42, 144; his letter rebuked and defended, 141

1530: letter answered by Henry, 142–43; reaction to the determinations, 143–44; reminded of Henry's passion for Anne, 146; favors making Ghinucci cardinal, 159

1531: to be shown the legatine depositions and the queen's *libellus*, 153; told of Catherine's consummation by Ancona, 161

1532: rebukes Henry for living with Anne (Jan.), 149; dispensations for Henry not known to Catherine's supporters, 146; issues another rebuke to Henry (Nov.), 149

1533: appoints Cranmer Archbishop of Canterbury, 165, 197, 231n; his ban on debate overridden in Convocation, 199; his dispensations relied on by Cranmer, 232–33, 256–57; marriage to Anne (11 July), 167–68, 214; in France with King Francis, 216

1534: allows a Neapolitan to marry his sister-in-law (Feb.), 170; his Consistory confirms Catherine's marriage (23 Mar.), 169; his death and tomb, 11n

1536: his dispensations nullified by Parliament, 256–57, 277

Clerk, John, D.Cn.L. (Bologna), Bishop of Bath and Wells in 1523 (d. Jan. 1541,

perhaps poisoned while returning from Cleves): writes of sack of Rome (1527), 29n; member of queen's counsel, conveys Henry's rebuke (1528), 62–63, cf. 82; cites queen to legatine court (1529), 78, 87–88, 89, 101; notarizes queen's appeals, 79, 88; her counsel at court, 87–88, 108; signs statement of 1 July 1529, 82; opposes determinations in Parliament (1531), 190–91; notarizes queen's legatine records, 76n, 88n, 168; authenticates 1503 treaty (1533), 196; opposes Henry's position in Convocation, 201–2; ambassador to Cleves (1540), 273

Clerke, Margaret, 165n

Cleves, 261, 268–69, 273. *See also* Anne of Cleves

Cleves, Duke of, brother of Anne, 273

Cleves, Duke of, father of Anne, 269

Cobham, Eleanor, 242

Cobham, Sir George Broke, Lord, 267, 274n

Cochlaeus, John, 198n

Code of Canon Law (1917), 233, 283n

coitus, as consummating marriage, *see* consummation; as criterion of affinity, *see* affinity; following betrothal creates marriage, 275

Compendious Annotation, A, 67–73, 115, 183

Compiègne, 38, cf. 158

compurgation, 148

concubinage, 17n, 35, 211, 226–27, 228, 242–43, 257

condition, *see* error

conditional contract of marriage, 103, 268, 272, 273–74

consanguinity, impediment of, 5–14, 22, 43, 44, 46, 48, 51, 107, 156, 213n, 249, 258, 263, 264n, 280, 282, 284–85. *See also* affinity, Innocent III, *and* Leviticus

consent, as criterion for marriage, 182, 185, 193, 228, *see also* affinity, contract, *and* public honesty; lack of, 14n, 265, 268, 270, 272, 273–74, 280, *see also* witchcraft

consistory, bishop's, 22n, 129, 216, 266, *and see* Ligham *and* Wootton; papal, 165–66, 168–69

consummation of marriage:

between Arthur and Catherine of Aragon:

—*before 1527*: affirmed by Arthur, 61, 122–23; denied by Arthur, 151; early denied by Catherine, 30, 150, 151, 233; affirmed by 1503 treaty (q.v.); denied by brief of Julius II (q.v.); denied by Isabella (q.v.); denied by Ferdinand (q.v.); suspected by Henry VII, 61–62, 153, 236; stated as dubious in bull of Julius II (q.v.); denied by Henry VIII, 30, 96, 107, 137, 145n, 150, 151, 233–35, 276

—*1527*: charged at Westminster trial and conceded by Bell for Henry, 24–25, 30, 109, cf. 33, 35–37; denied by Catherine, 31, 234; Henry realizes its import, 30–37; considered essential by Wakefield, 36–37

—*1528*: Wolsey not certain of, 56–57, 96, cf. 29–31, 234; discussed at Rome, 56–57, 137–38; Catherine denies and Wolsey advances proof of, 60–62, cf. 74; stated in *A Compendious Annotation*, admitted as presumed by Bishop West, 68–69, 70, 72, 73; denied by Catherine to Campeggio in confession, 60, 86, cf. 145; the brief's assertion protested by Catherine (7 Nov.), 64–65

—*1529*: assumed by Gregory Casale, 138–39; denied in Catherine's mandate (10 May), 136–37, 139–40, 144–45, 207; denied by Catherine under oath (16 June), 60n, 86, 107, 197, cf. 148, 187–88, 202, 237; denied by Catherine at legatine court (21 June), 85–86; charged at legatine court (25 June), 90–91; Henry's answer to charge in doubt, 91, 95–97, 109, 207, 209; debated in court, 74, 93–94, 96–97, 97–98, 99, 107, 108, 109, 111, 114–18, 122–23, 124, 130, 153–55, 214–15, 238, cf. 103; declared proven without further contrary proof (9 July), 109; Catherine's denial discussed with her by Henry (Oct.), 129–31, 137, 139, 152–53, 155, 173, 179; Henry challenged by Catherine and the pope to declare his opinion under oath, 131, 137, 139–40, 141–42, 144–45, 153, 179, 180

—*1530*: Henry privately denies knowledge of, 96, 145, 145n, 270; specified as essential in Cambridge and Oxford determinations, 176–77, 179; not specified by Orléans, 178; declared irrelevant by Angers theologians, 177; declared essential by Angers and Paris lawyers and Bourges theologians, 177–78, 187–88, 199, 205; presupposed but not specified by Paduan theologians, 145, 178; not specified by theologians of Bologna and Paris or Toulouse and Ferrara, 178, 199; given special attention by lawyers of Bologna, 178–79; implications of, for Henry, 179–80; considered nonexistent by pope, 141–42, 144; assumed in *consilium* to pope, 146; essential in assessing determinations, 144, 179, 187–88, 191

—*1531–33*: debated at Rome, 148–57, 159, 160, 161, 162, cf. 146–47

—*1531*: implied but declared nonessential in *Determinations* treatise (pub. Apr. and Nov.), 181–83, 193, cf. 223; denied to be essential by Fisher, 181, 183–86, 190; remissorials to prove lack of, 148, 192; proof of, discussed by Ortiz and Chapuys, 148; Catherine denies presumptions of (31 May), 191–92; witnesses against, found by Chapuys, 148–49, 192–93; Henry alleges it proved, 192; Henry knows its lack can be proved, 193; arguments for, sent by Henry to Rome, 153, 161, cf. 270; denied in Abel's *Invicta veritas*, 186–88; need for, questioned in a refutation of Abel, 188–89; University of Paris refuses to declare

inessential, 193, 217–18, cf. 204, 205

—*1532*: Henry sends queen's *libellus* to Rome as argument for, 103, 130, 153–55, 161, 179, 214, 238

—*1533*: treaty's assertion of, exploited by Henry, 162–63, 164, 196–97, 199, 210, 223, 236, 237; declared theologically irrelevant in Cranmer's *Twelve Articles*, 223–29, 231–33, 247–48; declared legally relevant and proved in *Twelve Articles*, 224, 233, 235–37, 247–48, 270, cf. 204, 207; discussed in both convocations, 200–203; asserted by Henry, 204, cf. 207; denied by Chapuys, 204–5; charged at Dunstable, 206; answered by Bell for Henry, 207; assertion of proposed, by Cranmer and Henry after Dunstable, 237–38; proofs of, sent to emperor's court, 214–15, 238; declared irrelevant by Spanish in Rome, 166, cf. 148; denied by Novati, 189

—*1534*: evidence for, still being collected, 165n; not referred to in Consistory sentence (23 March), 169; proofs against, doubted by Campeggio, 159, 169, 202; asserted by Parliament, 217; essential to Act of Succession, 219; debated by Catherine, 220–21

—*1536*: asserted in second Act of Succession, 247–48; Henry's current views of, 247–48

between Henry VIII and Anne of Cleves, 14n, 261, 270–71, 272–75

between Henry Percy and Anne Boleyn, 243, 252–53, 276, cf. 42, 50–51, 52, 255–56, 257–58

as criterion of affinity, *see* affinity; criterion of indissolubility, 14n, 16–17, 42, 49, 51, 228–32, 251–52, 254, 257–58, 262–63, 264–65, 274, 277, cf. 279; needed in external forum, 224, 227; not essential to marriage, 182, 185, 228, 232, 233, cf. 235; not possible in invalid marriage, 272; presumptions of, 61–62, 64–65, 70, 93–94, 97, 107, 109, 115, 122–23, 148, 151, 154, 191–92, 236–38, 270, 276, cf. 275; ways of, 235–36; without loss of physical virginity, 207, 224, 235–36, cf. 247

contract *per verba de futuro* (= betrothal, q.v.) or *per verba de praesenti* (= marriage): *de praesenti* considered *de futuro* until puberty, 105, 126, 269; *de praesenti* dissolves *de futuro*, 50, 107, 258, 263; coitus converts *de futuro* to *de praesenti*, 275. *See also* precontract

convocation, trials before, 26n, 271

Convocation: of Canterbury, under Archbishop Chichele, 26n, 271n; in 1533, 198–202, 204, 209–10, 212, 217, 218, 251n; in 1536, 246; of Canterbury and York jointly, to try the Cleves marriage, 4, 264–73; of York, 202–3, 210, 217, 218

Corpus iuris canonici, see Boniface VIII, canonists, Clement V, *Decretals of Gregory IX, Glossa ordinaria*, Gratian, "Tree of Affinity"

Cranmer, Thomas, D.Th., Archbishop of Canterbury in 1533 (d. 1556):
before 1529: first wife and loss of fellowship at Cambridge, 195
1529: first dealings with Henry, 175, 176n, 222–23, 229, 232, 235; and "local solution," 175, 175n, 222; first book and effect at Cambridge, 175–76, 225; possibly a chaplain of Boleyns, 175–76, 222, cf. 255
1530: with Wiltshire on embassy to Charles V, 175–76
1531: opinion of Reginald Pole, 194; revision and translation of *Determinations* treatise, 181, 200, 223
1532: as ambassador to Charles V, 194–95; second wife, 195; marriage invalid, 211; selected by Henry for Canterbury, 194–95, 222–23, 231n, cf. 175n
1533: returns to England, 196, 223; rumored to have married Henry and Anne, 196, 237; denies rumor, 213; appointment as archbishop approved at Rome, 165, 197; asks permission to authorize judicial proceedings, 197; writes *Twelve Articles* for Henry's spiritual benefit, 200, 223–33, 235–37, 247–48, 251–52, 258n, 262, 270, 274n, 275, cf. 204, 207, 258–59; writes it while awaiting approbation from Rome, 223; writes as theologian rather than canonist, 230n, cf. 227, 228–29, 232; proves that divinely prohibited affinity comes from marriage, not coitus, 147, 200, 224–29, 231–33, 251–52, 257; denies that unconsummated marriage can be dissolved by man, 228–29, 231, 232–33, 251–52, 256, 262–63, 264, 274n, cf. 257–58; says that even consummated marriage can be dissolved by religious vows, 231–33; establishes consummation of Catherine's first marriage, even without loss of physical virginity, 224, 233, 235–37, 247, 270, cf. 204, 207; on legal presumption, 224, 227–28, 236–38, 270; Convocation summoned in anticipation of his appointment, 198; his papal bulls arrive, and he is installed as archbishop, 200; makes protestation before taking oath of allegiance to pope, 233; has Convocation vote on law of affinity and fact of consummation, 200–202; does not urge private theology, 200; asks license of Henry to begin trial, 266; convenes Dunstable inquisition and annuls marriage, 4, 94n, 149, 202, 205–11, 212, 213, 214, 217, 220, 246, 281; in so doing acts as papal legate, 210–11; plans statement on queen's consummation, 237–38, 296–98, cf. 155; tries the marriage of Henry and Anne in a gallery of Lambeth Palace and validates it, 211–13, 214, 232; is unaware of Anne's precontract, 229, 255–56; relies on Clement VII's dispensations for Henry's first-degree affinity, 232–33, 256–57
1534: his sentence of annulment confirmed by Parliament, 217; sentence

rejected by Catherine, 220
1536: reaction to Anne Boleyn's arrest (3 May), 244–45, 251–52; conscience, 251–52, 262–63, 264, cf. 247–48; convenes inquisition into her marriage in a Lambeth Palace chapel, 244–47, 248–50, 253, 255; confesses Anne (16 May), 249–50, 252–53, 255–56; delivers sentence of annulment (17 May), 244, 245–46, 247–48, 249–50, 253, 259; possible grounds for sentence, 245–46, 247–59; confesses Anne again (18 May), 259; dispenses Henry and Jane Seymour from third-degree affinity *ex coitu illicito* (19 May), 259–60; still observing the purely ecclesiastical canons on marriage, 259; his faculty office, 264n, 267, cf. 278; his sentence confirmed by Convocation (June), 246; his sentence reported and confirmed in Parliament (July), 246–47, 248
1539–40: one of the commissioners for the Anne of Cleves marriage, 265, 266, 267–68, cf. 261
1540: examines act eliminating impediments of precontract, kinship, public honesty, and affinity, 261, 263; views on precontract, 262–63, 264; one of the "promoters" of the Cleves trial, 265–66; presides over trial, 266, 271; on fact-finding committee in trial, 267, cf. 271; does not pronounce sentence as metropolitan, 271–72
after 1547: and reintroduction of impediment of precontract, 264, 279; heads commission to reform canon law, 279; late views on marriage, 230n, 248, 249, 264, 279–81, 283; recantations under Mary, 251
Croke, Richard, D.Th., tutor in Greek to Henry VIII (d. 1558), 95, 144–45, 177, 202
Cromwell, Thomas, Secretary to the King and Lord Privy Seal, Earl of Essex in 1540 (d. 1540): and Chapuys, 129; and the "local solution" (1532), 175n, 198; and Act in Restraint of Appeals to Rome (1533), 198; and Dunstable trial, 207, 209, 211; and first Act of Succession (1534), 219n; and treason trial of Anne Boleyn (1536), 242–43, 253; investigates Percy precontract, 253, 255; present at Anne's annulment, 245; arranged marriage to Anne of Cleves (1539–40), 261; fall (1540), 261, 265; testimony on Cleves marriage, 265
Cuevas, Alonso, 150n

Darcy, Thomas Lord, 94–95, 217
Darius, Silvester, Auditor of the Rota, 157n, 158–59
Datary, Roman, 47
David and Abishag, 181–82, 184
Dean of the Arches, *see* Bell, Gwent, *and* Ligham
decretal bull, 54–55, 57–59, 65, 142, 174, 221
decretals, false, 6–7, 34, 225

Decretals of Gregory IX (1234):
   1.2. *De constitutionibus:* chap. 7,
Innocent III, *Quae in ecclesiarum,* 290;
chap. 9, Innocent III, *Cum M(artinus),*
293
   1.3. *De rescriptis:* chap. 7, Alexander
III, *Eam te,* 294; chap. 20, Innocent III,
Super litteris, 72, 295; chap. 28, Innocent
III, *Nonnulli,* 291; chap. 31, Honorius III,
Ad audientiam, 70–71
   1.6. *De electione et electi potestate,*
chap. 20, Innocent III, *Innotuit,* 290, 291
   1.9. *De renuntiatione,* chap. 10,
Innocent III, *Nisi,* 295
   2.13. *De restitutione spoliatorum,* chap.
13, Innocent III, *Litteris,* 26, 290
   2.23. *De praesumptionibus,* chap. 14,
Innocent III, *Litteras,* 294
   2.27. *De sententia et re iudicata,* chap.
12, Innocent III, *Cum olim,* 290
   2.28. *De appellationibus, recusationibus,
et relationibus:* chap. 54, Innocent III,
Sollicitudinem, 293; chap. 60, Innocent
III, *Cum cessante,* 294
   3.27. *De successionibus ab intestato,*
chap. 1, Council of Altheim, *Sed hoc,* 17n
   3.31. *De regularibus et transeuntibus ad
religionem,* chap. 16, Innocent III, *Ad
apostolicam,* 293
   4.1. *De sponsalibus et matrimoniis:*
chap. 2, Innocent III, *Praeterea,* 293n;
chap. 3, Eugenius III, *Iuvenis,* 72, 235–
36, 292, 293; chap. 4, Alexander III, *Ad
audientiam,* 67–71, 183, 185–86, 187; chap.
18, Urban III, *Cum in apostolica,* 40n;
chap. 21, Clement III, *Ad id quod,* 293;
chap. 26, Innocent III, *Tua nos,* 227, 293;
chap. 30, Gregory IX, *Is qui,* 107n–8n,
227, 294; chap. 32, Gregory IX,
Adolescens, 258n
   4.2 *De desponsatione impuberum:* chap.
2, "Nicholas I," *Ubi non,* 269n; chap. 3,
Isidore of Seville, *Puberes,* 292, 294; chap.
4, Alexander III, *Litteras,* 44; chap. 5,
Alexander III, *Accessit,* 44; chap. 6,
Alexander III, *Continebatur,* 44; chap. 7,
Alexander III, *De illis,* 105, 293; chap. 14,
Innocent III, *Tuae nobis,* 104
   4.4. *De sponsa duorum,* chap. 3, Alexander III, *Licet,* 229, 274
   4.5. *De conditionibus appositis in
desponsatione vel in aliis contractibus:*
chap. 3, Alexander III, *De illis,* 227; chap.
6, Innocent III, *Per tuas,* 293
   4.13. *De eo qui cognovit consanguineam
uxoris suae vel sponsae,* chap. 7, Innocent
III, *Fraternitati,* 226; chap. 11, Gregory
IX, *Iordanae,* 292
   4.14. *De consanguinitate et affinitate:*
chap. 3, Celestine III, *Quod dilectio,* 295;
chap. 6, Innocent III, *Quia circa,* 295;
chap. 8, Innocent III, *Non debet,* 7, 46,
107, 138, 156, 293
   4.15. *De frigidis et maleficiatis et impotentia coeundi,* cf. 271, 280; chap. 1,
Burchard of Worms, *Accepisti,* 294
   4.19. *De divortiis,* chap. 9, Innocent III,
Deus qui, 14–15, 139, 290
   4.20. *De donationibus inter virum et
uxorem et de dote post divortium
restituenda,* rubric, 291
   5.1. *De accusationibus, inquisitionibus,
et denuntiationibus,* chap. 24, Innocent
III, *Qualiter,* 4, 21–22, 78
   5.3. *De simonia, et ne aliquid pro
spiritualibus exigatur vel promittatur,*
chap. 31, Innocent III, *Licet,* 4, 21–22, 78

degrees of kinship, 5–6, 7, 9n, 44–45, 48–49,
   263–64, 280–81, 282–85. *See also* affinity
   and Leviticus
Denny, Anthony (later knighted), 270–71
depositions: at the legatine court, 74, 80n,
   95–97, 120–24, 125 (cf. 30), 126–27, 153,
   161, 165, 168, 199, 208–9, 236–38; for
   Catherine at Rome, 148–49, 192–93, *see
   also* remissorials; at Dunstable, 208; at
   Cleves trial, 267–68, 269–71, 274n, cf. 265
Derby, Edward Stanley, Earl of, 94
Derby, Thomas, Clerk of King's Council,
   119, 120, 188
Dereham, Francis, 275
determinations of the universities, 143–44,
   176–80, 187–88, 190–91, 193, 199–200,
   209–10, 214, 217–18, 219, 225, cf. 173–75,
   204, 205; dates of printing, 180, 181, 184n.
   See also consummation of marriage
   between Arthur and Catherine of
   Aragon (*1530*)
Determinations treatise (the king's white
   paper): written by Burgo, Edward Fox,
   and Stokesley in 1529, 180, 193, 200,
   262n; published in Latin (*Gravissimae
   . . . censurae*) in April 1531, 180, 184n;
   revised by Cranmer and translated by
   Cranmer and Elyot (pub. Nov. 1531),
   181, 200; on divorce and public honesty, 181–83, 222–23, 228–29, 262n; refuted by Fisher, Abel, and Novati, 12,
   181, 183–90, 224
Deuteronomy: significance of name ("second law"), 35; on doubtful cases, 231;
   on marriage, *see* levirate
dispensation (relaxation of law for special
   reasons): for divine law, *see* divine law
   and Leviticus; for marriage for Catherine
   of Aragon and Henry, *see* Julius II; for
   the same, suggested renewal of, 83, 139,
   141, 179, cf. 43; for a second marriage
   for Henry, *see* Clement VII (*1529*);
   given by God himself, 15, 106; granted
   by Wolsey as legate *a latere,* 22; granted
   by Cranmer, 259–60, 278; granted by
   Cardinal Pole, 282; invalid, implications
   of, 82, 140–41, 166, 179, 256–57, 282;
   papal—forbidden, voided, and revalidated by Parliament, 256–57
divine law: and affinity, *see* affinity; charged
   against Henry's marriage as possibility
   at Westminster trial, 24, 26, 28, 30, 66;
   charged at legatine court, 91, 97, 105–6,
   110, 123, cf. 74, 107, 113, 124; charged
   at Dunstable, 210, cf. 211; charge denied
   at Rome, 139, 141, 159, 165–66, 168–69;
   and dispensability, 1, 7–17, 24, 26, 28,

29, 32, 35, 37n, 43, 47–48, 51, 59, 66–67, 68–70, 106, 110, 123, 138–39, 141, 142, 143, 150, 152, 159, 164, 173–74, 176–80, 181–89, 199–203, 210–11, 215, 218–19, 220–21, 223, 224, 228–30, 231–32, 285; and public honesty, *see* public honesty

divine punishment, 24, 32–33, 234, 241–42, 247, 260, 263, 276–78

divorce: defined (as distinct from annulment), 16n; of Anne Boleyn, *see* Boleyn, Anne, relations with Percy; of Anne of Cleves after her annulment, 14n, 263, 265, 273–75; of consummated marriage, 229–32, 251, 264, 279–81, 283; of unconsummated marriage (= unconsummated precontract), 14n, 16–17, 42, 49, 51, 182, 228–32, 251–52, 254, 257–58, 262–63, 264–65, 274, 277, 279–80; by death and resurrection, 186. *See also* religious vows

Dorset, *see* Grey

dowry, Catherine of Aragon's, 106, 107, 126, 150, cf. 108n

Dunstable trial, 4, 94n, 149, 202, 205–11, 238, 266, cf. 95; records of, 4, 206, 214; sentence at, 210–11, 212, 213, 214, 214n, 217, 220, 246, cf. 218

Durantis, William, "the Speculator," Bishop of Mende (d. 1296), 13n, 22–23, 89–90, 102

Edward I, King of England, 15, 43, 46, 259

Edward III, King of England, 46

Edward IV, King of England, 38, 194, 242

Edward VI, King of England, 248, 260, 279, 282

Elizabeth I, Queen of England, 195–96, 241–42, 244, 245, 282–83, cf. 149, 167, 213, 275

Elizabeth of York, Queen of England, mother of Henry VIII, 13, 45, 194

Elyot, Sir Thomas, 181, 195

Emmanuel I, King of Portugal, 14

English Articles, 150–52, 155, 215; author of, 156–63; date of, 162–63

error of condition or of person, impediments to marriage, 280, cf. 272

espousals, *see* spousals

Essex, Mary Bourchier, Countess of, 119–20

Eugenius III, Pope (1145–53), 235–36. *See also Decretals of Gregory IX*, 4.1.3

Eugenius IV, Pope (1431–47), 11

external forum, 35, 224, 227, 236–38, cf. 270. *See also* consummation of marriage, presumptions of

Extractum registri, 77n, 80n, 85n, 88n, 136n, 137n, 150n, 168n

fact, factum, 9n, 24–25, 26–27, 68, 70, 77, 102, 103–4, 105, 111, 113–14, 125, 130, 137, 208, 209, 267, 273, cf. 112. *See also propositio omnium quae in facto consistunt*

Falier, Louis, Venetian ambassador, 75, 84–85, 86n, 87

Falk, William, 120

Faytor, John, D.C.L., Catherine of Aragon's proctor, 80

Featherstone (Fetherstonhalgh), Richard, M.A., tutor of Princess Mary, Archdeacon of Brecon and of St. David's (d. 1540), 188n, 202

Ferdinand I, King of Hungary, nephew of Catherine of Aragon, 150

Ferdinand II (the Catholic), King of Aragon and of Castile, King of Spain, 14, 15, 54–55, 97, 104–6, 115, 151, 162, 196, 197–98, 210, 237. *See also* Isabella *and* treaty of 1503

Ferrante (Ferdinand II), King of Naples (1495–96), 14

Ferrara, 178, 180, 217. *See also* determinations

Fisher, John, Bishop of Rochester, Cardinal in 1535 (d. 1535): Chancelor of Cambridge University, 98, cf. 35; consulted by Wolsey (1527), 29, 58–59, 66, 82–83, 173; guesses at annulment effort and encourages Catherine, 29n, 82–83; opposes papal trial, 81–84, 98–99; and Robert Wakefield, 35–37; and Bishop Staphileus, 158; included among counsel for Catherine (1528), 60, 82; present at Catherine's protestation against brief, 64; present at Catherine's appeal (16 June 1529), 78–79; advocate for Catherine at legatine court, 87–88, 108; speaks at June 28 session, 92–94, cf. 112, 118; submits treatise *Licitum* to court, 92, 97–98, 112, 137; replies to Gardiner's attack on *Licitum*, 98–99; present at session of 5 July, 101; confrontation with Henry in court during July, 81–84, 99; submits another treatise to court, 112–13; report of his being poisoned (1531), 190; treatise *Responsum*, 12, 181, 183–86, 190, 224; supposed author of *Parasceve*, 198n; votes against Henry's side in Convocation (1533), 201; attends Parliament against orders (1534), 216–17; attainder proceedings against, 217; challenged by Wakefield, 37n; author of seven books in defense of Catherine, 37n; executed, 251–52; early biography of, 75, 112n

Fitzgerald, Margaret, 44–45

Fitzroy, Henry, illegitimate son of Henry VIII by Elizabeth Blount, Duke of Richmond (b. ca. 1519, d. 22 July 1536), 33, 33n, 244

Fitzwalter (Fitzwater), Elizabeth, Viscountess, 119–20

Fitzwalter, Viscount, *see* Radcliffe

Flanders, 78, 135, 198. *See also* Lüneburg

Foix, John I, Count of, 11

force and fear, impediments of, 14n, 272, 280. *See also* witchcraft

fornication, *see* affinity from illicit coitus

forsan, 27, 64, 72, 97, 99, 108, 116, 117–18, 151–52, 155–56, 198, 215, cf. 86, 111

forum Dei (= internal forum, conscience), 35, 140, 211, 227–28. *See also* external forum

Fox, Edward, D.Th., secretary to Wolsey, Archdeacon of Leicester and king's almoner in 1531, Bishop of Hereford in 1535 (d. 1538): and Robert Wakefield, 37n; and negotiations of 1528, 52, 54–57, 113n, 157n; co-author of *Determinations* treatise (1529), 180, 193, 262n; fails in Paris missions to divinize public honesty (1531), 193, 217–18; votes on Henry's side in Convocation (1533), 202; responds to Chapuys's protest, 205; dead by 1540, 262n

Fox, Richard, D.C.L., Bishop of Winchester (d. 5 Oct. 1528), 30, 56, 124–25, 126–27

Foxe, John, 175, 283

Francis I, King of France, 66, 174–75, 216

Francis of Lorraine, 264n, 265, 267–69, 274

frigidity, *see* impotency

Gage, James, 208

Gardiner, Stephen, D.Cn.C.L., Wolsey's secretary, Archdeacon of Norfolk in 1529, Bishop of Winchester in 1531 (d. 1555): clerk of Westminster inquisition (1527), 23, 24n, 88; sent to pope at Orvieto (1528) to obtain new dispensation, 52, 54; to seek the decretal bull, 54, 57, 59, cf. 113n; to inquire into public honesty and argument of Henry's ignorance, 55–57, 100, 137, 157, 160; leaves Rome and arrives in London (22 June 1529), 88, 138–39; perhaps sits in legatine court as Wolsey's secretary, 88; treatise in Henry's name against Fisher's *Licitum*, 98–100, 113; sent to summon Bishop West from Ely, 74; reports on debate at Cambridge (1530), 176; argues point of consummation with Catherine (1531), 191–92; resists authorizing local annulment (1533), 197; votes on Henry's side in Convocation, 200–202; counsel for Henry at Dunstable, 206; sent on embassy to Charles and Francis, 216; opposed to Cromwell (1540), 265; prepares cases for Cleves annulment, 265; reviews draft of act on precontract and kinship impediments, 261, cf. 264–65; prosecutes Cleves annulment before Convocation, 266; on fact-finding committee, 267, cf. 271; reads sentence of annulment in Parliament, 273n

Gasparri, Pietro, Cardinal, 283n

Geminianus (Dominic of San Gimignano), canonist (d. before 1436), 137–38, 157n, 291n

Genesis on marriage, 7, 93–94, 225, 274

German views, 195. *See also* Lutherans

Germanic customs, 6, 33–34

Ghinucci, Jerome, Bishop of Worcester in 1523, deprived in 1534, Cardinal in 1535 (d. 1541), 144–45, 159–60, 177, 202

Gigli, Silvester, Bishop of Worcester (1498–1521), 105

Glass of the Truth, A, 123, 175n, 198

Glossa ordinaria to canon law: to Gratian, 291n; to *Decretals of Gregory IX*, 22n,

70, 156, 235–36, 269n, 291, 295n, cf. 155

Gloucester, Humphrey, Duke of, 242

Gratian of Bologna, *Concordia discordantium canonum* (or *Decretum*, ca. 1140), 5, 34, 69n, 289, 290, 291, 294

Gravissimae . . . censurae, 180, 184n. *See also Determinations* treatise

Greenwich, 24, 86n, 101, 109, 191, cf. 129, 192

Gregory I, Pope (Gregory the Great, 590–604), 6–7; Pseudo-, 6–7, 225

Gregory IX, Pope (1227–41), 69, 227 (ref. to CIC X 4.1.30), 258n. *See also Decretals of Gregory IX and Glossa ordinaria*

Grey, Thomas, Marquess of Dorset, 94–95, 112, 119

Groff (Chroiff), Henry de, 268

Gueldres (Gelder), Charles, Duke of, 268–69

Guildford, Lady Jane, 208

Guildford, Sir Henry, 94–95, 119

Gwent (Ventanus), Richard, D.Cn.C.L., counselor of Catherine of Aragon in 1529, chaplain to Henry and Dean of the Arches (and Official of Canterbury) in 1532, Archdeacon of London in 1534 (d. 1543), 112, 245, 266, 267

Hall, Edward, 38n, 66, 75, 81, 86, 107, 116, 124, 174

Hawkins, Nicholas, D.C.L., nephew of Bishop West, Archdeacon of Ely, Bishop-designate of Ely in 1533 (d. Jan. 1534), 194–95, 213, 214, 215n

Heath, Nicholas, D.Th., Bishop of Rochester in 1540 (later Archbishop of York), 261

Hebraic scholarship, 15, 35–37, 144, 173, 236. *See also* Jews

Hennage, Sir Thomas, 270–71

Henry IV, King of England, 9–10

Henry V, King of England, cf. 9

Henry VII, King of England: descent, 10, 194; and Catherine's suspected pregnancy, 61–62, 153, cf. 97; and his desire to marry Catherine himself, 151, 151n; and idea of Catherine's marrying Prince Henry, 26, 70, 126; and 1503 treaty (q.v.), 115, 196, 210; negotiations with Julius II, 104–5, 125; marries Prince Henry to Catherine in 1504, 104; and Prince Henry's protestation (1505), 126; death (1509), 27, 28, 54–55, 103–4, 108, 122, cf. 111, 152

Henry VIII, King of England:

before 1503: ancestors, 10, 13, 38, 43–46, 194, 258–59; born in 1491, 124, cf. 119; and delay in becoming Prince of Wales, 61–62, 153; and his father, concerning marriage to Catherine, 26, 70, 126

1503: betrothed at age 11 to Catherine, 103–4, cf. 26, 108, 111; and knowledge of dispensation, 54–57, 106, 110, 114, 160, 235–36; and young age, 27, 54–55, 58, 72, 106–7, 108, 110, 119, 122, 124, 152

1504: at age 13 marries Catherine *per verba de praesenti*, 58, 103–4, 111, 125, 126, 269, cf. 26, 28; marriage to be solemnized at age 15 (1506), 104, 111

1505: before turning 14, secretly protests against automatic "convalescence" of his marriage, 103, 105, 107, 111, 125–27, cf. 26–27, 28, 54, 58, 72, 74, 177, 209n, 258n, 269; still calls Catherine wife after protestation, 105

1509–27: becomes king, 103–4; solemnizes marriage to Catherine, 1–2, 54–55, 91, 104–5, 122, 206; consummates marriage, 24, 104, 151, 166, 233–35; assumes Catherine was virgin when he married her, 30, 95–96, 107, 137, 145n, 150, 151, 233–35, 276; and Elizabeth Howard, 47–48, 232, 249; his children by Catherine and his natural son, 32–33, 53; Mary Boleyn his mistress, 16–17, 34–35, 44n, 47–48, 146–47, 219–20, 232, 244–45, 248, 257, 277, 281; as Defender of the Faith, 12, 231; breaks up affair between Anne Boleyn and Percy, 254; in love with Anne, 1, 16, 38; scruples over incest, 1–2, 5, 10, 14–17, 21, 24, 32–33, 65–66 (cf. 29n), 74, 81–82, 83, 84, 92, 98–99, 137, 142, 146, 174, 211, 222–23, 234, 241, 247–48, 260, 276–78, 281, 283–84

1527: gives order for Bishop Richard Fox to sign deposition (Apr.), 125; defends his marriage in Westminster trial (May), 2, 4, 24–25, 94; by proxy admits consummation of Catherine's first marriage, 25, 30, 109, 276; new thoughts on public honesty and affinity from illicit coitus, 16–17, 31–38, 43, 46–49, 52, 67, 118–19, 147, 179–80, 190, 204, 207, 219–20, 222–24, 232–35, 247–48, 257, 276–77; his public and private justifications differ, 2, 35–37, 65–67, 190, 204, 207, 217–20, 222–24, 234–38, 246–48, 270, 276–77; silence on Catherine's virginity, 16, 37, 57, 130; shifts attack from indispensable divine law to technical flaws in bull, 66–67, 234; deception of Wolsey and secret missions to Rome, 38–41; effort to clear impediments between him and Anne, 38–53, 182, 251, 252, 254, 256, 277, cf. 232, 257–58; desire to remarry before annulment not bigamous, 39–40, 213; and dissolubility of unconsummated marriage, 16–17, 42, 49–51, 182, 229–31, 251, 252–53, 254, 257–58, 262–63, 264–65, 273–75, 277–78; desires protestation from Clement, 39, 41

1528: his book on the marriage read by Clement, 113; meetings with Campeggio (Oct.), 59; and marriage of his daughter to his son, 33n; visits Catherine and appoints counsel for her, 59–60; rebukes Catherine upon her revelation of the brief (Nov.), 62–63; speech at Bridewell (8 Nov.), 65–66, 81, 86n, 174; his reaction to the brief, 65, 67, 186; and inquiry into bigamy, 40

1529: cited to legatine court (1 June),

81–82, 84–86, 92; present in court (21 June), 81–82, 84–86, 92; addressed by cardinals in articles against the marriage (25 June) with charge of Catherine's consummation canceled, 90–92, 96–97, 207, cf. 111; his deposition submitted with allegation of dispensation (28 June), 95, 207, 208–9; as defender of the bond, 81, 94, 95, 116; his answer, if any, to charge of consummation not known, 91, 95–97, 109, 207, 209; his deposition listed among exhibits, 95n, 208–9; angered by Fisher, assigns Gardiner to respond in his name, 98; reads response in court and is countered by Fisher (July), 81–84, 99; his early denial of consummation cited in court, 107; his counsel attempt to prove consummation, 93–94, 117; his book submitted to court, 113; present at the last session (23 July), 127; reaction to adjournment, 128–29, cf. 173; secures promise from Campeggio and restricts movements, 96, 128; refuses to send powers of attorney to papal court, 143, cf. 161–62, 165, 173, 214; tells queen he will use public-honesty argument (Oct.), 129–31, 137, 139, 140, 152–53, 155, 173, 179; receives pope's letter of 7 Oct. with Catherine's challenge and delays response, 131, 141, 153; displeasure at letter imparted to pope, 141; and Cranmer, 175–76, 222–23, 233–35

1530: campaigns for academic support, 131, 142–43, 173–80; response to pope (July), 142–43; failure to respond to Catherine's challenge concerning her virginity, 131, 141–42, 144–46, 179–80; privately claims he could not tell if she was a virgin, 96, 145, 270, 276, cf. 193; says he does not remember, 145n

1531: his white paper published (Apr. and Nov.), 180–83, 184n, 190, 222, 223, *see also Determinations* treatise; sends councillors to argue consummation with queen (31 May), 191; receives two determinations against papal citation (June), 193; desire to try the marriage in local court and Warham's refusal, 175n, 193; offers the see of York to Pole and is refused, 193–94; sends arguments for consummation to Rome (July), 153; leaves Catherine for good and sends her a rebuke, 192; appoints Lee Archbishop of York, 194; fails in campaign for academic divinization of public honesty, 193, 217–18, 235, 277, cf. 174–75, 176–80, 204, 205; and Silvester Darius, 158–59

1532: rebuked by pope (Jan.), 149; sends queen's *libellus* to Rome as argument that she admitted consummation, 130, 153–55, 161, 179, cf. 103, 214, 238; and investigation of Percy contract (June), 253–54; as supposed contributor to *A Glass of the Truth*, 198n, cf. 175n; elevates Anne to Marquisate of Pembroke and goes on "honeymoon," 149, cf. 252; decides on Cranmer as Archbishop of

Canterbury, 194–95, 222, cf. 175n, 231n; threatened with excommunication (Nov.), 149; gets Anne pregnant, 149, 162, 195–96, 213

1533: marries Anne privately, 165, 196, 205, 211–13, 229, 237; rediscovers treaty and exploits statement of consummation, 124, 162, 164, 196–97, 199, cf. 210, 223, 236, 237; and Cranmer's *Twelve Articles*, 204, 207, 222–24, 229, 230, 232–35, 237, 247–48, 262; presses bishops to authorize local trial (Feb.), 197; and the restraint of appeals to Rome (March), 198, 204; reconvenes Convocation, 198; requires answer from Convocation, 201; states Catherine's consummation to Chapuys, 204, cf. 207; as Supreme Head, 203, 231n, 262–63, cf. 198; his permission for trial requested by Cranmer, 266; cited to trial at Dunstable, 205; refers Chapuys and his protestation to council, 205; empowers Bell as his proctor, 205, 206–9; does not respond personally to charges, 207; his legatine deposition exhibited, 208–9; his counsel at Dunstable, 206, 210; marriage declared null (23 May), 4, 210–11, 212–13, 217, 220, 246, 281; no longer insists on natural law, 211, cf. 143, 176, 178, 185, 199–200; intention of having Cranmer issue statement on consummation after trial, 237–38, 296, cf. 88, 155; has Cranmer set up trial to validate marriage to Anne, 211–13, 214, 232, cf. 218; perhaps remarries Anne, 211, 213; his excusator at Rome refused, 214; his excusator finally excluded (4 July), 165; appeals to a general council (5 July), 214; sends justification to Charles, relying on queen's *libellus* (6 July), 103, 214–15, 238; does not want war with Charles, 216; marriage to Catherine declared not against divine law at Rome, 165, 166, 168–69; excommunicated, but sentence not carried out (11 July), 167, 168; given till 1 Oct. to produce legatine records in Rome, 3–4, 76, 165–67, 169, 216; his deposition removed from legatine acts, 95, 209; missions to France and Germany, 216

1534: still collecting evidence for consummation, 164n; rejects French site for papal trial, 168; reconvenes "Reformation Parliament," orders opponents not to attend, 216–17; sent appeal by Cardinal Cajetan, 230–31; marriage to Catherine declared valid in Rome (23 Mar.), 169; and first Act of Succession, 217–20, 241, 248; marriage to Anne declared by Parliament to be approved by the universities, 217–18, cf. 160n; tries to have Catherine submit to the act, 220

1535: rebuked by Reginald Pole, 257

1536: disenchanted with Anne and suspects her of having used witchcraft, 241–42; reaction to death of Catherine, 241; new thoughts on divine displeasure,

241–42; constructs a case for nullity, 242–43; wishes to bastardize Elizabeth, 244; Anne's treasonous conduct toward him, 242–43, 255; reported lack of virility, 243, cf. 271; fear of supporting papal authority, 243–44; summoned to trial by Cranmer in chapel in Lambeth Palace, 244; his proctor and counsel at trial, 245, 250; marriage annulled (17 May), 4, 213, 246–47; current thoughts on his two marriages, 247–48, 251, 257; dispensed from third-degree affinity *ex coitu illicito* (19 May), betroths and marries Jane Seymour, 259–60

1537–38: and Duchess of Milan, 14n

1540: disappointed in Anne of Cleves, 261; cannot consummate marriage, 261, 270–71, cf. 14n, 273–74; seeks new annulment, 261; reasons for act eliminating the impediments of precontract and kinship, 261–65, 273–75; grants petition for annulment proceedings (6 July), 264, 265–66; deposition at trial, 267, 269–70; doubts Anne's virginity, 270, 276, cf. 273; marriage annulled (9 July), 4, 14n, 264, 266–73; justifies action to Duke of Cleves, 273–74; consummated fifth marriage intended to dissolve fourth in virtue of act on precontract, 263, 265, 273–74, cf. 14n

1540–42: marriage with Catherine Howard, 261, 262–63, 275–76, 277–78

1543: marriage to Catherine Parr, 276, 278

last thoughts on virginity, 276; his conscience and his marriages, summarized, 276–78; death (Jan. 1547), 279, cf. 248; his laws repealed, 279, 281–82, 284–85

Herbert, Edward, 1st Baron Herbert of Cherbury, 76

Hering, John, 208

Herod, King, 33, 71, 98, 285

Hogesteden, ambassador from Cleves, 268–69

Holland, Margaret, widow of John Beaufort, Earl of Somerset, dispensed to marry her nephew-in-law, Thomas, Duke of Clarence (1411), 9–10, 11, 13, 45–46

Hostiensis, Cardinal (Henry of Susa, Bishop of Ostia, d. 1271), 227, 293

Howard, Catherine, Queen of England, 261, 262–63, 275–76, 277–78, cf. 43, 259

Howard, Elizabeth, mother of Anne Boleyn, 47–48, 232, 249

Howard, Thomas, Duke of Norfolk: witness at legatine court (1529), 101, 112, 119, 122, cf. 111n; stops debate on determinations in Commons (1531), 190–91; wishes to try the marriage in secular court (Feb. 1532), 176; examines Percy on his precontract (June 1532), 253; professes ignorance of particulars of Anne's marriage to king (1533), 205; Lord High Steward in Boleyn treason trial (1536), 255; commissioner for Cleves marriage (1539–40), 265–66, 267–68; accuses Cromwell of treason

(1540), 261; petitions trial of Cleves marriage, 265–66; signs deposition for trial, 268

Hugh of St. Victor, theologian (d. 1141), 181–82, 184–85, 187

Hughes, Anthony, 267n

Hughes, John, D.Cn.L. (a married layman, d. 1543): employed in Wolsey's faculty office, 89; promoter at legatine court, 28n, 80, 89, 101, 102, 108–9, 110, 113–14, 119, 120, 124, 125, 127, 130, 137, 209; counsel for Henry at Dunstable trial, 206; on fact-finding committee in Cleves trial, 271

Hugo ("Henry") of Pavia, 69–71, 183, 185–86

Hussey, Sir John, 94, 112

illegitimation of Mary and Elizabeth, 219, 219n, 244, 247, 275, 281, 282, 283

impediments to marriage, *see* affinity, conditional contract, consanguinity, consent (lack of), error of condition or of person, force and fear, impotency, legal kinship, precontract, public honesty, spiritual kinship, *and* witchcraft

impotency, impediment of, 249, 271, 280, cf. 148–49, 192–93

incest, history of legal, 3, 5–14, 33–34, 233, 279–85. *See also* Henry VIII, scruples about incest (*1527*)

Innocent III, Pope (1198–1216): on affinity (ref. to CIC X 4.13.7), 226; forbids dispensations in Levitical degrees, 26; institutes the inquisition, 4, 21–22, 78; on marriage before puberty, 105; permits levirate, 14–15, 139, cf. 141; on presumptive consent (X 4.1.26), 227; reduces forbidden degrees of consanguinity, affinity, and public honesty, 7, 46, 107, 138n, 156. *See also Decretals of Gregory IX*

Innocent IV, Pope (1243–54), 139n, 141, 225

inquisition: *ex officio mero*, 4–5, 21–23, 77–78, 89–90, 102, 102n, 112n, 148, 205–6, 211–12, 242, 244, 250, 266; *ex officio mero, mixto, vel promoto*, 266. *See also* trials

Inquisition, Papal, in Spain, 11, 115, cf. 22n, 26n

instance trials, 4, 22n, 89–90, 102n, 112n, 211–12, 213n, 266, cf. 81

Isabella, Queen of Castile, 15, 237; attests to Catherine's virginity, 151, 162, 197; objects to Catherine's marrying Henry VII, 151n; receives brief before dying, 97, 104, 125; objects to statement of consummation, 97, 156, 198; death (26 Nov. 1504), 27, 28, 54–55, 104–5, 108, 122, cf. 111, 152

Islip (Yselip), John, Abbot of Westminster (d. 1532), 120, 124, 125

Iuvenis, see Decretals of Gregory IX, 4.1.3

Jaén, Cardinal of (Stephen Gabriel Merino, Archbishop of Bari, Patriarch of the West Indies, d. 1535), 167

James I, King of Scotland, 11

Jeanne of Valois, St., Queen of France (d. 1505, canonized 1950), 14n

Jews: expulsion of, 15; practices of, 12, 15, 106, 200, 225. *See also* Deuteronomy, Hebraic scholarship, levirate, Leviticus, Mosaic law

John the Baptist, 33, 71, 92, 98, 285

John III, King of Portugal, nephew of Catherine of Aragon, 150

John XXIII, Pope (Balthasar Cossa, 1410–15), 9–11, 12, 14

John XXIII, Pope (Angelo Roncalli, 1958–63), 10n

Jourdemayne, Margery ("the Witch of Eye"), 242

Julian, Pope (= Pseudo-Julius I), 225

Julius II, Pope (1503–13):

1504: hesitates to grant dispensation, 14, cf. 161; writes Henry VII that dispensation will be granted (6 July), 104, 125; sends brief of dispensation, dated 26 Dec. 1503, to dying Isabella (arrives 24 Nov.), 14, 58, 62n, 104, 125, 198; on Isabella's protest, inserts doubt of consummation (*forsan*) into bull, also dated 26 Dec. 1503, 97, 156, 198, *see also forsan*

1505: sends bull to England (Mar.), 105, cf. 1, 103

1527: his power to dispense doubted by Henry, 1, 14–16, 21, 32–33, 34–35, 65–66, 81, 83, 222–23, 230, 234–35; Henry searches for technical flaws in bull, 17, 35–37, 66, 234; power questioned in Westminster trial (May), 24, 26, 66, cf. 82; his bull submitted by Henry in defense of his marriage, 25; his bull attacked on technical grounds, 26–28; Fisher's views on dispensation, 29, 58–59, 82–83, 97; Wolsey's technical objections to bull, 29–32, 54–59, 61–62, 65, 66–67, 137–38, 157–58, 173–74, 234; doubt of power reported to Rome by Wolsey, 66–67, 173–74

1528: Catherine relies on bull and brief, 61–62; his power and bull's flaws discussed by West and opponent, 67–74; Henry expresses doubt of power and desire to test validity to Campeggio (Oct.), 59, 66; brief revealed by Catherine (Nov.), 62–64, 67; Catherine protests against brief's statement of consummation, 64–65; brief states claim to act "from other causes", 65, 85, 106; brief termed a forgery, 63, 67, 139, 160, 208, 215

1529: bull and brief objected to by Casale, 138–39; original of brief unobtainable by Henry, 67, 186; original of brief inspected by Lee and Ghinucci, 160, 208; bull and brief sent by Catherine to Rome, 196; dispensation cited by Henry at legatine court in defense of marriage (28 June), 95; bull and brief submitted by Henry's proctor (5 July), 101, 116, 238n; formal objections to bull, 101–2, 103, 108–12, 114, 115, 116–17, 121–22,

137; formal objections to brief, 101–2, 108, 111–12, 119, cf. 97; objections to bull answered by queen's counsel, 102, 103, 105–9, 110–11, 114, 115, 117–18, *see also libellus*, queen's; power to dispense questioned, 106, 110, cf. 91, 97, 105–6, 113, 123, 124; bull's *forsan* cited, 99, 108, 111, 117–18; brief's statement of consummation used by Gardiner, 99; brief's "other causes" cited, 107; his letters to Henry VII exhibited, 125; bull's silence on public honesty cited by Henry to Catherine (Oct.), 129–31, 139, 140, 153, *see also* public honesty; his dispensation discussed by Clement VII, 139–42, 143–44, 146

1530: his power questioned in universities, 143–44, 173–80, cf. 180–89, 193, 204, 205, 219–20, 220–21, 223

1531–33: defects of dispensations debated at Rome, 150, 151–56; his power questioned at Rome, 150, 152; brief's authenticity accepted by Henry's supporters, 152, 160, 215, 236–37, cf. 99

1533: his power denied by Cranmer in *Twelve Articles*, 224–28, 232; power questioned in both convocations, 199–203; his dispensation cited and submitted by Bell for Henry at Dunstable, 207, 208; his power denied by Cranmer at trial, 211; power questioned and flaws of bull and brief urged to emperor, 214–15

1533–34: power confirmed at Rome, 159, 165–66, 168–69, 220

1534: power denied by Parliament, 218–19; power denied by Tunstall to queen, 220–21

See also affinity (degrees of, and divine law), divine law (and dispensability), *and* public honesty (Henry's theology)

jurisdiction, ecclesiastical:
of archdeacons, 5, cf. 22–23; of bishops' consistories, 22n, 129, 216, 266, *see also* Ligham; of bishops, 193; of convocation, 271–72; of archbishops as metropolitans and *legati nati*, 81, 175n, 193, 206, 232–33, 271, cf. 197, 200, *and see* Ligham; of Wolsey as permanent *legatus a latere*, 3, 22–23, 24, 80, 89, 193; of specially commissioned *legati a latere*, 54, 77–78, 92, 283, cf. 26n, 61, 79, 84, *and see* legatine court; of pope, 23, 199, 232–33, *see also* canon law, Clement VII (Medici), dispensation, *and* papal trial; of pope, denied, 198, 205, 256, *see also* divine law and dispensability *and* Julius II; of a general council, 214, *and see* Lateran Council

assumed by Parliament, 198, 219, 256, 262, 263–64, 273, 274, 279, 281, 281n, cf. 175n–76n; of Cranmer and others under Henry as Supreme Head, 196–97, 198, 201, 219, 233, 259–60, 265–66, 271–73, 278

kings-of-arms, 125, cf. 258
Kingston, Sir William, 259
kinship, impediments of: by adoption, *see* legal kinship; by blood, *see* consanguinity; by coitus, *see* affinity; by marriage, *see* affinity *and* public honesty; by sacramental function, *see* spiritual kinship

Kite, John, former Archbishop of Armagh, Bishop of Carlisle and titular Archbishop of Thebes (d. 1537), 82, 101, 111n, 112, 121–22, 123

Knight, William, D.C.L., Archdeacon of Chester and of Richmond, Bishop of Bath and Wells in 1541 (d. 1547), secretary to Henry VIII, 38–42

Lambeth, parish church of, 208
Lambeth Palace chapel, site of Anne Boleyn's annulment trial, 244
Lambeth Palace gallery, site of validation trial of Anne Boleyn's marriage, 212
Landriano, battle of, 136
Lateran Council, Fourth, 7, 21–22
law, *see* canon, civil, divine, natural, *and* positive law; *see also* Parliament
lawyers, *see* canonists
Layton, Richard, D.C.L., Dean of York, 267
Lee, Edward, D.Th., the king's almoner, Archdeacon of Colchester and of Surrey, Archbishop of York in 1531 (d. 1544): examines original brief of Julius II in Spain (1529), 160, cf. 208; disputes with Catherine (1531), 191–92; appointed archbishop, 194, 195; refuses to try Henry's marriage, 194; inquisitor into Percy's contract (1532), 5, 253–54; resists authorizing a local trial (1533), 197; and Convocation of York, 202; forbidden to attend Parliament (1534), 216–17; disputes with Catherine, 220–21; at Convocation trial of Cleves marriage (1540), 266–67, cf. 271

legal kinship, impediment of, 43, 258, 285, cf. 263
legate: *a latere*, 22, cf. 54; *natus*, 211n. *See also* jurisdiction

legatine court at Blackfriars (1529):
papal commission for, 3, 59, 75, 77–78, 113n, 142, 157; inquisitional procedure in, 78, 89–90, 206–7
sessions of: (1) Monday 31 May, 3, 75, 77–78, 135; (2) Friday 18 June, 78–80, 85, 86, cf. 73–74; (3) Monday 21 June, 80–87, 88n, 92; (3a) Tuesday 22 June, 87–88; (4) Friday 25 June, 87, 89–92, 97; (5) Monday 28 June, 87–88, 92–97, 101, 114, 120–21, 122; (6) Monday 5 July, 74, 101, 108, 120–21, 122; (7) Friday 9 July, 101–2, 108–12, 122; (8) Monday 12 July, 109, 112, 120–21; (9) Wednesday 14 July, 112, 119–20; (10) Friday 16 July, 74, 120; (11) Monday 19 July, 120–25; (12) Wednesday 21 July, 74, 125–27; (13) Friday 23 July, 74, 127–28
Catherine's appearances in court, 79–80, 81, 84–87; her proctor, 80, cf. 87–88, 92, 234; Henry's appearances, 81–86, 92, 99, 127; his proctors, *see* Bell *and* Sampson; Catherine's motions against court rejected, 85, 87, 89; Catherine declared contumacious, 87, 89, 90, 92–93, 94, 95,

101; actions of Catherine's counsel, 72, 81–82, 84, 87–88, 92–94, 96–99, 102–3, 103–4, 105–9, 110, 112–13, 114, 117–18, 130, 138n, 153–54, 209, 214–15, 238; articles against marriage, 90–92, 120–22; the marriage charged with being against divine law, 91, 97, 105–6, 110, 123, cf. 74, 107, 113, 124; charge of consummation deleted from Henry's article, 91, 96–97, 207; Henry's deposition, 95–97, 109, 207, 208–9; Henry's allegation of papal dispensation in defense of marriage, 95; consummation of Catherine's first marriage discussed, 74, 90–91, 93–94, 95–98, 99, 107, 108, 109, 111, 114–18, 122–23, 124, 130; witnesses sworn in, 74, 94–95, 101, 112, 119, 120–21, 209, cf. 126; promoter's objections against bull and brief, 27n–28n, 102–3, cf. 105–8, 109–11; cardinal's articles against bull and brief, 101–2, 109–12, 120–22; public honesty discussed, 27n–28n, 73, 85–86, 99–100, 107, 109, 114–19, 121, *see also* public honesty; third articulation of objections by cardinals, 119, 120–22; depositions of witnesses submitted, 74, 80n, 120–24, 126–27, *see also* depositions; Henry's protestation produced, and fourth articulation by cardinals, 125–26; exhibits at court, 68n, 79–80, 83, 95, 98, 101, 112–14, 120, 124–25, 209, cf. 102–3; adjournment, 127–29, 165, 173

reaction in Rome, 136; queen's acts at court submitted to Rome (1531), 76n, 88n, 165–69; discussed by Chapuys (1533), 204; acts of court submitted to Dunstable court, 208–9; acts required in Rome by 1 Oct., 3–4, 76, 165, 167, 169, 216; record prepared by Clayburgh and Watkins, authenticated by Wootton (1 Oct.), 3–4, 75–128 (esp. 75–76, 79, 91, 95–96, 113, 124, 127–28), 207, 209, 216; events of 21 June and Henry's deposition removed, 76, 80, 95, 208–9

See also Campeggio, Catherine of Aragon, Henry VIII, Julius II, *and* Wolsey

Legh, Thomas, D.C.L. (later knighted), 206, 245

Leo X, Pope (1513–21), 11n, 22, 23n

levirate, law of (Deuteronomy 25), 14–16, 35, 99, 106, 113, 139, 139n, 141, 184–85, 185n, 186, 200, 202, 225, 284

Leviticus, prohibitions of: degrees named, 6n, 218, cf. 219, 247, 279, 280–81, 283–85; dispensed, before Henry's time, 9–15, during his time, 170, cf. 15, after his time, 283, cf. 284–85; and divine law, *see* affinity and divine law; Henry's reading of, 32–33, 34–35, 234–35, *see also* Henry VIII (*1509–27*: scruples over incest; *1527*: new thoughts on public honesty and affinity from illicit coitus); original meaning of, 12; and restriction to living relatives, 12, 71, 185, 185n, 218, 230, 284, cf. 37n, 199–200, 281; text of, 33, 35, 68, 68n, 187n, 224

libellus: as legal brief, 89–90, 212, 266, cf. 3,

102; queen's, 72, 102–9, 112, 114–15, 118, 130, 138n, sent by Henry to Rome, 103, 153–55, 161, 214, cf. 179, pressed upon Cranmer, 155, 238, sent by Henry to emperor's court, 103, 155, 214–15; as treatise submitted to court, 68n, 112–14, 209

Ligham, Peter, D.Cn.L., Dean of the Arches and Official of the Metropolitan Court of Canterbury in 1525, Commissary General of Canterbury (i.e., judge of diocesan consistory court) in 1532, still in 1534 (d. 1538), 76n, 88n, 92, 108, 112, 118, 168, 202

Livonians (Latvians), dispensed for levirate, 139n

Loazes, Ferdinand de, D.Cn.C.L., Apostolic Inquisitor against Heresy and Apostasy at Barcelona (wrongly identified with Cardinal John Garcias de Loaysa, Bishop of Osma and later Bishop of Sigüenza and Archbishop of Seville), 115–16

"local solution" (trial in England), 175, 175n, 193–95, 196–97, 198

Lombard, Peter, theologian, Bishop of Paris (d. ca. 1160), 106

Longland, John, D. Th., Bishop of Lincoln (d. 1547): and Henry's scruple (1527), 81–82; named at Westminster trial as future consultant, 29; cites Henry to legatine court (1529), 78–79; signs statement of 1 July, 82; attends legatine court, 111n, 112n; as late witness, does not testify, 119, 120; addresses Parliament on determinations (1531), 190–91; in Convocation (1533), 200, 202; Cranmer's assistant at Dunstable, 206

Lording, George, copyist of legatine record, 75, 91

lords, spiritual and temporal, letter of, to Clement VII (July 1530), 143–44

Lorraine, Duke of, 268–69; son of, *see* Francis of Lorraine

Louis XI, King of France, 11

Louis XII, King of France, 14n

Lüneburg, fictitious imprint of, 13n, 188n, 198n

Lutherans, views and influence of, 216, 252n, 280, cf. 195

Lyranus, Lyre, *see* Nicholas of Lyre

Mai, Michael, Charles V's ambassador in Rome, 135–36, 148–50, 157–59, 166, 167, 198

Margaret of Anjou, Queen of England (wife of Henry VI), 32

Margaret of Austria, 135

Marmaduke, Dr., chaplain to Wolsey, 158

marriage: jurisdiction over, 4–5, 21–23, 175, 175n, 193, 196–97, 198, 199, 256–57, 266, 281n, *see also* jurisdiction; Roman Catholic tribunals for, 40, 140–41, 166, *and see* trials; *see also* annulment, betrothal, clandestine marriage, consummation of marriage, contract, dispensation, divorce, impediments, precontract, *and* solemnization

Martin V, Pope (1417–31), 10–11, 12, 229n,
cf. 26n
Mary and Joseph, marriage of, 226, 228
Mary I, daughter of Henry VIII and
Catherine of Aragon (b. 1516), Queen of
England (1553–58): birth of, 104, cf. 32;
as princess, 65, 84; and marriage to half-
brother, 33n; illegitimated, 219, 219n,
244, 247, 281; as queen, 32, 194, 281–82
Mates, Peter, 119, 121
Matilda, Empress ("Lady of England and
Normandy"), 32
Mendoza, Iñigo de, imperial ambassador to
England: learns of Westminster inquisi-
tion (1527), 234, cf. 66n; and brief of
Julius II, 63–64; advises Catherine against
stressing virginity, 60, 73; and Catherine's
mandate (1529), 135
metropolitans, *see* jurisdiction
Milan, Duchess of (Christina, daughter of
Christian II of Denmark, niece of Charles
V), 14n
Montini, Floriano, Campeggio's secretary
and clerk of the legatine court, 77, 80,
86n, 92–94, 95, 144, cf. 112, 127
More, Sir Thomas: goes to France during
legatine trial, 82; as chancellor, 190–91;
resigns as chancellor, 175n; prevents his
attainder, 217; on Anne Boleyn, 245n;
early life of, *see* Rastell
Morice, Ralph, 175
Mosaic law, 7, 185. *See also* Deuteronomy,
levirate, *and* Leviticus
Moscosco, Dr., 174
Motta, B., papal secretary, 41
Muscetula (Muxetula), John Anthony,
imperial ambassador in Rome, 80n

natural law, 7, 143, 176, 178, 185, 199–200,
210–11, 224–25
Nicholas of Lyre (Lyra, Lyranus), Fran-
ciscan exegete (d. ca. 1340), 181–82,
184, 187, 224
Niño, Rodrigo, 145–46, 178–79
Noellet, William, Cardinal (d. 1394), 8
Norfolk, Agnes, Duchess of, 119–20, 208
Norfolk, Duke of, *see* Howard, Thomas
Norris, Henry, 245, 255, 259, cf. 242–43
Northumberland, Earls of, 45. *See also* Percy
Novati, Jerome, Auditor of the Rota in
1533, 189
Nun of Kent, *see* Barton
Nuremberg, 195

obreption, obreptitious (deliberate falsi-
fying), 97, 110, cf. 215, 292n
official (= ecclesiastical judge), 76n, 129,
168, 216, 266. *See also* Gwent *and* Wootton
Olisleger, ambassador from Cleves, 268–69
Orléans, 143, 178, 193, 199, 217. *See also*
determinations
Ormond, *see* Butler, Sir Piers, *and* Boleyn,
Sir Thomas
Ortiz, Dr. Peter, Charles V's proctor in
Rome, 146–47, 148–49, 159n, 168–70,
181, 192
Orvieto, 52, 54

Osiander (Hosemann), Andreas (d. 1552),
195
Owen, Sir David, 101, 112, 119, 120, 122
Oxford, Earl of, *see* Vere
Oxford, University of, 143, 175–77, 209,
217. *See also* determinations

Pace, Richard, secretary to the king, Dean
of St. Paul's (d. 1536), 35–36
Padua, 143n, 145, 177–78, 199, 217. *See also*
determinations
Paland, Elbert, Marshall of Cleves, 269
Palant the younger, 274n
Panormitanus (Nicholas Tudeschi), Abbot
of Palermo (d. 1445), 73, 116, 227, 229,
290, 291, 293
papal trial of Henry VIII's marriage to
Catherine of Aragon: advocation, 128,
136; preliminaries, 76n, 135–37, 143, 148–
50, 164–65, 165–66, 167–68, 173, 192–93,
214; formal sessions of Rota and Consistory, 165–67, 168–69, cf. 4
Parasceve (response to *A Glass of the
Truth*), 197–98, 198n
Paris, University of, 131, 143, 174–75, 178,
180, 188, 193–94, 199–200, 204, 205, 217.
See also determinations
Parker, Matthew, Archbishop of Canterbury
(1559–75), 283
Parliament:
of Henry VIII:
—*1531*: determinations discussed, 190–
91
—*1532*: urged by Norfolk to approve
secular trial of Henry's marriage, 176n
—*1533*: Act in Restraint of Appeals to
Rome (24 c. 12), 198
—*1534*: reconvened (Jan.), 216; Catherine's consummation and annulment
and Anne's marriage declared, Fisher and
Abel named in attainder of Elizabeth
Barton (25 c. 12), 160n, 217; further
papal dispensations prohibited (25 c. 21),
256; Act of Succession (25 c. 22), 6n,
217–20, 233, 279, repealed in 1536, 233,
246–47, again repealed in 1553, 281;
Campeggio and Ghinucci deprived of
bishoprics (25 c. 27), 160n
—*1536*: second Act of Succession (28 c.
7), 233, 245n, 246–49, 250, 251, 257, 277,
279, 281; papal dispensations invalidated
and revalidated with exceptions (28 c.
16), 256–57, 277
—*1540*: Dissolution of the Pretensed
Marriage with the Lady Anne of Cleves
(32 c. 25, 16 July), 273; Concerning
Precontract and Degrees of Consanguinity
(32 c. 38, 5 July), 46n, 256, 261–64,
273, section on precontract repealed in
1548, 264, 279, the whole repealed in
1553, 281–82, the section on degrees of
kinship resurrected in 1559, 282; attainder
of Featherstone, Abel, Powell, and others
(32 c. 59), cf. 188n; attainder of Cromwell (32 c. 62, 29 June), 261
—*1542*: attainder of Catherine Howard
(33 c. 21), 275–76

—*1544*: third Act of Succession (35 c.
1), 282n
  of other rulers, 194, 242, 264, 279–85
  passim
Parr, Catherine, Queen of England, 276,
  278, cf. 43, 259
Paul III (Cardinal Alexander Farnese),
  Pope (1534–49), 167n, 169–70
Paul VI, Pope (1963–), 188n
Pauline privilege, 232
peace, motive of, 28, 54–55, 58–59, 70, 72,
  106, 110–11, 122, 150, 152, 166, cf. 140
Penitentiary, Roman, 47
Percy, Henry, 5th Earl of Northumberland
  (d. 1527), 254
Percy, Henry, 6th Earl of Northumberland
  (d. 1537): kinship to Henry VIII, 44–46,
  258–59; alleged marriage to Anne, 44,
  50–51, 243n, 253–54, 277, cf. 252; investigated in 1532, 5, 253–55, 255–56; investigated in 1536, 243, 245, cf. 251, 252–
  53, 255–56, 276; present at Anne's treason
  trial, 255
Peter of Ancarano, canonist (d. 1416), 10,
  13, 14–15
Peter of La Palu (Paludanus, de Palude),
  O.P., theologian, Patriarch of Jerusalem
  (d. 1342), 225, 235
Peto (Peyto), William, M.A., Observant
  Franciscan, later Bishop of Salisbury
  (d. 1558), published, but probably did
  not write, the *Parasceve*, 198n
Philalethes Hyperboreus, 197–98, 198n
Philip II, King of Spain and of England,
  281–83
Pisan popes, *see* Alexander V *and* John
  XXIII (Cossa)
Pius II, Pope (1458–64), 12–13
Pole, Reginald, Cardinal in 1536, legate
  a latere to England, Archbishop of
  Canterbury in 1556 (d. 1558), 193–94,
  196, 257, 282
pollution (seminal emission), 226, 235, 271
pope: as Bishop of Rome, 231n, 257, 262,
  274; his dispensations invalidated, 256,
  277; and power to dispense from divine
  law, *see* divine law and dispensability
  and Julius II; *for individual popes, see*
  Alexander, Boniface, Clement, Eugenius,
  Gregory, Innocent, John, Julian, Julius,
  Leo, Martin, Paul, Pius, Urban, *and*
  Decretals of Gregory IX
positive law, 139, 141, 159, 165–66; *see also*
  affinity and divine law *and* public honesty, Henry's theology denied
Powell, Edward, D.Th. (d. 1540), 188n, 202
Poyntz (Poynes), Sir Anthony, 94–95
Praepositus (John Anthony of San
  Gregorio), Auditor of the Rota, Bishop
  of Alexandria, Cardinal, and Patriarch
  of Jerusalem (d. 1509), 70–71
precontract (= previous marriage): defined,
  49; as impediment to marriage, 5, 194,
  262; of Henry Percy (q.v.), Anne Boleyn
  (q.v.), and Anne of Cleves (q.v.), *see*
  Henry VIII (*1527*: and dissolubility of
  unconsummated marriage); impediment

revoked in 1540, 262–64; still held as
  binding by Convocation after revocation,
  264, 272–73; reinstated in 1548, 264, 279
presumptions of law, *see* consummation of
  marriage, presumptions of
promoter of the faith (devil's advocate), 23
promoter of the judge's office (promoter of
  justice), 23, 80, 89–90. *See also* Hughes
  (John) *and* Wolman
promotion of *ex officio* trial, 266
propositio omnium quae in facto consistunt,
  112, 112n, 120, 125, 127, cf. 267
Pseudo-Isidore, 6–7
puberty, *see* contract *and* Henry VIII (*1503
  and 1505*)
public honesty or decency: impediment
  arising from matrimonial contract, 16,
  27, history of, 33–34, 70; arises also
  from betrothal, 34, 44, 51–52; arises
  even from invalid contracts, 50; defined
  anew as affinity from illicit coitus, 233,
  259–60; included under affinity, 73, 107,
  115–16, 117–18, 156; regarded as affinity,
  146–47, 233; second and third genera of,
  156; termed quasi-affinity, 179
  between Anne Boleyn and Henry VIII,
  38–39, 43, 44–46, 49–52, 258
  between Catherine of Aragon and
  Henry VIII: dispensation to be sought
  by terms of 1503 treaty, 103; dispensation
  granted only for affinity, 30; arguments:
  (1) the Wolman objection against the
  bull (both affinity and public honesty
  present only affinity removed), 27, 30, 31,
  73, 107, 109, 114–16, 130, 137–38, 155,
  cf. 86, 99–100; (2) the Wolsey objection
  against the bull (only public honesty
  present and not removed), 30–31, 32, 33,
  35, 37–38, 55–56, 67, 73, 109–10, 111, 114,
  117–18, 121–22, 129–31, 137–38, 139, 140,
  152–56, 157, 173, 179, 214–15, 234, 248,
  cf. 116; (3) Henry's theology (public
  honesty in Levitical degrees is divine
  and indispensable), 31–33, 34–35, 67, 68–
  70, 71, 138–39, 178–79, 181–83, 190, 193,
  200, 219, 222–23, 224–33, 247–48, 257,
  276–77, 279, cf. 176–77, 281–82, 283; (4)
  Henry's theology denied, 16, 30, 35–37,
  70, 107, 118–19, 124, 139–40, 166, 178–79,
  179–80, 183–90, 193, 247, 263
  chronological survey of arguments:
  —*1527*: Bishop Fox's statement that
  only affinity had been dispensed, 30;
  Wolman's objection at Westminster
  inquisition, 27, 30, 31, 73, 109; Wolsey's
  argument and Henry's angry reaction,
  30–31, 32, 33, 37, 38, 117, 155, 234;
  Henry formulates his theology, 31–33,
  34–35, 52, 67, 119, 222, 234–35, 276–77;
  Wakefield's denial of his theology, 35–37
  —*1528*: Gardiner to discuss Wolsey's
  argument with Staphileus, 55–56, 100,
  137, 157, 160; Staphileus's probable response and Geminianus's version of the
  Wolman objection, 137–38; Henry's
  theology supported in Alexander III's
  Ad audientiam and argued in *A Com-*

pendious Annotation, 67–70, 71, 183;
Wolman argument in *Annotation* refuted by West, 72–73, 115–16
—*1529*: Casale urges Wolman argument
and divine status, 138–39; the uncleared
impediment denied by Catherine at
legatine court, 85–86; its divine status
implicitly denied by Gardiner, 99; Wolman argument alluded to by Gardiner,
99–100; Wolman argument raised by
Hughes and answered in queen's *libellus*,
27n–28n, 107, 109–10, 114–16, 130, 137,
154–55, 214–15, cf. 102; John Andreae's
form of the Wolman objection cited, 107,
114–15, 138; its divine status rejected by
queen's counsel and by theologians at
court, 107, 124; Wolsey argument formally
articulated by cardinals, 109, 111, 114,
117, 121–22, 130, 155, cf. 31–32, 97–98,
100; Wolman argument raised by Henry's
proctors, 116–17; Wolsey argument refuted by queen's counsel, 109–10, 117–18,
cf. 85–86; no witnesses testify on cardinals'
article, 121–22; Sanders's references to,
114, 116–18, 146–47; Henry threatens
Catherine with using the Wolsey argument in Rome (Oct.), 129–31, 137, 139,
140, 152–53, 155, 173, 179; Clement's
denial of divine status and probable reaction to Wolsey argument, 139–40, 179,
cf. 131, 143–44, 146–47, 155–56, 166;
Henry's theology set forth by Burgo,
Edward Fox, and Stokesley in treatise
later attached to determinations, 180, 181–
83, 190, 200, cf. 223; Henry's probable
discussion of his theology with Cranmer
at this time, 222–23, 233–35, cf. 175
—*1530*: Henry fails to get university
support for his theology, 176–79, cf. 144–
45, 187–88; Henry's current thoughts on
his theology and Wolsey's argument,
179–80
—*1531*: Wolman argument answered
by Loazes (5 June), 115–16; Henry's
theology in *Determinations* treatise (pub.
Apr. and Nov.) refuted by Fisher, 181,
183–86, 190, 224; Henry fails to get
Parisian support for his theology, 193,
217–18, cf. 204, 205
—*1532*: Henry sends queen's *libellus* to
Rome and rephrases Wolman objection in
Wolsey form, 153–56, 179; Henry's
theology in *Determinations* treatise refuted
by Abel, 186–88; Abel's attack not
answered, 188–89; Wolsey argument urged
at Rome in *English Articles*, 152–155;
probable reaction, 155–56, cf. 166
—*1533*: Cranmer sets forth Henry's
theology in *Twelve Articles*, 200, 223–33,
235, 247–48, 257, 279, cf. 259–60; Cranmer
does not defend Henry's theology in
Convocation, 200; Henry sends queen's
libellus and Wolsey argument to emperor's
court, 214–15; Henry's theology rejected
by Novati, 189
—*1534*: Henry's theology not exactly
reflected in Act of Succession, 219, 279

—*1536*: Henry's theology denied in new
Act of Succession, but perhaps still held
by him, 247–49, 256–57, 277, 279; Henry
and the Wolsey objection, 248
—*1540*: Henry's theology denied in
effect in act on matrimonial impediments,
263, 282
—*after 1547*: Henry's theology apparently combined with old view of affinity
from coitus by Cranmer and Parker, 248,
279, 280–81, 283; impediment of canon
law revoked in 1540 restored by Philip
and Mary and reabolished by Elizabeth,
282
Pucci, Laurence, Cardinal of the Church of
the Four Crowned Saints, 41–42, 55,
159–60

quasi-affinity, a name for public honesty,
179
Queritur, a treatise on Leviticus, 113n, 183n

Radcliffe, Robert, Viscount Fitzwalter
(Fitzwater), 94–95, 112, 119
Rastell, William, Judge, 47, 75, 188n,
cf. 112n
Ratisbon, 195
Ravenna, Cardinal Bishop of, *see* Accolti,
Benedict
Reformation of Ecclesiastical Laws, 279–81,
283
religious vows and the dissolution of mar-
riage, 14n, 59, 63, 231–32, 249–50, 251,
274, cf. 9n, 17n, 211
remissorials (remissory letters and reports),
148–50, 159, 162, 165, 168–69, 192, 234
Richard III, King of England, 13, 194, 242
Ridley, Robert, D.Th., 93–94, 97–98, 188n
Rochester: Diocese of, 112n; Bishops of, *see*
Fisher *and* Heath
Rochford, *see* Boleyn
Rojas, Francis de, Count of Salinas, 197
Roman law, *see* civil (Roman) law
Rome, sack of, 29n
Rota, Sacred Roman, 13–14, 149, 157–58,
160, 165–66, 189; Auditors of, *see* Accolti
(Peter), Antoninus, Campeggio, Capi-
suchi, Darius, Novati, Praepositus, Sandeo,
Simonetta, *and* Staphileus; Deans of,
157, 157n, 160
Rusticus, Nicholas, 119, 121

Sacheverell, Sir Richard, 101
St. John, Elizabeth, 44–45
Salviati, James, papal secretary, 78n, 86–87,
142
Sampson, Richard, D.Cn.C.L., Dean of the
Chapel Royal, Archdeacon of Cornwall
and of Suffolk in 1529, Bishop of Chichester in 1536, of Lichfield in 1543 (d. 1554):
told of Catherine's virginity and Wolsey's
public-honesty argument (1527), 31–32,
117, 234; Henry's proctor at legatine court
(1529), 79, 90, 95, 101, 108, 112, 116, 117,
120, 125, 128; shifts to Catherine's side
(reported Mar. 1530), 195; joins Gardiner
and others in dispute with Catherine

(1531), cf. 191–92; proctor for Henry in Boleyn annulment trial (1536), 245, 250; becomes Bishop of Chichester, 245; never Bishop of Westminster, 267n
sanatio in radice, 179, 212–13, 257
Sandeo, Felino, Auditor of the Rota, 13–14
Sanders (Sander), Nicholas, D. Th., author of *De origine ac progressu schismatis anglicani*, from 1576, left unfinished at his death (1581): original version extant in Rome, 47n; on Henry and Elizabeth Howard, 47–48, 249n; as authority on legatine court, 75, 108, 114, 116–19, 130, cf. 146–47
Scotus, John Duns, Franciscan theologian (d. ca. 1308), 7, 8, 9n
Seymour, Jane, Queen of England, 243, 247, 259–60, 276, cf. 43
Shorton, Robert, D.Th., formerly dean of Wolsey's chapel, queen's almoner, Archdeacon of Bath, member of queen's counsel in 1529 (d. 1535), 61, 79, 98, 202, 206
Shrewsbury, *see* Talbot
Simonetta, James, Bishop of Pesaro, Auditor and Dean of Rota, 157n, 168
Smeaton, Mark, 255, 259, cf. 242
solemnization of marriage (= wedding ceremonies in church), 53, cf. 16; and consummation, required for divinely forbidden affinity, 218, 247, 279; of Henry and Catherine of Aragon, set for 1506, takes place in 1509, 104, 111; of Henry and Anne Boleyn, in doubt, 196, 205, 211–13
Somerset, *see* Beaufort
Southampton, Sir William Fitzwilliam, Earl of, 265–66, 267–68
Spenser, Catherine, 45–46
spiritual kinship, impediment of, 43, 52–53, 258, 282, cf. 263
sponsa, contrasted with *uxor*, 68, 68n, 187n, cf. 224
spousals (= espousals, *sponsalia*), as referring either to betrothal or marriage, 49. *See also* contract
Standish, Henry, D.Th., Provincial of the Observant Franciscans, Bishop of St. Asaph in 1518 (d. 1535): member of queen's counsel (1528), 82; witnesses her appeal (16 June 1529), 78–79; speaks for her at legatine court (28 June), 87–88, 92, 94, 112, cf. 101, 118; signs document of 1 July, 82; speaks against university determinations in Parliament (1531), 190–91; votes on Henry's side in Convocation (1533), 202, cf. 200
Staphileus, John, D. Cn.C.L., Auditor of Rota, Bishop of Šibenik (Sebenico): editor of Geminianus's *Consilia* (1509), 137–38, 157n, 291n; on dispensability of Levitical degrees, 157n; mistakenly believed to be Dean of Rota, 40, 156–57, 157n; invited to England by Wolsey (1527), 157–58, 173; debated with Fisher, 158; used as character reference by Henry, 40; his advice sought by Wolsey on

public honesty (1528), 55–56, 137, 157, 158; his probable answer, 137–38; confident of an annulment, 166; death (22 July), 158, 158n; his treatise on Henry's marriage submitted to legatine court (1529), 113, 158
Stokesley, John, Archdeacon of Surrey and of Dorset, Bishop of London in 1530 (d. 1539): and Robert Wakefield, 37n; co-author of *Determinations* treatise (1529, pub. 1531), 180, 200, 262n; to be sent to Paris (1529), 174; addresses Parliament on determinations (1531), 190–91; pressed to authorize local trial (Feb. 1533), 197; presides over Convocation until Cranmer's instalment (Mar.), 198–200, cf. 212, 251n; votes on Henry's side (Apr.), 202; presents king's case to Convocation of York (May), 202–3; reports Cranmer's annulment of king's first marriage and validation of second (1534), 212–13, 218; balks at saying Convocation authorized second marriage, 218; repents of supporting Anne (1536), 252n; hesitates to express views of Anne's marriage, 251
Suffolk, *see* Brandon
summaria allegationis, 212, cf. 266
summary procedure, 77–78
surreption, surreptitious (suppressing information), 27, 97, 106, 110, 137–38, 139, 140, 152, cf. 76, 121

Talbot, George, Earl of Shrewsbury (d. 1538), 94–95, 111n, 112, 119, 120, 253–54
Talbot, Mary, wife of Henry Percy in early 1524, 5, 243n, 253–54, 258
Talcarne, John, B.Cn.C.L., 76n, 79, 88n, 168
Tancred of Bologna, 102n
Tarbes, Bishop of (Gabriel de Grammont), ambassador to England in Apr. 1527, Cardinal in 1530 (d. 26 Mar. 1534), 29n, 159, cf. 65, 81, 169, 174
Taverner, John, 120
Taylor, John, D.Cn.C.L., Archdeacon of Derby and of Buckinghamshire, Master of the Rolls (d. 1534), 95, 112, 120–22
theologians, 7, 11, 12–13, 16, 29, 33, 35, 51, 70, 107, 123, 124, 177–79, 179–80, 187–88, 196, 200–203, 209, 223, 227, 228–29, 230, 230n
Thirlby, Thomas, Bishop-designate of Westminster in Apr. or May 1540 (consecrated Dec. 1540), Bishop of Norwich in 1550, of Ely in 1554, deprived 1559 (d. 1570), 267, 267n
Thomas, St., *see* Aquinas
Thomas, Sir William, 94–95
Throgmorton, Sir George, 48
Torquemada (Turre Cremata), John de, O.P., theologian and canonist, Bishop of Sabina and Cardinal (d. 1468), 11–13, 15, 26, 225, 235, 285
Toulouse, 178, 180, 199, 217, *see also* determinations
treason, 217, 219–20, 242–43, 244, 250, 252, 254–55, 261, 275–76, cf. 188n, 256, 259
Treaty of Barcelona (29 June 1529), 136

treaty of 1503 (Anglo-Spanish): terms of, 104, 115, 162, 164, 196, 269; cited by Wolsey (1528), 61, 124; cited at legatine court by cardinals and probably by Hughes, and in queen's *libellus* (1529), 103, 111, 124; exhibited at legatine court, 124, cf. 162; its statement of consummation noticed by the Spaniards (1530), 162; its statement of consummation discovered by Henry (Jan. 1533), 124, 162–63, 164, 196, 223; submitted to board of scholars, 196–97; reaction of Catherine and Chapuys to discovery, 197; cited by Cranmer in *Twelve Articles*, 223, 236; copied by Watkins (12 Feb.), 124; to be shown to pope by Bonner, 164; displayed by Stokesley to Convocation, 199; cited by Cranmer in sentence of annulment (23 May), 210; cited by Cranmer in projected statement of consummation, 237

"Tree of Affinity," 114, 293

Tregonwell, John, D.C.L., later knighted, 245, 271, cf. 201

Trent, Council of, 17n, 283

trials, ecclesiastical:
    forms of, *see* canonization, convocation, inquisition, instance, *and* summary procedure; and jurisdiction, *see* jurisdiction
    matters tried: (1) heresy, 22, 26n, 93, cf. 11, 115, 242, 251; (2) magic (witchcraft), 5, 242; (3) marriage: in general, 5, 22–23, 40, 78, 140–41, 166, 213, 213n, 266; of specific marriages:
    —of Humphrey, Duke of Gloucester, and Eleanor Cobham (1441), 242
    —of Louis XII and Jeanne of Valois (1498), 14n
    —of Henry VIII and Catherine of Aragon at Wolsey's house (1527), *see* Westminster inquisition
    —of Henry VIII and Catherine of Aragon at Blackfriars (1529), *see* legatine court
    —of Henry VIII and Catherine of Aragon in Rome (1529–34), *see* papal trial
    —of Henry Percy and Anne Boleyn (1532), 5, 253–55, 255–56
    —of Henry VIII and Catherine of Aragon at Dunstable (Apr.–May 1533), *see* Dunstable
    —of Henry VIII and Anne Boleyn in gallery of Lambeth Palace (May 1533), 211–13, 214, 232
    —of Henry VIII and Anne Boleyn in chapel of Lambeth Palace (1536), 4, 244–59
    —of Henry VIII and Anne of Cleves (1540), 4, 264, 265–73

trials, secular: in general, 23, *see also* jurisdiction; for treason, of Anne Boleyn and associates, 244, 250, 252, 255, 256, 259, cf. 242–43, petitioned by More for himself, 217, *see also* attainder

Tunstall, Cuthbert, D.Cn.C.L. (Padua), Bishop of London, Bishop of Durham in 1530 (d. 1559): and Robert Ridley,

93; to be consulted on Henry's marriage (1527), 29, cf. 82; member of queen's counsel (1528), 62–63, 82; signs statement of 1 July 1529 and leaves for France on same day, 82; his treatise for the queen submitted to legatine court, 112–13; confirms report of Stokesley's mission to Paris, 174; absent from Parliament (1531), 190; opposes Stokesley in Convocation of York (1533), 203; forbidden Parliament (1534), 216–17; urges Act of Succession on Catherine, 220–21; commissioner for Cleves marriage (1539–40), 265–66, 267–68; reviews draft of act on impediments (2 July 1540), 261; petitions trial of Cleves marriage (6 July), 265; on factum committee at Cleves trial (7 July), 267, cf. 271

turpitude, meaning in Leviticus explained, 35, 99, 189, 224–25

uncle-niece, nephew-aunt marriages, 12–13, 14, 284–85

Urban III, Pope (1185–87), 40n

uxor, meaning of, 68, 68n, 187n, 224

vacation, harvest, 127–28, 165, 216, cf. 25, 78

Vannes, Peter, Latin secretary to Henry VIII, 136, 216

Vaughan, Stephen, 198n

Vaux, Thomas, 208

Venice, 15, 145, 177. *See also* Falier

verba de futuro or *de praesenti*, *see* contract

Vere, John de, 15th Earl of Oxford, Lord Great Chamberlain of England, 94–95, 121

Vergil, Polydore, canonist, Archdeacon of Wells (d. 1555), 93, 202

Veritatem rerum, treatise exhibited at legatine court, 113, 124

virginity: vows of, *see* religious vows; ways of losing, 235–36; Catherine of Aragon's, before marrying Henry, *see* consummation of marriage between Arthur and Catherine; consummation of marriage without loss of, 207, 233, 235–36, cf. 204, 224

vows, *see* religious vows

Voysey (Veysey), John, D.C.L., Bishop of Exeter (d. 1554), 82, 201–2

Wakefield (Wakfeld), Robert, B.Th., Orientalist (d. 1537), 35–37, 173, 202

Warham, William, D.C.L., Bishop of London in 1501, Archbishop of Canterbury in 1503 (d. 1532): and Henry VII, 126; Bedell his secretary, 202; consulted by Henry about his scruple (1527), 82, cf. 81; with Wolsey summons Henry to Westminster trial and acts as assessor, 24; suggested as legate in drafts of decretal bull, 57n; named to Catherine's counsel (1528), 62–63, 82; signs document of 1 July 1529, 82; witness at legatine court, 80n, 101, 122, 123, 126; receives university determinations (1530), 180; not in Parliament (1531), 190; refuses to try Henry's marriage, 175n, 193; examines Percy on his alleged marriage with Anne Boleyn (June 1532), 5, 253–54, 255–56; death of (22 Aug.), 194, 256

Watkins, Richard, B.C.L., notary of Canterbury, later king's prothonotary: clerk at legatine court (1529), 3, 75, 80, cf. 95, 112, 127; makes copy of 1503 treaty (Feb. 1533), 124; produces legatine acts at Dunstable trial, 208; compiles one-volume record of legatine court, omitting events of 21 June and Henry's deposition, 3–4, 75–76, 79, 80, 91, 121, 124, 209, 216; clerk at Cleves trial (1540), 267n

West, Nicholas, D.C.L., Archdeacon of Derby in 1486, Vicar General to Bishop Fox of Winchester in 1501, Bishop of Ely in 1515 (d. 28 Apr. 1533): at Henry's protestation (1505), 74, 126; defends Catherine in two treatises (1528), 67, 68n, 70–73, 115–16, 183, 258n; appointed counsel for Catherine, 73, 82; signs statement of 1 July 1529, 82; present at legatine court, 74, 101, 120, 124, 126, cf. 82; is sworn in and testifies (5 July), 74, 101, 119, 123–24; consistently holds the marriage not to be against divine law, 71, 74, 74n, 123; his treatises submitted to court, 68n, 74, 112–13; returns to Ely during trial and is taken ill, 74, 111; summoned by Wolsey to testify on the protestation, 74, 126–27; on deathbed during Convocation (1533), 202

Westminster, St. Peter's Church: site of Convocation trial of Cleves marriage, 266

Westminster inquisition: held in Wolsey's house (1527), 3, 21–29, 78, 81, 90; record of, by Clayburgh and Gardiner, 3, 23–24, 88, 113–14; Catherine hears of, 23, 31, 234; the marriage charged with perhaps being against divine law, 24, 26, 28, 30, 66; Henry by proxy admits consummation in Catherine's first marriage, 25, 30, 109, 276; Henry defends his marriage by citing the dispensation, 4, 24–25, 94; the promoter's objections, 26–29, 30, 31, 73, 102, 109, cf. 113–14, 125

Weston, Sir Francis, 255, 259

Weston, Sir Richard, 112

William of Paris (or of Auvergne), theologian, Bishop of Paris (d. 1249), 225

Willoughby, Sir Anthony, 119, 121

Wiltshire, *see* Boleyn, Thomas

Winchester, Bishops of, *see* Fox (Richard), Gardiner, *and* Wolsey

witchcraft, 5, 194, 241–42, 249, 271, 280

witnesses: legatine, *see* depositions *and* legatine court; needed to prove precontract, 243, 253, 256, 262

Wolman, Richard, D.C.L., Archdeacon of Sudbury (d. 1537): questions Bishop Fox (Apr. 1527), 30, 125, 126–27; promoter of Wolsey's office at Westminster inquisition (May), 25–29, 102, 113–14, 125; his public-honesty argument, 27, 30, 31,

73, 109, *see also* public honesty, Wolman objection; conveys Henry's rebuke to Wolsey for the latter's public-honesty objection, 32; votes on Henry's side in Convocation (1533), 202

Wolsey, Thomas, D.Th., Archbishop of York, Lord Chancellor, legate *a latere*, Bishop of Winchester *in commendam* in early 1529 (d. 29 Nov. 1530):
before 1527: as permanent legate *a latere* (from 1521), 3, 22–23, 24, 80, 89, 193; breaks up Percy-Boleyn affair at Henry's command (1522), 253–54
1527: unjustly suspected of instigating annulment, 21, 23, cf. 81, 84; twice consults with Fisher, 29; has Bishop Fox questioned (Apr.), 30, cf. 56; with Warham personally cites Henry to inquisition at Westminster, 24; does not cite Catherine but fails to keep the matter from her, 23, 31, 82–83, 234; presides over inquisition, 3, 21–29, 78, 90, 102, 276; appeals to his own conscience, 24, 81, cf. 55–57, 84; names bishops to be consulted and adjourns sine die (31 May), 29; sends Fisher's second letter to Henry (2 June), 29; Fisher refuses his request to say that Henry should ask pope's judgment, 81–84, 98–99; formulates his public-honesty objection, 30, 31, 32, 33, 37, 38, 117, 155; interview with Fisher (July), 58–59, 82; mission to France, 38, 58, 158; discovers Henry's intentions for Anne and his secret mission to pope, 38–40; wins over Staphileus, 157–58, cf. 173; returns from France to assist Henry in his papal campaigns, 38–39; convinces Henry that pope will not dispense him from present marriage, 39; is still deceived by Henry, 39–41; prepares with Henry new draft of dispensation, 39, 41, 42, 43–53, 182, 256; sends drafts of dispensation and of decretal bull to pope (5 Dec.), 173–74, cf. 54–55, 66–67
1528: is informed of Clement's suggestion that Henry remarry before annulment, 40; his objections to Clement's dispensation of Dec. 1527, 51; hears of Staphileus's debate with Fisher, 158; is aware that Clement knows of Anne, 52; sends Gardiner and Fox to Orvieto (Feb.), 52, cf. 54, 113n; appointed legate with Campeggio (Apr., renewed in June), 59, 77, cf. 55; knows Staphileus did not support him as legate, 157; has Gardiner press for decretal bull and consult Staphileus about public honesty and Ancona about Henry's ignorance (9 May), 55–58, 100, 137, 157, 160; in dark about Catherine's virginity, 56–57, 96, cf. 29–32, 234; tells Henry he will act only according to conscience (10 May), 58, 81; fears his downfall, 56–57, 59; responds to Catherine's arguments, 61–62, 98, 123, 151n; is aware of 1503 treaty, 61, cf. 103, 115, 124; proposes marriage of Princess Mary to half-brother Henry Fitzroy

(Oct.), 33n; consults with Campeggio and Henry, 59; visits queen with Campeggio (24 Oct.), 59; plans ruined by queen's revelation of brief (ca. 7 Nov.), 62; visits queen with Campeggio at Bridewell, 86n

1529: opens legatine court, cites king and queen to appear on 18 June (31 May), 3, 77, 89; in dark about queen's reaction (16 June), 78; hears queen's protests and appeals (18 June), 79–80, 85; appoints clerks and promoter, 80, 88, 89; addresses court (21 June), 81, 84, 85, 86n; his appeal to conscience reported to Rome by Campeggio, 81; concurs with Campeggio's denial of queen's motions, 85; rejects her new appeal, declares her contumacious, cites her to session of 25 June, 87, 89; hears petition of queen's counselors, perhaps appoints Gardiner to sit in court as his secretary (22 June), 87–88; declares queen contumacious and articulates objections against marriage (25 June), 90–92, 97; perhaps deletes question on consummation, 96, cf. 91; his conduct of trial criticized by Campeggio, 92; debates with Fisher and Ridley (28 June), 93–94; declares queen contumacious and receives witnesses on articles, 92, 94–95, 120, 121; announces that Henry in his deposition pleaded papal dispensation, 95; and Henry's deposition concerning consummation, 96–97; adjourns for week to plan strategy, 97–98, 100, cf. 101; devises bishops' statement of 1 July, 99, cf. 81–84; visits queen at Bridewell or Greenwich, 86n; declares queen contumacious for the last time (5 July), 101; receives bull and brief from Sampson and swears in further witnesses, 101, 120–21; hears objections to bull and brief by the promoter, 27n–28n, 102, 103, 105–8, 109–11, 113, 114, 115; receives *libelli* for queen and for king, 68n, 83, 98, 102–3, 108–9, 112–14, 124–25, 153–54, 238; articulates objections against bull and brief, including that of public honesty (9 July), 101–2, 109–11, 114, 122; receives witnesses on this second set of articles, assigns final term (12 July), 112, 120, 121; summons Bishop West to London, 74, 120, cf. 111; hears debate

on public honesty, 114, 116–18; modifies article on Henry's age, introduces new articles and swears in witnesses upon them, and postpones final term (14 July), 119–20; swears in more witnesses and further extends term (16 July), 120; receives depositions and other exhibits, including 1503 treaty, and extends term (19 July), 120–25; receives Henry's protestation and articulates objection, accepts West's testimony, and extends term (21 July), 125–27; present as Campeggio adjourns trial (23 July), 127–28; overlooks papal authorization to proceed during vacation, 78; still taken up with proceedings of trial (27 July), 128; in disgrace, 124, 129

1530: signs letter of lords to pope (June), 143; death, 191, 193
Woodville, Elizabeth, Queen of England, 38, 194, 242
Woodville, Richard, 43
Wootton (Wotton), Nicholas, D.Cn.C.L., D.Th., Official of the Consistory Court of London (d. 1567): authenticates Watkins and Clayburgh and their legatine record (1 Oct. 1533), 76, 209, 216; proctor for Anne Boleyn at annulment trial (1536), 245, 250; in charge of Cranmer's faculty office (from 1538), 267; ambassador to Cleves (1539 and 1540), 267, 273; signs Cranmer's dispensation allowing Henry to marry Catherine Parr without banns (1543), 278n
Wriothesley, Charles, son of Sir Thomas (Garter King-of-Arms), herald and chronicler, 245
Wriothesley, Sir Thomas, Garter King-of-Arms (d. 1534), 125
Wriothesley, Sir Thomas, 1st Baron Wriothesley of Titchfield (nephew of above), secretary to Henry VIII, later Earl of Southampton, 265, 267

York, Archbishops of, *see* Heath, Lee, *and* Wolsey; Convocation of, *see* Convocation

Zabarella, Francis, canonist, Bishop of Florence, Cardinal in 1411 (d. 1417), 225–26, 227, 235
Zalva (Salba, Zalba), Martin de, Bishop of Pamplona and Cardinal (d. 1403), 8, 9n, 229n